An Introduction to the Human Development and Capability Approach

Launched in September 2004, the Human Development and Capability Association (HDCA) promotes research from many disciplines on key problems related to poverty, justice and well-being. Frances Stewart is the current president of HDCA. Amartya Sen was the Founding President of HDCA 2004–2006; Martha Nussbaum was President of HDCA 2006–2008.

Mission

HDCA promotes high quality research in the interconnected areas of human development and capability. It is concerned with research in these areas across a broad range of topics where the human development and capability approaches have made and can make significant contributions, including the quality of life, poverty, justice, gender, development and environment inter alia. It further works in all disciplines – such as economics, philosophy, political theory, sociology and development studies – where such research is, or may be, pursued. While primarily an academic body, the Association brings together those involved in academic work with practitioners who are involved in, or interested in, the application of research from the fields of human development and capability to the problems they face.

Journal of Human Development and Capabilities

The *Journal of Human Development and Capabilities* is the peer reviewed journal of the Association. It publishes original works in economics, philosophy, social sciences and other disciplines that expand concepts, measurement tools and policy alternatives from the perspective of the human development and capability approach. It provides a forum for an open exchange of ideas among a broad spectrum of policy makers, economists and academics. Human development is becoming a school of thought and the Journal acts as a conduit for members and critics of this school.

Activities

The Association holds an annual conference, supports training activities, facilitates thematic groups on specific topics, and provides a forum in which collaborative research can emerge. It maintains a website which provides, among others: a comprehensive collection of bibliographic resources on the capability approach; tri-annual bulletins on core concepts and applications of the approach; information on thematic groups and their activities; video and teaching materials on subjects related to the capability approach, unpublished manuscripts, etc.

An Introduction to the Human Development and Capability Approach

Freedom and Agency

Edited by Séverine Deneulin
with Lila Shahani

publishing for a sustainable future

London • Washington, DC

International Development Research Centre
Ottawa • Cairo • Dakar • Montevideo • Nairobi • New Delhi • Singapore

First published by Earthscan in the UK and USA in 2009
Copyright © Human Development and Capability Association, 2009
Reprinted 2010

ISBN: PB 978-1-84407-806-6

IDRC publishes an e-book version of An Introduction to the Human Development and
Capability Approach (ISBN 978-1-55250-470-3)

For further information, please contact:
International Development Research Centre
PO Box 8500
Ottawa, ON K1G 3H9
Canada
Email: info@idrc.ca
Web: www.idrc.ca

Typeset by FiSH Books
Cover design by Susanne Harris
Cover images: Girls in Cajamarca, Peru © Maritza Paredes. Wase Friday market, central Nigeria
© Adam Higazi. Harvest season in Mekhong Delta, Vietnam © Zarni Maung. Students listening
to a lecture by Amartya Sen at the Sheldonian Theatre, Oxford, UK. © Oxford Poverty &
Human Development Initiative (OPHI).

For a full list of publications please contact:
Earthscan
Dunstan House
14a St Cross St
London, EC1N 8XA, UK
Tel: +44 (0)20 7841 1930
Fax: +44 (0)20 7242 1474
Email: earthinfo@earthscan.co.uk
Web: **www.earthscan.co.uk**

Earthscan publishes in association with the International Institute for Environment and
Development

A catalogue record for this book is available from the British Library

Library of Congress Cataloging-in-Publication Data
An introduction to the human development and capability approach : freedom and agency /
edited by Séverine Deneulin with Lila Shahani. – 1st ed.
    p. cm.
Includes bibliographical references and index.
ISBN 978-1-84407-805-9 – ISBN 978-1-84407-806-6 (pbk.) 1. Social psychology. 2. Human
behavior. I. Deneuline, Séverine, 1974– II. Shahani, Lila.
HM1033.I595 2009
302–dc22

2009013100

FSC
www.fsc.org
MIX
Paper from
responsible sources
FSC® C013604

Contents

List of Figures, Tables and Boxes

Figures

Tables

Boxes

List of Contributors

Editors

Séverine Deneulin is Lecturer in international development at the University of Bath. She researches on the conceptual foundations of the human development and capability approach and on the role of religion and values in development. She has published *The Capability Approach and the Praxis of Development* (Palgrave, 2006) and *Religion in Development* (Zed, 2009), and co-edited *Transforming Unjust Structures* (Springer, 2006). She is the Education Officer of HDCA. She holds a DPhil in Development Studies from the University of Oxford and an MA in Economics from the University of Louvain.

Lila Shahani is Editor for the Special Unit for South-South Cooperation at UNDP, where she previously held the positions of Policy and Partnerships Adviser and Communications Officer. She has also been responsible for the overall editing and research for several UNDP, ILO, UNICEF and Philippine government publications, and has also worked for a number of years in the Academic and Trade Editorial Department of Oxford University Press (US). She is currently finishing her DPhil in English language and literature at the University of Oxford, where her research focuses on comparative migration in the context of the Asian diaspora. She holds an MA in international relations from the Fletcher School of Law and Diplomacy at Tufts University.

Authors

Sabina Alkire is the Director of the Oxford Poverty and Human Development Initiative (OPHI), and the Secretary of the Human Development and Capability Association. Her publications include *Valuing Freedoms: Sen's Capability Approach and Poverty Reduction* (Oxford University Press, 2002), as well as numerous articles in philosophy and economics. Her research interests include: value judgements in economic decision-making and the conceptualization and measurement of individual agency (empowerment), particularly in South Asia. She has previously worked for the Commission on Human Security, coordinated the culture–poverty learning and research initiative at the World Bank, and developed participatory impact assessment methodologies with Oxfam and the Asia Foundation in Pakistan. She has a DPhil in Economics and an MSc in Economics for Development from the University of Oxford.

Proochista Ariana is Departmental Lecturer in global health and development at the University of Oxford. She has an MA in international health from Harvard University and a DPhil in International Development from the University of

Oxford. Her research pertains to the inter-relationship between health and development processes. She works with indigenous communities in Southern Mexico, and recently has extended her work to China and India. She has been involved with OPHI since its inception and with the organization of the Human Development Training Course for mid-career development professionals (co-organized with the Human Development Reporting Office, UNDP) since 2004.

Susan Johnson is a Lecturer in international development at the University of Bath. She has a background in economics and agricultural economics. She has researched and written extensively in the field of microfinance, expanding the analysis in the field to the institutional analysis of local financial markets, examining their social embeddedness in particular. She has also specialized in impact assessment and gender analysis. She was a lead researcher in the Imp-Act programme – a global three-year action-research programme to improve the quality of microfinance services and their impact on poverty, funded by the Ford Foundation. She has also been a researcher with the ESRC Wellbeing in Developing Countries research group, examining the relationship between well-being and markets.

Arif Naveed is Senior Research Fellow at the Mahbub-ul-Haq Human Development Center, Islamabad where he works on the South Asia Human Development Reports. He also teaches human development at the International Islamic University Islamabad as a visiting faculty member. Previously, he implemented various community development projects in rural Pakistan. He holds a Masters of Research in international development from the University of Bath and a Masters in economics from Quaid-i-Azam University.

Ingrid Robeyns is a philosopher and economist. She received her PhD from the Faculty of Economics and Politics at Cambridge University and is currently Professor in Practical Philosophy at the Erasmus University in Rotterdam. Her main research interests include: theories of equality and justice, the capability approach and feminist economics, and philosophy. She edited Sen's *Work and Ideas: A Gender Perspective* (Routledge, 2005, with Bina Agarwal and Jane Humphries) and *Measuring Justice: Primary Goods and Capabilities* (Cambridge University Press, 2009, with Harry Brighouse).

Maria Emma Santos is a Research Officer at the Oxford Poverty and Human Development Initiative (Department of International Development, University of Oxford) and a postdoctoral fellow at the Consejo Nacional de Investigaciones Cientificas y Tecnicas (CONICET), Argentina. Her research interests are the measurement and analysis of chronic and multidimensional poverty, and the quality of education, its determinants, and its role for poverty reduction. She is particularly interested in Latin American countries. She holds an MA in Economic Development from Vanderbilt University (US) and a Doctorate in Economics from Universidad Nacional del Sur (Argentina).

Randy Spence was previously the Director of Economic and Social Development Affiliates (ESDA). He worked from 1990 to 2005 with the International Development Research Centre (IDRC) of Canada as Senior Programme Specialist in economics and as Director of IDRC's Regional Office for Southeast and East Asia in Singapore. Prior to joining IDRC, he was a Senior Economist with the Canadian Department of External Affairs and the Department of Energy, Mines and Resources, as well as the Ottawa-based North–South Institute. He has worked on a long-range planning project in Kenya and as an economic advisor in the Tanzanian Ministry of Planning, and has taught economics at the Universities of McMaster and Guelph in Canada. He has a PhD in economics from the University of Toronto.

Elaine Unterhalter is Professor in education and international development at the Institute of Education, a college at the University of London which specializes in teaching, research and consultancy in education and related areas of social science and professional practice. She has authored *Gender, Schooling and Global Social Justice* (Routledge, 2007) and has co-edited a book with Melanie Walker on the capability approach and education. She has also published numerous articles on education, gender and social justice. She coordinates the Institute of Education research team with ActionAid to support research on girls' education in Tanzania and Nigeria, as well as the Oxfam-based Beyond Access programme on gender, education and development projects.

Sarah White is Director of the Centre for Development Studies at the University of Bath, where she teaches sociology and international development. Her research concerns the politics of how social identities are mobilized in development intervention. This is applied to a range of fields: child rights and child participation; gender, including men and masculinity; and race and culture. Her current research concerns well-being (ESRC-funded Research Group into Well-being in Developing Countries, 2002–2007) and religion (DFID-funded Research Programme Consortium into Religion and Development, 2005–2010) in India and Bangladesh.

List of Acronyms and Abbreviations

ADB	Asian Development Bank
AfDB	African Development Bank
CEDAW	Convention on the Elimination of all kinds of Discrimination against Women
CPA	Comprehensive Peace Agreement (Accra)
DESD	Decade of Education for Sustainable Development
EDE	equally distributed equivalent
EFA	Education for All
ESDA	Economic and Social Development Affiliates
ESRC	Economic and Social Research Council
EU	European Union
FBOs	Faith-Based Organizations
FGT	Foster–Greer–Thorbecke (indices)
FTAs	Free Trade Agreements
GATT	General Agreement on Tariffs and Trade
GDI	Gender-related Development Index
GDP	Gross Domestic Product
GEM	Gender Empowerment Measure
GGGI	Global Gender Gap Index
GNP	Gross National Product
HDCA	Human Development and Capability Association
HDI	Human Development Index
HIPC	Heavily Indebted Poor Country
HPI	Human Poverty Index
IADB	Inter-American Development Banks
IBRD	International Bank for Reconstruction and Development (World Bank)
ICCPR	International Covenant on Civil and Political Rights
ICT	Information and Communication Technology
IDRC	International Development Research Centre
ILO	International Labour Organisation
IMF	International Monetary Fund
IP	Intellectual Property
iPRS	interim Poverty Reduction Strategy
KA-DER	Association for Women in Politics (Turkey)
LEB	Life Expectancy at Birth
LURD	Liberians United for Reconciliation and Democracy
MDGs	Millennium Development Goals
MINUSTAH	United Nations Stabilisation Mission in Haiti

MODEL	Movement for Democracy in Liberia
NGOs	Non-Governmental Organizations
NHDA	*National Human Development Report*
NTGL	National Transitional Government of Liberia
ODA	Official Development Assistance
OECD	Organization for Economic Co-operation and Development
OPHI	Oxford Poverty and Human Development Initiative
PIU	Project Implementation Units (Afghanistan)
PRSP	Poverty Reduction Strategy Paper
R&D	Research and Development
ROSCA	Rotating Savings and Credit Association
TRIPS	Trade-Related Intellectual Property Arrangements
UN	United Nations
UNCTAD	UN Commission on Trade and Development
UNDP	United Nations Development Programme
UNESCO	United Nations Educational Scientific and Cultural Organization
UNIDO	UN Industrial Development Organization
WHO	World Health Organization
WIPO	World Intellectual Property Organization
WTO	World Trade Organization

Introduction

Background

In May 2006, a small group belonging to the Human Development and Capability Association (HDCA) met together for a few days at Oxford to work on making the association more dynamic, in the hopes of promoting 'research from many disciplines on problems related to impoverishment, justice and well-being'.[1] During general discussions about HDCA's role in the future, one member – Elaine Unterhalter – suggested that it might be a good idea to write a textbook on the human development and capability approach. The idea was enthusiastically embraced by the entire group.

As a consequence of that meeting, and in order to ensure ownership of the textbook project by its future users, a special working group – the 'education working group' – was created within HDCA to discuss teaching activities (and the development of teaching material) related to human development. Because of a generous grant from the UK Department for International Development to the Oxford Poverty and Human Development Initiative (OPHI at www.ophi.org.uk), which organized the meeting, more than 20 people from diverse disciplinary, geographical and professional backgrounds met in March 2007 at OPHI to discuss curricula, pedagogy, course contents, key readings, essential data, case studies, 'aha moments' and the textbook project itself.[2] The textbook proposal was thoroughly revised to include the group's feedback based on respective teaching experiences in various contexts.

While it was being completed, the textbook was significantly reworked and improved, once again, by the feedback of another international group of academics and policy-makers. In September 2008, a group participating in a human development training course organized by the Human Development Report Office of the United Nations Development Programme (UNDP) and OPHI worked on the textbook as their assignment.[3] Not only did they substantially improve the structure and content of the textbook; they also provided vivid personal accounts and policy case studies of their own.

Audience

The multi-disciplinary nature of the human development and capability approach does not lend itself easily to specialization for a targeted disciplinary audience. The approach touches on economics, politics, sociology, law, education, psychology, philosophy and other disciplines. This book is therefore correspondingly multi-disciplinary. Within academic institutions it is intended for use by undergraduates and post-graduates in development studies, education, politics, economics and social policy. As the human development and capability approach is also of considerable interest to development practitioners and policy-makers, the book has been deliberately shaped for practitioners in the field struggling to make policy decisions.

This textbook is thus designed for an eclectic readership. No prior knowledge of any specific discipline is necessary to understand its basic arguments. The textbook is bound to be used differently by different audiences, whether they happen to be students in development studies or the social science disciplines, development practitioners, civil servants or policy-makers. For example, students in development studies might wish to read the book from cover to cover, while students in social science disciplines might only read the first section (Chapters 1–3), followed by the chapters most relevant to their specific disciplines. The book is written so that each chapter can be read on its own, but it is important to note that chapters in Parts II and III cannot be readily understood without prior reading of Part I in its entirety.

A final word about context. Unlike other human development textbooks which have sprung from local realities and are used in the local context about which they have been written, this textbook is not context specific.[4] It aims at providing an accessible, pedagogical account of the human development and capability approach, and offers insights on how to use the approach in multiple contexts. It provides illustrations and case studies from a wide geographical spread, from Mexico to China, Uganda, Afghanistan and even Europe. This does not necessarily mean that the textbook is relevant only to a classroom composed of international students. Through its use of comparative case studies, the textbook is equally relevant for homogenous audiences. For example, students at a Mongolian university might be better informed about educational policies in their own country after learning about similar experiences in Africa. In the same way, practitioners and policy-makers from Central Asia might benefit from reading a policy case study on aid in Afghanistan.

Structure

The textbook is divided into three parts: Concepts, Topics and Policy. The first three chapters provide the conceptual foundations of the human development and capability approach. Chapter 1 discusses the importance – indeed, the unavoidability – of value judgements in development and public policy in general. It illustrates that different normative frameworks lead to different actions and consequences in people's lives. Chapter 2 introduces the fundamental principles of the approach, and constitutes the conceptual foundation for all subsequent chapters. Chapter 3 situates the approach within the context of other schools of thought and development thinking as a whole.

The second part is divided into separate topics and presents a human development angle into each one. There is no particular reason why the topics are arranged in this way, and they can be read in a non-linear fashion. Chapter 4 discusses the topic of economic growth and describes different views about the role of economic growth in promoting human flourishing. Chapter 5 reviews theories of justice and examines where the approach stands in relation to them. Chapter 6 deals with the topic of measurement, which is central to policy-making since it enables policy-makers to identify target groups in need of intervention. Chapter 7 analyses the role of institutions and markets in expanding people's opportunities to live the lives they value. Chapter 8 discusses democracy and political participation as mechanisms through which people become agents of their own destiny. Chapters 9 and 10 discuss two topics to which human development has often been reduced: education and health. Chapter 11 analyses how the topics of culture and religion have been addressed in development studies and critically discusses the contribution of the human development and capability approach. Other topics could have been added, such as a specific chapter on gender, or one on the environment, or another on conflict. However, we have limited ourselves to the topics above for practical reasons of time and length. It will be up to the teachers using this textbook to supplement the chapters with other topics relevant to human development.

The third part deals with policy considerations. Chapter 12 describes the many areas of policy that the human development and capability approach touches upon, and offers useful tools for policy analysis. Chapter 13 collects different policy case studies that can be used as a teaching method to prepare students in human development policy-making and practice.

Each chapter is divided into a similar structure:

- **Objectives**: the opening paragraph lays down the learning objectives that the user should have acquired after reading the chapter.
- **Key points**: these points are summarized at the beginning of each chapter to give the reader a quick glimpse of the chapter's central argument.
- **Boxes**: each chapter contains boxes that either convey stories illustrating a point made in the argument or reproduce excerpts from important material.
- **Questions**: each chapter ends with a series of questions for discussion to be used in seminars. Naturally, these are tentative only and each user is encouraged to add his or her own questions given the specific context in which the book is to be used.
- **Readings and further readings**: each chapter contains a list of readings which are divided between relatively accessible readings and more complex readings to suit a range of academic levels.

Acknowledgements

Copyrights of this textbook belong to the Human Development and Capability Association. However, HDCA is only what its members do. This textbook project would not have been completed without the generosity of members who shared their expertise in specific areas. Sabina Alkire has been a central person in HDCA since its birth in 2004; as Secretary of the Association, she has been one of its leading sources of dynamism and energy, and her writings have been a key reference on the human development and capability approach. She has authored most of the conceptual part of the textbook, and, as a pioneer in measuring freedom and agency, has written the measurement chapter, in collaboration with Maria Emma Santos (Chapter 6). She has also been present ever since the very inception of this textbook project in Oxford in May 2006 and offered continuous support. Randy Spence has offered his long policy expertise as economist for the chapters on economic growth (Chapter 4) and public policy (Chapter 12). Ingrid Robeyns has shared her expertise on the capability approach and theories of justice for the chapter on equality and justice (Chapter 5). Susan Johnson has worked for many years on access to markets in Africa and has contributed to writing the chapter on institutions and markets (Chapter 7). Elaine Unterhalter has shared many of the discussions of the capability and education HDCA thematic group in the chapter on education (Chapter 9). From his experience of rural Pakistan, Arif Naveed has suggested the central importance of health and nutrition and has provided invaluable assistance to Proochista Ariana who has written the chapter on health within very tight deadlines. In the midst of pressure to finish her doctoral studies in the area of public health, Proochista's organizational skills have also provided invaluable support to many HDCA and OPHI meetings. Finally, Sarah White has shared her expertise on culture and development for the chapter on culture and religion (Chapter 10).

Each chapter has also benefited from the contribution of many people who have generously provided edits and comments on specific or several chapters, or case studies and boxes. From their respective country experiences, Seyhan Aydinligil, Mustafa Aria, Khwaga Kakar and Wilmot Reeves have written policy case studies for Chapter 13. Melanie Walker has shared her research in pedagogy to provide some guiding notes about how 'to do what we teach' when teaching about human development. Michael Mawa, Pamela Mbabazi, Saidah Najjuma and Robert Esuruku and Jiantuo Yu have written case studies for Chapter 1. Wilmot Reeves, Pedro Flores, Seeta Prabhu and Saidah Najjuma have written boxes for Chapters 1, 2 and 5. Adriana Velasco and John Hammock have commented on the first part, and Adriana has kindly provided the pictures used for teaching human development in the Dominican Republic. Frances Stewart has commented on Chapter 3 and Colin Lawson on Chapter 4. Anna Hiltunen has facilitated the cover design, and Liz Bruton has been very efficient in posting several versions of draft chapters on the OPHI website. And of course, the participants of the March 2007 workshop and September 2008 course have provided invaluable comments and feedback on the work in progress. Their involvement would not have been possible without the generous support of the Oxford Poverty and Human Development Initiative (for the education workshop) and the team of the Human Development Report Office (for the human development course) which organized these two events. We also thank Oxford University Press for permission to reproduce the section 'Hunger amidst plenty' by Jean Drèze and Amartya Sen from *India:*

Development and Participation, 2002, pp. 336–40, and Palgrave Macmillan for permission to reproduce Box 1.1 'A great leap: from water reform to sanitation reform in 19th century Great Britain' from the UNDP, *Human Development Report*, 2006.

Two people have given special commitment to this project. Randy Spence has been very supportive, not only in contributing to chapters and commenting on material with efficiency and speed, but also in facilitating the open accessibility of the textbook with the International Development Research Centre of Canada. Lila Shahani's editorial expertise has also been invaluable: she carefully edited the entire manuscript, painstakingly going over every single line (occasionally re-writing certain sections entirely) to ensure clarity and comprehensibility throughout, and provided critical feedback on the text's overall structure and substance.

Finally, this textbook would not have seen the light of day without the graduate students of the Masters in International Cooperation and Development at the University of Bethlehem in Palestine. They have given me the motivation and energy to undertake and complete the task. I dedicate this textbook to them.

Notes

1   See the website of the Human Development and Capability Association at www.hd-ca.org.
2   The participants were: Seyhan Aydinligil (Turkey), Natal Ayiga (Uganda), Jim Chalmers (Australia), Elena Danilova (Uzbekistan), Zaid Eyadat (Jordan), Pedro Flores (Mexico), Alex Frediani (Brazil), Humayun Hamidzada (Afghanistan), John Hammock (US), Susan Holcombe (US), Solava Ibrahim (Egypt), Javier Iguiniz (Peru), Andrey Ivanov (Slovakia), Minquan Liu (China), Rosie Peppin-Vaugh (UK), Kusago Takayoshi (Japan), Elaine Unterhalter (UK), Adriana Velasco (Dominican Republic) and Melanie Walker (UK/South Africa). The workshop was organized by Sabina Alkire, Proochista Ariana and myself.
3   Khalid Abu-Ismail (Egypt), Robert Esuruku (Uganda), Khwaga Kakar (Afghanistan), Michael Mawa (Uganda), Pamela Mbabazi (Uganda), Saidah Najjuma (Uganda), Wilmot Reeves (Liberia) and Lila Shahani (Philippines/India).
4   To my knowledge, a human development textbook has been published in both English and Mongolian with UNDP Mongolia and local universities, and in Russian and English by UNDP Moscow and local universities. An Indian human development textbook is also being produced in collaboration with UNDP India.

Part I
Concepts

1

A Normative Framework for Development

Sabina Alkire and Séverine Deneulin

Aims of the chapter

- To show the importance of value judgements in development.
- To illustrate how value judgements – or normative frameworks – have a practical impact and shape policy making.
- To introduce the basic value of the human development and capability approach: that policies should promote human flourishing.

Key points

- Value judgements lie at the heart of development analysis and policy. However these value judgements are often not acknowledged.
- Public policy aims to create and sustain improvements. Different ideas about what should be improved lead to different policies (e.g. poverty reduction policies vary depending on how poverty is defined). In contrast with approaches that seek to improve the national economy, or people's resources, or their utility, human development argues that people's well-being should improve. Different policies ensue.
- Development policy involves uncertainty, trade-offs and complexity.
- The output or impact of any policy depends in part on the social, political, institutional, cultural and economic context.

The word 'development' has as many meanings as there are listeners. For some, development means more material prosperity: owning money, land and a house. For others, development concerns liberation from oppression. Some see development as a new word for neo-colonialism, and despise it. For still others, development is a holistic project of personal social and spiritual progress. In many contexts we speak of the 'development' of a child or the 'development' of new software as if development completes something as yet unfinished. But this too is simplistic, for in certain ways 'developing' countries are more mature than 'developed'. So the term is ambiguous and value laden. This textbook aims to present a people-centred meaning of development which is relevant to all countries, and to show its implications for development practice in many areas.

Regardless of any particular normative framework, many would view 'development' as a multi-dimensional and multi-sectoral process, involving social, economic and political change aimed at improving people's lives.[1] Development processes use and manage natural resources to satisfy human needs and improve people's quality of life. Note that those who hold these views may still range from Marxist to neoclassical. A region might be considered more 'developed' because its inhabitants command higher incomes per capita and because investment and employment rates are higher than other regions. In this context, economic growth and productive investment are the major concern of many development agencies. Other similar understandings of development add concerns for people's health and education as key ingredients to producing a more dynamic economy and higher material prosperity. Still others view development as enabling people to live lives they value. From this perspective, investment, employment and prosperity are some means, among others, of giving people such opportunities, although they are not the final goal. Despite the many differences, all the above have one common characteristic: they are normative. This chapter demonstrates that normative assumptions about what development is have important policy implications and practical consequences for people's lives. It concludes by introducing the human development approach.

Normative, positive and predictive

Development legitimately involves various kinds of analyses. Development policies or public policies are *normative* or ethical – based on value judgements – in that they clarify how groups ought to behave in order to create improvements. Should public policy aim at increasing economic growth only? Or should it give equal consideration to providing people free health care access, promoting gender equity and protecting ecosystems? These are questions that involve value judgements about what should be done. But development also requires learning from past experiences and analysing existing data. This is referred to as a *positive* approach to development, and relates to empirical studies, data analysis, hypothesis testing and other kinds of description and analysis. In addition, policy makers need to be able to *predict* how a situation could change in certain ways. For example, a development analyst might describe how many poor households exist in a country, and then try to predict or extrapolate how much a 5 per cent annual economic growth over five years will reduce the number of households that exist below a poverty line. Although distinct, *normative*, *positive* and *predictive* approaches are all interconnected, one needs to have positive and predictive analyses in order to make any normative assessments and vice versa. Yet normative analysis is fundamental and in some ways prior to predictive and positive analysis. Before describing the severity of poverty in a country, one needs a normative framework to define what poverty is – to choose its variables and measures. That is, before analysing poverty positively, one needs to make a value judgement about how poverty should be conceptualized. If poverty is defined as a lack of income this will have different implications for what governments and agencies should do to reduce poverty in comparison with a definition of poverty as unmet basic needs. The point is, normative approaches are central to the shaping of development policy, but are not sufficient to create it.

There are many ways in which normative frameworks affect policy decisions and outcomes. To name a few: they shape the data that we collect; they influence our analysis; they give certain topics greater or less political salience; they feed or hinder social movements; they may motivate professionals for moral or ethical reasons and they can be more or less philosophically credible.

All normative recommendations for development wrestle with common core issues: of uncertainty, of difficulties in prediction, of evaluating trade-offs and of identifying interconnections among variables and causal links. How can one take action on climate change? Should a country invest in wind turbines, solar panels or nuclear energy? We may not know which energy policy is the best option, given uncertainty about the future. In addition to uncertainty, trade-offs are more the norm than the exception in development policy-making. Should farmers in Kenya be encouraged to produce beans and flowers for European supermarkets? This creates employment for Kenyan farmers but also contributes to carbon emissions. How much should the Education Ministry of Tanzania allocate to achieving universal primary education and how much should they invest in the university sector? Policy-making often involves trade-offs between the pursuit of two valuable objectives.

Another difficulty for policy-making is the deep interconnection between different types of policies. The agricultural policy of encouraging flower cultivation for exports spills into employment policies in terms of job creation, which might then spill into gender policies – women may be empowered by moving from subsistence agriculture into business. Moreover, policies must navigate between different contexts and institutions, whether they are political, social or cultural. All must give some account of individuals' preferences, incentives and rewards, on the one hand, while guiding policies for firms, consumers, governments and international actors, on the other. Will an export-oriented agricultural policy strengthen local farmer cooperatives? Or will it give more power to multi-national agro-business companies? How stable or volatile is the demand for exports? What if the next government reverses the policy? Is encouraging another form of agriculture what local farmers actually value, and what benefits could it offer consumers who are the ultimate users of such products? Will women be empowered or constrained to menial jobs? To complicate matters further, one cannot predict the impact of policies without examining various cultural, political, economic and institutional contexts. The same agricultural policy of flower export will have a different impact in Kenya than in, say, Costa Rica.

John Neville Keynes (1891), who articulated the normative-predictive-positive distinction mentioned above, called policy 'the art of economics'. Policy-making in development no less than in economics is an art which resists scientific and technical modelling. It is also an art which profoundly depends on our normative assumptions. Whether one believes that the end of development is material prosperity, happiness or human freedom and fulfilment, these beliefs will shape the kinds of policies that are made and the reality in which we live.

To summarize: ideas about what development should be, matter. Different ways of understanding what development should improve lead to different policies and consequences.

The next sections present several examples of policy initiatives. We begin with quite a few concrete examples. Why? Instead of lecturing, we want readers themselves actively to analyse the situations and engage, throughout their study of human development, as agents in thinking practically about how to address various problems, and to keep in mind the various kinds of complexity that challenge all policy-makers. In the cases below, development policies reflect a dominant normative framework, in which public policy aims to increase economic prosperity, and predicts that improvements in other goals – such as better living conditions – automatically follow. The questions at the end of the chapter enable the reader to identify how normative frameworks actually make a difference in development policy and practice.

Case studies

Access to water in China

The Prefecture of Wuxi is one of China's most prosperous industrial towns.[2] It is also home to China's third largest freshwater lake, Tai Lake. Some 90 miles west of Shanghai, it has long been a source of life for millions of people. A famous scenic spot, the lake was immortalized in a popular song ('Beauty of Tai Lake') in the 1980s, which described its spectacular scenery at the time: 'Green reeds at the water's edge, rich in fish and shellfish at low tide, the lake water weaves through irrigation nets, the fragrance of fruit and rice floats around the lake.'

Unfortunately, the lake is nowadays frothing with pollution. In 2007, it was estimated that there were more than 20,000 chemical factories around the Tai Lake river basin. The lake is also located within a region that has experienced the highest level of urbanization in China. The population density of the Tai Lake area now exceeds 1000 inhabitants per square kilometre. Large amounts of industrial waste, urban sewage and chemical fertilizers end up in the lake water. The great volume of pollutants discharged into the lake causes water eutrophication. This leads to the formation of blue-green algae and renders the water undrinkable. The pollution reached its highest peak in May 2007, when a large bloom of blue-green algae so severely deteriorated the water quality that more than 2 million people were deprived of drinking water for nearly a week, cutting the town off from its natural water supply. According to senior officials of the Chinese environment regulating body, as temperatures rise, large-scale outbreaks of blue-green algae are very likely to occur in the future.

Since 1998, the Chinese government, from the central to the local level, has pooled many efforts to treat the water pollution in Tai Lake. By 2005, the Chinese government had pumped 10 billion Yuan[3] into the first phase of the plan to tackle pollution in the Tai Lake region. It is reported that the budget of the second phase amounted to 100 billion Yuan. However, despite all these efforts, water quality in the Tai Lake has not improved. The annual economic losses caused by the pollution were conservatively estimated to reach 5 billion Yuan.

The state of Tai Lake today epitomizes China's development process in the past three decades. The bloom of blue-green algae only reflects one of the many environmental challenges that China faces today. For a long time, growth in gross domestic product (GDP) has been seen as the only relevant indicator of development achievements. According to a report by the Ministry of Environment Protection published in 2006, the cost of environmental degradation caused by water pollution amounted to 286.28 billion Yuan in 2004, while environmental degradation caused by air pollution cost 219.8 billion Yuan. Total pollution-related losses accounted for more than 3 per cent of aggregate local GDP.[4] The opportunity cost of inaction remains very high. Not investing in tackling pollution now will result in greater economic losses in the future, a conclusion that the Stern Report on climate change amply demonstrated,[5] while the non-economic costs of pollution, such as loss of biodiversity and natural beauty, remain incalculable.

The Tai Lake ecological disaster triggered a nation-wide reflection on China's economic policies. After nearly 30 years of rapid economic growth, the Chinese have started to probe more fully into the meaning of economic growth and its relationship to quality of life. How to reassess the achievements of economic growth in the last three decades? Should public policy aim at an ultimate goal other than increasing economic prosperity? Is another normative framework for development needed?

While China has achieved extraordinary progresses in recent years – the Chinese are now wealthier, better educated and healthier than they have ever been – the environmental challenges mentioned above, along with other challenges like social and economic inequalities, call for major shifts in China's development policies and in its normative assumptions about what constitutes development. China's leadership is progressively acknowledging the situation and has formulated a bold new vision of development, described as the 'Scientific Development Approach', which roughly translates, in English, to the 'human development approach'. This approach highlights the fact that people should be the ultimate end of development. It calls for a balance between economic and social development and aims to build a harmonious society between and among human beings and in relation to their natural and social environment.[6]

Extractive industries in Peru

As it has been for centuries, the Peruvian economy in the 21st century is still based on mining, fishing and agriculture.[7] It is estimated that mining provides more than half of the Peruvian economy's annual export income. Peru is the world's second largest silver producer and Latin America's leader in gold output. The copper and zinc mine at Antamina in Ancash is the world's largest single investment project. Several billion dollars are also being invested in natural gas fields and old mines. All of these projects are run by foreign companies.

In the early 1990s, Peru began a structural adjustment process aimed at liberalizing its economy, leading to a boom in the mining sector. Rules governing the privatization of state-owned companies were established and labour laws were weakened significantly. Several provisions of the state environmental laws were also weakened early in Fujimori's first term. Moreover, the Land Law, which governs land ownership and use and establishes indigenous land rights, was modified in favour of mining investment.

These liberalization reforms greatly strengthened the position of the mining sector in the economy. During the greater part of the 1990s, this sector expanded significantly. Between 1991 and 1997, the area of land covered by mining concessions increased by over 700 per cent. By the end of 1999, mining rights had been assigned to approximately 12 per cent of the nation's territory. This expansion took place both in traditional mining zones and in areas that had never before experienced mining activity.

Despite these economic gains, mining has been very disruptive for the social and natural environment. Toxic chemicals such as cyanide and sulphuric acid are employed by the mining industry to extract minerals. The extraction process can also produce toxic by-products. These chemicals are not always transported or handled properly and spills are not uncommon. In 1999, residents of a village were exposed to mercury, a potent toxin, when a truck spilled its load. The residents, who present with symptoms that are consistent with long-term mercury poisoning, have never been compensated, nor have they received adequate medical treatment.

Environmental contamination is also frequently caused by inadequate tailings containment. Tailings are the rock wastes left behind following ore extraction. They often contain heavy metals, acid-forming minerals and residue from toxic chemicals used in the extraction process. Widespread water contamination caused by inadequate mine waste management has thus deeply affected Peru.

The arrival of a mining company can also have serious social consequences for local communities, including outright displacement. In some cases, communities are forcibly relocated to make way for mine development. In the case of the controversial Tambogrande gold mine in the department of Piura, such relocation was avoided. Construction of the mine required the relocation of approximately half the town. People refused to abandon their homes and, by uniting in opposition to the mine, successfully blocked the company's proposal.

Mining activity often involves the arrival of outsiders, which frequently generates tension within communities and threatens traditional practices. It is not uncommon for prostitution, alcoholism, domestic violence, family breakdown and health problems to increase in communities that coexist with mining.

Perhaps most devastating is the impact of mineral activity on the sources of the livelihoods of the affected communities, who are mainly farmers and livestock rearers. The impact of mining, specifically the loss of land and the contamination of water and soil resources, dramatically limits the ability of peasant communities to pursue traditional subsistence activities, thereby restricting their livelihood opportunities.

As with the previous story of Tai Lake in China, the pursuit of development in this context is based on certain normative assumptions about what development is. Mining has been chosen as a development strategy because of its positive effect on Peruvian GDP growth. Mining increases exports and builds on the comparative advantage of Peru in this sector. While economic gains would clearly benefit some, there were obvious trade-offs. What about the ability of peasant communities to cultivate the land of their ancestors? And what of the local communities' ability to live healthily? While the Peruvian government bases its development policies on a normative framework – that increasing quality of life comes through economic growth and that encouraging mining investment is one of the best strategies to achieve this aim – local people may have a different normative framework. For them, living healthy lives free of metal pollution, being able to farm the land in a sustainable way and being able to take part in indigenous festivals and religious ceremonies, may also be development outcomes they value but are unable to protect in the face of mining interests. Is there a way to bring these diverse views into a productive dialogue?

Forest protection in Uganda

On 12 April 2007, many Ugandans turned out in the streets of Kampala to protest against a government plan to sell 7000 hectares of forest land to a sugar company called Mehta, which was owned by an Indian family and which hoped to expand its sugarcane plantations considerably.[8] In this plan the government foresaw increased sugar production, increased exports and an engine for economic growth, growth that would eventually benefit all Ugandans. The land that was due to be sold was part of the Mabira Forest, home to several rare flora and fauna species and a nature reserve since 1932. The protest between demonstrators, who wanted to preserve the natural integrity of the forest, and the government, who hoped to encourage productive investment in the country, had turned violent. Three people died, including an Indian national.

The protest was organized by a group of environmentalists that included members of parliament, professional environmentalists, political activists and students. But the general public was quickly drawn into the protest. The mass media had covered the issue widely and the public was convinced that protecting the Mabira Forest was more valuable than sacrificing it for the sake of productive investment. Many demonstrators carried green leaves and placards to express their concerns about the forest and the environment in general. Some of the placards had telling messages. One placard read: 'Environment is life'. Another read: 'Government, listen to the voice of the people, Mabira is ours'.

Several arguments were made on the importance of protecting the forest. One of the daily newspapers in Uganda summed up the key argument as follows: 'Protagonists say (the) Mabira forest acts as [an] environmental filter zone for noxious gases, it buffers against soil erosion, it [hosts] endangered animal and flora species, and holds a variety of trees with high medicinal worth and hardwood timber worth hundreds of millions of dollars besides its aesthetic value...' (*Daily Monitor*, 5 May 2008).

Cultural, religious and traditional healers also joined the campaign to stop the destruction of the Mabira Forest for the expansion of the large-scale sugarcane plantation. The cultural leaders of Buganda, a tribe that lives on land where Mabira Forest is situated, petitioned the president in a letter to halt the process to give away the forest. Whereas the religious leaders prayed to God for the protection of the Mabira forest, traditional healers vowed to invoke the spirits of the forest to attack any action that is intended to cut down the trees of the forest. The leader of the Uganda Traditional Healers and Herbalists Association, Sylvia Namutebi, went to the forest to perform rituals to invoke the spirits.

As a result of these protests and outcries, Uganda's Cabinet suspended the proposal. However, one newspaper (*The New Vision*, 13 April 2007) noted that President Museveni scoffed at critics who opposed the forest give-away, saying he would not be deterred by people who do not see where the future lies. Even more recently, a Ugandan news agency quoted the president as saying that he still maintained his stand on the issue of Mabira during his 'State of the Nation Address' and that he believed that, with patience, the issue would be solved – i.e. that Ugandans would come to realize where the future of their country lies.[9]

'The Save Mabira Forest Crusade', as this movement came to be called, represents a historical moment in the development of modern Africa. Ugandans used cell phones and internet technologies to mobilize and organize street protests. One SMS message read: 'Save Mabira Forest, do not buy Lugazi sugar' and was circulated all over Uganda and beyond to mobilize civil action against the proposed project.

None of these cases are easy – trade-offs are unavoidable, and there are no simple answers. What is clear about this case is that the citizens of a developing country can mobilize and rally together on an issue that they feel has a direct and considerable impact on their quality of life. Here, the environment was inextricably linked to notions of development and well-being, which included considerations about health, food, history, religion and their overall relationship with nature. How can this loss be compared to the gain that others in Uganda and India and elsewhere might enjoy from the new sugar plantation?

The Heathrow expansion in London

The variety of normative frameworks for development is not only a reality in so-called developing countries.[10] It is a reality in industrialized countries as well and can have considerable consequences for people outside the national boundaries in which policy decisions are taken.

In London, the government has given its approval for building a third runway at Heathrow airport. Its major argument for the expansion is the impact the expansion would have on the British economy. London is an international financial centre and it is argued that the current airport capacity is unable to meet the air travel demand that such an international financial centre requires. It is believed that, without satisfactory airport facilities, businesses are likely to move out of London and the UK altogether. Another economic rationale for the expansion is the number of jobs that it would create. The government argues that these benefits more than compensate for the negative effects of building a third runway.

This economic project is, however, not without consequences. Air and noise pollution will increase. Areas in southwest London already cope with one plane taking off or landing every minute during the daytime. The government answers these complaints by arguing that technology will solve the pollution problem and that planes are likely to become much less noisy in the future. A village will have to be destroyed to make way for the expansion; 700 residents are likely to be resettled. The increase in air traffic is also contributing to CO_2 emissions, thereby accelerating climate change. While Western industrialized countries are mainly responsible for climate change, it is people in developing countries who have not contributed to the problem who suffer from it the most.[11]

As in Uganda, civil society organizations have rallied to protest against the government plan. In August 2007, a massive campaign was staged at Heathrow airport with activists camping on the site and creating travel disruption. They also produced detailed information which weakened the government's argument. The government's economic rationale was challenged on two fronts: first, the justification that the expansion is essential to London's economy does not match the empirical evidence of a link between airport capacity and business activities. Other European capitals have not expanded their major airports but international businesses did not necessarily relocate as a consequence. In contrast, despite Heathrow's poor customer performance – the disastrous opening of the new Terminal in April 2008 made international headlines, for example – new international businesses have settled in London. Second, the government overrates the contribution of the aviation sector to the economy. The industry is only the 26th biggest industry in Britain, half the size of the computer industry, and a tenth the size of banking and finance. Moreover, the industry is heavily subsidized: unlike petrol, there is no tax on aviation fuel and the industry is exempt from value added tax. Instead of creating new employment opportunities, the airport expansion is therefore likely to be a further burden on taxpayers.

In addition, civil society organizations have challenged the government's policy on environmental grounds. They have estimated that the annual climate change emissions from the third runway alone would be the same as Kenya's overall emissions. Considering further that 45 per cent of air strips within Europe are less than 500 kilometres in length, improving the high-speed railway network in Britain and within the continent would appear to be more economically and environmentally efficient as a whole.

Normative frameworks matter

The stories above lead us to ask basic questions about trade-offs between economic growth and quality of life, between policies that favour different groups of people, between the short term and the long term. Are poor people better off because of economic growth? On what grounds should their quality of life be assessed? Does economic expansion go hand-in-hand with a more limited access to safe water? Is mining in Peru a desirable way to generate higher income and employment? Is this the only criteria which should guide policy decisions? Is the expansion of air travel to be encouraged on the premise that its contribution to the country's economic output is necessary? How are economic benefits to offset environmental and social costs? Is displacement justified?

The stories highlight that each state of affairs is viewed differently by different groups and individuals. The Chinese government assesses China's economic development from a certain perspective. However, those who are negatively affected by economic growth assess it on the basis of other normative foundations. In Peru, the government undertakes mining activities on the basis of certain beliefs about economic development and the improvement of people's lives. In contrast, the people affected by mining activities have a different opinion about the contribution of mining to their lives, particularly when non-economic factors are taken into account. Equally, the Ugandan government assesses the value of forests from the perspective of job creation and certain types of economic incentives. However, other groups value the forests in a different light. Similar conclusions hold for the example of the Heathrow expansion plan: the government's prioritization of economic growth and productive investments does not match the general public's value of environmental protection and equal opportunities for future generations.

Disagreement is likely to be perennial. And it is not embarrassing at all that people do not agree. But there are better and worse ways to navigate between conflicts of interest and value, and there are policies that are better and worse at achieving the improvements they seek.

We can see here two sets of questions being asked by different groups, each relying on certain normative assumptions about what matters and what policies should be pursued. One set relates to *how the policy decision will affect economic output*. How much are the chemical companies in Tai Lake region to contribute to China's economic growth? How much is mining going to increase Peruvian exports and the country's GDP as a whole? How much is the destruction of parts of the Mabira forest going to contribute to the dynamism of the Ugandan economy? How much is the airport expansion going to contribute to job creation and Britain's economic growth? The other set relates to *how the policy will affect people's quality of life* – negatively or positively. Will economic growth enable the Chinese to live a life they value, such as living a healthy life free of contamination concerns? Will mining enable Peruvians to have dignified employment, send their children to school and enjoy better health? Will the giving away of protected areas to productive investment opportunities make most Ugandans better off? Is the airport expansion necessary to sustain the quality of life in Britain?

The stories clearly illustrate that what is considered to be 'development', and what is seen as a policy to improve people's lives, is inextricably linked with values about what matters. Whether development aims to improve economic growth or to advance human rights, human agency or human flourishing, the implications are both practical and far-reaching.

People first

To some, the idea that people should come first in social and economic processes appears a redundant truism. But development has long been sought and assessed in economic terms, with a particular focus on the annual growth of income per capita, instead of the consequences of this growth on the quality of people's lives. The two are distinct, as Box 1.1 illustrates.

The overwhelming focus on growth persists today. Economic growth is clearly a necessary component of development in most circumstances, although the rate of growth required might still be a source of debate. Furthermore, sustained economic growth is now widely recognized to be deeply interconnected with advances in health and education. Yet economic growth is still put forward regularly as the dominant normative framework for development, and other activities are justified insofar as they foster growth. In the following section, we critically examine several assumptions about economic growth and its contribution to human flourishing. These assumptions are briefly introduced here and will be discussed in further detail in subsequent chapters, particularly Chapter 4.

Box 1.1 Development and economic growth in Liberia

In 1944 the generous Open Door Policy was introduced by Liberia's 18th President, Dr W. V. S. Tubman. The policy was intended to attract foreign capital from many sources for a wide range of projects, including rubber tree plantations, lumbering and mining of iron ore. It was also intended to diversify the economy. As a guarantee to foreign firms, they were allowed to remit their earnings without any restrictions. The policy was very successful as the Liberian economy experienced extensive economic growth. For instance, the important iron ore sector attracted substantial foreign investment in the 1960s and the first half of the 1970s. By 1975, Liberia had become the world's fifth largest exporter of iron ore. In monetary terms, from 1946 to 1960, the Tubman Administration attracted over $500 million in foreign investment; exports rose from $15.8 million in 1948 to $82.6 million in 1960, an increase of 422.8 per cent; and Government revenue rose from $32.4 million in 1960 to $69.9 million in 1971, an increase of 115.7 per cent. The substantial economic growth recorded was an economic miracle.

However, Liberia's tremendous economic growth became characterized as 'growth without development', a phrase borrowed from Clower et al's *Growth without Development: an Economic Survey of Liberia* (1966, Northwestern University Press). According to Clower and his colleagues, 'the Liberian economy grew at a rate almost unparalleled anywhere else in the world (outstripped, in fact, only by Japan). Unfortunately, this growth did not lead to development, that is, to structural economic change absorbing larger numbers of Liberians in new productive activities and with more advanced training and skills. On the contrary, the returns from Liberia's economic growth, insofar as they accrued to Liberians, went almost exclusively to the small ruling minority of Americo-Liberians, thus reinforcing their political power and the economic and social divisions between the country's tribal majority'(pxv).

With time, Liberia experienced its first ever serious political street protest organized by the opposition on 14 April 1979. The opposition was mainly made up of sons and daughters of the tribal majority with few sympathizers from the elite who were marginalized themselves. This event was followed by the 12 April 1980 coup and a civil war that lasted from 24 December 1989 to 18 August 2003, when the Accra Comprehensive Peace Agreement (CPA) was signed by all warring parties, including both the Government and warring factions. Charles Taylor later went into exile due to pressure from warring factions fighting to oust his government and that of the international community (specifically President George Bush of the US who made a public pronouncement that Charles Taylor must go), and he was replaced by his Vice President, Moses Z. Blah.

As provided for in the CPA, a National Transitional Government of Liberia was inaugurated in October 2003, and it was charged with responsibility to oversee democratic elections in October 2005. Eventually, a democratically elected government was ushered into office on 16 January 2006 following the presidential and general elections in October 2005 and a subsequent run off in November 2005. Mrs Ellen Johnson Sirleaf was elected President, becoming the first ever democratically elected female president in Africa (see also Chapter 13).

This box was written by Wilmot A. Reeves.

Assumption 1: A high GDP per capita is necessary for human flourishing

The first assumption is that economic growth is desirable, in part, because it raises people's income, hence their quality of life. In many circumstances this is true, but not always and not necessarily. Empirical evidence shows no *automatic* connection between a high GDP per capita and the ability of people to flourish. Table 1.1 illustrates the link between GDP and some dimensions of human flourishing such as health, education and political freedom, in the case of Saudi Arabia and Uruguay, the Russian Federation and Costa Rica, and Vietnam and Morocco. Uruguay has a much lower GDP per capita than Saudi Arabia. Yet people live longer. Women are more literate. Fewer children die prematurely, and basic political rights and civil liberties (such as the right to vote and the freedom of expression and association) are fully respected. The contrast between the Russian Federation and Costa Rica yields similar conclusions: Russia is wealthier, but its inhabitants live much shorter lives in a much more constrained political environment. While Morocco has a higher GDP per capita than Vietnam, its illiteracy and infant mortality rates are much higher. The discrimination against women, as measured by the difference between the adult literacy and adult female literacy rate, is also much higher. When countries are arranged according to the Human Development Index – a composite index which measures progress in economic conditions, life expectancy and literacy — the wealthier countries in terms of GDP per capita are not necessarily better off when human dimensions such as health and education are taken into account. Saudi Arabia and Russia, the two richest countries of Table 1.1 in terms of economic development, are ultimately poorer than Uruguay and Costa Rica in human development terms.

Table 1.1 *Some human development indicators*

	Saudi Arabia	Uruguay	Russia	Costa Rica	Vietnam	Morocco
GDP per capita (PPPUS$)	15,711	9962	10,845	9481	3071	4555
Adult literacy rate (%)	82.9	96.8	99.4	94.9	90.3	52.3
Female literacy rate (%)	76.3	97.3	99.2	95.1	86.9	39.6
Life expectancy (years)	72.2	75.9	65	78.5	73.7	70.4
Under 5 mortality (0/00)	26	15	18	12	19	40
Political Rights/Civil Liberties [a]	7/6	1/1	6/5	1/1	7/5	5/4
Human Development Index	0.812	0.852	0.802	0.846	0.733	0.646

Source: Human Development Report 2007/2008, see www.undp.org
[a] Freedom House 2008 (with 1 being most free and 7 less free), see www.freedomhouse.org

Assumption 2: Families with a good income will not be deprived in other dimensions

Another widespread assumption is that not being poor in terms of income means not suffering from a lack in other matters too, such as health and education. However, empirical data often tell another story. In a pioneering study comparing different conceptualizations of poverty in Peru and India, Ruggieri, Saith and Stewart (2003) concluded that those who were poor in terms of income were not necessarily the same people who were poor in terms of education or nutrition. They obtained the following results: in India, 65 per cent of children who belonged to households below the monetary poverty line were not educationally poor (that is, were enrolled at primary school). In Peru, 93 per cent of children belonging to monetary poor households were not educationally poor, and 66 per cent were not nutritionally poor. However, 43 per cent of children in India who did not belong to monetary poor households were not enrolled at school. And 53 per cent of children from non-monetary poor families suffered malnutrition. Having an income, or belonging to a 'non-poor' household, is thus not a guarantee of avoiding malnutrition or receiving education, particularly where public services are weak or absent (we will come back to this in Chapter 6).

Table 1.2 *Poverty in different spaces: surprisingly different*

		Education		Nutrition/Health	
		Children	Adults	Children	Adults
Percent of people who are *not income poor* but are *capability deprived*	India	43	60	53	63
	Peru	32	37	21	55
Percent of people who are *not income poor* but are *not capability deprived*	India	65	38	53	91
	Peru	93	73	66	94

Source: Franco *et al* (2002) cited in Ruggieri, Saith and Stewart (2003)

Assumption 3: Economic growth will automatically reduce other kinds of poverty, such as malnutrition

In recent years, India and China have been celebrated as economic successes. The Chinese growth rate is nearly solely responsible for the fact that the Millennium Development Goal (MDG) of halving the proportion of people living on under $1 a day is likely to be met. It has therefore been assumed that sustained, high economic growth rates have had a tremendous impact on other kinds of poverty.

The rather counter-intuitive and disconcerting truth is that, at present, the expected spill-overs have been fairly scarce with respect to several key variables. Consider child malnutrition, which is one of the most critical indications of how well a country is doing. India has experienced 15 years of boundless economic growth. Yet, in 1998–1999, 47 per cent of children under the age of 3 were undernourished (weight for height was used as an indicator of malnutrition). In

2005–2006, that number remained resiliently and unacceptably high, at 46 per cent of all children under 3 remaining malnourished. Similarly, in 1998–1999, 58 per cent of children under 3 years of age had not received complete vaccinations; by 2005–2006, that number had barely decreased at all – 56 per cent of children were still not fully vaccinated. And anaemia had risen from 75 to 79 per cent in those same years.[12] Even in China, steady and impressive economic growth has been accompanied by startling health inequities and deprivations, particularly in rural areas.

Assumption 4: Data for income and expenditure are better than other poverty data

Critics of non-monetary indicators of development argue that income and expenditure data are the most reliable indicators of development. But, in fact, income and consumption or expenditure data are subject to a number of serious and widely-recognized difficulties. Income data in developing countries are often considered less accurate than consumption data, and are also more volatile (hence, less reflective) of sustained living standards (Deaton, 1997). Also, both consumption and income data have to be gathered item by item with varying recall periods, leading to potential errors. In addition, much consumption may be from non-market sources (public services, NGOs and community-based groups, home-grown food, home-made clothes, fire wood or dung collected, etc.) and the imputation of prices to these is not straightforward. Other challenges include the purchasing power parity rates across rural–urban areas or countries, the construction of 'equivalent' incomes for households of different sizes, and the determination of poverty lines.

Another assumption is that non-monetary indicators are of weak quality. However, the coverage and quality of non-monetary data has in fact improved tremendously in the last two decades. Regularized household surveys in developing countries have increased steadily since the 1980s, and the international pressure of meeting the MDGs has further accelerated this trend. Furthermore, a number of efforts to strengthen the capacities of national statistical offices have led to an increase in sample and data quality. Granted, the data are far from perfectly accurate, but analyses of poverty and deprivation increasingly draw on non-income variables as well as assets, consumption or income (see Chapter 6).

Assumption 5: It is easier to promote economic growth than human flourishing

Economic growth has been the focus of considerable study, policy prescriptions, strategies and political attention. But it has proven to be far more difficult to realize than most anticipated. In 2001, Bill Easterly drew attention to a 'puzzle' which he described as follows:

> In 1980–98, median per capita income growth in developing countries was 0.0 per cent, as compared to 2.5 per cent in

> 1960–79. Yet ... policies like financial depth and real over-
> valuation, and initial conditions like health, education, fertility,
> and infrastructure generally improved from 1960–79 to
> 1980–98. Developing country growth should have increased
> instead of decreased, according to the standard growth regression
> determinants of growth. The stagnation seems to represent a dis-
> appointing outcome to the movement towards the 'Washington
> Consensus'[13] by developing countries. (Easterly, 2001, p135)

In other words, although some economic growth policies had been implemented, they did not necessarily result in growth or economic development.

In 2005, the World Bank published a landmark report, *Economic Growth
in the 1990s: Learning from a Decade of Reform*.[14] The report observed that
growth performance was uneven across developing countries, but lower than
anticipated overall. It acknowledged that, 'Bank growth projections, as well as
growth projections by other forecasters, tend to be systematically over-
optimistic'. Further, it acknowledged that the unevenness of growth could not
be explained entirely by countries' adherence to advised policy reforms.
Indeed, some South and East Asian countries had achieved growth through
very different mechanisms. Although many country experiences and insights
were involved in the study, several central themes emerged. One was that the
1980s and 1990s had overlooked one determinant of growth of central
importance: institutions (see Chapter 7). The 2008 Commission on Growth
and Development examined the countries that achieved high and sustained
growth to establish what had caused it, and found considerable diversity in
strategies.[15] The point is that, although policy-makers in the 1980s and 1990s
had thought that the determinants of growth were clear – macroeconomic
stability, trade liberalization, privatization, deregulation, financial
liberalization and better public sector governance – growth proved to be, to
use Easterly's phrase, 'elusive'. Further, given the global 'credit crunch' in
September 2008, even those gains in growth proved more fragile than was
perhaps anticipated. Indeed, one of the advantages of human development
achievements is that, as section 1 suggested, they can be sustained even by
countries with relatively low incomes, and during economic downturns.

Assumption 6: Economic growth can be sustained without considerations for human flourishing

This assumption has been challenged by a study by Ranis, Stewart and
Ramirez (2000), who demonstrated that countries that have experienced
economic growth but whose population continue to suffer from low levels of
education and health were not able to sustain that growth in the long term.
Conversely, some countries with low levels of income per capita have been able
to provide an environment in which their inhabitants could attain good
educational and health standards. Ultimately, the only countries that were able
to sustain growth were those that had previously invested in the health and

education of their people. That education and health are instrumental in promoting economic growth is not however the sole reason for investing in these sectors, as Chapter 9 will discuss.

Human flourishing and the impact of policies on people's lives are the fundamental concerns of this textbook and the core of what is known as the 'human development and capability' approach. The next chapter presents the basic concepts of this people-centred approach to development.

Questions

1.1 What do you understand by the word 'development'? Draw a picture of your own conception of development.

1.2 Identify at least three concrete examples where economic development activities raise ethical questions. What possible positions might people take on each of these issues? How might they defend their respective positions? What information or assumptions do they rely upon? What value judgements would they (implicitly) be making? (This could be done as a role-playing exercise, where different parties defend their position taking into account their own respective value judgements).

1.3 How do normative frameworks affect policy decisions and outcomes? Can you give examples from your experience where a different normative framework would have led to other policy priorities and outcomes?

1.4 Why do you think the basic intuition that human concerns should be the ultimate goal of economic activity continues to be ignored in policy all over the world?

1.5 What are the main ideas and concepts which guide public policies in your country?

Notes

1   For an introduction to theories of development, see, among others, Cowen and Shenton (1996), Preston (1996) and Rist (1997).

2   Story written by Jiantuo Yu, Centre for Human and Economic Development Studies, Beijing University, China.

3   At the end of 2005, US$1 = 8.07 Yuan.

4   State Environment Protection Administration, *China Green National Accounting Study Report 2004*, Beijing.

5   The 'Stern Review on the Economics of Climate Change' can be downloaded from www.hm-treasury.gov.uk/independent_reviews_index.htm.

6   UNDP China Country Office, *China National Human Development Report 2007/8*, Beijing.

7   This section is taken from www.perusupportgroup.org.uk/key_extractive.html. With kind permission of Gabriela Drinkwater, from the Peru Support Group, for reproduction of the material.

8   Story written by Michael Mawa Mkumba University Uganda, Pamela Mbabazi Mbarara University Uganda, Esuruku Robert Uganda Martyr's University and Saidah Najjuma, Noejje University, Uganda.

9   www.eturbonew.com.
10   This section has been written on the basis of information contained in studies
     made by the Heathrow Association for the Control of Aircraft Noise available
     at www.hacan.org.uk.
11   See the *Human Development Report* 2007/2008 on climate change published
     by the UNDP at http://hdr.undp.org.
12   Focus Report (2006) *Focus on Children under Six*, reporting NFHS data from
     1998–1999 and 2005–2006. The document is available at
     www.crin.org/docs/sen_nutrition.pdf.
13   The 'Washington Consensus' refers to the policy package promoted by the
     Washington-based international institutions of the World Bank and
     International Monetary Fund. Gore (2000, p789) defines the 'Washington
     Consensus' as an approach which 'recommends that governments reform
     their policies and, in particular: (a) pursue macroeconomic stability by
     controlling inflation and reducing fiscal deficits; (b) open their economies to
     the rest of the world through trade and capital account liberalization; and (c)
     liberalize domestic product and factor markets through privatization and
     deregulation.'
14   Its contents can be accessed at www1.worldbank.org/prem/lessons1990s.
15   See www.growthcommission.org.

Readings

Crocker, D. (1991) 'Towards development ethics', *World Development*, vol 19, no 5,
     pp457–483
Easterly, W. (2001) 'The lost decades: Explaining developing countries' stagnation in
     spite of policy reform 1980–88', *Journal of Economic Growth*, vol 6, no 2,
     pp135–157
Gore, C. (2000) 'The rise and fall of the Washington Consensus as a paradigm for
     developing countries', *World Development*, vol 28, no 5, pp789–804
Preston, P. W. (1996) *Development Theory: An Introduction*, Blackwell, Oxford
Qizilbash, M. (1996) 'Ethical development', *World Development*, vol 24, no 7,
     pp1209–1221
Rist, G. (1997) *The History of Development: From Western Origins to Global Faith*,
     Zed Books, London
Sen, A. K. (1987) *On Ethics and Economics*, Basil Blackwell, Oxford
Ranis, G., Stewart, F. and Ramirez, A. (2000) 'Economic growth and human
     development', *World Development*, vol 25, no 2, pp197–209

Further Readings

Cowen, M. P. and Shenton, R. W. (1996) *Doctrines of Development*, Routledge,
     London
Deaton, A. (1997) *The Analysis of Household Surveys: A Microeconometric
     Approach to Development Policy*, John Hopkins University Press, Baltimore
Gasper, D. (2004) *The Ethics of Development*, Edinburgh University Press, Edinburgh
Gasper, D. (2008) 'Denis Goulet and the project of development ethics: Choices in
     methodology, focus and organization', *Journal of Human Development*, vol 9, no
     3, pp453–474
Goulet, D. (1995) *Development Ethics: A Guide to Theory and Practice*, Zed Books,
     London

Keynes, J. N. (1891) *The Scope and Method of Political Economy*. 4th Kelley and Millman Inc., New York, republished 1955

Ruggeri Laderchi, C., Saith, R. and Stewart, F. (2003) 'Does it matter that we do not agree on the definition of poverty?' *Oxford Development Studies*, vol 31, no 3, pp243–274

2

The Human Development and Capability Approach

Sabina Alkire and Séverine Deneulin

Aims of the chapter

- To introduce the key concepts and principles of human development and the capability approach.
- To understand the contribution of the approach to development thinking and policy.
- To identify the implications of the human development and capability approach for development at the micro and macro level.

Key points

- The capability approach contains three central concepts: functioning, capability and agency. A *functioning* is being or doing what people value and have reason to value. A *capability* is a person's freedom to enjoy various functionings – to be or do things that contribute to their well-being. *Agency* is a person's ability to pursue and realize goals she values and has reason to value.
- The human development and capability approach is multi-dimensional, because several things matter at the same time. Well-being cannot be reduced to income, or happiness or any single thing.
- The human development and capability approach combines a focus on outcomes with a focus on processes. Four key principles are: equity, efficiency, participation and sustainability.
- Improvements or progress are assessed in terms of capabilities, hence policies should promote capabilities.
- The selection of relevant capabilities depends on the situation. Public debate can be useful. Considering standard 'lists' also help groups not to overlook key areas unintentionally.

How would you define 'successful' development? Let us start with two oversimplifications. Consider first an approach to development in which the objective is to achieve and sustain high rates of economic growth. In this situation, the unit of analysis is evident: the economy. This may be the national economy or the economy of a particular region or sector. The currency of assessment is also clear: income now and in the future. Trade-offs, such as between environment protection and employment creation, or between this generation and the next, are resolved by market prices, exchange rates and discount rates; in some cases prices may be corrected for social, environmental and distributional concerns.

Now consider an approach to development in which the objective is to expand what people are able to do and be – what might be called their real freedoms. It puts people first. In this view, a healthy economy is one that enables people to enjoy a long and healthy life, a good education, a meaningful job, physical safety, democratic debate and so on. Notice two shifts from the earlier approach: first, the analysis shifts from the economy to the person. Second, the currency of assessment shifts from money to the things people can do and be in their lives, now and in the future.

In both situations, trade-offs surface. Policy must consider which groups of the population to focus on (*distribution*), and which period of time to prioritize (*dynamics*). In the second approach, there are also trade-offs to be considered between which aspect(s) of people's lives to focus on (*dimension*).

While each perspective takes a fundamentally different objective, they are not totally distinct; they overlap. Those who focus on people's lives are still vitally concerned with economic growth, macroeconomic stability, income poverty reduction and many other means of improving people's lives. And those focused on sustained growth still concern themselves with healthy, educated and skilled workers, and some modicum of peace and stability. Yet as has been discussed in the previous chapter, normative frameworks and ideas about what matters have enormous practical implications.

This chapter describes the second perspective, the people-focused one, otherwise known as the human development and capability approach. Human development has been pioneered by different people under different names and at different times. A focus on people's freedoms can be found in the notion of *ubuntu* in Southern Africa,[1] with liberation theology in Latin America and beyond,[2] with participatory development, community mobilization, rights-based approaches, sustainable livelihoods and many other ethical approaches to development. It is equally applicable in developed and developing countries. One of its leading voices is the philosopher and Nobel laureate in economics Amartya Sen, whose writings on the 'capability approach' provide the philosophical basis of human development and hence of this textbook. Later sections will present his foundational work and its basic terms and concepts. But, before moving to these, we begin by offering an overview of the key elements of human development.

Human development

A bird's-eye view

The idea of human development has been circulated in policy circles and public debate for the past two decades, with various degrees of persuasiveness, incisiveness and accuracy. One powerful vehicle of communication has been the annual *Human Development Report* produced by the United Nations Development Programme (UNDP). The first report was published in 1990, and all reports seek to articulate the human development perspective on one set of issues. In addition to the annual global report, roughly 100 different countries are producing their own *National* and *Regional Human Development Reports* today, with some of these countries producing state or provincial reports as well. These reports are intended to assess the quality of life of a population and be an advocacy tool for its improvement. The analysis draws upon data regarding health, education, nutrition, work, political freedoms, security, the environment and many other aspects of people's lives. In assessing the state of a population from a people-centred perspective, these reports have the political purpose of raising awareness and generating debate on public issues and concerns which would otherwise not be on the political agenda.

Box 2.1 Themes of global Human Development Reports to date

2009:	*Overcoming barriers: Human mobility and development*
2007/8:	*Fighting climate change: Human solidarity in a divided world*
2006:	*Beyond scarcity: Power, poverty and the global water crisis*
2005:	*International cooperation at a crossroads*
2004:	*Cultural liberty in today's diverse world*
2003:	*Millennium Development Goals: A compact among nations to end human poverty*
2002:	*Deepening democracy in a fragmented world*
2001:	*Making new technologies work for human development*
2000:	*Human rights and human development*
1999:	*Globalization with a human face*
1998:	*Consumption for human development*
1997:	*Human development to eradicate poverty*
1996:	*Economic growth and human development*
1995:	*Gender and human development*
1994:	*New dimensions of human security*
1993:	*People's participation*
1992:	*Global dimensions of human development*
1991:	*Financing human development*
1990:	*Concept and measurement of human development*

The *Human Development Reports* were the brainchild of Mahbub ul Haq, a Pakistani economist who wanted to see the world's economic and social progress assessed in a different way, moving away from the usual income and economic growth considerations that had come to characterize the World Bank's annual *World Development Reports*.[3] As ul Haq argued, a country that sells weapons should not be considered more 'developed' than a country that has chosen not to make weapons and export them, simply because the production of weapons makes the gross domestic product (GDP) of that particular country significantly higher. The following quote, taken from a speech given by Robert F. Kennedy on 4 January 1968, encapsulates the limitations of GDP as a measure of what makes life valuable:

> The Gross National Product of the United States is the largest in the world, but that GNP, if we should judge our nation by that, counts air pollution and cigarette advertising and ambulances to clear the highways of carnage. It counts special locks for our doors and jails that break them. It counts the destruction of our redwoods and the loss of our natural wonder and chaotic sprawl. It counts napalm and the cost of a nuclear warhead and armoured cars that fight riots in our streets. Yet the gross national product does not allow for the health of our children, the quality of their education or the joy of their play. It does not include the beauty of our poetry or the strength of our marriages, the intelligence of our public debate or the integrity of our public officials. It measures neither our wit nor our courage, neither our wisdom nor our learning, neither our compassion nor our devotion to our country. It measures everything, in short, except that which makes life worthwhile.[4]

Clarification of means and ends

Human development draws attention to 'what makes life worthwhile': people. In so doing, the appraisal of income growth itself is altered altogether. The limited value of income and wealth has been recognized for centuries. Aristotle argued that 'wealth is evidently not the good we are seeking, for it is merely useful and for the sake of something else' (*Nicomachean Ethics*, Book 1, chapter 5, 1096^a5–10). Going even further back in time, the first chapter of Amartya Sen's *Development as Freedom* relates a discussion described in an 8th century BC Sanskrit manuscript. A woman, Maitreyee, asks her husband 'if "the whole earth, full of wealth" were to belong to her, she (would) achieve immortality through it.' Hearing that she would not, Maitreyee asks, 'What should I do with that by which I do not become immortal?' (cited in Sen, 1999, p13).

That people matter does not mean that income does not. Income is obviously an important instrument in enabling people to realize their full potential. A 12-year old boy who wishes to pursue secondary education and become a doctor might have his dreams blighted by the fact that he has to

Box 2.2 The purpose of development

The basic purpose of development is to enlarge people's choices. In principle, these choices can be infinite and can change over time. People often value achievements that do not show up at all, or not immediately, in income or growth figures: greater access to knowledge, better nutrition and health services, more secure livelihoods, security against crime and physical violence, satisfying leisure hours, political and cultural freedoms and a sense of participation in community activities. The objective of development is to create an enabling environment for people to enjoy long, healthy and creative lives.

The human development paradigm covers all aspects of development – whether economic growth or international trade; budget deficits or fiscal policy; savings, investment or technology; basic social services or safety nets for the poor. No aspect of the development model falls outside its scope, but point of reference remains the widening of people's choices and the enrichment of their lives. All aspects of life – economic, political or cultural – are viewed from that perspective. Economic growth therefore becomes only one subset of the human development paradigm.

On some aspects of the human development paradigm, there is fairly broad agreement:

- Development must put people at the centre of its concerns.
- The purpose of development is to enlarge all human choices and not just income.
- The human development paradigm is concerned both with building human capabilities (through investment in people) and with using those human capabilities more fully (through an enabling framework for growth and employment).
- Human development has four essential pillars: equality, sustainability, productivity and empowerment. It regards economic growth as essential, but emphasizes the need to pay attention to its quality and distribution, analyses at length its link with human lives and questions its long-term sustainability.
- The human development paradigm defines the ends of development and analyses sensible options for achieving them.

Extract from Mahbub ul Haq (2004) 'The human development paradigm' in Fukuda-Parr and Shiva Kumar (eds) *Readings in Human Development*, Oxford University Press, New Delhi, 2nd edn, pp17 and 19.

work instead, in order to help pay health bills incurred by other family members. But income is not everything. The 12-year old would not have to work if there were adequate public health services for low-income families. And, in some cases, income does not help. A girl born in a well-to-do family might have her dreams of becoming a lawyer blighted because her family and community think it improper for her to work outside the home.

Values, priorities and public debate

The first *Human Development Report* in 1990 defined human development as 'both the process of widening people's choices and the level of their achieved well-being' (UNDP, 1990, p9). The purpose of development is to enhance people's capabilities, in the present and in the future, in all areas of their life – economic, social, political and cultural. It is here that human development rests fully on Amartya Sen's core idea of capabilities and agency. As these are very rich concepts, we will take time in the next section to introduce these terms with care. For the moment, let us continue with our swift tour through ideas of human development, by noting one feature: choices relate to our values and we have different values and often disagree, so human development also is, fundamentally, engaged in an ongoing conversation about what it would be most valuable for us to do next.

This issue of values is critical in the human development approach. What are the valuable choices that public policy should promote? Who defines what is valuable? How are deep disagreements resolved? What about values that seem reprehensible, ill-informed or harmful?

Because of human diversity itself, our respective values tend to be somewhat heterogeneous. Still, development in a given society tends to reflect its most cherished values – of equity, harmony with nature, peace and order, material wealth or children's well-being. The UK is the fourth largest global economy but a 2007 UNICEF report on child well-being in rich countries concluded that UK children had the lowest level of well-being among industrialized nations.[5] Not surprisingly, the report created substantial concern. This type of analysis helps people clarify what their values are, and what they might wish to change.

In 2007, a British TV channel brought a group from the small Pacific island of Vanuatu to make an anthropological study of British people. The trip was sparked by an alternative index of well-being in which Vanuatu ranked as the most 'developed' country on earth, while the UK came in at 108.[6] In one episode, the Vanuatu citizens spent half an hour in Central London during rush hour trying in vain to engage commuters in conversation. They could not grasp why people would pass each other like objects and rush like bees in a busy beehive. As a newspaper review of the series put it: 'This they thought was "crazy," a rejection of the most important things in life, which they believe to be "love, happiness, peace and respect."'[7] Human development raises issues of values, priorities and trade-offs so that people are better able to reflect profoundly on their circumstances and shape their respective societies.

Agency, voice and empowerment

One of the central goals of human development is enabling people to become agents in their own lives and in their communities. As Sen argues, in development activities 'the people have to be seen ... as being actively involved – given the opportunity – in shaping their own destiny, and not just as passive recipients of the fruits of cunning development programs' (Sen, 1999, p53). From this perspective, development relies on people's freedom to make decisions and advance key objectives. People themselves decide upon what kind of development they would like for themselves. When people and social groups are recognized as agents, they can define their priorities as well as choose the best means to achieve them. Referring to the choice between cultural tradition and poverty, on the one hand, and modernity and material prosperity, on the other hand, Sen (1999, p31) writes: 'If a traditional way of life has to be sacrificed to escape grinding poverty or minuscule longevity, then it is the people directly involved who must have the opportunity to participate in deciding what should be chosen.' While the principle of agency is clear, its implementation is more complex. Many decisions are made by groups rather than by individuals, and a person's ability to affect collective choices varies greatly in different contexts, as we shall discuss later.

Agency and the expansion of valuable freedoms go hand in hand (see Box 2.3). In order to be agents of their own lives, people need the freedom to be educated, to speak in public without fear, to have freedom of expression and association, etc. But it is also by being agents that people can build the environment in which they can be educated and speak freely, etc.

Box 2.3 Human development: Focusing on well-being and agency

The perspective of human development incorporates the need to remove the hindrances that people face through the efforts and initiatives of people themselves. The claim is not only that human lives can go very much better and be much richer in terms of well-being and freedom, but also that human agency can deliberately bring about radical change through improving societal organization and commitment. These are indeed the two central ideas that give cogency to the focus on human development. That focus relates, on one side, to a clearer comprehension of how – and in what ways – human lives can go much better and, on the other, to a fuller understanding of how this betterment can be brought about through a strengthening of human agency. I shall call them, respectively, 'the evaluative aspect' and 'the agency aspect' of human development.

Extract from Amartya Sen's foreword to *Readings in Human Development* (2003) by Fukuda-Parr and Shiva Kumar, pvii.

Plural information, multiple dimensions

The human development approach is inherently multi-dimensional and plural (see Box 2.4). While, in practice, most policies focus on one or several components of human development, the approach itself is potentially broad. It is about education as much as it is about health. It is about culture as much as it is about political participation. It deals with fiscal policy as much as health policy – higher taxes on alcohol and cigarettes could be as effective in giving people opportunities to live long and healthy lives as spending more on health services. It deals with agricultural policies as much as it deals with exchange rate policies – the devaluation of a currency may do more to promote exports and provide farmers with greater opportunities to earn a decent income than farm subsidies. It deals with educational policy as much as gender, environmental, industrial or technological policy. Human development thus relates to many aspects that concern people's lives, not only economic ones. It can therefore not be subsumed under one single academic discipline. It encompasses many disciplines, including economics, law, sociology, history, public policy, political science and philosophy.

Box 2.4 Accounting for human development

What does human development accounting, in fact, do? What is its special feature, its identifying characteristic? This is, at one level, an easy question to answer. Rather than concentrating only on some solitary and traditional measure of economic progress (such as the gross national product per head), 'human development' accounting involves a systematic examination of a wealth of information about how human beings in each society live (including their state of education and health care, among other variables). It brings an inescapably pluralist conception of progress to the exercise of development evaluation. Human lives are battered and diminished in all kinds of different ways, and the first task, seen in this perspective, is to acknowledge that deprivations of very different kinds have to be accommodated within a general overarching framework. The framework must be cogent and coherent, but must not try to overlook the pluralities that are crucially involved (in the diverse nature of deprivations) in a misguided search for some one measure of success and failure, some single clue to all the other disparate concerns.

Extract from Amartya Sen (2000) 'A decade of human development', *Journal of Human Development*, vol 1, no 1, p18.

Thus far we have focused mainly on the 'objective' of human development. Now we turn to the process. Mahbub ul Haq identified four procedural concerns or principles which have been used repeatedly in applying human development. They are: equity, efficiency, participation and sustainability. Of course other principles such as responsibility or respect for human rights also matter. But we will start with these four because they are often used:[8]

- *Equity* draws on the concept of justice, impartiality and fairness and incorporates a consideration for distributive justice between groups. In human development, we seek equity in the space of people's freedom to live valuable lives. It is related to, but different from, the concept of equality, which implies equality of all people in some space. In human development, equity draws attention to those who have unequal opportunities due to various disadvantages and may require preferential treatment or affirmative action. For example, the poor, differently-abled, women, ethnic minorities and other disadvantaged sections of the population may need special measures to enable them to have the same level of capabilities.
- *Efficiency* refers to the optimal use of existing resources. From a human development perspective, efficiency is defined as the least cost method of reaching goals through the optimal use of human, material, environmental and institutional resources to expand capabilities for individuals and communities. It is necessary to demonstrate that the

chosen intervention offers the highest impact in terms of people's opportunities. When applying this principle, one must conceive of efficiency in a dynamic context since what is efficient at one point in time may not necessarily be efficient in the long run.

- *Participation and empowerment* is about processes in which people act as agents – individually and as groups. It is about the freedom to make decisions in matters that affect their lives; the freedom to hold others accountable for their promises, the freedom to influence development in their communities. For example in the reform of an education system, human development would consider and try to draw upon the agency of children, parents, teachers, the local community, teachers unions, NGOs, the media, the ministry of education, the finance ministry, social movements and advocacy groups for education, and so on. Whether at the level of policy-making or implementation, this principle implies that people need to be involved at every stage, not merely as beneficiaries but as agents who are able to pursue and realize goals that they value and have reason to value.

- *Sustainability* is often used to introduce the durability of development in the face of environmental limitations but is not confined to this dimension alone.[9] It refers to advancing human development such that outcomes progress in all spheres – social, political and financial – endures over time. Environmental sustainability implies achieving developmental results without jeopardizing the natural resource base and biodiversity of the region and without affecting the resource base for future generations. Financial sustainability refers to the way in which development is financed without penalizing future generations or economic stability. For example, development should not lead countries into debt traps. Social sustainability refers to the way in which social groups and other institutions are involved and support development initiatives over time, and avoid disruptive and destructive elements. Cultural liberty and respect for diversity are also important values that can contribute to socially-sustainable development.

These four principles are not exhaustive, and later chapters consider the rights-based approach, and aspects of justice and responsibility, in greater detail. But these complete the swift mapping of human development. The next section focuses in further on key terms.

Going deeper: The capability approach

The human development approach has been profoundly inspired by Amartya Sen's pioneering works in welfare economics, social choice, poverty and famine, and development economics.[10] While Sen's works cover an extremely wide range of topics, his 'capability approach' has provided the basis of a new paradigm in economics and in the social sciences in general, so it is that approach upon which we concentrate.

In 1979, at Stanford University, Sen gave the Tanner lectures on human values called 'Equality of What?' He questioned the adequacy of measuring equality in the space of marginal or total utility, or primary goods. And he outlined for the first time his conception of capabilities, which has been developed in greater detail since. This section introduces the capability approach – its key terms, its contrast to other approaches and how various components interrelate.

In *Inequality Re-examined*, Amartya Sen writes: 'A person's capability to achieve functionings that he or she has reason to value provides a general approach to the evaluation of social arrangements, and this yields a particular way of viewing the assessment of equality and inequality' (1992, p5). The key idea of the capability approach is that social arrangements should aim to expand people's capabilities – their freedom to promote or achieve what they value doing and being. An essential test of development is whether people have greater freedoms today than they did in the past. A test of inequality is whether people's capability sets are equal or unequal.

Different phrases are used to try to communicate this basic idea in simple ways:

- The *Human Development Reports* describe the objective of 'expanding people's choices'
- Amartya Sen's 1999 book was entitled '*Development as Freedom*'
- Sometimes the words '*effective* freedoms' or '*real* freedoms' are used to emphasize that what matters is the actual possibilities not hollow promises or paper freedoms.

Box 2.5 Key terms of the capability approach

- **Functionings** are defined as 'the various things a person may value doing or being' (Sen 1999, p75). In other words, functionings are valuable activities and states that make up people's well-being – such as being healthy and well-nourished, being safe, being educated, having a good job, being able to visit loved ones. They are also related to goods and income but describe what a person is able to do or be with these. For example, when people's basic need for food (a commodity) is met, they enjoy the functioning of being well-nourished.
- **Capability** refers to the *freedom* to enjoy various functionings. In particular, capability is defined as 'the various combinations of functionings (beings and doings) that the person can achieve. Capability is, thus, a set of vectors of functionings, reflecting the person's freedom to lead one type of life or another ... to choose from possible livings' (Sen, 1992, p40). Put differently, capabilities are, 'the substantive freedoms [a person] enjoys to lead the kind of life he or she has reason to value' (Sen, 1999, p87).
- **Agency** is the ability to pursue goals that one values and has reason to value. An agent is 'someone who acts and brings about change.' (Sen, 1999, p19)

Functionings and capabilities

Formulations of capability have two parts: *functionings* and *opportunity freedom*. Sen's significant contribution has been to unite the two concepts. We start with functionings, which are being and doing activities that people value and have reason to value. For example, being nourished, literate and employed. However, functionings are not limited, which is why the human development approach applies to rich and poor countries, and to rich and poor people. Functionings also include playing a virtuoso drum solo, having a good reputation and a warm circle of friends. At one point Sen considered whether one should 'separate "material" functionings and capabilities (e.g. to be well-nourished) from others (e.g. being wise and contented)' and evaluate standards of living with reference to material capabilities. In the end he suggested that living standards encompass *all valued functionings*. 'It is possible that this way of drawing the line is a little too permissive, but the alternatives that have been proposed seem clearly too narrow' (Sen, 1987, p23). So functionings relate to many different dimensions of life – including survival, health, work, education, relationships, empowerment, self-expression and culture.

A vitally important phrase in the definition of functionings is 'value and have reason to value'. It sounds abstract but is of tremendous practical importance. Why? First, functionings are things people *value*. In other words, an activity or situation 'counts' as a functioning for that person *only* if that person values it. This encourages the participation and engagement of those people whose lives are at stake, in order to ascertain whether they will value changes that might ensue. Second, functionings are things people 'have reason to value'. The capability approach introduces value judgements explicitly. Why? In fact some people *do* value activities that are harmful, such as a psychopath who values the triumph of the kill as much as the victim would value not being killed. The phrase 'reason to value' just acknowledges that given our disagreements we do need to make some social choices. The issues that will be contentious are many and include female genital mutilation, domestic violence, censorship, discrimination, air travel and so on. The capability approach raises the issue of what process, group, philosophical structure or institution has the legitimate authority to decide what people have reason to value. But while the capability approach argues that public debate and critical scrutiny are often helpful, it stops well short of proposing one particular process as relevant in all contexts, and rather depends on the agency of people acting in those contexts to address these questions themselves and build up and share their repertoire of good practices.

Capabilities are the freedom to enjoy valuable functionings. So they combine functionings with a kind of opportunity freedom. Just like a person with a pocket full of coins can buy many different combinations of things, a person with many capabilities can elect between many different functionings and pursue a variety of different life paths. For this reason, the capability set has been compared to a budget set. Capabilities are thus described as the real and actual possibilities open to a given person. As T. H. Green wrote, 'We do not mean merely freedom from restraint or compulsion ... when we speak of freedom as something to be so highly prized, we mean a *positive power or capacity* of doing or enjoying something worth doing or enjoying' (cited in Sen, 2002b, p586).

Again, as Green's quote implies, capabilities include only possibilities that people really value. Truly evil or utterly vacuous activities are not capabilities (although they still exist and must be reckoned with, as we shall see). Some of Sen's descriptions of capability stress this, such as his description of capability as 'a person's ability to do valuable acts or reach valuable states of being' (1993, p30). Box 2.6 illustrates the distinction between functionings and capabilities.

Box 2.6 Capabilities and functionings in Mexico

In Mexico, as well as in other parts of the world, there are people who are in the business of dealing with 'second-hand goods'. These people go to apartment buildings and neighbourhoods to buy used things that people no longer want. This merchandise can vary from clothing, electronic appliances and tableware to CDs and toys. The profit in this business lies in buying things at a very low price and later going to open-air markets and selling them at a higher price. So the second-hand goods dealer is a collector of useless things that he can occasionally improve, which he then sells in various markets.

The case discussed here is that of Jorge Solís, who began to work as a second-hand goods dealer when he was 17 years old. This was because he and his mother were left on their own. His brothers and sisters had married and no one was there to help out with the household expenses.

People know that the second-hand goods dealer is in the neighbourhood when they hear him shouting: 'Old appliances you want to sell?' Consumers like me hear him and invite him to our homes to see what he is selling. One day, I saw Jorge through the window and I invited him in to see what merchandise he had.

Pedro: Sir, I didn't hear you shout. I want to sell several things.

Jorge: The thing is that I can't shout. I have a sore throat.

Pedro: Really? Have you taken some medicine for your sore throat?

Jorge: No, I don't have enough money to buy medicine.

Pedro: But if you don't buy any medicine, you won't get better and you won't be able to shout. As a consequence, we won't be able to hear you and we won't offer you our things.

Jorge: Well, yes, but there is no other way. I just hope that people see me even if they don't hear me shout, so that I'll be able to get something today and sell it.

What does this simple story illustrate? Jorge did not have the functionings required to be healthy and this restricted his possibilities of promoting his services and receiving a decent income. If Jorge does not have more money, he won't be able to buy the medicine he needs for his throat to heal, and the circle of restrictions will not be broken.

The fundamental lesson is that the basic functioning of enjoying good health can affect Jorge's capability set. Not having good health is also limited by the lack of instrumental freedoms, such as financial means and social security. For instance, Jorge had no access to affordable health services.

Jorge earns around $2500 Mexican pesos per month (US$250) and he spends this money on food. So how can he buy medicine if he gets sick? The last time I saw Jorge, he told me that his daughter is now working and she has registered him at the *Instituto Mexicano del Seguro Social* (IMSS Mexican Institute for Social Security) so he can now get free medical care. Lastly, I asked him if he planned to continue working in second-hand goods; his answer was: 'I couldn't work in anything else. What else could I do?'

This box was written by Pedro A. Flores Crespo.

Common misunderstandings 1: Choice

Through the years, a number of common misunderstandings of the capability approach, and relatedly of human development, have emerged. This section describes misunderstandings regarding the role of *choice*, and the extent of *individualism*.

A misunderstanding between 'capability' and 'choice' often surfaces, especially because the *Human Development Reports* use the phrase 'expand people's choices' instead of the rather cumbersome term of 'capabilities'. The phrase has the advantage of being simple English. But the term 'choices' is problematic because it does not introduce the issues of 'value' and 'have reason to value' that are central to capabilities. It is usually more important to be able to choose a career than to be able to choose between an array of rival brands of toothpaste, and human development needs to identify which choices are valuable. Also, the phrase 'expanding people's choices' seems to imply that more choices are always better – but this is not necessarily the case. Often people value having to make only a few good choices, rather than many cumbersome choices. As Sen writes, 'Indeed sometimes more freedom of choice can bemuse and befuddle, and make one's life more wretched' (1992, p59). Actually the capability approach recognizes that the goal is not to expand the number of choices – it is to expand the quality of human life. Also, the term choices itself is problematic because the desirability of individual choices varies by culture, and a high value of 'choice' is associated with western liberal individualism. People also sometimes value making some choices together – as a family or a community – and not individually. Also, in fact many capabilities are necessarily the outcome of joint process, not individual decisions. The term 'choice' obscures this – the capability approach's preference for terms like 'real freedoms' is an attempt to express the core objective in a culturally adaptable way.

In sum, 'expanding people's choices' does *not* mean that we focus on expanding *all* choices – regardless of their value, and as if the more choice the better. Furthermore, most choices affect more than one person and many are often made after discussion and consultation with others. So, in trying to 'expand people's choices' or real freedoms, we are not imagining that individuals are to make choices in isolation. Indeed, many capabilities can only be created and sustained by people acting together.

Common misunderstandings 2: Individualism

This brings up one further misunderstanding of Sen's capability approach and its relation to individualism. Often people argue that the capability approach is 'individualistic' and by this wrongly imply that it is a western liberal approach that presumes persons act alone rather than as members of groups. To clarify in what sense the capability approach focuses only on individuals it is useful to distinguish three kinds of individualism, only the first of which is advanced by the capability approach (Robeyns, 2005, p107; 2008, p90 all quotes):

- *Ethical individualism* 'postulates that individuals, and only individuals, are the *ultimate* units of moral concern... This, of course, does not imply that we should not evaluate social structures and societal properties, but ethical individualism implies that these structures and institutions will be evaluated *in virtue of* the causal importance that they have for individual well-being.'
- *Ontological individualism* holds that 'society is built up from only individuals and nothing (but) individuals, and hence is nothing more than the sum of individuals and their properties.'
- Explanatory or *methodological individualism* presumes 'that all social phenomena can be explained in terms of individuals and their properties.'

Many presume that the capability approach is individualistic because it focuses on what individual people (not groups) can do and be. First, we must point out that much of the work on the capability approach and human development as a whole has engaged groups specifically – women's groups, social movements, public actions, democratic practices and so on. Also, many choices are made by groups, not individuals. The capability approach thus does *not* defend methodological or ontological individualism. But even if we are highly interested in groups, the capability approach, as initially framed by Sen, takes the normative position of 'ethical individualism' – the view that what ultimately matters is what happens to every single individual in a society.

The reason Sen supports ethical individualism is that if the smallest fundamental unit of moral concern is any group, such as the family, the social group or the community, then analyses will systematically overlook any existing or potential inequalities *within* these units. For example, the deprivations particular to women and children have regularly been overlooked by analyses that focus on the household. Only if we probe into the well-being of each person do we have the possibility of discovering the relative under-nutrition, or subordination, of women.

A disagreement remains among a group of authors within the capability approach about the sufficiency of ethical individualism. Critics have questioned whether a rejection of ontological individualism is consistent with a commitment to ethical individualism. When human beings live together, they generate something truly collective, which is more than the sum total of their individual lives and cannot be reduced to individual characteristics. Assessing states of affairs only to the extent that they have a positive or negative effect on the well-being of each individual is therefore insufficient. This group recognizes that there may be something genuinely positive in the 'irreducibly social goods',[11] even if it has been generated by the oppression of some individuals. According to this argument, an orchestra performance has an intrinsic value even if some members are forced to play. The architectural beauty of pyramids in Egypt and medieval cathedrals in Europe provide other examples of irreducibly social goods which are of positive value to some, even if built by oppression and with terrible human cost. A full assessment of the situation from either view would trade off the contribution to future generations of people's capabilities to enjoy beauty or other irreducibly social goods, against the lack of capabilities of some workers. That trade-off is clearly contested, with those supporting irreducibly social goods implicitly giving a greater weight to the generations that use and enjoy a good, and others arguing for a greater weight – or even for human rights, hence certain absolute protections – to be given to those whose capabilities are curtailed by the activity.

While a nuanced consideration of individual capabilities seems sufficient to *evaluate* a state of affairs, recognizing the vital role of social norms, groups, movements and social institutions is essential for developing *policies* to advance capabilities. We shall return to this point shortly when we discuss the prospective or policy role of the human development and capability approach.

Why freedom? Capabilities not just functionings

As highlighted earlier, Sen's capability approach proposes that we identify functionings – the things (within reason) people value doing and being. The focus of development and policy is then to make people free to enjoy some combination of functionings, allowing them to expand their capabilities. But, some people wonder, why should we focus on freedoms so much? Do poor people really want to have the freedom to avoid hunger and discomfort? Do they not simply want to avoid hunger and discomfort? In most cases, yes, but what is distinctive about Sen's approach is the substantive role that freedom plays. Here are two of many reasons why freedom is important.

First, if we only focus on expanding functionings, we could do so by force, coercion, domination or colonialism. Most basic needs can be met in a prison, for example. Indeed, some countries have used force to advance functionings: for example, forced sterilization or the forced isolation of people who are HIV-positive. Focusing on freedom draws attention to social development and the value of empowerment, responsibility and informed public action.

Also, reasonable people sometimes choose to be deprived in one area of life in order to enjoy another kind of goodness. A person who is fasting is in a state of under-nutrition, which may seem very similar to starvation. But, in the one case, the fasting person *could* eat, although she chooses not to, whereas the starving person would eat if he could. Similarly, a student who could live well if he worked may instead endure poor and overcrowded housing conditions so that he might obtain a degree. People should be free to refrain from a functioning for good reasons if and when they so choose.

Note that, conceptually, 'there is no difference *as far as the space is concerned* between focusing on functionings *or* on capabilities. A functioning combination is a *point* in such a space, whereas capability is a *set* of such points' (Sen, 1992, p50).

Second, the notion of capability is also closely related to that of freedom. Sen defines freedom as 'the real opportunity that we have to accomplish what we value' (1992, p31). Freedom, he argues, has two aspects: opportunity and process. The opportunity aspect pays attention 'to the ability of a person to achieve those things that she has reason to value', and the process aspect pays attention to 'the freedom involved in the process itself' (2002b, p10). The notion of capability refers to the opportunity aspect of freedom, while the notion of agency, which is explained below, refers to the personal process of freedom.

Agency

The third core concept of the capability approach is *agency*. Agency refers to a person's ability to pursue and realize goals that she values and has reason to value. An agent is 'someone who acts and brings about change' (Sen, 1999, p19). The opposite of a person with agency is someone who is forced, oppressed or passive.

The agency aspect is important 'in assessing what a person can do in line with his or her conception of the good' (Sen, 1985, p206). Agency expands the horizons of concern beyond a person's own well-being to include concerns such as solidarity with the extreme poor. From this perspective, people can be active and creative, with the ability to act on behalf of their aspirations.

Agency is related to other approaches that stress self-determination, authentic self-direction, autonomy, self-reliance, empowerment, voice and so on. The strong collective desire for agency suggests that development processes should foster participation, public debate and democratic practice.

Agency is inescapably plural in both concept and measurement. In Sen's view:[12]

1   Agency is exercised with respect to the goals the person values and has reason to value.
2   Agency includes effective power as well as direct control, that is, it includes not just individual agency, but what one can do as a member of a group, collectivity or political community.
3   Agency may advance well-being or may address other goals – for example, relating to the good of one's family or community, of other people and of art and the environment.

4   To identify agency entails an assessment of whether the agent's goals are in some way reasonable – a person who harms or humiliates others would not, in this view, be exerting agency.

5   The agent's responsibility for creating or sustaining a state of affairs should be incorporated into his or her evaluation of how to act as an agent.

Box 2.7 Agency and well-being, freedom and achievement

Suppose two sisters, Anna and Becca, live in a peaceful village in England and have the same levels of achieved well-being. Both believe that the power of global corporations is undermining democracy, and that governments should give greater emphasis to global justice. Anna decides to travel to Genoa to demonstrate against the G8 meetings, while Becca stays at home. At that moment, Anna is using her freedom of agency to voice some of her political concerns. However, the Italian police do not like the protesters and violate Anna's civil and political rights by beating her up in prison. Anna's achieved well-being has obviously been considerably lowered. Anna is given the option to sign a piece of paper declaring that she committed violence and is a member of an extreme-left organization (which will then give her a criminal record). If she does not sign, she will be kept in prison for an unspecified length of time. Anna therefore has a (highly constrained) option to trade her freedom of agency for a higher achieved well-being. Becca had the same potential agency but chose not to use it. She is concerned about human rights violations and the hollowing of democracy itself, but does not wish to sacrifice her achieved well-being for these goals.

Such an example shows that the distinctions Sen makes are important because, in evaluative exercises, one has to ask whether the relevant dimension of advantage is the standard of living, achieved well-being, agency achievement, well-being freedom or agency freedom. The central claim of the capability approach is that whatever concept of advantage one chooses to consider, the informational base of this judgement must relate to the space of functionings and/or capabilities, depending upon the issue at hand. Sen's claim is that well-being achievements should be measured in functionings, whereas well-being freedom is reflected by a person's capability set. A focus on agency will always transcend an analysis in terms of functionings and capabilities, and will take agency goals into account. However, it is typical of Sen's work that he does not defend this as a closed theory or dogma: there can be good reasons to include other sources of information as well.

Extract from Ingrid Robeyns (2005) 'The capability approach – a theoretical survey', *Journal of Human Development*, vol 6, no 1, pp102–103.

Compare and contrast

Human development and the capability approach arose in conversation with other approaches to development. At that time – and, indeed, even now – many were suggesting that social arrangements and development itself should focus on maximizing income, assets and other commodities in the interests of achieving happiness. This section compares and contrasts human development with competing approaches.

Income, happiness and commodities are obviously important. The problem is that, if policies aim *only* to increase one of these, they might unintentionally create distortions. This is because policies that focus on only one objective tend to ignore everything else. For example, if a programme aims to maximize individual happiness alone, it may celebrate the achievement of a deeply joyous political prisoner, without feeling any obligation to address the unjust detention in which the prisoner finds himself. A more thorough analysis of the situation might appreciate the prisoner's tremendous inner strength, on the one hand, *while* working immediately to help free her, on the other.

The capability approach argues that focusing on capabilities is a more direct and accurate way of expanding what people really value. Focusing on capabilities introduces fewer distortions. We therefore compare and contrast the capability approach with other approaches to the evaluation of well-being that inform development policy.

With happiness

Much conventional economics is based on a utilitarian approach. It assumes that the most desirable action is the one that increases people's psychological happiness or desire-fulfilment the most. This view has made a tremendous comeback in recent years, drawing on new data on happiness and life satisfaction. Richard Layard (2005), for example, thoughtfully examines how our entire economic system could evolve if our steady and enduring purpose were to maximize a nation's happiness, instead of its income.

This approach has tremendous appeal. Happiness seems to invite a deeper reflection upon our material goals and values. It helps people see these goals from a different perspective. Sen and others writing on the capability approach consider happiness to be 'a momentous achievement' to be celebrated. But when you look beyond the headlines, some concerns continue to arise.

First and perhaps most importantly, our mental utility may not track in any predictable fashion the things we really *value*. A poor, devout widow may become serenely reconciled to her circumstances, but this does not mean that she would not value *also* having warm socks and pain medication for her arthritis. Alternatively, a middle-aged man may become a hospice volunteer following the death of his mother because he wishes to share with others the inner peace he has found as a result of having come to terms with her terminal illness. In doing this, he may share the pain and tragedy of others' lives, so his 'happiness' would be lower than if he did not do hospice work at all. But he would not wish for any other kind of life.

Second, happiness levels may obscure significant deprivations. Sen notes that people whose deprivations deserve systematic attention may often not be utility-deprived:

> Consider a cripple.... Suppose that he is no worse off than others
> in utility terms despite his physical handicap because of certain

> other utility features. This could be because he has a jolly disposition. Or because he has a low aspiration level and his heart leaps up whenever he sees a rainbow in the sky. Or because he is religious and feels that he will be rewarded in [the] after-life, or cheerfully accepts what he takes to be just penalty for misdeeds in a past incarnation. The important point is that, despite his marginal utility disadvantage, he no longer (has) a total utility deprivation. (Sen, 1980, p217)

His happiness rating, being durably independent of his quality of life, would therefore not provide a very good policy indicator of the requirements needed to address his deprivations.

Third, self-reported utility may often be biased by information and social circumstances. As Sen (2002a) pointed out in the *British Medical Journal*, the state of Kerala, which had almost universal education and a life expectancy of 74 at the time, also had the highest self-reported morbidity in India. In contrast, Bihar, one of India's poorest states, with a life expectancy below 60, had the lowest rate of self-reported morbidity. The objectively healthy state was subjectively health-poor and vice versa. How do we evaluate this? It seems that the low self-reported morbidity in Bihar occurred because people had less ability to assess their own health situation, and had less hope of doing anything to remedy it. Subjective data, whether on happiness or morbidity, is therefore conditioned, to a great degree, for example by our knowledge, aspirations and peer group.

With resources
Many other approaches to development focus instead on cultivating different kinds of resources; these may be assets, property rights or basic needs, such as housing, food, clothing, sanitation and so on. These approaches recognize the fundamental importance of commodities and material goods to our well-being in the short- and long-term. They identify valid connections between resources and capabilities, and argue that, in order to expand capabilities and sustain these expansions, certain resources are required. In many cases, these analyses are utterly apt, and will form, as we shall see, an integral aspect of the human development approach.

But measuring resources is still different from measuring functionings. The capability approach argues that we will inadvertently make mistakes if we try to give everyone the same resources, because people's ability to convert the same resources into functionings varies a lot. To take a simple example, the same *amount* of rice (or other good), will be converted into radically different levels of physical vigour by a child, a disabled teenager, an agricultural worker or an elderly person. Similarly, people who are physically impaired require greater resources to achieve mobility. Clearly, people have different abilities to convert resources into capabilities and, if policies equalize resources, they will disadvantage certain groups (in the case of food, labourers, pregnant women, those with allergies or with a high metabolism) in significant ways. For this reason, we should aim for greater equality in the space of functionings and capabilities directly.

Sen identifies five vital factors that are often overlooked when we focus on income and resources instead of capabilities (1999, pp70–71):

1   *Personal heterogeneities* (a pregnant woman will have different nutrition requirements from an elderly woman);
2   *Environmental diversities* (pensioners in Scotland will need a different income to keep warm in winter than pensioners in Dar es Salaam);
3   *Institutional variations* (parents in a country with good free public education will require a different income to educate their children than parents in a country without free public education or with poor quality schools);
4   *Differences in relational perspectives* (the material requirements for appearing in public without shame when having guests depends on local customs); and
5   *Distribution within the family* (the family income might not be spent to feed the children adequately but instead to buy the parents' drinks).

In order to assess people's well-being, further information is therefore needed on other aspects of people's lives – their health, education, nutritional status, dignity, autonomy and so on.

Another problem is that people value things other than increased resources. The process of maximizing resources may have social and environmental costs (changes in culture and lifestyle) that people have good reason to reject. In the words of the 1990 *Human Development Report*: 'The basic objective of development is to create an enabling environment for people to enjoy long, healthy and creative lives. This may appear to be a simple truth. But it is often forgotten in the immediate concern with the accumulation of commodities and financial wealth' (p9).

Putting it all together

A bicycle provides a good example of how these different concepts relate. A person may own or be able to use a bicycle (a resource). By riding the bicycle, the person moves around town and, we assume, values this mobility (a functioning). However, if the person is unable to ride the bicycle (because, perhaps, she has no sense of balance or is not permitted to ride), then having a bicycle would not in fact result in this functioning. In this case, the access to the resource coupled with the person's own characteristics (balance, etc.), creates the capability for the person to move around town when she wishes. Furthermore, let us suppose that the person enjoys having this capability to leap upon a bicycle and pedal over to a friend's house for lunch – thus having this capability contributes to happiness or utility.

Resource	–	Functioning –	Capability	–	Utility
bicycle		mobility	ability to		pleasure
			move around		

The bicycle example illustrates how the various concepts are all related to one another when they coincide nicely. The question is: which concept do we focus on? Which will be distorted most (or least) often? The capability approach argues that utility can be distorted by personality or adaptive preferences; functionings can be enjoyed in a prison or stifled environment; and a bicycle can be useless if you cannot balance, so *capability* represents the most accurate space in which to investigate and advance the various forms of human well-being.

The capability approach

The capability approach has often been mistaken for a theory of justice, which it is not (see Chapter 5). So what is it? Basically, while human development and the capability approach require positive, normative, predictive and policy analyses, two roles have been more visible to date: an evaluative (normative) role, and a prospective (policy) role.[13]

Simply put, the normative or evaluative role examines which capabilities have expanded:

> [T]he capability *approach* is a proposition, and the proposition is this: that social arrangements should be evaluated according to the extent of freedom people have to promote or achieve functionings they value. If equality in social arrangements is to be demanded in any space – and most theories of justice advocate equality in some space – it is to be demanded in the space of capabilities. (Alkire, 2005, p122)

For example, the Human Development Index is used to rank countries according to their achievements in key functionings. Similarly, Robeyns refers to the capability approach as a 'broad normative framework for the evaluation and assessment of individual well-being and social arrangements':

> [T]he capability approach is not a theory that can *explain* poverty, inequality and well-being; instead, it rather provides a tool and a framework within which to *conceptualize* and *evaluate* these phenomena. Applying the capability approach to issues of policy and social change will therefore often require the addition of explanation theories. (Robeyns, 2005, p4)

The *Human Development Reports*, both nationally and globally, represent a good example of the prospective or policy approach. Prospective analyses ask 'which policy should be implemented'. A *prospective* application of the capability approach is a working set of the policies, activities, courses of action and recommendations that seem, at any given time, most likely to generate considerable capability expansion and human development. The set of policies should be considered together with the processes by which these policies were generated, and situated in terms of the contexts in which they will be more likely to deliver these benefits.

Selecting capabilities or functionings

As we have seen, the capability approach is incomplete. It relies on the agency and involvement of people in different contexts to specify which capabilities to focus on, for example. As noted earlier, the development process should be assessed according to the extent to which it expands the 'capabilities that people have reason to choose and value'.

Because of its resistance to overt prescription, the capability approach is open to many different forms of specifications regarding what constitute valuable capabilities. Even if it was not necessarily erroneous to look for a complete ordering of what constitutes human well-being, it cannot be identified in practice. This is what Sen calls the 'fundamental and pragmatic reasons' (Sen, 1992, p49) for incompleteness.

However, the task of specifying capabilities – for example in a participatory Poverty Reduction Strategy, in a national or local plan, for an NGO project, or for inclusion in an international multi-dimensional health measure – faces two challenges: a challenge of *omission* and a challenge of *power*. In terms of omission, groups may inadvertently overlook a capability that is quite important. Having a list of capabilities others in a similar situation have selected can help people to clarify their own set, and may bring to mind important capabilities they might have overlooked or not dared to hope for. In terms of *power*, there is always a danger that the powerful – be these economic elite, a particular ethnicity or gender or family or party – will select capabilities that advance their views, perhaps at the expense of minority voices.

Many authors work to address these concerns. The most prominent of these, Martha Nussbaum, has proposed a list of ten central human capabilities that, she argues, should be the basis of constitutional guarantees. In her view, having a list of capabilities is vital to avoid the issues of *omission* and *power*. She notes that, 'just as people can be taught not to want or miss the things their culture has taught them they should not or could not have, so too can (they) be taught not to value certain functionings as constituents of their good living' (Nussbaum, 1988, p175).

Since what people consider to be valuable and relevant can often be the product of structures of inequality and discrimination, and because not all human freedoms are equally valuable, Nussbaum argues that one might need to go beyond the incompleteness of Sen's capability approach so that equal freedom for all can be respected.

She grounds her version of the capability approach on what she calls an 'internalist essentialist' position. Insofar as we recognize human beings as human, there should be an essentialist basis for any view about what constitutes human life and what deprives it of its full human character. Her list of central human capabilities is as follows (Nussbaum, 2000, pp78–80):

1   *Life*: Being able to live to the end of a human life of normal length; not dying prematurely.
2   *Bodily health*: Being able to have good health, including reproductive health; to be adequately nourished; to have adequate shelter.
3   *Bodily integrity*: Being able to move freely from place to place; to be secure against violent assault, including sexual assault and domestic violence; having opportunities for sexual satisfaction and for choice in matters of reproduction.
4   *Senses, imagination and thought*: Being able to use the senses, to imagine, think and reason; being able to use imagination and thought; being able to use one's mind in ways protected by guarantees of freedom of expression with respect to both political and artistic speech, and freedom of religious exercise; being able to have pleasurable experiences and to avoid non-beneficial pain.
5   *Emotions*: Being able to love, to grieve, to experience longing, gratitude and justified anger, not having one's emotional development blighted by fear and anxiety.
6   *Practical reason*: Being able to form a conception of the good and to engage in critical reflection about the planning of one's life (this includes liberty of conscience and of religious observance).
7   *Affiliation*: (A) Being able to live with and toward others, to recognize and show concern for other human beings, to engage in various forms of social interaction; to be able to imagine the situation of another (this includes freedom of assembly and political speech). (B) Having the social bases of self-respect and non-humiliation; being able to be treated as a dignified being whose worth is equal to that of others (this includes non-discrimination).
8   *Other species*: Being able to live with concern for and in relation to animals, plants, and the world of nature.
9   *Play*: Being able to laugh, to play and to enjoy recreational activities.
10 *Control over one's environment*: (A) Political: Being able to participate effectively in political choices that govern one's life; having the right of political participation, protections of free speech and association. (B) Material: Being able to hold property (both land and movable goods), and having property rights on an equal basis with others; having the right to seek employment on an equal basis with others; having the freedom from unwarranted search and seizure. In work, being able to work as a human being, exercising practical reason and entering into meaningful relationships of mutual recognition with other workers.

Sen has no objection to Nussbaum's project of eliminating the incompleteness of his approach, as long as no one's list is seen as 'the only route' (1993, p47). He also supports sharing best practices in identifying important capabilities. Fixing one pre-determined authoritative list, however, undermines people's agency. Setting a fixed and forever list of capabilities, he argues, would be 'to deny the possibility of fruitful participation on what should be included and why' (Sen, 2004, p77). Robeyns and Alkire have thus focused on different aspects of the *process* of selecting capabilities, to which we return in Chapter 6.

The key questions to keep in mind when selecting capabilities are: (1) which capabilities do the people who will enjoy them *value* (and attach a high priority to); and (2) which capabilities are relevant to a given policy, project or institution?

Questions

2.1 How does income help you to achieve things you value and have reason to value? What functionings do you value that income does not influence?

2.2 If you were to assess the well-being of people in your country, what information would you include? Why?

2.3 How do you go about selecting which capabilities a national poverty measure in, say, Nepal should focus on?

2.4 Tartal is a high-income country.[14] Its per capita GDP is 19,000 (PPP US$), which places it below the IMF's classification of an 'advanced economy', but its growth rate is 2 per cent per annum, suggesting a promising future in terms of development. Nevertheless, despite these statistics, there are a vast number of cultural and ethnic groups that have not equally shared in Tartal's growth performance.

The country gained its independence in 1887 and adopted a new constitution in 1901. After a tumultuous political history during most of the 20th century, it deposed a 20-year dictatorship in 1982 and established democracy in 1985. Since then, the country has attempted to use its abundance of resource-rich land to modernize, globalize and achieve greater economic development.

Tartal's current population is 150 million, with about 60 million under the age of 25 and a population growth rate of 1 per cent. Almost 70 per cent of its residents reside in rural areas, although there has been recent migration to large cities that has increased the urban population dramatically. The largest metropolitan city is the capital of Mani, with a population of 10 million; the second largest city is Safa, with a population of 7 million. Both cities are on the Pacific coastline, emphasizing the divide between an urban, prosperous coast and a rural, impoverished interior.

About 50 per cent of the population is considered 'white' or of 'mixed' European ancestry, while another 50 per cent of the population is considered indigenous. Although Tartal is one of the world's largest economies, it has high levels of poverty, illiteracy and persistent malnutrition. While the average income is very high, the way in which this income is distributed within the country remains highly unequal, with the top 10 per cent of the population accounting for 30 per cent of the country's income, and with a mere 1 per cent of the country's income going to the poorest 10 per cent. Also, the women in Tartal are severely restricted in terms of their 'freedoms' to choose in economic, social and cultural realms. Only 8 per cent of parliamentary seats are held by women.

The fast pace of economic growth has also been at the cost of environmental considerations: the environment is polluted with industrial effluents; agriculture is affected by the overuse of chemicals; and forests are depleted. The biodiversity of the country is threatened by ignorance and a neglect to preserve the country's rich natural resources.

The country's democratic system of governance is not fully participatory, with the media being stifled and people not having a say in the major decisions that affect their lives. The adult literacy rate is estimated at 65 per cent but it remains at only 30 per cent among indigenous people. This illiteracy further heightens the critical lack of indigenous participation in government.

Questions for discussion:
• In what areas of human development has Tartal excelled, and where does it continue to fall short?
• What data would you use to assess the success of Tartal's development?

Notes

1   The term *ubuntu* originates in the Bantu language and conveys the meaning that one is only a human being through one's relationship with others. It has often been used for reconciliation in post-apartheid South Africa, and stresses the importance of caring for others and harmony between people.
2   Liberation theology has its roots in Latin American Christianity in the 1960s, and is centred upon the question: how do we make sense of a compassionate and loving God in a world marked by poverty, oppression, injustice, inequality and environmental destruction? Islam also has its own form of liberation theology.
3   For an intellectual biography of Mahbub ul Haq, see Ul Haq and Ponzio (2008).
4   Available at www.commonwealthclub.org/archive/20thcentury/68-01kennedy-speech.html
5   The report is available at www.unicef.org/media/files/ChildPovertyReport.pdf.
6   New Economics Foundation (2007), 'The Happy Planet Index: An index of human well-being and environmental impact', www.neweconomics.org/gen/
7   *The Independent*, 8 September 2007.

8   The description of the four principles has been written by Seeta Prabhu.
9   This principle could be ranged under the 'equity principle' as it deals with intergenerational equity.
10   Amartya Sen's curriculum vitae can be found at www.economics.harvard.edu/faculty/sen, and his autobiography at http://nobelprize.org/nobel_prizes/economics/laureates/1998.
11   See Deneulin (2006) and Gore (1997) for a discussion on 'irreducibly social goods' in the context of the capability approach.
12   These are drawn from Sen (1985); see also Alkire (2008).
13   Alkire (2008).
14   This question was written by Seeta Prabhu.

Readings

Alkire, S. (2002a) 'Dimensions of human development', *World Development*, vol 30, no 2, pp181–205

Alkire, S. (2005) 'Why the capability approach', *Journal of Human Development*, vol 6, no 1, pp115–133

Fukuda-Parr, S. and Shiva Kumar, A. K. (eds) (2003) *Readings in Human Development*, Oxford University Press, Delhi

Layard, R. (2005) *Happiness: Lessons from a New Science*, Allen, London

Nussbaum, M. (2000) *Women and Human Development*, Cambridge University Press, Cambridge

Robeyns, I. (2005) 'The capability approach – A theoretical survey', *Journal of Human Development*, vol 6, no 1, pp93–114

Sen, A. K. (1980) 'Equality of what?', in S. McMurrin (ed.) *Tanner Lectures on Human Values*, Cambridge University Press, Cambridge

Sen, A. K. (1987) *The Standard of Living*, Cambridge: Cambridge University Press

Sen, A. K. (1989) 'Development as capability expansion', *Journal of Development Planning*, vol 19, pp41–58, reprinted in S. Fukuda-Parr and A. K. Shiva Kumar (eds) (2003) *Readings in Human Development*, Oxford University Press, Oxford

Sen, A. K. (1992) *Inequality Re-Examined*, Clarendon Press, Oxford

Sen, A. K. (1999) *Development as Freedom*, Oxford University Press, Oxford

Sen, A. K. (2000) 'A decade of human development', *Journal of Human Development*, vol 1, no 1, pp17–23

Sen, A. K. (2002a) 'Health: Perception versus observation', *British Medical Journal*, no 324, pp859–860

Sen, A. K. (2004) 'Capabilities, lists and public reason: Continuing the conversation', *Feminist Economics*, vol 10, no 3, pp77–80

Ul Haq, M. (1995) *Reflections on Human Development*, Oxford University Press, New York

Ul Haq, M. (2003) 'The human development paradigm', in S. Fukuda-Parr and A. K. Shiva Kumar (eds) *Readings in Human Development*, Oxford University Press, Oxford

Ul Haq, K. and Ponzio, R. (eds) (2008) *Mahbub ul Haq: An Intellectual Biography*, Oxford University Press, Delhi

UNDP (1990) *Human Development Report*, Oxford University Press, New York, available at http//hdr.undp.org/en

Further Readings

Alkire, S. (2002b) *Valuing Freedoms*, Oxford University Press, Oxford

Alkire, S. (2008) 'Using the capability approach: Prospective and evaluative analyses', in S. Alkire, M. Qizilbash and F. Comim (eds) *The Capability Approach: Concepts, Measures and Applications*, Cambridge University Press, Cambridge

Alkire, S., Qizilbash, M. and Comim, F. (eds) (2008) *The Capability Approach: Concepts, Measures and Applications*, Cambridge University Press, Cambridge

Deneulin, S. (2006) *The Capability Approach and the Praxis of Development*, Palgrave, Basingstoke

Evans, P. (2002) 'Collective capabilities, culture and Amartya Sen's *Development as Freedom*', *Studies in Comparative International Development*, vol 37, no 2, pp54–60

Gasper, D. (1997) 'Sen's capability approach and Nussbaum's capabilities ethic', *Journal of International Development*, vol 9, no 2, pp281–302

Gore, C. (1997) 'Irreducibly social goods and the informational basis of Sen's capability approach', *Journal of International Development*, vol 9, no 2, pp235–250

Nussbaum, M. (1988) 'Nature, function and capability: Aristotle on political distribution', *Oxford Studies in Ancient Philosophy*, Supplementary Volume, pp145–84

Nussbaum, M. (1993) 'Non-relative virtues: An Aristotelian approach', in M. Nussbaum and A. Sen (eds) *The Quality of Life*, Clarendon Press, Oxford

Qizilbash, M. (1996) 'Capabilities, well-being and human development', *Journal of Development Studies*, vol 33, no 2, pp143–162

Robeyns, I. (2008), 'Sen's capability approach and feminist concerns', in Alkire, S., Qizilbash, M. and Comim, F. (eds) *The Capability Approach: Concepts, Measures and Applications*, Cambridge University Press, Cambridge

Sen, A. K. (1985) 'Well-being agency and freedom: The Dewey lectures 1984', *Journal of Philosophy*, vol 82, no 4, pp169–221

Sen, A. K. (1993) 'Capability and well-being', in M. Nussbaum and A. Sen (eds) *The Quality of Life*, Clarendon Press, Oxford

Sen, A. K. (2002b) *Rationality and Freedom*, Harvard University Press, Cambridge, MA

Sen, A. K. (2002c) 'Symposium on *Development as Freedom*: Response to commentaries', *Studies in Comparative International Development*, vol 37, no 2, pp78–86

3
Ideas Related to Human Development

Séverine Deneulin

Aims of the chapter

- To comprehend how the notion of freedom is understood in the human development and capability approach, on the one hand, and in market liberalism, on the other.
- To situate the human development and capability approach in the context of related people-centred development ideas, such as basic needs, human security and human rights.
- To highlight the distinctions and complementarities between the human development and capability approach and these related development ideas.

Key Points

- Both human development and neoliberalism endorse the idea of freedom, but the former sees freedom as positive freedom, while the latter only sees it in negative terms.
- There are key ingredients for spreading ideas: using moral narratives, conveying the narrative to a wide audience, achieving academic excellence, building an intellectual community and wider networks to support the idea, and engaging in politics.
- The human development approach adds a greater emphasis on freedom and participation, as well as more robust intellectual foundations, to the basic needs approach.
- The human rights approach shares a common vision with human development, but the latter places greater emphasis on the institutional requirements for promoting human rights.
- Human security expands on the idea of human development to include the notion of risk.

'Ideas change history'. This was the theme of the 2007 conference organized by the Human Development and Capability Association at the New School in New York. The conference blurb read as follows:

> The special theme of the conference will be on the spread of ideas and their social impact. *The ideas of economists and political philosophers, both when they are right and when they are wrong, are more powerful than is commonly understood. Indeed the world is ruled by little else' (Keynes).* As the famous quote by Keynes reflects, breakthrough ideas in economics and political philosophy can change history, but what are the processes that shape their spread? Ideas spread and have impact through three channels: academia, government policy and social movements. What has been the experience of progressive ideas in the past and what are the prospects for (the) human development and capability approach in shaping development policy? What is the likely intellectual trajectory of capability and human development?

Indeed, ideas do have the power to change history. Without the idea of equality between men and women, or the equality between races, the world today would look very different. It is the idea of equality between genders that granted women the right to vote and be educated. It is the idea of equality between races that put an end to the institution of slavery.

The idea of capability, as opposed to utility, forces us to assess policy from a different perspective. As we have already discussed in the first chapter, ideas about what matters profoundly influence human actions. Ideas underpin normative frameworks, which in turn underpin public policy. This chapter explores the relationship between the ideas contained in the human development and capability approach and other related ideas in development thinking.

The human development and capability approach does not have a monopoly on 'people-centred' development theories emphasizing that the ultimate goal of policy and development is human flourishing. The basic needs approach held this idea as early as the 1970s. Equally, the human rights approach holds core human development ideas as being sacred, such as the right to non-discrimination, to be free from hunger, to be educated, etc. More recently, the idea of human security, with its emphasis on freedom from violence, fear and insecurity – all critical to the human development approach – has also received much attention. How do these ideas compare with one another? And how do such ideas influence policy? These are the types of questions this chapter attempts to address. But, before doing so, we begin by examining how the notion of freedom differs in the human development and capability approach, on the one hand, from that espoused in market liberalism, on the other. It is critical that these distinctions be clarified at the outset, given the centrality of freedom to both approaches and to prevent any unnecessary confusion.

Human development and market liberalism: Freedom compared

In Chapter 2, we saw that the idea of freedom – as expressed in the concepts of capability and agency – is the core idea of the human development and capability approach.[1] But advocates of unbridled market liberalism are also heralds of the idea of freedom. For them, increasing people's choices and freedoms in life also constitutes their main policy objective. That both human development and market liberalism – understood here as the economic ideology that markets should be restricted as little as possible – endorse freedom and human choices as central values, has led to some confusion about the distinctions between them. There are, however, fundamental differences between the two. For market liberalism, freedom means first and foremost being free from interference. For example, one is less free if the money one earns is taken off in high taxation, even though that money is used for providing public goods, such as a national security system. Similarly, one is less free when regulations restrict the trading of goods across borders, even though the restrictions might improve the quality of life of poor farmers in developing countries.

From this perspective, it is possible to be free while starving to death at the same time. In 1943, a famine struck Bengal, a region in the north-eastern part of India, which is now in part the country of Bangladesh. More than three million people died. As Sen has observed in his writing on famine, this did not happen because people were prevented from trading, were systematically abused by the military or because of food shortages (the amount of *available* food in fact rose) – but because an economic shock cut the earnings of people in a wide range of jobs (for example, those in the fishing industry) and left them unable to buy the food they needed. Sen (1981) has been able to demonstrate a strong link between democracy and the reduction of famine. In countries with a free press, and with political oppositions able to unseat unpopular regimes, government takes the action necessary to make sure everyone is fed. Given the opportunity, people use their *political* freedom to counteract the inequalities generated by uncontrolled 'economic freedom' (see Chapter 8 for more on this).

For the human development and capability approach, freedom is not only negative freedom, such as freedom from interference, but also positive freedom: the freedom to do or be what one values. In order to enjoy the freedom of being fed, some freedoms sometimes have to be restricted. In the example above, the freedom to buy and sell can be limited to allow others to have what they need to live and flourish. Or the freedom of some to speculate on the housing market can be limited so that others can buy affordable housing. In other words, the freedom that matters is not the freedom from interference from others, but the freedom that one has to live a good and worthwhile life. According to the human development and capability approach, expanding this freedom should be the primary goal of public policy. A consequence of this is that economic and social policies become deeply intertwined. The economic policy of increasing interest rates, for example, has consequences for the freedom of those who go into debt simply to meet the basic costs of living. When human freedom is used to assess economic policy, the policy itself cannot be analysed without overlooking its social effects.

That human freedom is the ultimate objective of public policy does not suggest that one could, or should, get rid of the market economy. The freedom to buy and sell, the capability to participate in markets, remains an important freedom (Sen, 1999, p112). But other freedoms are important as well. Market freedom is only one kind of human freedom. It is not an absolute that necessarily justifies inaction in the face of human needs or non-market aspirations. If the free exchange of goods is only one freedom among many which we have reason to value, then the marketplace should not *dictate* society's shape but should instead be seen as a *tool* to help realize the kind of society human beings have reason to value. For example, extensive freedom in market transactions may result in environmental loss (if an increase in the volume of goods bought and discarded is not accompanied by a recycling policy) or in reduced access to health-care facilities by lower income groups (if the privatization of health services is accompanied by lower public investment in the public health system).

Unlike market liberalism, which prescribes the openness of economies and other ready-made policies irrespective of context, the human development and capability approach is not prescriptive about public policy.[2] It never prescribes a policy as being 'good' for any country. Its richness lies in providing an analytical framework to make appropriate policies in given contexts, within the overall objective of promoting human freedoms. For example, if a country subsidizes the provision of gas, this may appear to be a desirable social policy, since it lowers family expenditure, reduces wood and carbon consumption, and thereby promotes environmental sustainability. But, on the other hand, industries that use gas would be advantaged over other industries, creating a distortion in the market. And what was initially a subsidy to help poor families may turn out to be a government transfer to a group of industries. Thus, what is at first sight a good policy to help fight poverty and protect the environment might in the end be an inefficient and inequitable measure. Although the human development and capability approach is not policy prescriptive, its policies are guided by the questions: Is this policy efficient? Is it equitable? Is it sustainable? Does it promote empowerment?

Human development and market liberalism may have the same concerns for 'choice' and 'freedom', but their underlying philosophies and ensuing policies are quite different. Table 3.1 summarizes the major differences. For human development, choice is understood in terms of the valuable things that people are able to be or do. For market liberalism, in comparison, valuable choices are those that satisfy people's preferences. Consider the example of importing cheap goods from China. For market liberalism, this increases people's choices in the sense that consumers in importing countries have a wider variety of goods to buy from, and they have a choice to buy the commodities at a cheaper price. But the human development and capability approach asks additional questions. Is it a valuable choice to be able to buy, say, toys made in China for a third of the price of toys made in Europe (because of low wages) and to be able to choose from a selection of 100 instead of 50 toys? In contrast to market liberalism, human development asks us to also examine the valuable choices available to the Chinese workers who have produced these goods. The cheap price paid may be a reflection of exploitative labour conditions.

Table 3.1 *Human development and neoliberalism compared*

Human development	neoliberalism
• Expansion of human freedoms as objective	• Maximization of economic welfare as objective
• Freedom of choice – understood as human capabilities and functionings	• Freedom of choice – understood as utility and satisfaction of preferences
• Emphasizes all human rights	• Emphasizes political and civil rights
• Is guided by concern of equity and justice	• Is guided by a concern for economic efficiency
• Health and education are intrinsically valuable	• Health and education are seen as investment
• Important state functions	• Minimal state
• People as ends and as focus of concern, economic growth is only a means to an end	• People as means and markets/economic growth as a focus of concern
• Poverty as multidimensional deprivation	• Poverty defined as below income line
• Multi-disciplinary and pragmatic	• Economic and dogmatic
• The non-monetary and economic focus leads to weak data	• Good quality data but neglect of non-economic issues

Source: adapted from Jolly (2003)

✳ good example.

Both human development and market liberalism oppose discrimination but one does it for reasons of efficiency, while the other does it on the basis of human rights. For example, the exclusion of women from labour markets is seen by human development as a denial of women's right to employment. For market liberalism, in contrast, the exclusion of women from labour markets is a denial of greater economic opportunities, such as a more creative and dynamic workforce that could lead to higher economic performance.

While both agree on the importance of the state, human development advocates a much larger role for states. For market liberalism, it is not the role of the state to ensure a minimum level of well-being for its population. However, as we have highlighted above, the principle of non-intervention often requires greater scrutiny given the lack of equity and justice it often engenders. Within the human development and capability approach, market freedoms go hand in hand with freedoms in other spheres, such as freedom in the political sphere. This is why political and civil rights, on the one hand, and economic and social rights, on the other, are inextricably linked. That some groups enjoy the right to non-discrimination more than others is often the consequence of political action to overcome discrimination.

Another distinction is that market liberalism believes that everything can be measured in terms of utility, income and opportunity cost. In contrast, human development recognizes that well-being is multi-dimensional. There are some dimensions that cannot be compared monetarily: for example, if one chooses to work hard during weekends, at the expense of time spent with one's family, market liberalism assumes that the two activities can be compared on a single scale, namely, the amount of extra money one can earn by doing so. Human development recognizes that the fulfilment one derives from work, and the fulfilment one derives from family relationships, remain incommensurable. An additional income can therefore not 'compensate' for the loss of quality in one's family life. This is not merely a matter of 'opportunity cost': the benefit of extra work and the loss of family life cannot be reduced to a single monetary measure.

Human development is thus fundamentally distinct from market liberalism even if both share, on the surface, the same concern for human freedom. This has led to a confusion between the human development approach and human resources, a core concept in market liberalism. Both approaches perceive health and education as being the central focus of public policy, but there remain fundamental differences between them. Paul Streeten (1994) highlights the following: first, he writes, human development is concerned 'with the unproductive, the lame ducks, and the unemployables: the old, infirm, disabled, and chronically sick', while human resources are not. Second, the human resources approach tends to treat people as passive 'targets' and not as 'active, participating agents'. Third, seeing education and health as ends (instead of means to other ends) entails different educational curricula and health programmes. The human resources approach focuses on vocational training aimed at the labour market, while human development aims at education for its own sake and for understanding and transforming the world. Fourth, both have a gender focus, but for very different reasons. The human resources approach argues that it is important for a well-functioning economy for women to participate in labour markets. Human development advocates women's rights in general, whether it leads to economic returns or not. In sum, for human development, promoting education and health does not have to be justified on the grounds of productivity or efficiency. Even if a certain educational programme does not yield high economic returns – funding a school for disabled people vs. funding a vocational secondary school – it may be worthwhile.

How the idea of freedom spread

The idea of freedom as conceived by market liberalism – freedom as non-interference from government – had a tremendous influence on the world in the post-World War II period, particularly from the 1980s onwards, with Ronald Reagan and Margaret Thatcher as its major protagonists in politics, and the Bretton Woods institutions – the International Monetary Fund and the World Bank – as its major advocates in the arena of international development. This conception of freedom did not however spread in a 'natural' way. It was a conscious strategy orchestrated by a set of individuals. In a paper examining how the idea of freedom in the context of market liberalism spread, Alkire and Ritchie (2007) highlight the following ingredients necessary for the spread of ideas, all of which market liberals deployed in order to spread their idea of freedom all over the world. Exploring how this idea was disseminated may offer some insights about how other ideas, such as those in the human development and capability approach, might equally be spread.

The first element necessary in spreading an idea is the use of moral narratives. In 1945, Friedrich von Hayek published the *Road to Serfdom*. This was a clearly and accessibly written book – it was published by the Reader's Digest – that outlined a moral case for laissez-faire market economics. The post-war context was one that saw the rising influence of Communism in Europe and elsewhere in the world. Within that political context, the *Road to Serfdom* tried to defend the moral case for upholding the values of human dignity and freedom against its alternative: the model of a state-controlled economy. The book narrates the kind of society that could emerge if different economic and social policies were at play. It specifically depicted scenarios about what might happen if collectivist policies were to be implemented.

The second ingredient is that of targeting 'second-hand traders'; that is, once the narrative has been written, it has to be disseminated to an audience. Hayek makes the distinction between the producers of ideas and the second-hand traders. These are the people who communicate ideas to a mass audience (journalists, novelists, entrepreneurs and film-makers). The narrative is thus not restricted to an academic community but is shared with people who are able to bridge the academic world and that of mass media.

Third, ideas need to be sustained by an intellectual community. At first, the advocates of free market liberalism had a difficult time finding employment in universities, and their ideas were not well-received in a world where many young people were actively flirting with communism. So they set out to develop an international community of scholars who shared similar principles. They met once a year in Switzerland and became known as the Mont Pélerin Society. Its mission statement is as follows:

> The Mont Pélerin Society is composed of persons who continue to see the dangers to civilized society outlined in the statement of aims. They have seen economic and political liberalism in the ascendant for a time since World War II in some countries but also its apparent decline in more recent times. Though not necessarily sharing a common interpretation, either of causes or consequences, they see danger in the expansion of government, not least in state welfare, in the power of trade unions and business monopoly, and in the continuing threat and reality of inflation.[3]

In addition, intellectual communities need to be given academic credence. This has been the role of the University of Chicago, where the first chairs in free market economics were endowed. The academic community was able to permeate the policy world with its ideas through a policy think-tank, namely the Institute of Economic Affairs, which was founded by the donation of a businessman (a chicken farmer) who had been inspired by the ideas in *The Road to Serfdom*.

A fourth ingredient is that of fostering talent and investing in senior and junior members to disseminate ideas further. This was done through additional donations to universities from the business world to create lectureships and research positions for people who endorsed the idea of freedom as non-interference. Another way in which students at universities were exposed to such ideas was through the publication of accessible policy papers by the Institute of Economic Affairs,[4] such as the Hobart papers, which summarized in simple terms how various issues could be tackled by market liberalism, such as the role of the state, taxation, housing and the provision of public goods, etc.

A final, crucial ingredient is political engagement with political parties and interest groups willing to take these ideas on board. For example, the spread of neoliberalism in Chile in the 1970s had a lot to do with: (1) a group of Chicago-educated Chilean economists who worked closely with General Pinochet to manage the Chilean economy; and (2) powerful interest groups, such as landowners, who had a stake in the idea of freedom as non-interference. In the UK, there was also very close collaboration between the Institute of Economic Affairs and the government of Margaret Thatcher during the 1980s.

But freedom as non-interference was not the only prevalent development idea during this period. Other ideas more related to the human development and capability approach were also present, namely the idea of basic needs, but the idea did not achieve the kind of momentum that freedom in market liberalism did because all the necessary preconditions for its successful spread were not gathered.

The basic needs approach

The idea of freedom as non-interference did not capture the imagination of development economics overnight. An early influence in development thinking was that of economic growth as the key mechanism for eliminating poverty and securing better living conditions for people, thereby increasing human choices (Srinivisan, 1994; Streeten, 2003). It was believed that an increase in wealth would endow people with greater opportunities to live the kind of lives they chose to live. Streeten (2003, p68) gave three justifications for this belief: (1) that 'through market forces – such as the rising demand for labour, rising productivity, rising wages, (and) lower prices of the goods bought by the people – economic growth would spread its benefits widely and speedily'; (2) 'progressive taxation, social services and other government interventions would spread the benefits downwards'; and (3) poverty should not be a concern in the early stages of development, since what mattered was to build the productive capacity of the economy first.

This concern for economic growth should not be confused with market liberalism. When, in 1961, the United Nations General Assembly adopted its first 'Development Decade', its initial objective was to intensify its efforts to support both developed and developing countries in their efforts to achieve 'self-sustaining growth ... and social advancement' in their respective countries and 'to create conditions in which the national incomes of ... developing countries would (increase) by five per cent yearly by 1970 and would continue to expand at this annual rate thereafter' (Emmerij et al, 2001, p44). These aims were of course compatible with those of socialist economies. The state was thereby granted a strong interventionist role in the economy in order to set up the conditions for high economic growth and to achieve the necessary savings rate for investment.

The idea of economic growth as the major objective of development was increasingly questioned by the narrative that began to unfold in the 1970s. The narrative was as follows: economic growth tended to concentrate income and wealth in the hands of the few, increasing human choices of a few and leaving many in destitution. The academic community first reacted by trying to find alternative ways of linking economic growth with redistribution policies by publishing studies such as the 1974 'Redistribution with Growth' by the Institute of Development Studies at Sussex University. But the academic community remained unable to find a sufficient number of allies in the political world. Because governments were themselves part of the elite and reluctant to redistribute the benefits of growth towards the poor, it was difficult to put this alternative approach into practice. Further and more successful attempts at finding an alternative to economic growth were made at the end of the 1970s, with the establishment of the 'basic needs' approach.

The idea of the satisfaction of basic needs as the primary objective of development emerged from work on employment at the International Labour Organisation (ILO) in the early 1970s. An analysis of data on employment conditions in developing countries demonstrated that economic growth and employment were not necessarily a guarantee of freedom from poverty. Indeed, many hard-working people remained unable to have their basic human needs – health, food, education and others – met. In 1977, the ILO published a report on *Employment, Growth and Basic Needs* which formally introduced the idea of basic needs as the objective of development policy for the first time. The idea acquired further policy influence when taken up by the then World Bank President Robert McNamara, who set up a special commission to work explicitly on basic needs. The work of that commission, led by Paul Streeten, was published in 1981, and became known as the basic needs approach, which was defined as 'an approach that attempts to provide the opportunities for the full physical, mental and social development of human personality and then derive the ways of achieving this objective' (Streeten, et al, 1981, p33).

Although the basic needs approach initially emphasized that the objective of development was to provide the conditions for a full human life (material, social, cultural and political), it primarily focused, in operational terms, on the minimum requirements for a decent life – health, nutrition and literacy – and the goods and services needed to realize it, such as shelter, sanitation, food, health services, safe water, primary education, housing and related infrastructures.

Although the idea of basic needs emerged as a practical response to poverty in developing countries, it lacked sound formal and theoretical foundations. It therefore also lacked the backing of a wider intellectual community, which would have been instrumental in disseminating its ideas. Economic and social narratives had also shifted in the 1980s, which did little to buttress the idea of basic needs in the policy arena. The turmoil of the debt crisis in the 1980s, and the imposition of macroeconomic stabilization and adjustment policies that drastically restricted states in their ability to provide basic social services for their people, essentially brought the basic needs approach to a standstill. Box 3.1, written by one of its main proponents, further explains the rise and eventual demise of the approach.

Box 3.1 The Basic Needs Approach

The best shorthand way of describing basic needs is:
incomes + public services + participation.

The basic needs approach is a reminder that the objective of development is to provide all human beings with the *opportunity* for a full life. It goes behind abstractions such as money, income or employment. These aggregates have their place and function but … are useless if they conceal the specific, concrete objectives that people themselves seek. It appeals to members of national and international aid-giving institutions and is therefore capable of mobilizing resources, unlike vaguer (although important) objectives, such as raising growth rates to 6 per cent, contributing 0.7 per cent of GNP to development assistance, redistributing for greater equality or narrowing income gaps.

As the basic needs concept entered the North–South dialogue, all sorts of misconceptions and misinterpretations grew around it. First, it was said that basic needs are confined to basic commodity bundles. Second, it was the thought that the role allotted to the state was too powerful, both in determining what basic needs are and in providing for them being met, and that this type of paternalism (was) both inefficient and unworthy. Third, it was held that there was a neglect of opening up opportunities to people: access to jobs, income, assets, credit (and) power (was) neglected in favour of so many calories, so many yards of cloth.

During the 1980s, and while stabilization and adjustment policies were pursued, new concerns were incorporated (into) the development dialogue: the role of women (and children), the physical environment, population, habitation, human rights, political freedom and governance, empowerment [and] corruption. The basic needs approach was regarded as too narrowly focused on commodity bundles delivered to people by the government, and it had to carry the ballast of past misinterpretations.

Extracts from Paul Streeten (2003) 'Shifting fashions in development dialogue', in S. Fukuda-Parr and S. K. Kumar, *Readings in Human Development*, Delhi: Oxford University Press, pp72–75.

It was only in the early 1990s that the essential ideas behind the basic needs approach – that providing the ideal conditions for a full human life require a multi-dimensional and non-monetary conception of well-being, which should be the ultimate goal of development – was reintroduced to the public policy arena. Amartya Sen's groundbreaking theoretical work on equality and poverty measurement, welfare economics and social choice theory[5] – with Mahbub ul Haq playing the critical role of translating these ideas into practicable policy through the creation of the *Human Development Report* and the Human Development Index in 1990 (Fukuda-Parr and Kumar, 2003) – firmly established the importance of the human development and capability approach in policy and development circles.

The human development approach offers three additional dimensions to basic needs: first, it is based on a much stronger philosophical foundation, thanks to Sen's pioneering work in welfare economics and social choice, which questioned utility as the primary marker for judging states of affairs. Second, it blurs the distinction between developed and developing countries. It is a framework as relevant for assessing the quality of life of people in the US as it is for, say, Sierra Leone, while basic needs had little application in industrialized countries. Finally, human development places a greater emphasis on human freedom and participation (although the latter was initially a feature of the ILO's basic needs approach, it eventually became less of a priority).

Human rights

In addition to the idea of basic needs, another influential idea in policy circles in tune with the core principles of the human development and capability approach was human rights. Indeed, one could argue that seeing humans as ends of the development process was not the sole purview of the human development paradigm alone. It was, in fact, the central concern of the Universal Declaration on Human Rights as early as 1948: all humans should be free and equal in dignity and rights (Article 1), such as the right to work, the right to education, the right to health, the right to vote, the right to non-discrimination, the right to a decent standard of living, etc. Like many ideas in international policy, human rights evolved as a response to post-war narratives. The Declaration was written in the hopes that the atrocities committed during wartime would never be repeated again. While political philosophers had long espoused the centrality of human rights, 'second-hand traders' like journalists, and the political engagement of individuals like Eleanor Roosevelt and public entities like the United Nations (UN), gave it enormous momentum after World War II.

There are significant connections between the human rights approach and that of human development and capability. As the opening sentence of the 2000 *Human Development Report* on human rights puts it: 'Human rights and human development share a common vision and a common purpose – to secure the freedom, well-being and dignity of all people everywhere' (UNDP, 2000, p1).

In a briefing on the capability approach and human rights, Polly Vizard defines a human right as 'a claim to a fundamental benefit that should be enjoyed universally by all people everywhere on the basis of equality and non-discrimination.'[6] She highlights five underlying human rights principles:

1   *universality*: they apply to all people everywhere by virtue of their humanity;
2   *equality*: the benefits of human rights should be enjoyed on the basis of equality and non-discrimination;
3   *inalienability*: human rights cannot be transferred or taken away;
4   *indivisibility*: civil, political, economic and social rights are indivisible – one cannot give priority to one over the other; and
5   *interdependence*: economic, social, civil and political rights are deeply interdependent.

She notes that a characteristic aspect of the idea of human rights is that of 'assignment of responsibility'. Human rights are usually conceived in terms of corresponding notions of obligations and duties. If there is a human right to, say, freedom of conscience, then there are obligations on behalf of states and other institutions to ensure that people are free to hold opinions they believe to be true. The idea of human rights thus focuses on the question: who should be doing what for whom? Given that human rights are inscribed in international law, nation states are therefore the primary duty holders for enforcing human rights. States have the main responsibility for providing an adequate legal framework and institutions that guarantee a respect for human rights.

The major similarity between the two approaches is that both are based on the maxim that individuals should not be treated as a means but as an end. Human life, and its quality and dignity, should be the criteria according to which states of affairs, as well as economic, political and social arrangements, should be assessed. The human rights approach enhances human development with its stronger focus on obligations and duties, while the latter remains an evaluative framework for assessing states of affairs. In contrast, human development does not focus on the state and legal institutions alone. Ensuring that people live flourishing human lives – through the protection of, say, their freedom of conscience, movement or association – is after all not only the role and responsibility of the state: it is also the role of multiple entities, such as civil society organizations, businesses and individuals. If a country passes a law that ensures the right of every child to education, the human development approach will go beyond that right and look at the institutional framework that allows that right to be fulfilled. It will look at the economic, social, political and cultural institutions that constrain or enhance the fulfilment of that right.

According to Sen (2005), the idea of capabilities is distinct from the idea of rights in the sense that the former refers to the *opportunity* aspect of freedom alone, while the latter also refers to its *process* aspect. Let us consider two people who do not enjoy going out in evenings: one of them, a political dissident, has been put by the government under house arrest after 5pm every day and must be accompanied by government agents to all her meetings and walks. The concept of capability tells us that both could go out if they chose to. However, the concept of human rights includes in addition the process aspect in the freedom these two have: the political dissident does not enjoy the right of free movement. A focus on capabilities only can sometimes violate basic principles of equity. Sen offers the example of women living longer than men: if, in order to promote equality of capability to be healthy between men and women, women were denied health care, this would actively constitute gender discrimination, which is a violation of human rights.

Another aspect that the concepts of capability and human rights do not share is that of sensitivity to *means*. Two people might enjoy the same right of freedom of movement, but if one were disabled, she would require different means in order to be able to enjoy that right. The idea of capability includes differences in means requirement: the capability to move freely would require different resources for a blind person (such as special signs at train stations). The human rights approach does not necessarily take such differences into account.

Another difference between the idea of human rights and human development is that the latter emphasizes both the intrinsic and instrumental character of civil and political rights. They are not only good for their own sake, but they are also instrumental in promoting human flourishing, as will be discussed in Chapter 8.

These differences suggest that both approaches are complementary and can in fact reinforce one another. In the words of the 2000 *Human Development Report*:

> Human rights express the bold idea that all people have claims to social arrangements that protect them from the worst abuses and deprivations – and that secure the freedom for a life of dignity. Human development, in turn, is a process of enhancing human capabilities – to expand choices and opportunities so that each person can lead a life of respect and value. When human development and human rights advance together, they reinforce one another – expanding people's capabilities and protecting their rights and fundamental freedoms. (UNDP, 2000, p2)

The report highlights the mutual enrichment of ideas of human rights and human development (UNDP, 2000, pp1–2): first, human rights draw attention to the accountability of governments and other institutions, to respect, protect and fulfil the human rights of all people. Second, the idea of human rights requires a large set of legal instruments in order to enforce these rights and secure people's freedoms. Third, human rights add moral legitimacy to the objectives of human development. Given that the rights to education, health, non-discrimination and so forth are inscribed in international legislation, this gives moral legitimacy to the objective of development, which is about promoting people's health, education and so forth. Fourth, the idea of human rights draws attention to the people who lack these rights. It gives to human development a sense of prioritization. Social and economic policies should be oriented towards those who are deprived of basic human rights. As for the contribution of human development to human rights, the report argues that human development brings a 'dynamic long-term perspective to the fulfilment of rights', and 'directs attention to the socio-economic context in which rights can be realized – or threatened'. Human development focuses on the institutional factors that violate human rights and tries to find ways of changing these constraints, and of mobilizing resources, so that human rights can be guaranteed, because legislation alone is not sufficient to ensure the protection and provision of these rights.

Human security

Along with human rights, another idea that was increasingly prominent during the 1990s was human security. The idea of security has long been central to the military world. Again, narratives that unfolded in the 1990s played a role in emphasizing the importance of security considerations beyond the military arena. Indeed, the rise of internal conflicts in many developing countries led to an increasing consolidation of security and development goals. Under-development, poverty and injustice have also been considered as breeding grounds for civil conflicts. Development, along with the reduction of poverty and inequality, was therefore seen as a way of achieving security and peace.

Emerging from this changing context, human security attempted to overcome the limitations of conventional interpretations of security to generate responses that were sufficiently adequate for dealing with the new sources of insecurity in the post-Cold War period. Human security essentially highlights the fact that a military solution is not necessarily the answer to insecurity. The 1994 *Human Development Report* shifted the focus of security from the protection of the state and its borders by military means to the protection of individuals from a wider range of threats to their well-being. It defined human security as including 'safety from such chronic threats as hunger, disease and repression, and protection from sudden and hurtful disruptions in the patterns of daily lives, whether in homes, jobs or communities' (UNDP, 1994, p1). The report divided human security into seven main categories: economic security (such as job security), food security, health security, environmental security, personal security, community security and political security.

Human security is thus much more than the absence of violent conflict:

> Human security in its broadest sense embraces far more than the absence of violent conflict. It encompasses human rights, good governance, access to education and health care, and ensuring

that each individual has opportunities and choices to fulfil his or her own potential… Freedom from want, freedom from fear and the freedom of future generations to inherit a healthy natural environment – these are the interrelated building blocks of human, and therefore national, security'. (Commission on Human Security 2003, p4)

Box 3.2, written by Amartya Sen and taken from the *Human Security Report* (Commission on Human Security, 2003) explains the similarities and differences between the ideas of human security, human rights and human development.

Box 3.2 Development, rights and human security

Human security is concerned with reducing and – when possible – removing the insecurities that plague human lives. It contrasts with the notion of state security, which concentrates primarily on safeguarding the integrity and robustness of the state and thus has only an indirect connection with the security of the human beings who live in these states. That contrast may be clear enough, but in delineating human security adequately, it is also important to understand how the idea of human security relates to – and differs from – other human-centred concepts, such as human development and human rights. These concepts are fairly widely known and have been championed, with very good reason, for a long time, and they too are directly concerned with the nature of human lives. It is thus fair to ask what the idea of human security can add to these well-established ideas.

Human development and human security

The human development approach, pioneered by the visionary economist Mahbub ul Haq (under the broad umbrella of the UNDP), has done much to enrich and broaden the literature on development. In particular, it has helped to shift the focus of development attention away from an overarching concentration on the growth of inanimate objects of convenience, such as commodities produced (reflected in the GDP or the GNP), to the quality and richness of human lives, which depend on a number of influences, of which commodity production is only one. Human development is concerned with removing the various hindrances that restrain and restrict human (life) and prevent its blossoming. A few of these concerns are captured in the much-used 'human development index' (HDI), which has served as something of a flagship for the human development approach. But the range and reach of that perspective have motivated a vast informational coverage presented in the UNDP's annual *Human Development Report* and other related publications that go far beyond the HDI.

The idea of human development, broad as it is, does, however, have a powerfully buoyant quality, since it is concerned with progress and augmentation. It is out to conquer fresh territory on behalf of enhancing human lives and is far too upbeat to focus on rearguard actions needed to secure what has to be safeguarded. This is where the notion of human security becomes particularly relevant. Human security as an idea fruitfully supplements the expansionist perspective of human development by directly paying attention to what are sometimes called 'downside risks'. The insecurities that threaten human survival or the safety of daily life, or imperil the natural dignity of men and women, or expose human beings to the uncertainty of disease and pestilence, or subject vulnerable people to abrupt penury related to economic downturns, demand that special attention be paid to the dangers of sudden deprivation. Human security demands protection from these dangers and the empowerment of people so that they can cope with – and, when possible, overcome – these hazards.

There is, of course, no basic contradiction between the focus of human security and the subject matter of the human development approach. Indeed, formally speaking, protection and safeguarding can also be seen as augmentations of a sort, to wit, that of safety and security. But the emphasis and priorities are quite different in the cautious perspective of human security from those typically found in the relatively sanguine and upward-oriented literature of the human focus of development approaches (and this applies to human development as well), which tend to concentrate on 'growth with equity', a subject that has generated a vast literature and inspired many policy initiatives. In contrast, focusing on human security requires that serious attention be paid to 'downturns with security', since downturns may inescapably occur from time to time, fed by global or local afflictions. This is in addition to the adversity of persistent insecurity of those whom the growth process leaves behind, such as the displaced worker or the perennially unemployed.

Even when the much-discussed problems of uneven and unequally-shared benefits of growth and expansion have been successfully addressed, a sudden downturn can make the lives of the vulnerable thoroughly and uncommonly deprived. There is much economic evidence that, even if people rise together as the process of economic expansion proceeds, when they fall, they tend to fall very divided. The Asian economic crisis of 1997–1999 made it painfully clear that even a very successful history of 'growth with equity' (as the Republic of Korea, Thailand and many other countries in East and Southeast Asia had) can provide very little protection to those who are thrown to the wall when a sharp economic down-turn suddenly occurs. The economic case merely illustrates a general contrast between the two perspectives of *expansion with equity* and *downturn with security*. For example, while the foundational demand for expanding regular health coverage for all human beings in the world is tremendously important to advocate and advance, that battle has to be distinguished from the immediate need to encounter a suddenly growing pandemic, related to HIV/AIDS or malaria or drug-resistant tuberculosis. Insecurity is a different – and in some ways much starker –problem than unequal expansion. Without losing any of the commitment that makes human development important, we also have to rise to the challenges of human security that the world currently faces and will long continue to face.

Human rights and human security

There is a similar complementarity between the concepts of human rights and human security. Few concepts are as frequently invoked in contemporary political debates as human rights. There is something deeply attractive in the idea that every person anywhere in the world, irrespective of citizenship or location, has some basic rights that others should respect. The moral appeal of human rights has been used for varying purposes, from resisting torture and arbitrary incarceration to demanding the end of hunger and the unequal treatment of women. Human rights may or may not be legalized, but they take the form of strong claims in social ethics. The idea of pre-legal 'natural' or 'human' rights has often motivated legislative initiatives, as it did in the US Declaration of Independence or in the French Declaration of the Rights of Man in the 18th century, or in the European Convention for the Protection of Human Rights and Fundamental Freedoms in the 20th century. But even when they are not legalized, affirmation of human rights and related activities of advocacy and monitoring of abuse can sometimes be very effective, through the politicization of ethical commitments. Commitments underlying human rights take the form of demanding that certain basic freedoms of human beings be respected, aided and enhanced. The basically normative nature of the concept of human rights leaves open the question of which particular freedoms are crucial enough to count as human rights that society should acknowledge, safeguard and promote.

This is where human security can make a significant contribution: by identifying the importance of freedom from basic insecurities – new and old. The descriptive richness of the considerations that make security so important in human lives can, thus, join hands with the force of ethical claims that the recognition of certain freedoms as human rights provides. Human rights and human security can, therefore, fruitfully supplement each other. On the one hand, since human rights can be seen as a general box that has to be filled with specific demands with appropriate motivational substantiation, it is significant that human security helps to fill one particular part of this momentous box through reasoned substantiation (by showing the importance of conquering human insecurity). On the other, since human security as an important descriptive concept demands ethical force and political recognition, it is useful that this be appropriately obtained through seeing freedoms related to human security as an important class of human rights. Far from being in any kind of competition with each other, human security and human rights can be seen as complementary ideas.

One of the advantages of seeing human security as a class of human rights is the associative connection that rights have with the corresponding duties of other people and institutions. Duties can take the form of 'perfect obligations', which constitute specific demands on particular persons or agents, or of 'imperfect obligations', which are general demands on anyone in a position to help. To give effectiveness to the perspective of human security, it is important to consider who in particular has what obligations (such as the duties of the state to provide certain basic support) and also why people in general, who are in a position to help reduce insecurities in human lives, have a common – though incompletely specified – duty to think about what they can do. Seeing human security within a general framework of human rights can, thus, bring many rewards to the perspective of human security.

To conclude, it is important, on one side, to see how the distinct ideas of human security, human development and human rights differ, but also to understand why they can be seen as complementary concepts. Mutual enrichment can go hand in hand with distinction and clarity.

This is a reproduction of Box 1.3 of the Human Security Report which was written by Amartya Sen (Commission on Human Security, 2003), available at www.humansecurity-chs.org.

Other related ideas

The Millennium Development Goals

Another development idea that has been at the forefront of policy agendas for the past decade has been the Millennium Development Goals (MDGs). At the Millennium Summit held in New York in September 2000, 189 UN member states adopted the Millennium Declaration, which consisted of eight goals that have to be achieved by the year 2015. These goals are divided into 21 targets with 60 indicators against which progress is tracked.[7] When possible, indicators are disaggregated according to male/female, urban/rural and other variables, such as ethnicity or language. The MDG targets and indicators can thus be seen as a partial roadmap for human development. They are human development goals, although they do not reflect all of the dimensions of human development (see Table 3.2).

Unlike policy ideas that are first introduced to the wider public by a community of like-minded academics, the MDGs were designed by an international political community as a tool to monitor development progress. The campaign received a lot of media attention, especially with the 'Global Call to Action' in 2005, which was better known in Europe as the 'Make Poverty History' campaign. Unlike human development, the MDGs do not include concerns for empowerment and participation (except in relation to gender empowerment), equity and distributional issues, and the sustainability of development advances across time. The MDGs also lack explanatory value and analytical power.

Despite these weaknesses, the MDGs remain useful for the human development approach.[8] First, MDG indicators enable us to analyse the reality and evolution of a country's development within a broader frame than the one offered by income or GDP per capita. MDGs are related to the human development approach but are limited to the most basic aspects of human well-being. Second, MDGs offer a frame of high-priority and limited interventions. This aspect is essential for public policies in developing countries, which must face numerous problems simultaneously, but have limited resources and capabilities. Third, they establish relatively realistic objectives and a time-line in which to achieve them. In addition, they are accompanied by a set of homogenous monitoring indicators, which facilitate the analysis and comparison of country and regional performances. Fourth, MDGs reaffirm the commitment of developed countries to support the developing world. The flow of international aid is necessary if these countries are to overcome poverty and increase the well-being of their respective populations. The MDG framework encourages worldwide cooperation and solidarity. It highlights that governments are accountable not only for reducing poverty or promoting basic health and education, but also for promoting gender equality and empowering women, ensuring environmental sustainability, providing access to affordable and essential drugs, making available the benefits of new technologies, and

Table 3.2 *Correspondence between key capabilities and the MDGs*

Key capabilities for human development	Corresponding MDG
Living a long and healthy life	Goals 4, 5, 6: reducing child mortality, improving maternal health and combating major diseases
Being knowledgeable	Goals 2, 3: achieving universal primary education and promoting gender equality in education
Having a decent standard of living	Goals 1, 7: reducing poverty and hunger and ensuring environmental sustainability
Enjoying political and civil freedoms to participate in the life of one's community	Not a goal, but an important global objective included in the Millennium Declaration

Source: Seeta Prabhu, mimeo document

providing universal access to reproductive health. Another positive aspect of this is that civil society has stepped into this public discourse to demand the achievement of these goals, giving them greater agency and contributing to the overall empowerment of society as a whole.

Sustainable development

Another idea that has been prominent in the past two decades has been sustainable development, that is, an economic development that is compatible with the capacity of natural resources to sustain such development in the long run – Ghandi famously said that the world would need six planets if it were to sustain consumption levels similar to those of the US. The 1987 Brundtland Commission Report, *Our Common Future*, coined sustainable development as 'development that meets the needs of the present without compromising the ability of future generations to meet their own needs.' The two key concepts (p. 43) are: (1) needs (the essential needs of the world's poor should be given overriding priority); and (2) limitations (the ability of the environment to meet present and future needs is however limited).

In a paper that compares the idea of human development with that of sustainability, Anand and Sen (2000) argue that human development brings to sustainable development, in addition to its concern for equity between generations, an equal concern for equity within generations. The demand for sustainability is part of the universal character of human development. Human development is about promoting the freedoms that people have reason to choose and value in both future and present generations. This universalism entails that deprivations and sufferings of both current and future generations be given equal attention. As Anand and Sen (2000) write, 'that universalism also requires that in our anxiety to protect ... future generations, we must not overlook the pressing claims of the less privileged today. A universalist approach cannot ignore the deprived people today in trying to prevent deprivation in the future.' They continue, 'there would be something distinctly odd if we were deeply concerned for the well-being of the future – and as yet unborn – generations while ignoring the plight of the poor today.' Putting the concern for inter-generational equity above the principle of intra-generational equity would amount to 'a gross violation of the universalist principle'. Human development 'certainly demands such impartiality'.

Another point that Anand and Sen insist on is that the market cannot be the only solution for ensuring sustainable development. The concern for universalism 'demands that the state ... serve as a trustee for the interests of future generations'. There is a wide role for the state, through taxes, subsidies and regulation to 'adapt the incentive structure in ways that protect the global environment and resource base for people yet to be born'.

As with human rights and human security, sustainable development therefore shares many similarities with the human development and capability approach. Indeed, the principle of sustainability is a core human development principle. But the human development and capability approach offers a much broader framework for analysis and action, such as evaluative and institutional tools to address the challenges of development and sustainability.

Questions

3.1 Draw the similarities and differences between the ideas of human development, market liberalism, basic needs, human rights, human security, Millennium Development Goals and sustainable development.
3.2 How does concern for inter-generational and intra-generational equity relate? Discuss the possible trade-offs.
3.3 What is the most influential idea in public policy in your country? Why and how has this idea acquired so much policy influence?
3.4 In your opinion, what would be required to make the human development and capability approach influential in the policy decisions of government, multi-national companies and business organizations in your country?
3.5 Can you think of organizations that already implement human development principles in their activities and practices?

Notes

1   This section draws from an article written by Angus Ritchie in the first issue of *Maitreyee*, the e-bulletin of the Human Development and Capability Association, March 2005, available at www.hd-ca.org (section 'e-bulletin').
2   This paragraph has been written by Adriana Velasco.
3   See www.montpelerin.org.
4   See www.iea.org.uk.
5   Desai (1991) attributes two parallel sources to human development: (1) the pioneering works made in equality and poverty measurement by Anthony Atkinson and Amartya Sen; and (2) the search for a non-economic measure of development pioneered in the 1960s with the social indicators school in Scandinavian countries.

6   The briefing is available at www.hd-ca.org (section 'educational resources', category 'educational material').
7   See http://mdgs.un.org/unsd/mdg/
8   This paragraph has been written by Adriana Velasco.

Readings

Alkire, S. and Ritchie. A. (2007) 'Winning ideas: Lessons from free-market economics', *OPHI Working Paper* 6, Oxford Poverty and Human Development Initiative, available at www.ophi.org.uk

Anand, S. and Sen, A. K. (2000) 'Human development and economic sustainability', *World Development*, vol 28, no 12, pp2029–2049

Commission on Human Security (2003) *Human Security Now*, available at www.humansecurity-chs.org

Desai, M. (1991) 'Human development: Concepts and measurement', *European Economic Review*, vol 35, pp350–357

Emmerij, L., Jolly, R. and Weiss, T. (2001) *Ahead of the Curve?: UN Ideas and Global Challenges*, University of Indiana Press, Bloomington

Fukuda-Parr, S. and Kumar, S. K. (eds) (2003) *Readings in Human Development*, Oxford University Press, Delhi

Jolly, R. (2003) 'Human development and neo-liberalism', in S. Fukuda-Parr and S. K. Kumar (eds) *Readings in Human Development*, Oxford University Press, Delhi

Sen, A. K. (1981) *Poverty and Famines*, Clarendon Press, Oxford

Sen, A. K. (1999), *Development as Freedom*, Oxford University Press

Sen, A. K. (2005) 'Human rights and capabilities', *Journal of Human Development*, vol 6, no 2, pp151–166

Srinivasan, T. N. (1994) 'Human development: A new paradigm or reinvention of the wheel?', *The American Economic Review*, vol 84, no 2, pp238–243

Streeten, P. (1994) 'Human development: Means and ends', *The American Economic Review*, vol 84, no 2, pp232–237

Streeten, P. (2003) 'Shifting fashions in development dialogue', in S. Fukuda-Parr and S. K. Kumar (eds) *Readings in Human Development*, Oxford University Press, Delhi

Streeten, P., Burki, S. and Stewart, F. (1981) *First Things First: Meeting Basic Human Needs in Developing Countries*, The World Bank, Washington, DC

UNDP (1994) *Human Development Report: New Dimensions of Human Security*, Oxford University Press

UNDP (2000) *Human Development Report: Human Rights and Human Development*, Oxford University Press

World Commission on Environment and Development (1987) *Our Common Future*, Oxford University Press, New York

Further Readings

Alkire, S. (2003) 'A conceptual framework for human security', *CRISE Working Paper* 2, available at www.crise.ox.ac.uk/pubs/workingpaper2.pdf

Blundell, J. (2007) *Waging the War of Ideas* (3rd edn), Institute of Economic Affairs, London

Gasper, D. (2005) 'Securing humanity: Situating "Human Security" as concept and discourse, *Journal of Human Development*, vol 6, no 2, pp221–246

Sen, A. K. (2004) 'Elements of a theory of human rights', *Philosophy and Public Affairs*, vol 32, no 4, pp315–356

Stewart, F. (1985) *Planning to Meet Basic Needs*, Macmillan, London

Stewart, F. (2006) 'The evolution of economic ideas: From import substitution to Human Development', in V. FitzGerald and R. Thorp (eds) *Economic Doctrines in Latin America*, Palgrave, Basingstoke

Part II
Topics

4

Economic Growth

Randy Spence

Aims of the chapter

- To critically evaluate economic growth theories from the perspective of the human development and capability approach.
- To understand the linkages between economic growth and human flourishing.

Key Points

- Economic growth is only one of several necessary ingredients for promoting human flourishing.
- GDP fails to measure human flourishing for two main reasons: (1) income is a poor measure of well-being; and (2) it masks inequity in the distribution of income and material consumption.
- In aiming for efficiency and growth, distributional equity, stability and public engagement, post-war economies came close to the objective of human flourishing. In comparison, the policies in the past three decades, which have tended to focus more narrowly on efficiency and growth alone, have been characterized by major inequity, insecurity and environmental damage.
- Finding the 'best' growth and development path requires trial and error. Many theories and approaches are valuable, but no single approach or model suffices completely.

In the first chapter, we detailed some unverified assumptions regarding the relationship between economic growth and human flourishing. We noted that the positive link between the two is not as obvious as one might think. There are countries that have experienced high rates of economic growth but not necessarily an expansion in valuable capabilities. We cited the example of India which, after 15 years of steady economic growth, still shows no decrease in the rate of malnutrition among its children. This chapter explores in a more systematic way the mechanisms through which economic growth leads to the expansion of valuable capabilities.

This chapter is divided into three sections: the first section reviews how economic growth has been treated in the history of economic thought. It illustrates that there are divergent views among economists about the role of economic growth in the promotion of human flourishing. The second section discusses various economic growth theories that have been prevalent since the 1950s and are still called upon today to support economic growth as a key development objective. It argues that considerations about what constitutes economic growth and human flourishing, what factors cause or facilitate them, and how they are related depend upon the respective ideological positions, theories and historical experiences of different societies. The final section analyses the specific contribution of the human development literature to the growth debate.

Concluding with questions and points of discussion, the chapter assists readers in forming their own respective opinions. There is no canonical view about the relationship between economic growth and human flourishing. Short historical reviews of economic thought and experience inevitably tend to be both selective and interpretive, and this one is no exception. But the chapter attempts to be as broad as possible. Readers are advised to read widely on the basis of the literature provided here and elsewhere, and to draw their own conclusions.

Growth in the history of economic thought

Classical economists

Some of the major classical economists were: Adam Smith, David Ricardo, Thomas Malthus, John Stuart Mill and Karl Marx. As Europe moved from feudalism into capitalism, the major preoccupations of classical economics were about the relationships between laissez-faire policies – free markets with everyone pursuing their own personal gain – and the development of society itself, where issues such as power, class, individual equity, governance and the emergence of democracy played a critical role. Most classical British economists were interested in the same key questions: what propelled economic growth and what determined its distribution? The 19th century saw the development of laissez-faire economies, with workers and goods free to move, and workers' organizations free to advance their own respective interests.

In establishing the theory of comparative advantage, Ricardo made economics even more concerned with efficiency: all economies can gain by specializing in the production of goods that they are better at producing, and by trading them with other countries. For example, given that Portugal is more abundant in land suitable for growing vines, and England more abundant with land for grazing sheep, one country has an advantage in specializing in wine production and the other in wool.[1] Adam Smith's demonstrations of specialization, self-regulating markets and 'the invisible hand' are well known. But classical economists were invariably political, and economic considerations were rarely divorced from political and ethical concerns. Smith was very clear that there were many internal and international conditions necessary if market-regulated economies were to work, such as the ability to 'see the world through the eyes of other people', which was fundamental to the pursuit of justice, a central theme in Smith's works (Rothschild, 2001).

Of the classical economists, Marx was the most focused on labour, although all the classical British economists (and intellectually Marx was one) used various labour theories of value. Marx's theory holds that the value of goods and services is ultimately based on human labour input. He predicted that socialism would replace capitalism, as the workers would 'rise and abandon their chains'. But the 20th century failed to play out this prediction. This convinced many that a socialist state which provided incentives, minimized rent-seeking behaviour based on position rather than a contribution to the economy, avoided state control and repression, and that was efficient and stable enough to avoid economic collapse or drastic political reform, has yet to be found. Despite this, Marx foresaw many of the problems and opposition that the expanding global dominance of market forces and industrial power would encounter.

Pre-World War II: National Accounting

Along with major experiments in centrally-planned economies, the development of the theory of efficient market functioning continued, and national economic accounts were developed and refined to provide detailed data on production, consumption and the trade of goods and services – and of factors of production – across all domestic economic sectors[2] and in trade with other countries. Aggregate measures of domestic or national production and income, and their change from year to year, became the standard measures of economic growth.

Gross domestic product (GDP) is the total value-added in production of goods and services within an economy in a year.[3] Value is added at each stage of the production of a product,[4] by factors of production (land, labour and capital), which are paid for accordingly. GDP is therefore equal to total national income (Y) – paid to factors in the form of wages, interest, rents and profits (w, i, r and p). These incomes are spent each year on household consumption of final goods and services (C), investment (I), government spending (G) and net exports (exports minus imports or X–M):

$$\text{GDP} = Y = w + i + r + p = C + I + G + (X–M)$$

The distribution of income depends on who in a society owns which factors of production: land/resources, labour/skills or capital (plant and equipment).

Measuring economic growth performances, with GDP as a primary measure, requires national accounts. But GDP, while certainly useful and important, has several serious drawbacks, as a measure of both economic activity and well-being. As a measure of material consumption, income and expenditure, the figures leave out many components, including environmental damage, activities in the informal sector that dominate in many countries (the informal sector accounts for 85–90 per cent of the Indian economy, for example), household and reproductive work, and non-profit activities such as volunteering. Furthermore, all public sector activity is valued at cost, as there are no markets and prices for most public services. Moreover, GDP is the economy-wide total and does not give information about what happens at the individual- or household-level. More individual income or consumption data are needed. Another severe limitation of GDP is that it does not take into account certain variables that matter for human flourishing. Neither income nor expenditure measure the *well-being* people obtain from such goods and services. Thus, Bill Gates is not necessarily millions of times better off than the average American. People derive well-being not only from consuming goods and services, but also from peace, meaningful employment and fulfilling relationships, etc. (see Chapter 2).

Polanyi vs. Hayek

In his *Great Transformation*, Karl Polanyi (1944) analysed the development of markets from early history to the great transformation of the 1900s, particularly the separation of their control first from monarchs and then from guilds in the 18th and 19th centuries. State intervention was to be minimized, except where markets failed. In this regard, Adam Smith's *Wealth of Nations* (1776) had been an important landmark. Polanyi argued that labour should not be seen just as another commodity for sale, both because of the intrinsic value societies place on labour (work as part of human dignity) and because markets tend to fail in promoting human flourishing on their own (education and health are not best provided only by the free functionings of markets but also by public provision). He argued that effective regulation at macro and sectoral levels were urgently needed. The great transformation thus included building the capacities of both government and market institutions. Like Marx, Polanyi saw the end result as the socialist state, but also predicted opposition and problems for its opposite – the global rule of market forces and industrial powers.

Fredrick von Hayek, a rival and ideological opponent of Polanyi's, had a strong influence in setting out the case for market efficiency and minimal government intervention. He saw in the price system the key allocative mechanism in an efficient market economy. *The Road to Serfdom* became a seminal publication for market liberalism, as has already been discussed in Chapter 3. Governments, which had substantially expanded during both World Wars, did not contract in the post-war era and had begun to develop obvious pockets of inefficiency. But, instead of demanding efficiency in core public sector functions, neoliberals demanded that the role of government be minimized instead.[5]

The elegant calculus of neoclassical economics has been highly influential in promoting this view. In seeking to maximize their 'utility' by consuming goods and services, consumers express to the production system exactly what they want – voting with their wallets. In seeking to maximize profits, producers make what people want as efficiently as possible, given the resources available to the economy at any given time (natural resources, labour, capital and knowledge). At the 'margin' of everyone's efforts, wages, interest, rents and profits received by factory owners exactly equal the value of their contribution to economic production. There are no 'excess' profits in a competitive system, beyond market-determined payments for the contributions of all resource owners.

This efficient equilibrium occurs because of price mechanisms. The prices of production factors, as well as those of goods and services, are constantly adjusting themselves to reflect changes in consumer demand or production costs.[6] These adjustments, however, only work under conditions of perfect competition, that is, large numbers of producers and consumers, no market power exercised by any groups of producers or consumers, no barriers to trade of goods or factors, equal information available to all market participants and many other conditions. These never fully exist in real markets, of course (see Chapter 7). In reality, many situations of imperfect competition tend to exist. In addition, the idea of efficient market operation only applies to goods that are individually consumed, and there is a further set of public goods, like health, education, law/justice, the environment, equity and security that comprise about a quarter of the GDP of most economies.[7]

Keynes and Schumpeter

Keynes' *General Theory of Employment, Interest and Money* (1936) helped to formalize important traditions of economic thought. While neoclassical economics is about the (static) efficiency of resource allocation, it does not explain how production grows. According to Keynes, the principal mechanism in market economics is savings and investment. People hold back income from consumption in a year, and use it to increase the production capacity of the economy in the future – investing it in capital (building plant and equipment) and education (building skills and knowledge). He argues that the rate of saving is one of the main drivers of growth in market economies. Thus the growth theory of the post-war period focused on the rate of saving, and the productivity of the new capital in raising income.

Keynes focused more on the imbalances which arose between intended savings and investment, and between money demand and supply, and on the nature of instabilities and disequilibria that could result from these imbalances – notably unemployment and other factors. The Great Depression had reinforced the importance of stability, in addition to efficiency, and had demonstrated that growth could be de-railed and in fact entirely undone by severe macroeconomic instability. To this day, debate has continued about how governments can best achieve greater stability. Keynes was also influential in the creation of the Bretton Woods institutions after the war – the International Bank for Reconstruction and Development (IBRD, now the World Bank group) and the International Monetary Fund (IMF). These were designed to promote stability, reconstruction and liberalization in global finances. The General Agreement on Tariffs and Trade (GATT), which resulted from the failure of governments to create an International Trade Organization at the Bretton Woods negotiations, was directed almost entirely at trade liberalization.

These institutions have been central in maintaining strong market economies and a liberalization agenda in global economic and development relations, reflecting the views and interests of the US and European countries, who continue to remain the dominant financial contributors in the international arena today. But although Keynes and 'Keynesian economics' were very influential, arguing for a public sector role in stabilizing market economies, the Bretton Woods institutions and WTO still maintain a strong non-interventionist agenda. We will return to these issues later.

Another influential perspective on economic growth in the immediate post-war era was Schumpeter's *Capitalism, Socialism and Democracy* (1944). While critiquing Marx, he argues that capitalism will 'decompose' for a number of reasons, including monopolistic practices, the destruction of the institutional framework of capitalist societies, a 'growing hostility' to excessive materialism and 'the process of creative destruction' inherent in capitalism. Current thinking on growth and development, as will be detailed below, takes somewhat similar views. The rapid growth of countries as large as China – with successes, failures, experimentation and enormous learning curves – reinforce the view that there is no general or single (capitalist) model of economic growth and development. Creative destruction also recalls an earlier focus on technological change as a central driver of economic growth. Factors that generate and facilitate technological development and change (innovation) have become major analytic concerns, particularly in the past two decades.

Public economics

Public finance, better understood as public economics, underwent extensive development in the mid-20th century. It is mainly concerned with the principal operations of governments, public goods provision (expenditure), public revenue raising (taxation and borrowing) and economic stabilization. The most well known public finance economists include Richard and Peggy Musgrave, Ursula Hicks, Kenneth Arrow and Paul Samuelson. Public economics defines the principal functions of government as efficiency, equity, stabilization, public engagement and participation.

One major failure on the part of markets in allocating resources efficiently is in the area of public goods and services. It is not efficient for many individuals and groups in a society, for example, to have their own respective defence forces or legal and justice systems; once in place, these services generally tend to be available to everyone and are collectively consumed. Less completely collective in consumption are, for example, education and health, where the benefits of services go mainly to the individual student or patient, although if an individual is healthy or well-educated, many others (as family, friends, co-workers or fellow citizens) also benefit. In such cases, markets either fail to produce the services or allocate too few resources. Public financing and provision of these services is necessary from the point of view of pure 'efficiency'.

Environmental degradation involves a similar kind of collective consumption and market failure. Global warming occurs because we collectively release too much carbon into the atmosphere. We collectively consume the ability of the atmosphere to absorb carbon because, in the short-term, no one has to pay. In the longer-term, however, we all pay. But, because market forces do not assign the costs to individuals, collective action is needed. A public economics solution to this would be for all countries to agree upon maximum global carbon emissions levels annually, and to then assign these global quotas to countries on the basis of a collective agreement that favours poorer countries. The latter would get higher allocations than they currently need if, for example, quotas were based on population. They could then sell part of their quota. A true marginal cost of burning carbon would be established, and poor countries would gain.

A second category of market failure lies in the concentration of market power (imperfect competition) in the hands of a few sellers or buyers. In the cases of monopoly and oligopoly (when there is one or very few dominant sellers), consumers pay too much and the dominant producer(s) earn/s monopoly profits. In reality, almost all markets have some degree of market concentration. For the more extreme cases, where consumer welfare is strongly affected, countries use competition policy instruments and related regulation to break up or reduce monopolies/oligopolies and increase the efficiency of the economy's operation. An insufficient capacity to employ competitive policies leaves consumers in many developing countries open to the monopolistic tendencies of both domestic and foreign producers.

A second function of government, in addition to correcting market failures, is to establish equity, for a purely market economy does not redistribute income and wealth. The only significant avenue open to individuals is to save and invest, so that their income and consumption can increase over time. This is particularly hard to do for poor people whose consumption is already too low to permit survival, let alone savings. Most societies therefore redistribute resources from the rich to the poor, and the tools of public economics analyse the different redistributive options – mainly types of government taxes and expenditures – in terms of their redistributive results and economic efficiency. A progressive income tax (the higher the income, the higher the tax rate) is a favoured instrument in many countries where the tax system is strong enough to implement it. Subsidizing health care and education for poorer segments of the population is also frequently done, as it is often politically more feasible to redistribute 'opportunity' (e.g. via education) than to redistribute income.

The third function of governments, ensuring economic stability, has been especially highlighted by the structural adjustment experiences of the 1970s and 1980s. The negative consequences of economic instability, such as high price inflation and exchange rate volatility, can be very large for both economic growth and human flourishing. The principal stabilizing instruments governments have are: monetary policy, fiscal policy (taxation and expenditure) and financial sector regulation. Experience suggests that frequent intervention by governments to stabilize markets is often destabilizing because it is anticipated by market actors and because of lags of recognition, action, policy implementation and impact in the processes of intervention.

As a result, steady and conservative monetary and fiscal policies have been practised in most advanced economies, together with firm financial sector regulation.[8] In particular, money supply is kept growing at the growth rate of the real economy, and the government deficit is kept to a very small percentage (2–4 per cent) of the GDP. With today's complex and global financial markets, traditional tools of monetary policy intervention are used more frequently to expand or contract money supply, such as fixing the rate at which the central bank lends to other banks, or specifying the amount of reserves banks are required to keep on deposit at the central bank. Extraordinary measures are used under extraordinary circumstances, such as the nationalization of some banks during the 2008–2009 financial crisis.

Finally, while leadership remains an important role of government, public engagement and participation have not been sufficiently emphasized in the many countries that practise neoliberal economic policies. They have been more prominent in centrist and social democratic countries (e.g. in Scandinavia), and are making a comeback in others where opposition to corporate lobbies as the main shapers of public policy is rising.

The possibility of social choice

In his Nobel lecture of this title, Amartya Sen observed:

> Arrow's 'impossibility theorem' (formally the 'General Possibility Theorem') is a result of a breathtaking elegance of power, which showed that even some very mild conditions of reasonableness could not be simultaneously satisfied by any social choice procedure, within a very wide family. Only a dictatorship would avoid inconsistencies, but that of course would involve: (1) in politics, an extreme sacrifice of participatory decisions, and (2) in welfare economics, a gross inability to be sensitive to the heterogeneous interests of a diverse population. (Sen, 1999, p351)

The search for workable theories and processes of social choice became one focus of Sen's work, and that of many others. With neither market economy mechanism nor reasonable voting or decision rules for the making of public choices on a range of basic areas – from what public goods and services to provide to the provision of the non-economic freedoms – the development of pragmatic theory and practice has drawn on several sources; from the conclusion of Sen's lecture:

> Addressing these problems fits well into a general program of strengthening social choice theory (and 'nonobituarial' welfare economics). In general, informational broadening, in one form or another, is an effective way of overcoming social choice pessimism and of avoiding impossibilities, and it leads directly to constructive approaches with viability and reach. Formal reasoning about postulated axioms (including their compatibility and coherence), as well as informal understanding of values and norms (including their relevance and plausibility), both point in that productive direction. Indeed, the deep complementarity between formal and informal reasoning – so central to the social sciences – is well illustrated by developments in modern social choice theory. (Sen, 1999, p366)

Economic thought at the periphery

The underlying theory of the mixed economy was developed mainly among the more advanced economies of the Organization for Economic Co-operation and Development (OECD) states. The experiences of other countries were very different, and economic thought about growth reflected these differences. One body of 'opposing' views to liberalization and free markets is that of 'dependency theory'. This theory emerged in Latin America in the 1950s and borrowed significantly from Marxist analysis.[9] According to dependency theory, the economies of colonized countries – the periphery – were doomed to provide raw materials for the colonizing centre, where goods were manufactured and prosperity grew. This meant that the economy at the periphery was characterized by low productivity, leading to low savings, investment and growth and a vicious circle of underdevelopment. Because resources flew from periphery to centre, the latter enriched itself at the expense of the former. Post-World War II attempts in Latin American countries to develop domestic industry behind high tariff barriers – so-called 'import-substitution policies' – reflected this kind of thinking. These policies tended to develop inefficient industries which could not compete in global markets, and were mostly abandoned by the late 1970s. However, opposing neoliberal forces imposed by the political, economic and military elites in Latin America were also characterized by failures.

Other analyses of growth became influential during this period as well. Gunnar Myrdal won a Nobel Prize in 1974, the same year as Hayek, for his penetrating analysis of the interdependence between economic, social and institutional phenomena. His ten-year study of poverty in Asia, *Asian Dream: An Inquiry into the Poverty of Nations*, published in 1968, resulted in the prediction that high population growth would stunt economic growth. Rapid development would be possible only with population control, wider distribution of agricultural land and investment in health care and education. One reason his predictions could not be verified was the heavy investment in health and education in East Asia prior to this period, which led to growth spurts in the second half of the 20th century. In addressing the relationship between human development and economic growth, Myrdal was a pioneer in the field of economics. As we will later discuss, it has now been established that there can be no long-term economic growth without investing in health and education (Ranis et al, 2000).

There are other influential theories of growth that are based on developing country experiences but which remained unrecognized by the 'mainstream' – because development economics was generally regarded with some disdain in economics departments in Western universities. The dual sector model of Sir Arthur Lewis, in *Economic Development with Unlimited Surplus of Labour* published in 1954, posited that there was surplus labour in developing countries, particularly in agriculture, and that the movement of labourers to higher productivity jobs in manufacturing could be an important and ongoing source of growth. China's current economic growth experience exemplifies this. The experiences of other countries also underscore that labour productivity in manufacturing is typically much higher than in agriculture. Movement from agriculture to industry is thus one of the few sources of rapid economic growth. Exports of manufactured goods may also be typically needed to provide markets for rapidly growing production. This *export-oriented* growth has had a strong emphasis in neoliberal economic policy.

Of the many other theories of economic growth which deserve mention, the theories advanced by Rostow and Hirschman still bear relevance today. In his *Stages of Economic Development: A Non-Communist Manifesto* (1960), Walt Rostow put forward the view that there are five stages of economic growth: the traditional society, the preconditions for take-off, the take-off, the drive to maturity and high mass consumption. He argued that these stages apply to both communist and capitalist countries. He analysed the effects of different kinds of conflict and war on progression from stage to stage. While criticized for oversimplification, his theory retains both empirical and intuitive merit. It also emphasizes the building of capacities involved in growth – in agriculture and industry, in social overhead capital, and in political coalitions and non-economic factors – a view increasingly found in recent development thinking.

Albert Hirschman, in *The Strategy of Economic Development* (1958), theorized that most countries lacked the capacity to pursue investment and growth on a broad basis across economic sectors. With a shortage of entrepreneurship (rather than capital) as the binding constraint to growth, and with many factors typically inhibiting entrepreneurs in poor countries, Hirschman argued that investments should be strategically focused on a few sub-sectors – notably in manufacturing – in order to create profitable opportunities for further investment. This theory of 'unbalanced growth' is reflected in current thinking about agglomeration economies, and their importance in the rapid growth of East Asian countries.[10] Hirschman's view is quite the opposite of Rostow's, which involves a 'big push' rather than a series of small strategic movements.

Contemporary approaches to economic growth

Economic growth theories

Robert Solow received a Nobel Prize in 1987 for his contribution to the theory of economic growth. His theory relates to explanations of the sources or determinants of growth in the supply or production side of an economy. It starts with the idea of production functions, namely that the quantity of output (Q) in any sector is a function of the amounts and qualities of inputs or factors of production. These typically are land and natural resources (R), labour (L) and physical capital, such as buildings and machines (K):

$$Q = f(R, L, K)$$

With detailed data for an economy's sub-sectors, it should then be possible to 'explain' the growth of output by the growth in quantities and qualities of inputs. Any residual is attributed to 'technological change', that is, shifts in the production functions not due to factor inputs. Solow's results challenged economists who thus far had seen savings and capital accumulation as the main determinants of economic growth. As he succinctly summarized in his Nobel lecture:

> The main result of that 1957 exercise was startling. Gross output per hour of work in the US economy doubled between 1909 and 1949; and some seven-eighths of that increase could be attributed to 'technical change in the broadest sense' and only the remaining eighth could be attributed to conventional increase in capital intensity. (Solow, 1987)

Over the next 50 years, much work was done to set out the conditions of steady growth with aggregate supply and demand in balance, and to examine ways in which technology and knowledge were 'embodied' in capital or in labour (people). These approaches, however, mainly took the primary explanatory variables of growth – the rate of technological change and the rate of savings – as being exogenous and largely unexplained.

Not surprisingly, efforts over this period to explain technological change were also active, culminating in 'endogenous' growth theory since the 1980s (Romer, 1990). Two of the key factors underlying technical change, not surprisingly, are education and research and development, with the latter subsequently broadened to 'innovation'. We return to these factors later, particularly in terms of what factors influence innovation in all sectors and levels of the economy. In sum, the growth theory of the past 50 years brought attention back to technology, ideas and knowledge, and thus to the capabilities of people, in the form of education and innovation.

Evolutionary theory and behavioural economics

The seminal 1982 work of Richard Nelson and Sidney Winter, *An Evolutionary Theory of Economic Change* – building on earlier thinkers, including Throsten Veblen and Joseph Schumpeter – refuted the idea of rational profit-maximizing firms and put forward an evolutionary process by which firms adapt their technologies and processes to changing market conditions, succeeding or going bankrupt according to the success of their respective paths to adaptation. Evolutionary economics stresses the importance of new ideas and knowledge-generation, the adoption of ideas through (market) selection and learning processes, the importance of organizational capabilities and behaviour, and the inter-dependency and irreversibility of these evolutionary growth processes.

Such approaches apply not only to firms and industries, but also to political, social, legal and other institutions. In enumerating consequences of evolutionary thinking, Geoffrey Hodgson (2007, pp336–7) includes as a priority 'the development of an ontology of institutions, leading to refined definitions and classifications of institutional types, the building of a theory of institutional evolution, and an enhanced understanding of the role of institutions, culture and technology in economic growth and development'. Chapter 7 will discuss the role of institutions and institutional economics in greater detail.

Behavioural economics considers 'rational' welfare-maximizing behaviour unrealistic, and introduces insights from psychology into explanations of market decisions and public choice. Daniel Kahneman received a Nobel Prize in Economics in 2002 for having integrated insights from individual and social psychology into economics, especially concerning human judgement and decision-making in contexts of uncertainty (Kahneman and Tversky, 1979).[11] In general terms, the main forms of what neoclassical theory classifies as 'irrational' behaviour occur because people's rationality is bounded or limited, as is their resolve and self-interest. Resulting behaviours include overconfidence, undue optimism, loss aversion, inequity aversion, reciprocity, herd instinct, resorting to rules of thumb, habit and cognitive frames. Important behavioural insights include the notions that: the savings rates of individuals can be dramatically increased by long-term programmes that require no immediate sacrifice of consumption;[12] drug and substance abuse can be reduced by changing the environment and alternatives faced by users (Green and Kagel, 1996); and habit change and loss aversion can result in small penalties being very effective in environmental matters (a habit-changing policy with extremely successful results has been the introduction of a small charge for plastic shopping bags, for example).[13]

As markets often do not operate efficiently in terms of economic growth and human flourishing, policies designed to improve outcomes depend strongly on knowledge of human behaviour and institutional change – the clearer and more specific the knowledge, particularly with respect to the human and institutional (cognitive and organizational) environments in question, the better.

Neoliberalism

Despite the many developments that have taken economic thinking beyond it, neoclassical theory has been the dominant force in international economic relations since the mid 1970s, influencing economic policies imposed by Western powers and the International Financial Institutions (IFIs).[14] Neoclassical economics has also influenced successive negotiating 'rounds' under GATT and its current successor, the World Trade Organization (WTO); trade barriers have been dramatically reduced worldwide. But it is only in the latest Doha round that much attention has been given to the critical needs of poorer developing countries, particularly with regards to access to essential medicines.[15]

Neoliberal policies focused primarily on the privatization of public ventures, the deregulation of markets, trade and financial sector liberalization, and generally minimizing the size and role of government in the economy. Countries that could escape the dictates of the IFIs generally did so, however. These included East Asian countries in particular, where governments followed liberal economic policies in leveraging global markets, but intervened heavily through investment in education, health, technology and innovation. Their very rapid growth reflects the success of these home-made policy combinations, as well as cumulative skill in experimentation and learning.

In Latin America, the ability of countries to follow their own paths was also at stake (Seers 1983). Chile was a particularly dramatic example. Neoliberal policies were imposed by the Pinochet regime (1973–1980) with the overt backing of the US and economists from the University of Chicago.[16] A period of high economic growth followed – above 7 per cent per annum – and growth has slowed to a still favourable rate of about 4 per cent since 2000. Chile, however, remains a relatively inequitable country in terms of income distribution, with about 30 per cent of the population living at European standards of living, while the rest remain poor. We will return to questions about growth and trickle-down economics, including the best timing for increases in economic growth, its translation to better equity outcomes, and its role in promoting human flourishing.

During the past 30 years, advanced Western countries have continued to pursue mixed economic strategies in ways that were quite different from the neoliberal policies many of them promoted and imposed in the developing world. Some serious mistakes were made internationally by failing to address the capacity constraints that prevented developing countries – particularly in Africa – from achieving the potential benefits of liberalized economies, and from failing to understand that policies not made and owned domestically ultimately have little chance of success.

The World Bank and the IMF, for example, imposed neoliberal policies during the structural adjustment programmes of the 1970s and 1980s. While unavoidable in nature, the speed and extremity of these policies left many of the 'losers' of economic structural change destitute, particularly those who were already poor to begin with (Cornia et al 1988). Little thought was given to adjustment assistance or to potential political backlashes and instability. Similarly, IMF policies imposed to correct financial crises were in many cases too contractionary, causing unnecessary damage to economies and individuals. Privatizations – in telecoms, for example – often resulted in private monopoly operators replacing public monopolies, with no increase in competition, no increase in service and no reduction in communications costs to consumers.

The continuing production and export of arms on a very large scale has also been particularly damaging to both economic growth and the promotion of human flourishing. In a recent study of *The Bottom Billion People of the World*, Collier (2007) estimates that 'the cost of a typical civil war to the country and its neighbours can be put at about $64 billion' (p32), that 'the expected time before a failing state achieves decisive change is fifty-nine years ... and the cost of a single failing state over its entire history of failure, to itself and its neighbours, is around $100 billion' (p75).

Growth of what and for whom?

Much of the history of economic thought is oriented towards the aggregate growth of the economy and average income per person (GDP/P) – but not to improving the well-being of individuals. Neoclassical economics, however, begins with individuals and defines well-being as the *value* (price times quantity) of consumption of (material) goods and services, for each individual and for the society as a whole. As Chapter 2 has already argued, the value of income or consumption for an individual is not necessarily a good representation of his/her well-being.

The human development and capability approach defines well-being in many dimensions. Growth therefore has different meanings, and has to be aggregated in different ways to get measures for an economy and the sub-groups within it. This is being done in many places, but not yet on a global scale. Efforts are being made in the Philippines, for example, where half of the local governments have adopted a community-based monitoring system that collects data every 3 years for every household for 16 indicators of income, employment, health, education, security and community involvement. Geographical Information Systems (GIS) software is then used to map the data. By scrolling through GIS maps created over time, one can see changing school attendance rates, access to safe water or health care, income, incidents of violence, etc.[17] This is a different but very tangible definition of growth, and one that can be highly useful to communities and governments tackling very serious issues.

In focusing on individuals rather than aggregates or averages, the human development and capability approach *incorporates* a strong dimension of equity and sustainability. Most economic literature addresses aggregate growth before distribution. That second question – growth for whom? – has of course been the battleground of economies and societies, whether in terms of class, income deciles, ethnic or religious groups, or groupings of countries. The capability approach does not ignore the importance of groups but, by focusing on individuals, it targets redistribution at that level. This is not too conceptually different from the mixed economy approach of most OECD countries, where for example progressive income tax is used to redistribute income among income groups, from richer to poorer. But the capability approach further demands a multidimensional understanding of well-being/ deprivation and a wider range of normative or ethical judgements about the relative importance of different kinds of deprivations – material consumption, health, security, empowerment, etc. – on an ongoing basis.

Along with mixed economy policies, the capability approach has many other allies in economic thinking. Behavioural economics is a natural ally because it recognizes and measures well-being/poverty and designs equity-oriented policies. There are many such links in present-day theoretical and applied policy research. In this context, the capability approach is also more process-oriented and less 'model'-oriented than most mainstream economics. Processes of informed public discourse are essential in making ongoing choices, and theories and principles of social justice and social choice are a major part of this knowledge base. There are clearly links with institutional economic thinking in the sense that the cognitive and organizational frameworks of these decisions – and the ways in which they change over time – are central to promoting the well-being and freedoms of both individuals and groups. Innovation systems thinking and experience is also a natural ally of the capability approach, as will be further explored below.

Box 4.1 The Commission on Growth and Development

The Commission on Growth and Development, supported by the World Bank and by countries and foundations, issued its report on 21 May 2008. The report focuses on economic growth in GDP and GDP per capita, and to a considerable extent on the rapidly growing developing economies of the past 25 years. It emphasizes, however, that economic growth is not an end in itself, but a means to human development, equity, security and empowerment. It also emphasizes that there are many balances to be struck by any society in order to begin and sustain a process of rapid growth as a mechanism to promote human flourishing. Human development writ large is both the output and one of the most important inputs of economic growth.

Building the capability of individuals and the capacities of systems, groups and institutions – market, public and non-profit – is also a useful way of looking at economic growth and development. The latter in this sense is defined by what an economy knows how to do in producing goods and services and promoting human freedoms. This building takes decades of cumulative progress, and can be lost very quickly in periods of conflict or instability. An effective political consensus is needed, 'reform teams' have been effective in many countries in facilitating agreement and changes in perspective.

Finding the 'best' path is experimental and demands quick learning and response. No single approach or model suffices. Approximately 13 countries have succeeded in the past 25 years in sustaining growth at 7 per cent or more – Botswana, Brazil, China, Hong Kong, Indonesia, Japan, Korea, Malaysia, Malta, Oman, Singapore, Taiwan and Thailand. Another dozen have experienced growth of over 6 per cent over the past 25 years. Common ingredients of success include the following, which are discussed in detail in the Commission's report:

- fully exploiting the world economy (trade, finance, education/knowledge and technology);
- maintaining macroeconomic stability;
- high rates of savings and investment (including in health, education and infrastructure);
- market allocation of resources (including competition, labour and capital mobility);
- equity and equality of opportunity, women in education, and in labour and capital markets, regional development, bottom-up strategies, social protection and risk mitigation;
- technology- and knowledge-acquisition and development;
- effective environment and energy management; and
- committed, credible and capable governments.

The Commission Report also discusses in detail new challenges now facing less advanced countries: 'global warming; the falling relative price of manufactured goods and volatile relative price of commodities, including energy; swelling discontent with globalization in advanced and some developing economies; the ageing of the world's population; and a growing mismatch between global problems and weakly-coordinated international responses'.

Commission on Growth and Development (2008, p9).

Innovation systems

Innovation systems can be defined as 'the network of institutions in the public and private sectors whose activities and interactions initiate, import, modify and diffuse new technologies', or 'the elements and relationships which interact in the production, diffusion and use of new, and economically useful, knowledge.'[18]

Focusing on innovation systems thinking and research is often done by the leading creative and technical sectors of society. This high-tech concentration is often on platform technologies like biotech, information and communication technologies (ICTs) and, increasingly, nano-technology – and their application to the production of goods, especially for export sectors. Innovations and innovation systems are however equally important for (and in) the 'bottom of the pyramid' (Prahalad, 2006). For example, poor Thai farmers discovered, on their own initiative, how to grow organic rice with lower cost and labour input than green revolution varieties, and got a little help from regional universities on using organic inputs from forests. Mobile phone networking is another innovation that has led to large changes for many poor populations in terms of the expansion of markets, social business and public services. Examples include: individuals arranging microfinance and insurance by mobile phone and the increase in personal security measures. In fact, an entire range of economic services has begun to emerge – finance, insurance, marketing and distribution (farmers and fishers connecting with markets, reduced middleman margins), employment services (drivers, casual workers), personal services, public tele-health and education services.[19] These developments are important, and have a lot to do with the diffusion of ICTs, a key globalization driver and knowledge carrier:

> Telecommunication infrastructure (and the pricing of services) is of particular importance. Telecommunication plays a variety of crucial roles in the public and private sector. It can aid education, transparency initiatives, and the delivery of government services. It can also raise productivity by disseminating price information to farmers, fishermen, and other producers. Telecommunication promotes widespread access to financial services. It also enables trade in services (a rapidly growing area of commerce) and links to global supply chains. (Commission on Growth and Development, 2008, p36)

Building innovation systems is necessary to strengthen and broaden the processes of development. Key actors are: the private and non-profit sectors at all levels, government and education institutions (especially tertiary). While the public subsidy of specific industrial *outputs* violates considerations of efficiency and international trade, societies can and do subsidize or invest heavily in *inputs*, particularly people – in a wide variety of ways, including education and health services for individuals, research and development (R&D) funding, tax and other incentives, support for start-up commercial ventures and public goods production. The judicious management of intellectual property and an ability to balance public and private interests have also become increasingly important to innovation.

But countries have different strategies and are at different stages. China, for example, is in the process of moving some 500 million people from agriculture and rural employment to largely urban manufacturing. It is dominating world production and the export of consumer goods, lending money from trade surpluses back to importing countries so they can continue to import, and developing high-tech sectors for subsequent stages of development. Chile is just embarking on a second round of developing its innovation and education systems, gradually raising R&D activity to the 1–3 per cent of GDP level typical of wealthier countries, and raising tertiary education access from 30 per cent to 60–70 per cent of the entire population.

Most countries, including poor ones, are engaged in both high-tech and 'bottom of the pyramid' R&D aimed at solving their more immediate problems and helping to generate economic growth.

In an increasingly multi-polar global economy, with China and a few other (primarily East Asian) economies dominating consumer goods trade, sources of comparative advantage for less advanced economies remain constrained. At the same time, exporting offers major growth potential beyond domestic demand growth. Agriculture export would be a better option for many poor countries were it not so heavily protected by wealthier countries. Resource industries – petroleum, minerals and gems, forestry, horticulture and wine, and fisheries, for example – offer enormous potential for countries that are able to manage their revenues well, but otherwise resource revenues can be a curse. Industries producing for domestic demand are also important, such as non-traded goods and services, including those at the bottom of the pyramid.

Economic growth as a means to human flourishing

Do economic growth and human flourishing go together?

Yes and no. Material well-being is an integral aspect of individual flourishing. The growth of consumption of goods and services is therefore a necessary part of human flourishing. Many might agree that the growth of total or average consumption or income would be an improvement if there were no losers, or if winners actually compensated losers through redistribution mechanisms (tax, public education and services, etc.). However, most societies make decisions that tend to worsen equity for a variety of reasons: those in power care little about equity or believe that it eventually comes with growth ('trickle down'), or can be addressed once a growth process is already in place. Rapid waves of growth and technology advances tend by their nature to worsen distribution initially, so a basic issue for societies is how much equity they can and should pursue over time. Singapore eliminated poverty and unemployment in a generation of rapid growth but there were special circumstances (see question 4.5). For the most part, Latin America has not done well on growth or equity. Figure 4.1 shows regions that have high levels of income inequality, as measured by the Gini coefficient (the closer to 0, the more equitable; the closer to 1, the less equitable); for more on this see Chapter 6.

If one goes beyond material well-being to include other dimensions – political, social or cultural – there are certainly more possible differences between economic growth and human flourishing. There was significant economic growth in the USSR, but very few would claim flourishing in the comprehensive suppression of political freedom. American suppression of some basic civil liberties (like the 90-day detention without trial) during the recent Bush era was by comparison a mild negative in terms of human flourishing, but a negative nonetheless. States that severely suppress the freedoms of minorities tend to experience a widespread loss of security. In

Figure 4.1 Gini coefficients in the world

Source: United Nations Human Development Report 2007–2008.

short, there is more to human flourishing than economic growth – notably the provision and distribution of material and non-material dimensions of well-being across people and generations.

Factors of economic growth

There are many factors that influence economic growth, and this number increases as the view is expanded from economic growth (GDP per capita) to include equitable growth and individual well-being in its many dimensions. A short list of causal, fundamental and enabling factors includes:

- high rates of savings and investment (including micro-credit and foreign investment);
- technological change acquisition and development (developed locally and imported);
- innovation systems (education, ideas, entrepreneurship, collaborating institutions, financing and incentives, innovation/application in commercial, non-profit and public sectors);
- human development dimensions (health and education in particular);
- export development (leveraging foreign demand, technology, knowledge and education);
- efficient resource allocation in domestic market, public sectors and labour mobility;
- committed and capable governments, efficient public services and regulation, and effective environmental management;
- external and internal trade and finance that is as 'free' as possible;
- equity and equality of opportunity – including gender equality – in education, labour and capital markets, access to assets;

- efficient infrastructure and public goods provision, competition policy, redistribution, social protection and risk mitigation, support of bottom-up, local development;
- stability: peace, effective governance, sound macroeconomic policy, enabling and effective law and regulation;
- institution building and change – both organizations and knowledge bases – private, non-profit and public sectors, including processes of informed public discourse;
- improved understanding of contexts of well-being and the behaviour of individuals and groups; and
- from the global community: arms reduction, financial management and stability, global environmental management and protection, progressive and coherent economic policy, effective peacekeeping and development cooperation or assistance.

It is much easier to list key ingredients than to prioritize them in any society's actual context, or to suggest how to proceed with the recipe when some, or many, ingredients are still missing. Many challenges arise when a growth and development process is begun.[20] There are also many challenges regarding the balance and timing of growth dimensions, sustaining sufficient political and social consensus, and sequencing in its many dimensions.[21] The external environment may be hostile rather than supportive, and the support of the global community (in terms of arms reduction, financial management, etc.) quite limited.

The relationship between economic growth and human flourishing

The first chapter established that there is no automatic link between economic growth and human flourishing. Countries with a high GDP per capita, such as Saudi Arabia, do not necessarily exhibit high human development achievements, for example. It is not because income per capita rises that one will necessarily observe corresponding increases in life expectancy, literacy and other human freedoms.[22] Economic growth does indeed provide the resources to sustain improvements in human development, but only if it is accompanied by many other things, including higher public expenditures on health and education, and particularly female education.

Ranis et al (2000) highlight four factors that influence the extent to which economic growth contributes to human flourishing. First, there is household activity, especially the households' propensity to spend their after-tax income on items that contribute most directly to the promotion of human flourishing, such as food, potable water, education and health. The extent to which households spend on these goods depends on who controls the expenditures in the household (greater female control over household income and greater female education often mean higher spending on such goods). Second, the extent to which economic growth increases the incomes of the poor depends on income distribution in the country itself, and the extent to which economic growth is capable of generating employment for low-income groups and rural households. Third, the level of government activity influences the translation of economic growth into improved quality of life. This depends on the public expenditure ratio, the social spending allocation ratio (the proportion of total government expenditures going to the education and health sectors), and the social priority ratio (the proportion of total social expenditures going into primary areas, such as basic education). These three ratios are determined especially by the tax capacity of the government, the size of military expenditures, corruption and the level of decentralization in the government. Finally, NGOs can be an important factor in promoting human flourishing.

But the relationship between economic growth and human flourishing is not only uni-directional: it goes in both directions. Ranis et al (2000) highlight the following mechanisms through which improvements in human flourishing contribute to greater economic growth: (1) Health, primary and secondary education and nutrition raise the productivity of rural and urban workers; (2) secondary education facilitates the acquisition of skills and managerial capacity; (3) tertiary education supports the development of basic science, the appropriate selection of technology imports, and the domestic adaptation and development of technologies (see the discussion above on ICTs); (4) secondary and tertiary education represent critical elements in the development of key institutions, such as government, the law and the financial system; (5) a better educated workforce is more creative, leading to greater technological innovation (see above); and (6) a better educated female workforce leads to reduced fertility rates, and hence higher economic growth per capita. Ranis et al (2000) however qualify the role of education in promoting economic growth: for education to lead to economic growth, one needs a certain quantity and quality of foreign and domestic investment so that employment opportunities can be created. Figure 4.2 summarizes the bi-directional relationship between progress in human development and economic growth.

Gathering evidence for 76 countries over 30 years, Ranis et al (2000) classify country performance into four categories: virtuous, vicious and two types of lop-sidedness – lopsided either with strong human development but weak economic growth (HD-lopsided), or lopsided with strong economic growth but weak human development (EG-lopsided). In the virtuous cycle, human development enhances growth, which in turn promotes human development, and so on. In the vicious cycle, poor performance on human development tends to lead to poor growth performance, which in turn depresses human development achievements and so on. On the other hand, HD-lopsided may happen when good human development performance does not generate good economic growth, due to a dearth of complementary resources arising from low investment rates. However, Ranis et al conclude that such a scenario does not persist in the long-term. Countries can thus move in all directions except from EG-lopsided to the virtuous cycle. In other words, unless concern for human development is included in policies aiming

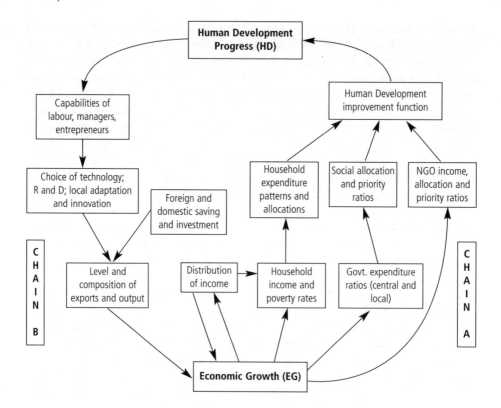

Figure 4.2 Causal chain between human development and economic growth

Source: Gustav Ranis, HD Insights, UNDP Human Development Report Office, Issue 6, March 2007; see also: http://www.econ.yale.edu/~granis/

at promoting economic growth, the latter cannot be sustained in the long term, and hence improvements in human flourishing cannot take place in the future.

Figure 4.3 traces the experience of different countries. In the 1960–2001 period, East Asian countries tended to experience a virtuous cycle, sub-Saharan Africa a vicious cycle, and Latin America a HD-lopsided development pattern.

The findings of Ranis et al demonstrate that economic growth is essential to human development, but it all depends on the kind of growth and the strength of existing mechanisms for translating growth into human flourishing. Echoing the findings above, the 1996 *Human Development Report* enumerates the following ingredients to enable economic growth to contribute to human flourishing:[23]

• equity: equal distribution of economic opportunities;
• job opportunities: opportunities for productive and well-paid work;

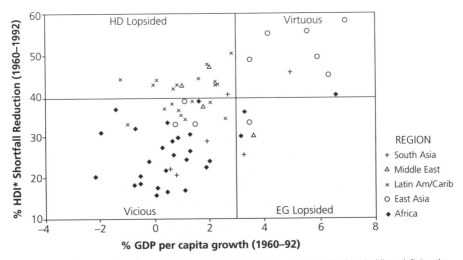

Figure 2. *Classification of country perfomance (1960–92). Note: The horizontal and vertical lines defining the four quandrants represent developing country averages weighted by population.*

Figure 4.3 Human development and economic growth performance: Cross-country evidence

Source: Gustav Ranis, HD Insights, UNDP Human Development Report Office, Issue 6, March 2007; see also: http://www.econ.yale.edu/~granis/

- access to productive assets: equal access to assets, such as land, physical infrastructure and financial credit;
- social spending: channelling a major part of public revenue into high priority social expenditure;
- gender equality: investing in women's capabilities and empowering them;
- population policy: creating the conditions for slower population growth;
- good governance: those in power giving high priority to the needs of the whole population, and people participating in decision-making at many levels; and
- active civil society: non-governmental organizations and community groups playing a vital role in enhancing human development.

Without appropriate public policies, economic growth can end up being *jobless* without increased employment opportunities; *ruthless* with benefits going mainly to the rich rather than the poor; *voiceless* without an expansion of empowerment and political engagement; *rootless* by stifling rather than encouraging cultural diversity; and *futureless* by depleting natural resources rather than being environmentally friendly.

Questions

4.1 It has been argued that, in advanced economies, the post-World War II generation became prosperous largely because of the movement toward gender equality, women going to work and double-income families. Economies were growing, and asset prices (especially housing) adjusted slowly, so that families experienced ease in finding jobs, high incomes and low living costs. Could a similar process be possible for developing countries if internal changes were made which support rapid growth in labour force participation for women? Discuss.

4.2 The Philippines regularly monitors the well-being of certain communities in terms of 16 indicators of income, employment, health, education, security and participation, for a cost of about $1 per person per year. It successfully uses this information to substantially reduce severe deprivations. Other countries could do this too, for the cost is low and the benefit high. Sketch some of the ways the municipality or district in which you live might benefit from a regular picture of the well-being of individuals and households.

4.3 Agriculture should be a comparative advantage and source of growth for many poor countries that are endowed with plentiful land and farm labour. But advanced economies protect their markets and farmers by trade barriers. With rising world food demand and prices, could agriculture become a stronger growth engine for the poor? If so, how? Who would benefit most – their food consumers or producers, or consumers in advanced economies?

4.4 Fast-growing economies have a lot of imbalances to sort out – e.g. equity and environmental management – and play a growing role in international affairs and institutions. What can reasonably be expected of them in terms of the provision of global public goods, such as arms reduction, financial management and stability, global environmental management and protection, progressive and coherent economic policy, effective peacekeeping and development cooperation or assistance?

4.5 In the mid-1970s, Singapore shifted its economy from low labour cost and polluting goods production to highly-skilled and technology sectors. Among its key policy moves were the raising of the minimum wage, heavy investment and subsidy of tertiary training, subsidy of skilled labour via low-cost housing, and the creation of a national fund that collected about one third of incomes and invested them in housing, infrastructure and pensions. Economic growth accelerated, and poverty and unemployment were eliminated. Although prosperity had been achieved in a generation and poverty eliminated, some argue that political opposition and freedoms were severely suppressed at the same time, and that the former does not justify the latter. What are your views about the priority, if any, between economic growth and political freedoms? Are political freedoms likely to emerge with substantial periods of prosperity?

4.6   We are very timid in what we ask for. In the global economy, we asked mainly for average economic growth in the past four decades, and we got it. We did not ask for equity and environmental conservation, and we got inequality and environmental damage in large measure. How could we ask for more and get it? Which countries do you think have the least inequality and greatest sustainability, along with economic growth and material prosperity?

4.7   One of the key reasons for the growth *and* distribution success of agricultural reforms in Vietnam was that the de-collectivization process was generally done equitably, resulting in the equitable distribution of land. This fact, coupled with a supporting public environment, proved crucial for the uptake of new crops and technologies. Vietnam's relatively highly developed human resource base and education/research system at the time of economic liberalization, have also been essential assets in managing the thousands of private and public sector adjustment processes. To move to a virtuous development path, do countries weak in education and human capabilities need to focus on these first, or can they pursue fast market economy growth and policies at the same time?

4.8   'I believe that economics would be a more productive field if we learned something important from evolutionists: that models are metaphors, and that we should use them, not the other way around' (Paul Krugman).[24] In what ways does your knowledge of the capability approach influence your views about the relationship between economic growth and human flourishing?

Notes

1   It is worth underlining that potential gains from trade may be shared by trade partners or may be realized by some at the expense of others. The conditions for mutual benefit include full employment in trading countries, perfect mobility of factors of production within countries, immobility of factors of production between countries, negligible transport costs and perfect competition. In other words, these are the standard assumptions that allow the perfectly efficient allocation of productive resources in an idealized free market.

2   Standard classifications today list sub-sectors and industries within several broad sectors: natural resources (agriculture, forestry, fishery and mining); infrastructure (energy, communications, transport, etc.); manufacturing (food/resource processing, consumer and capital goods) and services (financial, business and personal). Public services (education, health, justice, etc.) are not separated from private services but are disaggregated.

3   The word 'gross' in GDP means 'gross of depreciation' – that is, the depreciation of the economy's capital stock during the year is not netted out, as is done for net domestic product.

4   Shoes sold to consumers are produced from many inputs – leather, rubber, lace, tools, etc. Each is made by an industry that adds value to what it acquires from other industries. So the total final value is the sum of the values added at each intermediate stage.

5   Such terms ('neo-classical', 'neoliberal' and 'neo-conservative') are often used to refer to those who emphasize the operation and efficiency of markets, and base economic policies entirely on market principles and interests. The term 'liberal' in economic thought has generally been associated with market-oriented economic policy, retaining, however, concerns for equity and the corrective role of social policy.

6   Microeconomics expresses this equilibrium as a system of differential equations for the utility-maximizing consumers and profit-maximizing producers. At the macro level, (computable) general equilibrium models fit this simplified behaviour and perfectly competitive market structure to the particulars (national accounts) of a given country.

7   Public goods are characterized by non-excludability (no one can be excluded from consuming the good), and non-rivalry (a person's consumption does not reduce the benefits of someone else's consumption).

8   The financial crisis of 2008 has, however, been attributed in large part to insufficient and inappropriate financial regulation.

9   Well known contributors include Raúl Prebisch, Paul Baran and Andre Gunder Frank, who wrote *Capitalism and Underdevelopment in Latin America* in 1967.

10   Agglomeration economies occur where initial clusters of industries develop, together with their support infrastructure and human capital, making further investment more attractive for both domestic and foreign investors.

11   These insights were mainly taken from both laboratory and field experiments; see Kahneman's Nobel lecture and autobiography at http://nobelprize.org/nobel_prizes/economics/laureates/2002/.

12   See the blog of Harvard Professor Greg Mankiw at: http://gregmankiw.blogspot.com/2006/06/behavioral-economics.html

13   New Economics Foundation, 'Behavioural economics: Seven principles for policy makers', July 2005, at www.neweconomics.org/gen/

14   These are mainly: the International Monetary Fund (IMF), World Bank (IBRD) and regional development banks – Asian (ADB), African (AfDB) and Inter-American (IADB).

15   The balance between protection of and access to intellectual property (IP) is a central debate in an increasingly knowledge-based global economy. Multilateral arrangements under the WTO – in TRIPS (trade-related intellectual property arrangements) – have often been superseded by the more protectionist measures in bilateral free trade agreements of the US and EC. A good IP reference can be found at www.iprsonline.org.

16   The best known elaboration of this economic policy perspective was set out in Milton Friedman's *Capitalism and Freedom,* which was published in 1962.

17   For GIS maps in the Philippines, see a PowerPoint presentation by Celia Reyes entitled 'Community-based measurement and monitoring poverty', at www.ifpri.org/2020Chinaconference/day3/presentations/G2-4_CReyes.ppt.

18   These definitions are taken from the 1997 OECD report on national innovation systems at www.oecd.org/dataoecd/35/56/2101733.pdf.

19   For more information, see the work of LIRNEasia at www.lirneasia.net/projects, of Research ICT Africa at www.researchictafrica.net, and of Dialogo Regional sobre Sociedad de la Informacion at www.dirsi.net/english.

20   The Commission on Growth and Development is tackling this matter directly, through study and interaction among leaders of advanced and failed countries. Analyses and experience in overcoming conflict and governance failures have

grown substantially in the past decade. Paul Collier (2007) assesses conflict, governance, resource revenue and landlocked traps, making recommendations for international and advanced-country actions.

21 Sequencing of trade and financial 'liberalization' are often analysed, but sequencing also involves a more pervasive, micro and ongoing set of timing questions under (severe) resource constraints – privatization and competition policy, development of different sectors/areas of comparative advantage and growth potential, education priorities, health-care and services priorities.

22 The software 'gap minder' shows that countries that have experienced economic growth have not necessarily made much progress in terms of human development. See http://hdr.undp.org/external/gapminder/2005/2005.html.

23 This summary of the 1996 HDR was written by Seeta Prahbu.

24 'What economists can learn from evolutionary theorists' at www.mit.edu/~krugman/evolute.html.

Readings

Barro, R. and Sala-i-Martin, X. (2003) *Economic Growth*, MIT Press, Cambridge

Boozer, M., Ranis, G., Stewart, F. and Suri, T. (2003) 'Paths to success: The relationship between human development and economic growth', *Economic Growth Center Discussion Paper 874*, Yale University, www.yale.edu/leitner/SSRN-id487469.pdf

Collier, P. (2007) *The Bottom Billion: Why the Poorest Countries are Failing and What Can Be Done about It*, Oxford University Press, Oxford

Commission on Growth and Development (2008) *The Growth Report: Strategies for Sustained Growth and Inclusive Development*, www.growthcommission.org

Cornia, G. A., Jolly, R. and Stewart, F. (eds) (1988) *Adjustment with a Human Face: Ten Country Case Studies*, Oxford University Press, Oxford

Galbraith, J. K. (1991) *A History of Economics*, Penguin, London

Harvey, D. (2005) *A Brief History of Neoliberalism*, Oxford University Press, Oxford

Nelson, R. and Winter, S. (1982) *An Evolutionary Theory of Economic Change*, Harvard University Press, Cambridge, MA

Prahalad, C. K. (2006) *The Fortune at the Bottom of the Pyramid*, Wharton School Publishing, Philadelphia, PA

Ranis, G. and Stewart, F. (2002) 'Economic growth and human development in Latin America', www.eclac.org/publicaciones/xml/2/19952/lcg2187i-Ranis.pdf

Ranis, G., Stewart, F. and Ramirez, A. (2000) 'Economic growth and human development', *World Development*, vol 28, no 2, pp197–219

Rothschild, E. (2001) *Economic Sentiments*, Harvard University Press, Cambridge, MA

Samuelson, P. (1948) *Foundations of Economic Analysis*, Harvard University Press, reprinted as P. Samuelson and W. D. Nordhaus (2004) *Economics*, 18th edn, McGraw-Hill, Columbus, OH

Schumpeter, J. A. (1987) *History of Economic Analysis*, Routledge, London

Sen, A. (1999) 'The possibility of social choice', *American Economic Review*, vol 89, no 3, pp349–378

Solow, R. (1987) 'Growth theory and after', Nobel Prize Lecture available at http://nobelprize.org/nobel_prizes/economics/laureates/1987/solow-lecture.html

UNDP (1996) *Human Development Report: Economic Growth and Human Development*, Oxford University Press, New York

Further Readings

Acemoglu, D. and J. Robinson, (2008) 'The role of institutions in growth and development', Commission on Growth and Development paper, www.growthcommission.org

Aghion, P. and Howitt, P. (1997) *Endogenous Growth Theory*, MIT Press, Cambridge, MA

De la Croix, D. and Michel, P. (2002) *A Theory of Economic Growth*, Cambridge University Press, Cambridge

El-Erian, M. and M. Spence, (2008) 'Growth strategies and dynamics: Insights from country experiences', Commission on Growth and Development paper, www.growthcommission.org

Green, L. and Kagel, J. H. (1996) *Advances in Behavioral Economics*, Volume 3, Greenwood Publishing Group, Santa Barbara, CA

Hodgson, G. M. (2007) 'The revival of Veblenian institutional economics', *Journal of Economic Issues*, vol 47, no 2, pp325–342

Kahneman, D. and Tversky, A. (1979) 'Prospect theory: An analysis of decisions under risk', *Econometrica*, vol 47, no 2, pp263–291

Kanbur, R. (2008) 'Globalization, growth and distribution: Framing the questions', Commission on Growth and Development paper, www.growthcommission.org

Mkapa, B. W. (2008) 'Leadership for growth, development and poverty reduction: An African viewpoint and experience', Commission on Growth and Development paper, www.growthcommission.org

Rodrik, D. (2008) 'Normalizing industrial policy', Commission on Growth and Development paper, www.growthcommission.org

Romer, P. (1990) 'Endogenous technological change', *Journal of Political Economy*, vol 98, no 5, ppS71–S102

Schmid, A. A. (2004) *Conflict and Cooperation: Institutional and Behavioral Economics*, Blackwell, Oxford

Seers, D. (1983) 'Structuralism and monetarism in Latin America: A reappraisal of a great debate, with lessons for Europe in the 1980s', in K. Jansen (ed.) *Monetarism, Economic Crisis and the Third World*, Routledge, London

5

Equality and Justice

Ingrid Robeyns

Aims of the chapter

- To link the capability approach with theories of equality and social justice.
- To investigate how the capability approach differs from John Rawls' theory of justice.
- To introduce the underlying purpose and main ideas of theories of justice.
- To highlight the role of the capability approach in developing theories of justice.
- To examine the implications of a capability-based approach to justice for policy design and other intervention strategies.

Key points

- Equality and justice are related but distinct values.
- There are crucial differences between the capability approach to justice and Rawls' *Justice as Fairness*, yet the philosophical debate concerning their precise differences continues.
- The capability approach can be developed into partial or complete theories of justice, but this requires much more philosophical work than just embracing functionings and capabilities as metrics of justice.
- The capability approach is particularly well-suited to looking at justice for disadvantaged groups, such as women.
- The capability approach leads to several distinct recommendations, but much more work still needs to be done to see how the capability approach can be put into practice and how its policies and interventions can be effectively evaluated.

This chapter aims to introduce the contribution of the capability approach to the literature on theories of equality and social justice. As described in the second chapter, the capability approach is a broad normative framework for the evaluation and assessment of individual well-being and social arrangements, the design of policies, and proposals about interventions and social change in society. It is used in a wide range of fields, including development studies, welfare economics, social policy and political philosophy. This chapter highlights the role that the capability approach can play in one of these fields – the literature on theories of justice, and the related question concerning what implications follow for justice-enhancing interventions and policies. This literature in large part falls within the domain of normative political philosophy, but there is some overlap with the work being done by welfare economists and other scholars.[1] The chapter does not provide a complete overview of the literature on the capability approach and social justice, and is not aimed at an audience of advanced philosophy students, but rather hopes to introduce some key issues to an interdisciplinary audience.

The first section sketches the nature of contemporary academic literature on theories of justice, and includes a brief discussion of how the concepts of equality and justice are related. The second section discusses the main outlines of John Rawls' theory of justice, which is generally regarded as the most important and influential contemporary theory of justice. The third section presents the main critique by capability theorists on Rawls and, alternately, two Rawlsian critiques on the capability approach. Studying these critiques will give us a sense of how these theories differ. The fourth section poses a question about what is needed for the construction of a complete capability theory of justice. Next, we examine how the capability approach deals with justice for disadvantaged groups, particularly justice between women and men. The final section explores the implications of a capability-based approach to justice for policies and other intervention strategies.

A brief description of the literature on theories of justice

Justice is essentially a contested concept: there is no generally-accepted definition or description of justice, and thus no consensus on what the appropriate subject matter of theories of justice is or should be. This does not of course mean that nothing can be said of it at all. David Miller's description of social justice is a good starting point. He contends that when arguing about justice, we are discussing:

> how the good and bad things in life should be distributed among the members of a human society. When, more concretely, we attack some policy or some state of affairs as (being) socially unjust, we are claiming that a person, or more usually a category of persons, enjoys fewer advantages than that person or group of persons ought to enjoy (or bears more of the burdens than they ought to bear), given how other members of the society in question are faring. (Miller, 1999, p1)

Theories of justice do not, however, cover the entire spectrum of moral issues. Social justice theorists generally agree that there are parts of morality that fall *outside* the scope of justice. Charity is such a case: you may not have a moral duty to help someone, but may nevertheless decide to help that person as an act of charity. One might argue, for example, that it is not a matter of justice for people with median incomes to donate money for a children's playground, but at the same time we would applaud it if people with such incomes would do this as a matter of charity or because they are committed to the value of communities.

Can we describe justice, and theories of justice, by their properties, as philosophers often do? First, justice is a property that has been ascribed to both individuals and institutions: justice is a virtue of individuals in their interactions with others, and justice is also a virtue of social institutions (Barry and Matravers, 2004). Thus, we can say that a certain society is more or less just, or we can say that the behaviour of some persons is just or unjust. Theorists of justice tend primarily to discuss the justice of social arrangements, that is, of social institutions broadly defined; justice as an individual virtue is sometimes regarded as a matter of ethics rather than of political philosophy (although not every political philosopher would agree with this way of demarcating justice from ethics). Moreover, an increasing number of theorists define social institutions so broadly that they also include institutions such as the family, systems of class and caste, or even social norms; under such broad definitions, conceptualizing justice as a virtue of institutions includes much of what we would also think of as justice as a virtue of persons.

Second, the terms 'social justice' and 'distributive justice' are generally used interchangeably. Often the term 'justice' is used as a shorthand to cover both, but this may be misleading since there are debates related to justice that fall outside the scope of social justice, such as retributive justice, which deals with crime and just punishment (Barry and Matravers 2004).

Third, there are several different schools within social justice theories. Barry and Matravers (2004) identify conventionalism, teleology, justice as mutual advantage, and egalitarian justice. *Conventionalism* is the view that issues of justice can be resolved by examining how local conventions, institutions, traditions and systems of law determine the divisions of burdens and benefits. Barry and Matravers rightly point out that this approach, which in a modern version has been defended by Walzer (1983), can lead to the acceptance of grossly unjust practices by certain communities because they are generally endorsed, even if they may be seen as unjust if judged on the basis of values and ideas not currently present (or dominant) in that society. *Teleology* is the view that social arrangements should be justified in reference to some good that they are ultimately leading towards: some examples are utilitarianism, natural law theory or Aquinas's Christian philosophy. For teleological theories, what justice is follows from an account of the good, and thus the account of justice depends on the account of the social good itself. A criticism of teleological theories is that they necessarily rely on an external source, such as utility, the natural law or God's authority. Teleological accounts of justice therefore necessarily depend on notions of the ultimate good (whether or not this is derived from religious sources). But in pluralistic societies characterized by the presence of different religions and non-religious citizens, it becomes hard to see how justice can be derived from notions of the good that are not accepted by all. Many contemporary political philosophers therefore argue that teleological theories cannot be defended since people have competing ideas of the good, and we cannot call upon a generally-accepted external source that will tell us which idea of the good should be imposed on all.

The third and fourth schools, in comparison, share a commitment to some form of liberalism that recognizes the diversity of acceptable definitions of the good life which just societies should accept. These schools experienced a major revival after the publication of John Rawls' *A Theory of Justice* in 1971, which is generally regarded as the single most important work on social justice in the last century. Rawls turned to the *social contract tradition*, where justice is understood as the outcome of mutual advantage. The core idea is that rules of justice are ultimately more beneficial to everyone than if each were to pursue her own advantage on her own. Some of these theories (though not Rawls'!) take the relative power or bargaining strength as given, and therefore one may question whether in situations of unequal bargaining power, justice will be done (Nussbaum 2006). The other liberal school of justice is *egalitarian justice*, which is premised on the idea that people should be treated with equal respect and concern (Dworkin 2000). The most basic claim of these theories is that people are equals in a moral sense: each person should be seen as being of equal worth. Yet that general and abstract claim can be further developed in many different ways, and it is in specifying these further details that philosophers disagree. It tends to require equality of something, but not necessarily equality of outcome in the material sphere (in fact, plain equality of resources is a claim very few theorists of justice would be willing to defend, since people have different needs, are confronted with different circumstances and, if they are given the same opportunities, are likely to make different use of them). Hence, John Rawls' theory of justice can be seen as an egalitarian theory of justice, but so are theories that come to very different substantive conclusions, such as Robert Nozick's (1974) entitlement theory. Other major contemporary theorists of justice who can be labelled 'liberal egalitarian' are Brian Barry (1995), Philippe Van Parijs (1995), and Ronald Dworkin (2000), among many others – although there is also a substantial literature within analytical political philosophy that criticizes these theories (e.g. Anderson 1999).

While all four schools of social justice receive wide support, it is primarily liberal egalitarian theories that are discussed in relation to the capability approach. Even within this group, there is a strong internal diversity: the only real uniting feature is that all these theories endorse the principle that there should be considerable (although by no means absolute) scope for individuals to determine their own life plan and notion of the good.[2]

Of the four schools of social justice, only the last two regard justice and equality as being closely related values. Under conventionalism, justice is guided by existing traditions, conventions and institutions, even if they do not treat people as equals in a plausible sense. Teleological theories also do not equate justice with some idea of equality; instead, the idea of the good is more important, even if it implies that people are not treated as moral equals. In some theories of conventionalism and teleology, social justice may be consistent with a notion of equality, but this is not necessarily the case for all these theories. The social contract tradition and liberal egalitarianism, in contrast, derive their principles of social justice from a fundamental idea of people as moral equals, as beings with equal moral worth. However, the notion of equal moral worth does not necessarily lead to the notion of equality of resources or another type of equality of outcome (see further below on what equality of resources and outcomes suggests). Social justice and equality are related in these theories, but not always at the level of material inequality, but rather at a more fundamental level of treating people as moral equals or with equal respect and concern.

For a proper understanding of mainstream philosophical literature on theories of justice, it is helpful to know that the literature itself is highly abstract, and often rather detached from questions about policy design or political feasibility. Sen (2006) has recently criticized such theories, and in particular Rawls' theories, for being overly transcendental. Such ideal theories give an account of the perfectly just society, but do not tell us what needs to be done to get closer to that very ideal, how we can make the world less unjust, and which of two situations might be more unjust than the other. Another problem with contemporary theories of justice is that they are often based on so-called idealizations or strong assumptions, which may introduce significant biases or exclude certain groups of people. They also tend to make such theories too far removed from practical applicability. For example, it has been argued that Rawls' theory is unable to account for our sense of duty towards the severely disabled, as will be further examined below. Some have argued that these theories do not offer much guidance on how we can move to a more just society by making feasible improvements, that is, they do not tell us what kind of actions or policies need to be implemented to move us in the direction of this utopian vision of a just society (Sen, 2006; Pierik and Robeyns, 2007). When we try to apply contemporary theories of justice to the actual reality of our chaotic and often messy world, there are all sorts of complications that need to be taken into account, such as trade-offs between different values, power imbalances between different social groups, unintended consequences of justice-enhancing interventions and policies, or interests of individuals and groups that may conflict with concerns for justice (e.g. a desire for re-election on the part of government administrations). However, there is certainly no consensus on whether these problems are inherent to ideal theories: the distortive nature of these simplifying assumptions may well be a *contingent* problem of ideal theory itself. This is a very topical debate and it remains unclear whether the outcome will change the way theories of justice are constructed in the next few decades (Sen, 2006; Robeyns and Swift, 2008). It may well be that we will be seeing a turn towards more non-ideal, empirically-informed, 'directly useful' theories that are easier to translate into practice; this would in any case be in line with what a human development perspective would recommend, and capability theorists working on justice are among those who most strongly advocate this turn to practice.

Rawls' theory of justice in a nutshell

The previous section indicated the central importance of Rawls' theory in contemporary debates on theories of social justice. This section describes the essence of Rawls' theory, and its implications for the capability approach.[3] Rawls' theory of justice, which he called 'Justice as Fairness', was gradually developed in a series of articles, and especially in his book *A Theory of Justice* (originally published in 1971 and in a revised edition in 1999), which is considered by many political philosophers to be one of the most important texts on moral and political philosophy in the 20th century. Although one does not need to know Rawls' work to discuss issues of justice in public debates, it is impossible to understand the contemporary academic literature on theories of justice without having a minimal knowledge of Rawls' theory.

What were the central issues Rawls hoped to address? Social institutions and societal practices, such as the constitution, legislation, the labour market or the institutions of the welfare state can be exploitative and unfair, and often provoke resentment among the people who have to live under these practices and institutions. Rawls was trying to provide an answer to the question: how can we organize society in such a way that the principles of societal cooperation are fair and therefore acceptable to everyone? It is in this sense that Rawls regards his work as being in the social contract tradition, since he wants to investigate the basic structure of a just society which is organized to each person's mutual advantage. Rawls used the term 'the basic structure of society' to refer to the totality of the social institutions and practices. He defines the basic structure of society as 'the way in which the main political and social institutions of society fit together into one system of social cooperation, and the way they assign basic rights and duties and regulate the division of advantages that arise from social cooperation over time' (Rawls, 2001, p10). Rawls argues that the basic structure is the proper object of our concern since, by focusing on the basic structure of justice, we could accommodate issues of both equality and freedom. If we could manage to find a way to make the basic structure of society fair, then people could freely live according to their own ideas of the good life within this just structure, which would begin with the notion of citizens as moral equals.

How can we find out what such a fair society would look like? Rawls asks us to participate in a thought-experiment, what he calls the 'original position'. We are asked to step out of our current place in society, and plant ourselves in the original position, which is situated behind a 'veil of ignorance'. This veil takes away our knowledge of our actual place in society, and any information about our sex, the colour of our skin, our social positioning, our profession, our natural abilities such as intelligence or strength, and so on and so forth. We also do not know our conception of the good life. The reason for this is that Rawls does not want to develop a theory that is skewed in favour of one particular notion of the good life. People in the original position do, however, know all the general facts about their society, such as basic economic and political principles, human psychology, and the relations between people and their respective social backgrounds.

Once we are in this position, we can decide upon the principles of justice that should govern our society. The aim of introducing the original position and its veil of ignorance is that we will not try to favour a set of socio-political rules and institutions that tend to favour the kind of person that we are in the actual society. In other words, the original position is set up in such a way that the moral conditions for a just society are in fact met: we will not choose principles that are biased in favour of people with the talents, skills and personal characteristics that we have, nor will we prefer social institutions that are in favour of people who share our notion of the good life. As the parties in the original position have no information about their place in society, circumstances or life plans, the agreement that they will reach in the original position regarding the principles of justice will be fair to everyone. Rawls believes that the principles of justice so reached would be stable, since they are (hypothetically) chosen under conditions of freedom and equality, and thus command enduring support by all.

Once in the original position, we are offered a menu of possible principles of justice from which we must choose. Rawls argues that we will choose from this menu those principles that it is most rational for us to choose, given the information that we have. Once in the original position, he singles out the following two principles that it will be rational for us to choose:

1 Each person has the same indefensible claim to a fully-adequate scheme of equal basic liberties, which scheme is compatible with the same scheme of liberties for all.
2 Social and economic inequalities are to satisfy two conditions: (2a) first, they are to be attached to offices and positions open to all under conditions of fair equality of opportunity; (2b) and second, they are to be to the greatest benefit of the least-advantaged members of society (2b is called 'the difference principle') (Rawls, 1999, pp42–43).

The basic liberties are: 'freedom of thought and liberty of conscience; political liberties (for example, the right to vote and to participate in politics) and freedom of association, as well as the rights and liberties specified by the liberty and integrity (physical and psychological) of the person; and finally, the rights and liberties covered by the rule of law' (Rawls, 1999, p44). Rawls repeatedly stressed that the two principles had to be seen as working in tandem. The first principle, the principle of equal basic liberties, has priority over the second principle; in addition, (2a), the principle of fair equality of opportunity, has priority over the difference principle (2b).

Applying the difference principle requires interpersonal comparisons of relative advantage. Rawls holds that a person's advantage should be specified by social primary goods, which are all-purpose means that every person is presumed to want, as they are useful for a sufficiently wide range of ends. The social primary goods can be classified into five groups (Rawls, 1999, p386):

1   the basic rights and liberties;
2   freedom of movement and choice of occupation;
3   powers and prerogatives of offices and positions of authority and
    responsibility;
4   income and wealth; and
5   the social bases of self-respect.

The parties in the original position do not know which notion of the good life they will endorse; they do not know whether they will want to change their views on the good life over a lifetime; and they do not know their own natural abilities. They will therefore choose general all-purpose means that will be suitable for all comprehensive doctrines of the good life, and that will also allow them to revise their conception of the good, if they should wish to do so. In response to some of the critiques of the first edition of *A Theory of Justice*, Rawls stressed that it is not real persons who are assumed to want those primary goods, but rather persons in their capacity as citizens with a political conception of a theory of justice. These persons should reason as citizens debating in the public arena, and not defend their own private interests, debating institutional rules that affect everyone as members of the same polity. Rawls thus makes a rather strict distinction between the public and the private spheres of life – something that has led to criticism by feminists, communitarians and several others.

Due to the priority of the first principle over the second – the principle of fair equality of opportunity (2a) over the difference principle (2b) – the first three groups of primary goods are effectively equalized among all persons before the difference principle plays any substantive role. This leaves us with only income and wealth, and the social basis of self-respect (categories 4 and 5) to identify the persons or groups in society who are worst-off. Rawls arguably considers the social basis of self-respect to be the most important primary good. He proposes that the best way to provide the social basis of self-respect is by treating every citizen as an equal, that is, by giving every citizen the same rights and liberties. Thus, Rawls seems to suggest that, if both the principle of justice and the principle of equality of opportunity are met, then everyone is provided with the same social basis of self-respect. As a consequence, the difference principle will make interpersonal comparisons based on estimating lifetime expectations in terms of income and wealth.

Since Rawls was deeply concerned with the possibility that people with very different moral views on the good life can come to a reasonable agreement on the principles of political justice, he stressed that the conception of justice must be readily available to all, and that the information necessary to make a claim of injustice must be verifiable by all and preferably easy to collect (Rawls, 1999, pp370–371).

Rawlsian justice versus the capability approach

We now turn to a comparison between Rawls' theory of justice and the capability approach. We will do this by presenting one major critique by capability theorists of Rawls' account of justice, and the latter's critique of the capability approach.[4]

The most well-known critique was formulated by Sen in his 1979 Tanner lecture, which bore upon the Rawlsian conceptualization of a person's advantage, the identification of the worst-off in terms of primary goods, and the consequences of this for some individuals with special needs or special characteristics. Sen's critique started with his claim that justice as fairness dealt in an unsatisfactory way with severely disabled people (Sen, 1980, pp195–220). The difference principle, which determines how well-off someone is in terms of income and wealth *alone*, would not justify any redistribution to the disabled on the grounds of their disability. Rawls' strategy has been to postpone the question of our obligations towards the disabled, excluding them from the development of the theory and the principles of justice altogether. The underlying reason is that Rawls prefers to focus on classical problems that have recurred in the history of political thought. Justice as fairness addresses what he regards to be the fundamental question of political philosophy, namely, 'what principles of justice are most appropriate to specify ... when society is viewed as a system of cooperation between citizens regarded as free and equal persons, and as normal and fully cooperating members of society over a complete life' (Rawls, 2001, p176, note 59). Rawls certainly does not want to deny our moral duties towards the people who fall outside the scope of his theory, but he thinks that we should first work on a robust and convincing theory of justice for the 'normal' cases and only then try to extend it to the 'more extreme cases' (ibid.). The neglect of the needs of the disabled is thus not so much situated in the conceptualization of social primary goods, but rather determined by the limited scope of justice as fairness as a social contract theory between 'normal and fully cooperating members of society'.

However, Sen's critique of the inflexibility of primary goods goes beyond the case of the severely disabled. He believes that the more general problem with the use of primary goods is that it cannot adequately deal with the pervasive inter-individual differences between people, since people have 'very different needs varying with health, longevity, climatic conditions, location, work conditions, temperament, and even body size' (Sen, 1980, pp215–216). Sen's critique of primary goods boils down to the fact that primary goods cannot adequately account for inter-individual differences in people's abilities to convert these primary goods into what people are able to be and do in their lives. In contrast, Sen argues that we should focus directly on people's beings and doings, that is, on their capabilities to function. Primary goods are the means with which one can pursue one's life plan. But the real opportunities or possibilities that a person has to pursue her own life plan are not only determined by the primary goods that she has access to, but also by a range of factors that determine to what extent she can turn these primary goods into valuable states of being and doing. Hence, Sen claims that we should focus on the extent of freedom that a person has, that is, her actual capabilities.

Rawls has acknowledged that his theory does not account for justice towards the severely disabled. The question is whether it is possible to include the physically and mentally disabled by extending the social contract drawn up in the original position. If that is not possible and the only way to deal with them is in an *ad hoc* fashion, then the question becomes whether this should be considered to be unacceptable. There is a substantial literature grappling with this question, and philosophers disagree on whether or not Rawlsian theory can ultimately be sufficiently adapted.

Let us now turn to two important Rawlsian critiques of the capability approach. Rawls has argued that the capability approach entails a comprehensive notion of the good, in contrast to the political liberalism of justice as fairness (Rawls, 1988, p456; Sen, 1992, pp82–83). Rawls suggests that the capability approach relies on a particular conception of the valuable ends in life, and therefore does not respect the many comprehensive views of the good life that citizens of a plural society might endorse. Political liberalism, in contrast, claims to be fair despite different comprehensive conceptions of the good, and only endorses principles of justice that citizens with diverse and conflicting comprehensive notions of the good can endorse as the result of an overlapping consensus.

Sen (1992, pp82–83) has argued that Rawls' claim that the capability approach would endorse one unique view of the good is ultimately mistaken. The capability approach holds that the relevant focus is on the combination of capabilities that a person can access, in other words, a focus on a person's capability set. And this capability set 'stands for the actual freedom of choice a person has over alternative lives that he or she can lead' (Sen, 1992, p114). An interpersonal comparison focusing on a set of achieved functionings would endorse a comprehensive notion of the good, but this is precisely what Sen and Nussbaum have stressed repeatedly: as a matter of principle, the focus is not on achieved functionings, but on *capabilities to achieve* those functionings.

But is this reply sufficient? One possible response to Sen's defence is that the capability approach fundamentally relies on specifications in the list of valuable capabilities and, as such, imposes a specific view on the good life. One may argue that by listing the capabilities that are going to count for purposes of social justice, we are imposing a comprehensive notion of the good life itself. If a particular functioning is important to my notion of the good life, and is not included in the list of capabilities, then the conceptualization of justice will be biased against my notion of the good life.

It is well-known that Sen has refused to endorse one particular list of capabilities and, as such, stays clear from facing this problem, while Nussbaum has proposed and defended a list of capabilities that a capability-based theory of social justice might promote (see Chapter 2). The objection (that the selection of capabilities could indirectly entail the endorsement of a comprehensive notion of the good life) thus seems only relevant for Nussbaum's version of the capability approach, and not for Sen's – although some critiques have argued that Sen's capability approach also contains an implicit comprehensive conception of the good life (see note 4). Nussbaum's capabilities approach aims to specify capabilities as the fundamental constitutional entitlements that every person in every country should be guaranteed, and that are thus non-negotiable. Nussbaum believes that her list can be obtained as part of an overlapping consensus of people as citizens who have otherwise diverse views of the good life, but not everyone is convinced that this argument is in fact valid. Nevertheless, this leaves unanswered the question of whether one can select relevant capabilities in a manner that can be justified *both* in terms of the process by which the selection takes place, *and* in terms that respect all acceptable notions of the good life that people might endorse. This is an area in which more work still needs to be done.

The second major Rawlsian critique on the capability approach is the charge that it does not meet the publicity criterion. It has been argued, both by Rawls (1993, p182) and more recently by Pogge (2002a), that a theory (or principles) of social justice should be based on the publicity criterion and be workable, that is, inequalities and injustices should be able to be assessed by the public and should not need to rely on impossible amounts of information. As Rawls (1993, p182) puts it, 'What is crucial is always to recognize the limits of the political and the practicable ... we must respect the constraints of simplicity and availability of information to which any practicable political conception (as opposed to a comprehensive moral doctrine) is subject.'

Brighouse (2004) has summed up the advantages of social primary goods constituting a publicly measurable metric as follows:

> First, citizens can see more readily whether justice is being done if we have a public way of measuring it. Second, the theory can guide policymaking more clearly, because policymakers can see what the relevant deficits are. Finally ... citizens can hold policy-makers accountable for their successes and failures, by looking at the publicly-measurable outcomes of the policies. (Brighouse, 2004, p82)

Certainly, the capability approach has some difficult questions to answer: are capabilities indeed too difficult to measure or assess in such a public fashion? Would they really require too many different types of information? Would this then make the capability approach as a theory of social justice unworkable? So far, these questions have not yet been answered. Sen has repeatedly stated that capabilities can form the informational basis for a theory of justice, but he has never developed such a theory himself. So we are left with the open question of how to select capabilities without imposing a notion of the good life, and whether the publicity requirement poses an insurmountable obstacle. Note also that these are not just philosophical questions: they are very pertinent if we consider the practical application and policy relevance of a capability theory of justice beyond the urgent cases of extreme poverty relief or emergency assistance.

What conclusion can be drawn from this debate between Rawls and the capability theorists? Capability theorists have often claimed that the capability approach is a superior framework to Rawlsian justice. From the discussion above, it is fair to say that the literature does not allow us to draw such a conclusion as yet. There are still many differences between the Rawlsian framework and the various interpretations of the capability approach – all of which have not been sufficiently analysed, nor have all the Rawlsian critiques been satisfactorily answered.[5] For the moment, where forthcoming work in this area will lead the debate remains an open question.

What do we need for a capability theory of justice?

The previous two sections demonstrated that Rawls' theory of justice and the capability approach to justice differ in several ways: one important difference is that the capability approach is not, as of now, a complete theory of justice. Nussbaum's work comes closest to offering us a capability theory of justice, but even her account remains incomplete in several critical ways. Moreover, it would be a mistake to think that there can be only one capability theory of justice; on the contrary, the open nature of the capability framework allows for the development of a family of capability theories of justice. In the next section, we will discuss what is needed if we want to create such a theory.

A first important question that any theorist of justice needs to ask is: 'justice of what?' or 'equality of what?' A minimalist interpretation of the capability approach states that it *only* specifies an evaluative space, that is, it only answers the question 'in which dimensions should we evaluate justice, inequality, poverty, etc.' In the literature on social justice, there are several terms used to indicate precisely what we are assessing or measuring: the metric of advantage, the currency of justice, or the informational basis for interpersonal comparisons. The most influential metric of justice is resources, although it is often held by capability theorists that capabilities provide a better metric of interpersonal comparison than resources. However, 'resources' is a term that is used to cover a number of different categories.

One can distinguish between five different types of resources that have been criticized by capability theorists: a first type is GNP per capita. Despite its widely discussed shortcomings, it has been one of the few statistics available for each country and is therefore extensively used in research on global poverty and inequality. In theories of justice, however, it remains largely absent. A second type is individual disposable income. Welfare and development economists who work on the microeconomic aspects of development focus on individual disposable income or, in case one is looking at people who live partly in a subsistence economy, on direct consumption. Again, this measure is not often defended as the best metric of justice by theorists of justice. Nevertheless, equivalized household income, which serves as a proxy for individual income and which adjusts the income of the household to take account of the number of people in it, is often used by welfare economists who want to conduct empirical research on unjust inequalities. A third type is individual entitlements to material goods. This notion extends individual disposable income by including an estimate for non-market production and the provision of public goods. This extended account of resources is used in more fine-grained micro studies in welfare economics but still not very much in theories of justice. A fourth type is that of Ronald Dworkin's impersonal and personal resources (Dworkin, 2000). Impersonal resources are equivalent to individual entitlement to material goods. Personal resources are personal bodily and mental resources, like intelligence, physical and mental abilities and disabilities, and so forth. A fifth type is that of Rawlsian social primary goods, which were discussed earlier. They are a combination of individual disposable income (type 2) and certain civil and political human rights, opportunities, and the social basis of self-respect. Note that Rawls does not include Dworkin's personal resources.

Based on this simple classification, we can conclude that there is a significant difference in how different scholars understand the term 'resources' – the difference between economists and political philosophers, in fact, is particularly striking. An important consequence is that capability critiques of 'resourcism' (i.e. resource-based theories of justice) relying on one of these types cannot automatically be extended to another type, since they can be so different. Within theories of justice, the main arguments are with Rawlsian resourcists and with defenders of Dworkinian resourcism.[6] Other possible metrics are needs, basic needs or the many different types of subjective welfare. A full capability theory of justice would need to show why it works better as a metric of justice than all these other metrics. Many capability theorists tend to believe that the superiority of functionings and capabilities has been proven, but critics like Pogge (2002a) have shown that further substantiation is required.

Another major choice that has to be made when developing a capability theory of justice is to decide on whether we want it to be an outcome or opportunity theory, that is, whether we think that we should assess injustices in terms of achieved functionings, in terms of capabilities or a mixture of both. At the level of theory and principles, most theorists of justice endorse the view that justice is achieved when all have equal genuine opportunities. Translated into capability language, this would imply that capabilities are the relevant metric of justice, and not functionings. However, not everyone subscribes to this view. There are a few political theorists who keep arguing for equality of outcome, rather than opportunities. In the capability literature, Marc Fleurbaey (2006) has argued against the view for taking only capabilities into account and defends a focus on 'refined functionings' (being the combination of functionings and capabilities). In addition to these theoretical arguments, there can also be non-theoretical considerations for focusing on functionings (or in combination with capabilities), related to data availability or measurement limitations, for example, or because the specific area warrants a focus on functionings, as may be the case with children.

A third issue which needs to be solved if one hopes to develop a capability theory of justice is to decide and justify which capabilities matter the most. There are at least two ways of answering this question: either through procedural approaches, such as criteria from which the relevant capabilities are derived, or by defending a specific list of capabilities. This selection of relevant capabilities for the purposes of justice can be done both at the level of ideal theory (without taking issues of practical feasibility and implementation into account), at the level of abstract principles (Anderson, 1999; Nussbaum, 2000, 2006) or at an applied theoretical level, which is useful for practical assessments of injustice (Wolff and de-Shalit, 2007).

Fourth, a capability theory of justice needs to specify where the line between individual and collective responsibility is drawn, how it will be decided, where and by whom. There is a remarkable absence of discussion on issues of responsibility in the capability literature, in sharp contrast to political philosophy and welfare economics, where this is one of the most important lines of debate, certainly since the publication of Dworkin's work on justice and equality. Nevertheless, whether or not one chooses to discuss it explicitly, any concrete capability policy proposal can be analysed in terms of the division between personal and collective responsibility – but this terminology remains largely absent from the capability literature altogether. This may in part be explained by the fact that much of the work on capabilities deals with global poverty, where issues of responsibility seem to be less relevant since it would seem rather grim to suggest that the world's most destitute people are individually responsible for the respective situations they are in. Philosophical puzzles, such as the issue of expensive tastes (for expensive wine, caviar, fast cars, etc.) are simply beyond the radar screen of the child labourer or the poor peasant. However, while this may be a valid justification for the absence of any discussion on personal responsibility among capability scholars concerned with poverty, it does not absolve theorists of justice, who deal with justice in affluent societies (or affluent sections of poor societies) as well. The question of responsibility is also relevant in the debate on global justice, since there have been fierce exchanges between those who hold that citizens of affluent societies are in part responsible for global inequality and poverty in developing countries, and those who think that this responsibility is in fact much more limited (Pogge, 2002b).

This brings us to a related issue: a theory of justice generally specifies not only rights but duties. However, capability theorists have remained largely silent on the question of who should bear the duties for expanding selected capabilities. Nussbaum passionately advocates that people all over the world should be entitled, as a matter of justice, to threshold levels of all the capabilities on her list; but, apart from mentioning that it is the government's duty to guarantee these entitlements, she does not address the question of who precisely should bear the burdens and responsibilities for realizing these capabilities. A related question is whether governments are the only agents of justice-enhancing change, or whether others have duties too (individuals, families, groups, communities, institutions and so forth).

Finally, a theory of justice needs to explain on what basis it justifies its principles or claims of justice. For example, in Rawls' theory of justice, the two principles are justified by the thought-experiment of the original position, which they are based on. Dworkin's egalitarian justice theory starts from the meta-principle of equal respect and concern, which he then develops with the notion that the distribution of burdens and benefits should be sensitive to the ambitions that people have, but should not reflect the unequal natural endowments individuals are born with. If capability scholars want to develop a full theory of justice, they will also need to explain on what basis they hope to justify their principles or claims.

Gender justice and justice for marginalized groups

Many scholars have used the capability approach to study inequalities or injustices between social groups, such as men and women, or justice for indigenous people, tribal groups, religious minorities, *dalits* and so forth. The capability approach is particularly well-suited to studying these dimensions of justice for a number of reasons. First, it is an empirically-based approach which does not rely on simplifying assumptions that basically brush these dimensions of disadvantage and oppression under the carpet by introducing unjustified assumptions (idealizations), such as those discussed in the first section. Second, it uses a multi-dimensional metric of justice, so that it does not only focus on either subjective assessments or material inequalities. The problem with subjective assessments is that people get used to their respective circumstances. Therefore, how deprived groups adapt to their objectively poor circumstances and many deprivations will not be fully reflected in their subjective judgements. Privileged people also get used to their circumstances, and thus their subjective self-assessment may be much more modest than one would expect, given their objective circumstances.

However, the human development and capability approaches need to more effectively combine the focus on capabilities, as normative units of evaluation, with theories that explain the causes and workings of the social structures of group oppression, such as gender, caste or class. Although most capability scholars embrace theories of social explanation, it is in principle possible to use the capability approach in combination with individualistic or libertarian theories that explain these group inequalities. An important part of the debate about gender equality, caste equality, class equality or other types of equality for disadvantaged groups will therefore inevitably focus on these explanatory theories, rather than on inequalities in advantage in terms of their levels of functionings and capabilities.

In using the human development and capability approach for analysing group inequalities, one has to take special note of the selection of capabilities themselves. Some groups may score much better on one capability than others, and the omission of a certain capability from the analysis might therefore have important consequences for our normative judgements about group inequalities. For example, economists typically discuss gender inequality in terms of material resources (income, wages), but gender issues cannot be properly assessed if the distribution of care work is not included in the analysis, since care work is highly gendered.

From theories of justice to just practices and policies

Since, as we saw at the beginning of this chapter, theories of justice are mainly developed at the level of ideal theory, the capability approach to social justice and equality may not be particularly useful in telling us what justice-enhancing strategies and policies to develop. Indeed, this has sometimes been phrased as a serious concern, namely, that theories of justice are too abstract and do not help us with social justice struggles on the ground. One may well argue that we roughly know what is going wrong and we need political action rather than more and more detailed theorizing. Moreover, some think that the subtleties of the theories of justice are easily abused in reality in order to justify gross inequalities, as may have been the case with philosophical discussions on individual responsibility. For example, a book by Brian Barry (2005) exemplifies this concern with the direct application of theories of justice to political change and the reform of the welfare state, rather than with further philosophical refinements of theories of justice. Related charges have been specifically aimed at the capability approach as well. For instance, it has been argued that not enough attention has been paid to issues of social power in the capability writings on justice, and Feldmann and Gellert (2006) have underscored the importance of recognizing the struggles and negotiations by dominated and disadvantaged groups if social justice is ever to be realized. Such questions of power politics, effective social criticism, successful collective action, historical and cultural sensitivities, and the negotiation of competing interests are indeed largely absent from the philosophical literature on theories of justice. These ideal theories develop *standards* of a just society, but often do not tell us what institutions or policies are necessary if just societies are to be constructed, nor do they tell us what social and political processes will help advocates implement these social changes in concrete ways.

But the capability approach can be linked to more concrete justice-enhancing policy proposals that have been developed. For one thing, the Millennium Development Goals can be understood as being a practical, albeit truncated, translation of the capability approach in practice. In fact, at the level of severe global poverty, any concrete poverty-reduction strategy which conceptualizes poverty in a capability sense is, for most accounts of justice, a concrete justice-enhancing strategy, since these theories would include the absence of severe poverty as a principle of justice.

If we move from the area of poverty-reduction strategies to the question of just social policies in countries or regions with higher levels of affluence, we then observe that there are much fewer actual examples of justice-enhancing policies that have been explicitly grounded in, or associated with, the capability approach. Yet many concrete policies and interventions could be interpreted as such, or are consistent with the capability perspective itself. One example relates to a policy of providing, regulating and/or subsidising child-care facilities. This can arguably be justified as a prerequisite for gender justice in capabilities since, due to gender norms, women will in effect not be able to develop themselves professionally if they are not supported in their need for decent quality-regulated (and possibly subsidised) child-care facilities. Mothers at home may be materially well-off if their husbands earn a good income but, if they do not have the genuine opportunity to hold jobs, then their capability sets are severely constrained and gender justice in capabilities cannot be achieved. An income metric which assumes equal sharing in the household may not detect any moral problem, but a capability metric will claim that women will have less freedom than men, since the provisions are not there to ensure that both parents can hold jobs, and gender norms and other gendered social mechanisms make it difficult for men to volunteer to stay at home with their kids.

Another example concerns a justice-enhancing intervention that was set up by a small group of citizens in Utrecht, a large city in Holland (but, as the example will show, it could be any city with immigrants who speak another language). It is well known that the children of immigrants are disadvantaged at school since they are very likely to enter school with a much weaker knowledge of the Dutch language than non-immigrant children. For this reason, a group of citizens decided to set up a network of volunteers to read books to small immigrant children in their own homes. In this way, they effectively reduced the gap in educational opportunity between immigrant children and non-immigrant children. This example also illustrates that justice-enhancing strategies are not confined to public policy, but can also be initiated by persons and groups at the grassroots.

But, despite the many possibilities of using the capability approach to practice justice-enhancing strategies, capability scholars have been criticized for having their priorities wrong: by focusing so much on the metric of justice and on human diversity in the conversion of resources into capabilities, their approach draws attention away from huge inequalities in terms of resources (income, wealth) and therefore helps to preserve the (unjust) status quo. Pogge (2002a) has specifically argued that the capability approach – Sen's work in particular – overemphasizes the role of national and local governments, thereby neglecting the huge injustices created by the global economic system and its institutional structures, such as global trade rules. Pogge may have a point in his charge that capability theorists have paid insufficient attention to these issues, which have been discussed at length in the philosophical literature on global justice. But one might also argue that this is orthogonal to the issues about which the capability approach to social justice is most concerned, namely, how to make interpersonal comparisons of advantage for the purposes of social justice. One could, quite plausibly, hold the view that, since most capability theorists are concerned with human well-being, they should invest their energies in addressing the most urgent cases of injustice, investigate their underlying causal processes and mechanisms, and concentrate on the development of solutions. This is not, however, a valid critique of the capability approach as a theory, nor does it recognize the role that the approach *can* play in substantive debates about global justice and inequality. One should simply not take the capability approach for being more than it is: an evaluative approach that draws our attention to people's beings and doings, and their real freedom to be who they value being, and do the things they value doing.

Questions

5.1 Which are the four main theoretical schools of social justice? Can you identify existing social policies or justice-enhancing interventions that are based on each one of these schools or approaches?

5.2 How do the concepts of equality and justice relate, and how do they differ?

5.3 Explain the essence of Rawls' theory of justice in your own words.

5.4 Take one social group (e.g. women, ethnic or religious minorities, *dalits*, scheduled tribes and castes, disabled people, the elderly, gays, etc.). Describe the main concerns of justice for that social group from a human development and capability perspective.

5.5 What are the most important issues of justice in your country or community? How would a human development and capability perspective analyse that issue?

5.6 Do you know a policy in your country that is based, either explicitly or implicitly, on the capability approach?

Notes

1 For an accessible introduction to contemporary political philosophy, see Swift (2001).

2 It is noteworthy, however, that some critics have argued that Sen's capability approach also contains an implicit (and fairly comprehensive) conception of the good life, which leads us to question how well it is situated within the tradition of

liberal egalitarian theories of justice (see e.g. Arneson 2000 or Deneulin 2002).

3   For a lengthier introduction to Rawls' work on justice, see Richardson (2006).

4   There are other capability critiques on Rawls, including critiques regarding the limited scope of Rawlsian theory and its contractarian nature. See Nussbaum (2006) and Brighouse and Robeyns (2010).

5   For example, most critiques by Pogge (2002a) remain as yet unanswered. Some responses are forthcoming in Brighouse and Robeyns (2010).

6   For the difference between capabilities and social primary goods, see the previous section. For the difference between capabilities and Dworkinian resources, see Williams (2002) and Pierik and Robeyns (2007).

Readings

Barry, B. and Matravers, M. (2004) 'Justice', in E. Craig (ed) *Routledge Encyclopedia of Philosophy*, available online at www.rep.routledge.com/article/S032

Brighouse, H. and Robeyns, I. (eds) (2010) *Measuring Justice: Primary Goods and Capabilities*, Cambridge University Press, Cambridge

Deneulin, S. (2002) 'Perfectionism, Liberalism and Paternalism in Sen and Nussbaum's Capability Approach', *Review of Political Economy*, vol 14, no 4, pp497–518

Nussbaum, M. (2000) *Women and Human Development*, Cambridge University Press, Cambridge

Nussbaum, M. (2006) *Frontiers of Justice: Disability, Nationality and Species Membership*, Harvard University Press, Cambridge MA

Pierik, R. and Robeyns, I. (2007) 'Resources versus capabilities: Social endowments in egalitarian theory', *Political Studies*, vol 55, no 1, pp132–152

Pogge, T. (2002a) 'Can the capability approach be justified?' *Philosophical Topics*, vol 30, pp167–228

Pogge, T. (2002b) *World Poverty and Human Rights*, Polity Press, Cambridge

Rawls, J. (1999) 'Social unity and primary goods', first published in 1982 in A. K. Sen and B. Williams (eds) *Utilitarianism and Beyond*, Cambridge University Press, Cambridge. Reprinted in S. Freeman (ed) (1999) *John Rawls Collected Papers*, Harvard University Press, Cambridge, MA, 359–387

Rawls, J. (1988) 'The priority of the right and the idea of the good', *Philosophy and Public Affairs,* vol 17, no 4, pp251–276. Reprinted in *Collected Papers*, 449–472

Rawls, J. (1999) *A Theory of Justice* (1st edn 1971), Harvard University Press, Cambridge, MA

Rawls, J. (2001) *Justice as Fairness: A Restatement*, Harvard University Press, Cambridge, MA

Sen, A. K. (1980) 'Equality of what?', in S. McMurrin (ed.) *The Tanner Lectures on Human Values*, University of Utah Press, Salt Lake City

Sen, A. K. (1990) 'Justice: Means versus freedoms', *Philosophy and Public Affairs*, vol 19, pp111–121

Sen, A. K. (1992) *Inequality Re-examined*, Clarendon Press, Oxford

Sen, A. K. (2006) 'What do we want from a theory of justice?', *Journal of Philosophy*, vol 103, no 5, pp215–238

Further Readings

Anderson, E. (1999) 'What is the point of equality?', *Ethics*, vol 109, no 2, pp287–337

Arneson, R. (2000) 'Perfectionism and politics', *Ethics*, vol 111, no 1, pp37–63

Barry, B. (1995) *Justice as Impartiality*, Clarendon Press, Oxford

Barry, B. (2005) *Why Social Justice Matters*, Polity Press, Cambridge

Brighouse, H. (2004) *Justice*, Polity Press, Cambridge

Dworkin, R. (2000) *Sovereign Virtue: The Theory and Practice of Equality*, Harvard University Press, Cambridge, MA

Feldman, S. and Gellert, P. (2006) 'The seductive quality of central human capabilities: Sociological insights into Nussbaum and Sen's disagreement', *Economy and Society*, vol 35, no 3, pp423–452

Fleurbaey, M. (2006) 'Capabilities, functionings and refined functionings', *Journal of Human Development*, vol 7, no 3, pp299–309

Miller, D. (1999) *Principles of Social Justice*, Harvard University Press, Cambridge, MA

Nozick, R. (1974) *Anarchy, State and Utopia*, Basic Books, New York

Nussbaum, M. (2003) 'Capabilities as fundamental entitlements: Sen and social justice', *Feminist Economics*, vol 9, nos 2/3, pp33–59

Rawls, J. (1993) *Political Liberalism*, Columbia University Press, New York

Richardson, H. S. (2006) 'John Rawls', *Internet Encyclopedia of Philosophy*, online at www.iep.utm.edu/r/rawls.htm

Robeyns, I. and Swift, A. (2008), 'Social justice: Ideal theory, non-ideal circumstances', *Social Theory and Practice*, special issue, vol 34, no 3

Swift, A. (2001) *Political Philosophy: A Beginner's Guide for Students and Politicians*, Polity Press, Cambridge

Van Parijs, P. (1995) *Real Freedom for All. What (if Anything) can Justify Capitalism*, Oxford University Press, Oxford

Walzer, M. (1983) *Spheres of Justice*, Basic Books, New York

Williams, A. (2002) 'Dworkin on capability', *Ethics*, vol 113, no 1, pp23–39

Wolff, J. and de-Shalit, A. (2007) *Disadvantage*, Oxford University Press, Oxford

A very good, freely available on-line source for philosophy is the *Stanford Encyclopaedia of Philosophy*, which has comprehensive entries on such names and terms as 'John Rawls', 'distributive justice,' 'egalitarianism', and so forth.

6
Poverty and Inequality Measurement

Sabina Alkire and Maria Emma Santos

Aims of the chapter

- To introduce the concepts of poverty and inequality.
- To familiarize readers with the key measures of monetary poverty and inequality.
- To present key multi-dimensional measures of poverty.
- To raise awareness of the importance of measurement tools as well as of their underlying concepts for policy use.

Key Points

- Poverty and inequality can be considered in different spaces: incomes, resources or functionings.
- Poverty measures (a) choose the space for analysis, (b) identify which people are poor and (c) summarize a society's poverty status in an aggregate number.
- Inequality measures (a) choose the space for analysis, (b) consider the entire distribution of people, from poorest to richest, (c) summarize the inequality of the distribution in a single number.

Note to the Reader: This chapter is structured differently from others, and readers will want to use the chapter in different ways. Some people are a bit daunted by numbers and economics, while others find the precise language and concise description of key measures to be practical and helpful. Readers of this textbook will come from *both* groups. Therefore we have structured the chapter as follows. First of all, we have endeavoured to describe all measures simply, using examples and non-technical language whenever possible. Still, if you are new to quantitative methods and want a completely non-technical overview, please *skip the shaded sub-sections and shaded boxes*. If you have some familiarity with terms and notation, please read the chapter straight through.

The importance and limitations of measurement

Chapter 2 observed that the human development approach was multi-dimensional, and that the selection of valuable capabilities will be done again and again, so that relevant capabilities are used in each context. Traditionally, poverty and inequality have been measured in the space of income. However, those advancing human development often wish to undertake quantitative analyses of achieved functionings in addition to income or consumption. The development of quantitative multi-dimensional measures of poverty and inequality is a new but rapidly-developing area and this chapter will provide some introduction to it.

Importance

Numbers, as Székely (2006) observed, can move the world. Good measures allow us to compare poverty and inequality across time and between groups, and contribute to policy design. The collection and summarizing of data in aggregate measures is part of an informed, rigorous and pragmatic approach to policy. This has been called 'evidence-based policy-making' by the *Human Development Measurement: A Primer* (Human Development Report Office, 2007).

Given how measurement affects policy analysis and formulation, decisions regarding whether one or multiple dimensions are considered, which indicators are used, and how the data are aggregated, are important because they influence who benefits from responses to poverty and inequality. Moreover, measures of poverty and inequality are important tools for advocacy. One strong motivation for undertaking data analysis is to support the formulation of more effective policy. Sound policies are grounded in sound analyses.

Yet because human development and the capability approach move beyond the metric of income, their measurement raises particular challenges. In the quote below Sen articulates well the challenges of developing a measure of capability living standard. The same tensions apply to measures of capability poverty, or indeed inequality.

> There are two major challenges in developing an appropriate approach to the evaluation of the standard of living. On the one hand, it must meet the motivation that makes us interested in the concept of the living standard, doing justice to the richness of the idea… On the other hand, the approach must be practical in the sense of being usable for actual assessments of the living standard. This imposes restrictions on the kinds of information that can be required and the techniques of evaluation that may be used.
>
> These two considerations – *relevance and usability* – pull us, to some extent, in different directions. *Relevance* may demand that we take on board the inherent complexities of the idea of the

living standard as fully as possible, whereas *usability* may suggest
that we try to shun complexities if we reasonably can. Relevance
wants us to be ambitious; usability urges restraint. This is, of
course, a rather common conflict in economics, and while we
have to face the conflict squarely, we must not make heavy
weather of it. (Sen, 1987, p20)

For this reason, in addition to quantitative measures, on which this chapter
focuses, human development also seeks the rich insights that arise from
qualitative interviews, participatory analyses, life histories and ethnographic
research. These qualitative techniques are often used alongside quantitative
techniques at every stage – in the selection of dimensions, in the triangulation
of findings, in the identification of research hypotheses, and in the
mobilization of a local response to deprivation. They provide powerful keys to
understanding the causes of poverty, as well as methods of coping with
adversity. Human development analyses are more accurate, powerful and
locally effective when they combine quantitative measures with participatory
and qualitative research.[1]

Limitations

At the same time, the goal is not to *measure* poverty – but to *reduce* it. And
too often interest in measurement seems to supplant practical action. This is in
part because in some places more attention is placed on poverty measurement
than causal analysis, or political response. Harris (2007) argues that
mainstream poverty research has generally failed to address the dynamic,
structural and relational factors that give rise to poverty. He warns of the risk
that poverty research depoliticizes what is essentially a political problem.

Green and Hulme (2005) advance a similar argument. Poverty, they argue,
is often conceptualized in such a way that it is not seen as the product of social
relations. The technical measurement of poverty can seem to dissociate it from
the social processes of the accumulation and distribution of wealth. Then, the
profoundly political task of counting the poor is made to seem scientific and
the value judgements which Sen argues should guide poverty measurement, are
not explicitly faced. The political aspects need direct attention.

It might be relevant in this regard to re-invigorate aspects from the early
developments of economic theory. The study of (the laws that governed) the
distribution of wealth among landlords, capitalists and labourers was of
primary importance, as can be seen in the work of Ricardo (1817) and Marx
(1867). Indeed, such tradition was continued in many distributional studies
later on, in what is called the study of *functional* income distribution. Those
analyses report what percentage of the total income (or gross national product)
generated in an economy goes into rents, profits and wages in return for the
different factors of production. Although such studies may help to 'unveil'
underlying social relations, they provide a partial picture of distributional
issues, since households or individuals may own more than one factor of

production. That is probably why the study of the *personal* income distribution, which looks at what each person in a distribution earns regardless of the source from which it was obtained, gained increasing attention and eventually displaced the former approach. Ideally one should consider all distributional issues and look for unifying frameworks.[2]

In summary, we understand that quantitative poverty and inequality measurement is – although important – limited. It is just one building block of distributional analysis and policy design and implementation. Furthermore, poverty measurement needs to be accompanied by analyses of the social processes, structures and relationships that create poverty (and, we might add, by practical and political action to confront poverty). Thus while the remainder of this chapter focuses enthusiastically on inequality and poverty measurement, it does so fully recognizing the limitations of this task, and the need for complementary methods both of research and of action.

Income-based measures of inequality

Box 6.1 Terms

In this chapter we discuss how to measure inequality, poverty and well-being. Although the three concepts may be familiar and are indeed related, their measurement entails different procedures.

- **Inequality** measures consider the *entire* distribution (in one or several indicators) and provide a value that summarizes the inequalities between every person or household's achievements.
- **Poverty** measures focus on the part of the population that falls short of some minimum level, often called a poverty line (in one or several indicators) and provide a value that summarizes deprivation in that society.
- **Well-being** measures (sometimes called welfare, quality of life or standard of living) consider the *entire* distribution of achievements (in one or several indicators) and provide a value that summarizes the level of well-being in the population. Typical examples are the gross national product (GNP) per capita and the Human Development Index (HDI).

When measures of poverty, inequality and well-being include only one domain – usually income or consumption, they are called *uni-dimensional* measures. When they combine several domains, they are called *multi-dimensional* measures.

Income, consumption and assets data: pros and cons

Until recently, the measurement of inequality and poverty referred exclusively to uni-dimensional measures using data on income, consumption, expenditure or wealth/assets. There are considerable distinctions between these kinds of data. Usually consumption data are favoured as being more useful and more accurate for the construction of poverty and inequality measures in developing countries (Deaton and Grosh, 2000) but in practice this varies by region and by the adequacy of the survey. In Latin America and the US, for example, income-based measures are more common. Asset-based measures and wealth indices based on asset data are generally used when neither consumption nor income data are available and often require a different treatment, so we focus on consumption and income data here. For simplicity, we will refer in a general way to *income* and by this mean both kinds of data, but this does *not* indicate a preference for income over consumption or expenditure.

Monetary measures are criticized for several reasons. First, unless the data are deliberately enriched, they assume that markets (and therefore prices) exist for all goods, and ignore the existence of public goods and access to non-market education and health services, for example. Second, they overlook people's differing 'conversion factors' between income and functionings. 'An older, or more disabled, or more seriously ill person may need more income (for assistance, for prosthetics, for treatment) to achieve the same functionings (even when that achievement is at all possible)' (Foster and Sen, 1997, p212).[3] Third, having a certain amount of income does not guarantee that the individual will allocate it to the basic goods and services considered necessary to lead a non-impoverished life (addicts, for example, might not). Fourth, the indicator used is usually the total (per-capita or equivalent) household income, but this overlooks inequalities in intra-household distribution, in which some members may receive less because of their gender, age or status in the household. Finally, income data are usually deeply flawed due to missing observations and misreporting. Although different imputation techniques have been developed to correct for this, these data problems have an undoubtedly detrimental effect on the reliability of money-metric based estimates.[4]

Despite these disadvantages, the practical methodologies for measuring inequality and poverty in the income spaces have been solidly developed and provide the basis for extensions to other dimensions and spaces. Moreover, money-metric measures of inequality and poverty have proved to be useful in practice, satisfying Sen's 'usability' requirement mentioned in the previous section.

Inequality measurement: Two tools

As soon as you have chosen which kind of data to use, you can study the *distribution* of this indicator for different groups (for example residents of countries or regions). A distribution shows how much each person or household earns or consumes within the same time period.

Example of two distributions:

State A		State B	
Person 1	2	Person 1	5
Person 2	7	Person 2	1
Person 3	6	Person 3	9

We study the distribution in order to answer this question: Which of the two distributions is more equal? We can compare State A and State B using one of two tools: inequality *rankings* or inequality *measures*. Rankings such as Lorenz dominance provide a rule for comparing distributions, whereas measures such as the Gini coefficient apply a function or mathematical formula to each distribution and generate a number that indicates its level of inequality (Foster, 2006a, p276).

Inequality rankings: the Lorenz criterion

The Lorenz criterion (also called Lorenz dominance) constitutes a partial inequality *ranking* rule. It is based on a graphic tool called the Lorenz curve (Lorenz, 1905), simple and visual. To construct the Lorenz curve of a distribution, you first order people from poorest to richest. For example, State A would be (2,6,7). The curve depicts the cumulative share of total income (in the vertical axis) received by each cumulative share of the population (p in the horizontal axis). Each point of the curve indicates the share of total income received by the poorest p share of the population (see Box 6.2). A perfectly equal distribution would be such that the Lorenz curve would coincide with the 45° line, so that the poorest p of the population receive p of total income (for example, the poorest 10 per cent of the population receive 10 per cent of total income, and so on). A perfectly unequal distribution would be such that the Lorenz curve runs along the horizontal axis and up the vertical axis on the right (with everyone receiving zero income except for one person who receives all the income). Then, the Lorenz criterion judges a distribution A more equal than another B if the Lorenz curve of A lies above that of B for some p and nowhere below for all p (Foster 2006a, p276). The ranking is partial because the criterion remains silent if two Lorenz curves cross.[5]

Box 6.2 The Lorenz curves: an intuitive overview

1. Order the distributions of each group from poorest to richest. So A = (2,6,7) and B = (1,5,9).
2. Create the cumulative distribution as below.
3. Plot the cumulative share of population against the cumulative share of income to see the Lorenz Curves for each group.

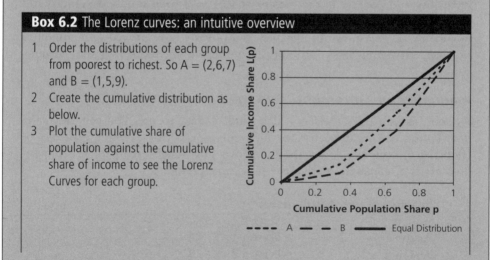

Cumulative population share	Cumulative income share L(p)	
p	A	B
0	0	0
1/3 (1 person out of 3 people)	2/15 = 2 + 6 + 7	1/15
2/3	2 + 6 = 8/15	6/15
3/3	2 + 6 + 7 = 15/15	15/15

4 In the graph, it can be seen that the Lorenz curve of A is always above that of B, closer to the equal distribution line, and that the curves do not cross. Therefore A is ranked as more equal than B. In other words, A 'Lorenz-dominates' B.

Inequality measures: Gini, Atkinson and Generalized Entropy

As opposed to the Lorenz criterion, inequality measures provide a complete ranking. All pairs of distributions can be compared. Several inequality measures have been proposed in the literature. However, not all of them are desirable from either a technical or a policy perspective. There is now a broad consensus regarding four properties that an inequality measure should satisfy in order to be used in practice and give an accurate representation of inequality, which are briefly introduced in Box 6.3.

Box 6.3 Key properties of inequality measures

There are four basic properties that an inequality measure should satisfy. These are: *symmetry, replication invariance, scale invariance* and *transfer*. Suppose that we represent an income distribution among n individuals with a vector $y = (y_1, y_2, ..., y_n)$, where each element y_i is the income of individual $i = 1, ..., n$. Let $I(y)$ denote the level of inequality of distribution y according to a given inequality measure I.

- By **symmetry** (also called anonymity), an inequality measure should be invariant to *who* receives each income (for example, $I(2,4) = I(4,2)$).
- By **replication invariance** (also called population principle), an inequality measure should be invariant to replications of the population such that the level of inequality does not depend on the population size (for example $I(2,4) = I(2,2,4,4)$).
- By **scale invariance** (also called zero-degree homogeneity or relative income principle) an inequality measure should be invariant to proportional changes of all incomes in a distribution such that the level of inequality does not depend on the total income in a distribution (for example $I(2,4) = I(4,8)$).
- By **transfer** (also called the Pigou–Dalton principle following Pigou 1912 and Dalton 1920), an inequality measure should increase whenever there is a regressive transfer (from a poorer to a richer person, preserving total income) between two individuals (for example $I(1,5) > I(2,4)$) (and inequality should decrease whenever there is a progressive transfer).

A measure satisfying these four basic properties is called a **relative inequality measure**.

Foster (1985) proved that only the inequality measures that satisfy the four mentioned properties will rank two distributions in the same way as the Lorenz criterion; they are said to be *Lorenz-consistent* inequality measures. That means that whenever the Lorenz criterion judges a distribution A more equal than another B, all relative inequality measures will agree with this judgement. However, whenever the Lorenz criterion cannot decide (because the Lorenz curves cross), the relative inequality measures can still provide a ranking, but the ranking of different measures may differ, as each one satisfies different additional properties.[6]

The Gini coefficient

Among the 'good' measures of inequality (that is, those satisfying the four basic properties), is the Gini coefficient (Gini, 1912), which is the most common measure of inequality, and is reported by most countries.[7] In this measure, all possible pairs of incomes in the distribution are compared. The higher the Gini coefficient, the more unequal the distribution.

There are different equivalent formulas for the Gini. One particularly easy method makes use of the Lorenz curve (see Box 6.4). The Gini is the ratio of the area between the diagonal (equal distribution) and the Lorenz curve, to the entire area in the triangular region below the diagonal. So when distributions are perfectly equal, the area between the diagonal and the Lorenz curve is zero (since the Lorenz curve *is* the diagonal), therefore the Gini coefficient is zero. When distributions are perfectly unequal the area between the Lorenz curve and the diagonal is the entire triangular region below the diagonal, hence the Gini coefficient is one.

While the Gini is clearly the best known measure, it does have some weaknesses – for example it cannot be decomposed into an inequality *between* population groups component and an inequality *within* population groups component.[8] Two other prominent inequality measures are the Atkinson Index, and the Theil Indices. The last ones are part of a class of measures known as Generalized Entropy measures, and which *can* be decomposed.

There are other common ways of representing inequality such as the ratio of the share of income owned by the richest 90 per cent of the population to the poorest 10 per cent (the 90:10 ratio; it can be any other two richest and poorest shares), and the percentage of income that goes to the bottom 20 per cent of the population, which are easy to interpret. However, they are less rigorous and informative as they ignore the parts of the distribution not specifically considered in the measures as well as changes that may occur within the considered shares (they violate one of the four basic properties: transfer).

Formula for the Gini coefficient

Following the notation introduced in Box 6.3, if vector y represents an income distribution among n individuals, the Gini coefficient can be expressed with the following formula:

(1)
$$G = \frac{\sum_{i=1}^{n} \sum_{j=1}^{n} |y_i - y_j|}{2n^2 \mu}$$

where μ denotes the mean income of the distribution y ($\mu = \sum_{i=1}^{n} y_i/n$). Note that it adds the absolute value of the difference between all the possible pairs of incomes y_i and y_j, and divides it by 2 because each income difference is counted twice, and by total population and income (so that the Gini is replication and scale invariant).

Box 6.4 How to calculate the Gini coefficient

Given distribution B = (1, 5, 9) of Box 6.2, an easy way to calculate the Gini coefficient is the following:[9] Using a table, the absolute value of all the possible differences can be calculated.

	1	5	9
1	0	4	8
5	4	0	4
9	8	4	0

The sum of all the entries of the table (which is obviously symmetric) corresponds to the numerator of expression (1). Then, the Gini coefficient is given by:

$$G = \frac{2(4 + 8 + 4)}{(2)(3^2)(5)} = 0.35$$

In terms of the Lorenz curve, it can be verified that the Gini coefficient is given by

$$G = \frac{L}{OCD} = 2L$$

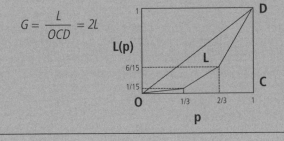

An introduction to General Means

Two other important inequality measures, Atkinson's measures and Generalized Entropy measures, are based on the *general means* of order β, where β refers to the exponent to which each person's income is raised (Foster and Shneyerov, 1999). We will explain the general means, also called β-means, first. Using the same notation as before, the β-means are given by the following expression:

$$(2) \qquad \mu_\beta = \begin{cases} \left[\dfrac{1}{n}\sum\nolimits_{i=1}^{n}(y_i)^\beta\right]^{1/\beta} & \beta \neq 0 \\[2ex] \prod\nolimits_{i=1}^{n}(y_i)^{1/n} & \beta = 0 \end{cases}$$

When $\beta = 1$, the expression is reduced to the arithmetic mean. When $\beta > 1$, higher weight is given to higher incomes, hence the β-mean is greater than the arithmetic mean, approaching the maximum income as β approaches ∞ (infinity). When $\beta < 1$, higher weight is given to lower incomes, therefore the β-mean is lower than the arithmetic mean, approaching the minimum income as β approaches $-\infty$. When $\beta < 1$, the general means constitute a powerful tool to capture inequality in a distribution. For a given value of β, the more unequal a distribution is, the lower will be the β-mean with respect to the arithmetic mean. For a given distribution, the more one wants to penalize inequality, the lower should be the β value used. In this range, two cases are well known: when $\beta = 0$, the β-mean is called the *geometric mean*, and when $\beta = (-1)$, it is called the *harmonic mean*.

Box 6.5 Example of general means

We continue with the same example used for the Lorenz curves, to exemplify the calculation of the general means. Consider two states A and B, with distributions: A = (2,6,7) and B = (1,5,9). We first present an example on how to calculate some members of the β-means and then compare the two distributions with a graph.

Arithmetic Mean The arithmetic mean ($\beta = 1$) for State A is as follows:

$$\mu_1 = \frac{2 + 6 + 7}{3} = 5.$$

Geometric Mean If we choose $\beta = (0)$ – which is called the 'geometric mean' – then the formula is a bit different (only for this case). Given that there are 3 people in State A, its geometric mean is the product of the 3rd root of each achievement:

$$\mu_0 = \left[(2)^{1/3} \times (6)^{1/3} \times (7)^{1/3}\right] = 4.38$$

Harmonic Mean If $\beta = (-1)$ the general mean (called the harmonic mean when $\beta = (-1)$) is defined -for State A- as

$$\mu_{-1} = \left[\frac{(2)^{-1} + (6)^{-1} + (7)^{-1}}{3}\right]^{-1} \quad \text{which equals} \quad \left(\frac{1/2 + 1/6 + 1/7}{3}\right)^{-1}$$

which equals $\quad \dfrac{3}{1/2 + 1/6 + 1/7} = 3.71$

So calculating general means is actually much easier than it seems. Note that to calculate the general means achievements have to be scaled to take strictly positive values.

The graph depicts the values of the β-means for different values of β for the two states A and B. Note that the β-means for the two states are the same when β = 1, given that the two distributions have the same arithmetic mean. Also note that in both cases, when β < 1, the β-means are lower than the arithmetic mean, because in both states income is unequally distributed and, for this range of the parameter values, lower incomes receive a higher weight. Note moreover that in this range, the β-means for distribution B are lower than those for distribution A because B has a more unequal distribution than A. On the other hand, when β > 1, B has a higher β-mean than A because the higher incomes receive a higher weight.

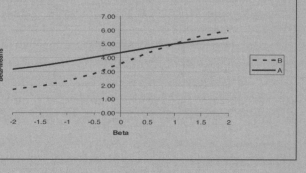

Atkinson's parametric family of inequality measures

The general means with β < 1, correspond to what Atkinson (1970) called the '*equally distributed equivalent* (EDE) *income*'. EDE is the per capita income level that if assigned to all individuals produces the same social welfare level as the actual distribution.[10] The more unequal a distribution is, the lower will be the β-mean (that is, the EDE income) with respect to the arithmetic mean. Atkinson's (1970) family of inequality measures is then given by

$$(3) \quad A_\beta = 1 - \frac{Y_{EDE}}{\mu} = 1 - \frac{\mu_\beta}{\mu} \quad \text{with } \beta < 1$$

measuring the percentage loss in welfare due to inequality. In a perfectly equal distribution, everyone receives the mean income, $\mu_\beta = \mu$, and inequality is zero. As a distribution tends towards being perfectly unequal (with only one person tending to accumulate all the income and the others tending to have zero), inequality tends to one.[11] In the middle, 'if $A_\beta = 0.3$, for example, it means that if incomes were equally distributed, we would need only 70 per cent of the present national income to achieve the same level of social welfare (according to the particular social welfare function)' (Atkinson, 1970, p250).

One advantage of these measures is that they are a *family*. Policy-makers can adjust the value of parameter β explicitly depending on how much they value equality. Intuitively, β is inversely related to the degree of inequality aversion a policy-maker or society has. The lower the value of β, the higher the aversion to inequality and the greater the importance placed on the poor.

Generalized Entropy measures

The formula for the next class of measures, the generalized entropy class, is as follows:[12]

(4)
$$GE_\beta = \begin{cases} \dfrac{1}{\beta(1-\beta)} \dfrac{1}{n} \sum_{i=1}^{n} \left[1 - \left(\dfrac{y_i}{\mu} \right)^\beta \right] & \beta \neq 0, \beta \neq 1 \\[2em] \dfrac{1}{n} \sum_{i=1}^{n} \dfrac{y_i}{\mu} \ln\left(\dfrac{y_i}{\mu} \right) & \beta = 1 \\[2em] \dfrac{1}{n} \sum_{i=1}^{n} \ln\left(\dfrac{\mu}{y_i} \right) & \beta = 0 \end{cases}$$

This broad class of measures encompasses different particular inequality measures. For $\beta < 1$, the measures are a monotonic transformation of *Atkinson's measures*. For $\beta = 1$, the measure is the *Theil index*, originated in the information theory. For $\beta = 0$, the measure is the *Theil second measure*, also known as the mean logarithmic deviation. For $\beta = 2$, the measure is a multiple of the squared coefficient of variation (which is the variance divided by the squared mean). Parameter β is – again – an indicator of inequality aversion and of the measure's sensitivity to transfers at different parts of the distribution. When $\beta = 2$, the measure is 'transfer neutral' (a transfer of a given size between two individuals has the same effect at high and low incomes). When $\beta < 2$ (which includes the two Theil measures and Atkinson's transformations), the measures give higher weight to transfers at the lower incomes. Finally, when $\beta > 2$, the measures stress transfers at higher incomes in a kind of 'reverse sensitivity'. Clearly, in this range, the indices are not useful measures of inequality.[13] The main advantage of the generalized entropy measures over the Atkinson's family of measures is their decomposability.[14]

Income poverty measurement: Two steps

In a seminal paper, Sen (1976) highlighted two steps in poverty measurement: *identification* and *aggregation*.

1 At the identification step one needs to determine *who* are the poor, and the population is divided into two groups: poor and non-poor.

Identification: Who is Poor?

poverty

2   For aggregation (which means putting together) one needs to select a poverty index. Aggregation summarizes overall poverty into one meaningful number.

> Poverty in our country is 0.30. Last year it was 0.25. In my state it is 0.15, but in the South it is 0.40.

Aggregation:
How poor are we?

Poverty measurement has usually been done in the space of income or consumption. However, a prior step to measurement involves choosing the space (and variables) (Sen, 1976, p229). For example, we could consider a poverty measure based on nutritional outcomes, or a multi-dimensional approach can be taken, as we will discuss in the following sections. In this section we present the framework for income poverty measurement.

Income poverty measurement: Identification

A key tool for identifying the poor is a *poverty line*, often also called a poverty threshold or cut-off. A monetary poverty line is the minimum amount of money considered necessary to lead a non-impoverished life. People whose income level is below the poverty line are considered poor, and people with an income at or above it are non-poor. Poverty lines are usually denoted by z.

> **Example:** Consider four people, with incomes (7, 2, 4, 8), and a poverty line of 5. The two persons who have less than 5 (2 and 4) are poor. If a 1 means the person is poor, and a 0 means they are non-poor, after identification we have (0,1,1,0). It is that easy.

The difficult step in identification is setting the poverty line. There are three types of poverty lines:

• **Absolute poverty lines:** identify the minimum income level required for all individuals. Absolute income poverty lines are often constructed calculating the monetary value of the set of food items that provide the amount of calories required by an 'equivalent adult' (about 2100 calories a day) and augmenting this cost by some proportion to account for non-food items also considered necessary.[15] Usually a *food poverty line* and *total poverty line* are distinguished. Absolute poverty lines have the advantage that they are comparable over time (with the appropriate price adjustments) and across countries (even when the food items differ, the set is supposed to provide a certain amount of calories). This is the approach officially adopted by the US and most Latin American countries. The World Bank uses a version of this methodology and is currently using a (lower) poverty line of US$1.25 a day and a (higher) poverty line of US$2 a day.

- **Relative poverty lines:** identify the poor based on a context-dependent poverty line. Relative poverty lines are usually some fraction of an income standard, such as the mean or the median. The idea is that individuals in more affluent societies need higher income levels to lead a non-impoverished life than individuals in less affluent contexts.[16] This approach has been adopted by most countries of the European Union (EU). While the concept of relative poverty sounds appealing, it can have some counter-intuitive implications: if all incomes in a society suddenly dropped sharply by exactly the same extent, leaving most of the society in a destitute situation from an absolute point of view, relative poverty would not change.
- **Hybrid poverty lines:** combine an absolute with a relative poverty line.[17]

The choice of which poverty line to use, and where to set the threshold (whether based on international convention or a national one, whether to use a food poverty line or a basic consumption basket, etc.), is a value judgement and a political choice. It also depends on the purpose of the poverty measure. Note that although the poverty line may divide the population into two neat groups, it may exaggerate differences between individual people. There may not be a marked difference between a person whose income is just a tiny bit above the poverty line and another just below it.[18]

Income poverty measurement: Aggregation

The next step is to aggregate the information we have about poor persons into a *poverty measure*, or poverty index.[19]

> **Definition:** a poverty measure is an index $P(y;z)$ that gives the level of poverty of distribution y, according to the poverty line z.

The most common poverty index is the **headcount ratio**, which reports the percentage of the population who are poor. For example, '32 per cent of people in Tartal are poor'. However as Box 6.6 discusses, the headcount ratio is a flawed measure. The most common way to improve the headcount ratio draws on what are called the Foster–Greer–Thorbecke (FGT) indices. This is a family of indices, which includes the headcount ratio as one of its members, but it has the advantage that other members of this family provide better incentives for policy-makers to address the very poorest of the poor. All members of the FGT family can be decomposed by district, ethnicity, rural–urban or any other categories of the population.

Two are widely used:

1. **Poverty Gap (FGT-1):** reflects the *depth* of poverty as well as the *headcount ratio*
2. **Squared Poverty Gap (FGT-2):** reflects the *headcount ratio*, the *depth* of poverty and the *inequality* among the poor. This measure prioritizes the poorest of the poor.

Box 6.6 Poverty measures and policy incentives

Headcount Poverty measures encourage policy-makers to reach out to the persons closest to the poverty line, not to the extreme poor.

In selecting which poverty measure to use, it can be helpful to think through the incentives that the measure provides to policy-makers. Clearly politicians will wish, in their annual speech, to report the biggest reduction in poverty they can. And poor people also might value such progress!

 poverty

Which poverty measure will help policy makers to focus on the persons most in need?

The headcount ratio is the most commonly used poverty measure worldwide. However it provides incentives for politicians to lift those persons who are closest to the poverty line over it. If a politician instead elects to help the extreme poor, the extra effort required will not improve the new headcount ratio. If we use the Poverty Gap measure (FGT-1) instead, the politician is equally proud of raising an extremely poor person's income by $10 as raising a person who is $10 below the poverty line above it. If we use the Squared  Poverty Gap measure (FGT-2), the politician has a far *bigger* triumph to report in her speech if she has helped the very poorest person than if she helped the poor person close to the poverty line.

Box 6.7 Key properties of poverty measures

As for inequality, many authors have identified the set of properties that a poverty measure should satisfy.[20] Not surprisingly, some of those properties are essentially the same for both poverty and inequality; others are specific to poverty measurement. **Symmetry** and **replication invariance** are also required for a poverty measure, such that the poverty level does not depend on who is poor or on the total size of the considered population. **Scale invariance** is also required, although in this context it demands the poverty measure not to change when all incomes *and* the poverty line change in the same proportion.[21] Two new properties are specific to poverty measurement. One of them, called the **focus** axiom, requires the poverty measure to be concerned exclusively with those who are poor. That is, an increase in the income of a non-poor person should not change the poverty level. The other principle, **monotonicity**, requires the poverty measure to increase whenever a poor person's income decreases. The **transfer** property from inequality measurement is also required in poverty measurement, but restricted to the set of the poor (we are not interested in what happens to the non-poor), so that if there is a progressive transfer between two poor people, poverty should decrease.[22] Two additional properties are particularly relevant for poverty measures. These are **subgroup consistency** and **additive decomposability**. **Subgroup consistency** demands that whenever poverty decreases (increases) in a given subgroup of the population, and the poverty level of all other groups remains unchanged, overall poverty should decrease (increase). One can imagine the discouragement to policy-makers if huge gains in reducing poverty in a specific region, or among a specific ethnic group, were not reflected in a reduction in the overall poverty level. **Additive decomposability** goes even further and requires the overall poverty level to equal the weighted sum of subgroup-poverty levels, where the weights are the population shares of each subgroup. A decomposable measure allows analysts to determine the percentage contribution of each specific subgroup to overall poverty. A decomposable measure is always subgroup consistent, but the converse is not true.[23]

The Foster–Greer–Thorbecke (FGT) poverty measures

This section presents the class of poverty measures that has been most widely used in empirical applications, which is the Foster, Greer and Thorbecke (1984) (FGT) class of poverty indices.[24] The headcount ratio is a special case of the FGT indices as we shall see. As well as being robust, this is a very easy class of measures to understand and to compute.

Given an income distribution $y = (y_1, y_2,...,y_n)$ and a poverty line z, start by calculating the normalized gap for each individual in the distribution. For incomes that are below the poverty line, the normalized gap is the distance between the poverty line and the income value, measured in poverty line units. For incomes that are above the poverty line, their income is replaced by z, the income at the poverty line (recall the focus axiom, we are not interested in incomes of the non-poor), so their normalized gap is simply zero. The normalized gaps are given by:

(5)
$$ g_i = \begin{cases} \left(\dfrac{z - y_i}{z} \right) & y_i < z \\ 0 & y_i \geq z \end{cases} $$

Now construct a vector $g^\alpha = (g_1^\alpha, g_2^\alpha,...,g_n^\alpha)$ where each element is the normalized gap raised to the power α, with $\alpha \geq 0$. The FGT class of measures are just the mean of that vector:

(6)
$$ P_\alpha(y;z) = \mu(g^\alpha) \qquad \alpha \geq 0 $$

Example: Consider four people whose incomes are $y = (7,2,4,8)$ and the poverty line $z = 5$.

The Headcount Ratio P_0

Let's consider first the case of $\alpha = 0$. Each gap raised to the 0 power just gives us a value of 1 if the person is poor and 0 if non-poor, so we can call the g^0 vector the *deprivation vector*. In this example: $g^0 = (0,1,1,0)$, indicating that the second and third persons in this distribution are poor. The mean of this vector – the P_0 measure – is one half: $P_0(y;z) = \mu(g^0) = 2/4$, indicating that 50 per cent of the population in this distribution is poor. This measure is known as the headcount ratio (or poverty incidence). Undoubtedly, it provides very useful information. However, as noted by Watts (1969) and Sen (1976), it gives neither information on the depth of poverty nor on its distribution among the poor. For example, if the third person became poorer, experiencing a decrease in her income so that the distribution became $y = (7,2,3,8)$, the measure would still be one half; that is: it violates monotonicity. Also, if there was a progressive transfer between the two poor persons, so that the distribution was $y = (7,3,3,8)$, the P_0 would not change either, violating the transfer principle. Certainly, the headcount ratio's insensitiveness to the depth and distribution of poverty is not a minor issue. It has direct policy implications. If this was the official poverty measure in a country (and unfortunately that is very often the case), a government interested in maximizing the impact of resources on poverty reduction would have all the incentives to allocate them among the least poor, those that are closer to the poverty line, leaving the lives of the poorest poor unchanged.

The Poverty Gap P_1 (or FGT-1)

Consider now the case of $\alpha = 1$. The $g^1(y)$ vector, which may be called the *normalized gap vector*, is for the example above, $g^1(y) = (0,3/5,1/5,0)$. The aggregate poverty measure P_1, is the mean of the normalized gap vector. In our example $P_1(y;z) = \mu(g^1) = 4/20$. As opposed to the headcount ratio P_0, the P_1 the measure *is* sensitive to the depth of poverty. It satisfies monotonicity. If the income of the third individual decreased so we had $(7,2,3,8)$ the normalized gap vector would now be $g^1(y) = (0,3/5,2/5,0)$ and P_1 would increase to $P_1 = 5/20$. All measures with $\alpha > 0$ satisfy monotonicity. However, a transfer from an extremely destitute person to a less poor person (who still is poor) would not change P_1, since the decrease in one gap would be exactly compensated by the increase in the other. Therefore, by being sensitive to the depth of poverty (i.e. satisfying monotonicity), the P_1 measure does make policy-makers want to decrease the depth of poverty (even if the poor person does not become non-poor). But because of its insensitivity to the distribution among the poor, the P_1 measure does not provide extra incentives to help the poorest poor.

The Squared Poverty Gap P_2 (or FGT-2)

Finally, consider the case of $\alpha = 2$. The $g^2(y)$ vector, which may be called the *squared gap vector*, is for the given example $g^2(y) = (0,9/25,1/25,0)$. The aggregate poverty measure P_2 is the mean of the normalized gap vector: $P_2(y;z) = \mu(g^2) = 10/100$. The P_2 measure is sensitive to the depth of poverty: if the income of the third person decreases in one monetary unit, the squared gap vector becomes $g^2(y) = (0,9/25,4/25,0)$, increasing the aggregate poverty level to $P_2 = 13/100$. Moreover, it is also sensitive to the distribution among the poor: if there is a transfer from the third to the second individual of one monetary unit $(7,2,4,8)$ becomes $(7,3,3,8)$, the squared gap vector becomes $g^2(y) = (0,4/25,4/25,0)$, decreasing the aggregate poverty level to $P_2 = 8/100$. By squaring the normalized gaps, the biggest gaps receive a higher weight, which has the effect of emphasizing the poorest poor and providing incentives for policy-makers to address their situation urgently. All measures with $\alpha > 1$ satisfy the transfer property.[25]

It is worth repeating that all measures of the FGT family are decomposable in subgroups of population, allowing the identification of each group's contribution to overall poverty.

Measuring development and well-being: The Human Development Index (HDI)

The inadequacy of income for representing people's well-being has been the central message of the human development and capability approach. Among the alternative indices to assess people's well-being, the *Human Development Reports* (HDR) have focused on four indices: the Human Development Index (HDI), the Human Poverty Index (HPI), the Gender related Development Index (GDI) and the Gender Empowerment Measure (GEM). In this section we will discuss the HDI, its critiques and possible amendments, and leave the HPI for discussion in the next section. Note that the HDI is not a poverty index (it does not use poverty lines) but rather reflects overall well-being.

The Human Development Index (HDI)

The HDI summarizes a country's total achievement in three dimensions of human development: health, education and standard of living. Within these dimensions, the indicators used are life expectancy at birth (name it H) to represent long lasting and healthy life, a weighted average of the literacy rate and the combined gross enrolment rate (name it E) to represent educational achievement, and per capita GDP adjusted for purchasing power parity to represent command over resources for a decent life (name it Y). In the computation of the index, the logarithm of the per capita GDP is used rather than the per capita GDP itself. This is to reflect the diminishing returns of income on development: as income increases, the enhancing effect of additional income increments on human development decreases (that is, 'human development does not require unlimited income' (HDR 2007/2008, Technical Note 1)). The three indicators are normalized according to some goalpost values, so that they range between 0 and 1.[26] The HDI is then obtained as the simple average of the three indicators.

(7) $HDI = [H + E + Y]/3$

It is worth noting that each of the indicators that compose the HDI are essentially the average or mean values of the corresponding variable (health, education and income) in the population. We can name the distribution of each of those variables in the population as h, e and y.[27] Given that the HDI is the average of these three indicators, the HDI is a 'mean of means' (Foster, Lopez-Calva and Székely, 2005):

(8) $HDI = \mu[\mu(h),\mu(e),\mu(y)]$

The power of the HDI lies in its simplicity and political content. It enables cross-country comparisons about their states of 'development' on other grounds than income per capita. However, there has been a lot of dispute surrounding the index. Among several, there are three salient critics: (1) the (arbitrary) selection of dimensions and indicators, (2) the (arbitrary) selection of weights and (3) the insensitiveness of the HDI to inequalities in the distribution of human development in the population.

The selection of dimensions and indicators

The construction of the HDI was driven to a great extent by the cross-country data available in 1990, as well as the need to generate a simple compelling policy message. Only three dimensions and four indicators are involved. However the HDI has been so powerful that many have come to associate human development only with health and education in addition to income. This led Fukuda-Parr to title an article 'Rescuing the Human Development Concept from the HDI' (Fukuda-Parr, 2000). The HDI does not include all capabilities that might be of interest. However, in addition to the composite indices (the HDI, the HPI, the GDI and the GEM), the *Human Development Reports* include a plethora of other data, which complement the information provided by the indices. Yet human development remains associated mainly with health and education.

The HDI – supposedly intending to measure objectives of human development (*ends*) – has also been criticized for retaining income as one of the relevant dimensions, because in the human development approach income is regarded exclusively as a *means*. The justification given is that the income variable serves 'as a surrogate for all the dimensions of human development not reflected in a long and healthy life' (HDR, 2007/2008, Technical Note 1).

Also, achievements across countries vary deeply in terms of the HDI indicators, which raises issues of policy relevance. Access to knowledge in the UK might not be adequately captured by literacy rates. Analogously, the ability to live healthy lives in the US might be more adequately represented in an obesity rate than infant mortality rate. While the HDI and HPI evolved two forms to improve their relevance to rich countries, issues remain.

Others criticize the specific choice of indicators because they are highly correlated with one another; choosing indicators with lower correlations would have created a more powerful index in some ways. Yet others argue that the HDI would have been of greater policy relevance if its indicators moved more swiftly in response to policy than life expectancy, and were all either stock or flow indicators.

Box 6.8 Beyond the HDI: What dimensions might matter?

In an attempt to go beyond the HDI, Ranis, Stewart and Samman (2006) identify 11 categories of human development. These are: **mental well-being, empowerment, political freedom, social relations, community well-being, inequality, work conditions, leisure conditions, economic stability, political security** and **environment conditions**. Within each category, they identify several existing internationally comparable indicators and estimate the correlations between each of them and the HDI. They find that a few of the considered indicators are highly correlated with the HDI, and therefore not worth including. However, most indicators in each category have little correlation with the HDI and could be included, as when assessing human development (p342).

The problem of the availability of cross-country data in these areas remains. A practical attempt to increase the data available on 'Missing dimensions' of human development is led by the Oxford Poverty and Human Development Initiative (www.ophi.org.uk). Its 'Missing Dimensions' work seeks to develop internationally comparable indicators and to add modules on these dimensions in standardized survey instruments. The selected missing dimensions of well-being are (Alkire, 2007, p348): **employment**: particularly informal employment and safety at work; **empowerment or agency**: the ability to advance goals one values and has reason to value; **physical safety**: focusing on security from violence to property and person, and perceived violence; **the ability to go about without shame**: to emphasize the importance of dignity, respect and freedom from humiliation, and **psychological and subjective well-being**: to emphasize meaning, its determinants, and satisfaction.

The selection of weights

A second criticism of the HDI has been the arbitrary set of weights. Why does the literacy rate weights twice the gross enrolment rate within the education indicator? And within the HDI, why are all dimensions equally weighted? There is also a tension between the perception that the dimensions are equally weighted, and the fact that the normalization process introduces less visible inequalities in weights between the dimensions.[28]

Inequalities in human development

A third salient criticism is that the HDI fails to capture inequality in the distribution of human development across the population. One possibility to highlight inequalities would be to compute the HDI for different populations. Most frequently, the available data are aggregate; that is, they are the average values *H*, *E* and *Y* for a population. This is a problem because to highlight inequalities one needs data for each person or household. One way forward is to use the mean achievement of some population group, such as income quintile, gender, race, caste, religion or geographical area (so that one could use a mean value of *H*, *E* and *Y* for each group). For example Grimm et al (2006) suggest that the HDI be calculated for each income quintile to show transparently the inequality in HDI among economic classes. The quintile-based measure is a very simple and intuitive way to explore inequality, but faces challenges in matching income quintiles to health and education outcomes. Income fluctuates more than health and education, and also the inequalities in income are higher, so this measure implicitly gives income inequality a greater weight than inequalities in other dimensions.

Another possibility would be to slightly adapt the structure of the HDI to capture inequalities. To do this we require data for *each* person or household. This means we would need to replace life expectancy – which is estimated for a population – with some other health variable. The basic idea is very simple and is as follows. The HDI is a 'mean of means' – the average life expectancy, average educational outcomes and average income for a population are themselves averaged (added up and divided by 3) to obtain the HDI. If we construct the HDI *exactly* as before, but instead of using a simple average (the mean – which refers to the distributionally-neutral arithmetic mean) use a mean that pays more attention to the achievements of the poorest, then the HDI will *automatically* reflect inequality. Such a structure has been proposed by Foster, Lopez-Calva and Székely, 2005 (FLS from now on), and is described in Box 6.9.

Box 6.9 An inequality adjusted HDI

Foster, Lopez-Calva and Székely (2005) propose an inequality adjusted HDI that satisfies a number of desirable principles, and is easy to compute. There are two steps to calculate it from individual or household level data.

First take the β-mean of the distribution of each of the HDI variables (recall the HDI just uses the 'average' – the arithmetic mean – for each dimension). A value of β < 1 needs to be used (usually either β = 0 or β = −1) because then if the variable is perfectly equally distributed among people, the β-mean equals the arithmetic mean, but if there is inequality, the β-mean will be lower than the arithmetic mean (note that if β = 1, the original HDI is obtained). So now the component indicators for each dimension are the β-means rather than the 'averages' or arithmetic means of that dimension.

Second, to aggregate these indicators in an index of human development, whereas the HDI uses the average or arithmetic mean of the three dimensions, take the β-mean of the three, using the same value of β as before. If more than one value of β is reported, a *family* of human development indices is obtained. Whereas the HDI is a mean of means, the inequality adjusted HDI is a 'general means of general means'.

(8) $$HDI_\beta = \mu_\beta[\mu_\beta(h), \mu_\beta(e), \mu_\beta(y)] \qquad \text{for } \beta \leq 1$$

In this way, when $\beta < 1$, this index not only penalizes inequalities in the distribution of a certain outcome across the population (in the first step), but it also penalizes uneven developments *across* dimensions (in the second step). The value of the index for a country with similar values of $\mu_\beta(h)$, $\mu_\beta(e)$, and $\mu_\beta(y)$ will be higher than the value for a country with very different levels of the three β-means.[29] Also, this measure is the same if you aggregate instead first across dimensions for each person or household, and then the β-mean across people.

Notwithstanding these critiques, as well as others, the HDI has been highly successful in doing what it was created to do, to dethrone GDP and direct attention to social achievements. This index has been essentially created as a strategic and political tool. In his preface to *Readings in Human Development*, Sen calls the HDI an 'instrument of public communication'. However, after almost two decades of use, it may be helpful to develop additional measures of both progress and poverty that address some of the criticisms, especially as data collection procedures have been improving both in terms of the number and type of covered dimensions, and of internationally comparable indicators.

Multi-dimensional poverty measurement

Since the advent of the HPI in 1997, multi-dimensional poverty measures have risen to prominence. This is due partly to the energy of the human development approach, and Sen and others' writings regarding the ethical importance of expanding different capabilities. It is also due to the wide availability of better data. Better poverty measures are in demand. Efficient poverty reduction entails analysis of the interconnections between different kinds of deprivation that trap poor people in poverty. And the targeting of benefits to the poorest requires measures to identify those who suffer multiple deprivations at the same time.

The interest in multi-dimensional poverty measures is driven by three goals:

- **National poverty measures**: Income-based poverty lines are increasingly regarded as insufficient, and many countries are also constructing indices of multiple deprivation that better capture the well-being or deprivation of their citizens over time.
- **Identify beneficiaries for targeted public programmes**: In many countries, certain public services are targeted to the poor, but targeting methods based on income data alone can be error-ridden. Multi-dimensional measures can be cheaper and more accurate.
- **Evaluate progress**: Multi-dimensional measures can be constructed for monitoring and evaluation, and can contribute to assessing the impacts of policies and programmes.

Multi-dimensional measures are not perfect. But they are improving. A useful measure needs to be:

- understandable and easy to describe, so it facilitates policy-making and public debate;
- flexible, so it can fit different purposes and contexts;
- technically robust;
- operationally viable given existing data; and
- easily replicable by analysts in country (Székely, 2006).

Of course measurement alone is not enough. It needs to be complemented by causal analyses, as well as political engagement.

Steps to constructing a multi-dimensional measure

When measuring multi-dimensional poverty, several choices need to be made, some of which are common to the uni-dimensional case and some of which are specific to the multi-dimensional case. Several have already been mentioned. In what follows, we will briefly describe each practical step that needs to be taken to construct a multi-dimensional poverty measure.

Choice of the unit of analysis

A first decision regards the unit of analysis. Is it the individual, the household, cities, regions, countries? None is perfect. Frequently the household is selected (for reasons of data availability) and all members of a household identified as poor are considered poor. This ignores intra-household distribution of resources as well as variations in inherently personal variables such as nutrition, empowerment and health. All units have strengths and weaknesses.

Order of aggregation

There are two kinds of poverty measures. Some aggregate first across people and then across dimensions (HPI). These can use data from any source, but they cannot look at the breadth of poverty each person or household suffers. Others aggregate first across all dimensions for the same person or household, and then across people. These are very appealing because they consider the multiplicity of deprivations every household or person suffers. The difficulty is that they require data from the same survey instrument. Choosing the order of aggregation influences the possible measures, as only a few measures are path independent (have the same value regardless of the order of aggregation) such as FLS' HDI_β.

Choice of dimensions

Another crucial choice regards the selection of dimensions. As we have seen, the capability approach does not prescribe one list of capabilities that should be considered. The dimensions often vary depending on the context and purpose of the measure. As Sen observes (1996, pp57–58), 'in dealing with extreme poverty in developing economies, we may be able to concentrate, to a great extent on a relatively small number of centrally important functionings and the corresponding basic capabilities . . . In other contexts, the list may have to be longer and more diverse.'

Nussbaum (2003) argues in favour of her list of ten central human capabilities (in the case of constitutional guarantees) to assure that the capability approach carries critical force. Even if hers and other conventions are useful to stir the imagination, Sen (2004) reiterates the need to engage public debate, and not fix a list from the sidelines which is deaf to public reasoning and to the particularities of that measurement context.

Alkire (2008) noted that most researchers have drawn implicitly on one or more of five selection methods. These are:

1   *Existing data or convention*: To select dimensions mostly because of convenience or a convention, or because these are the only data available with the requisite characteristics. If one is not gathering data directly, this is a necessary but insufficient reason.
2   *Theory*: To select dimensions based on implicit or explicit assumptions about what people do value or should value. This can be useful, if combined with 3 or 4.
3   *Public 'consensus'*: To select dimensions using a list that has achieved a degree of legitimacy due to public consensus. Examples include human rights, the MDGs, and the Sphere project (a set of minimum standards in disaster response) or national plans. This is useful, particularly in combination with 4 or if various actors can publicly scrutinize them.
4   *Ongoing deliberative participatory processes*: To select dimensions on the basis of ongoing purposive participatory exercises that regularly elicit the values and perspectives of stakeholders. This is useful if participation is relatively wide and undistorted.
5   *Empirical evidence regarding people's values*: To select dimensions on the basis of empirical data on consumer preferences and behaviours, or psychological studies of which values are most relevant. This can be useful in combination with 3 or 4 (but not alone).

Clearly, these methods overlap and the choice of methods will rightly vary by context.

Robeyns (2006) strongly advocates that however dimensions are selected, researchers, analysts and government officials should write up explicitly in their papers or reports the process they used in order to foster public debate and feedback. She suggests that the write-ups should *explicitly formulate* why the dimensions or indicators are claimed to be things people value and have reason to value. They should *justify the methodology* by which dimensions were selected. And they should articulate the dimensions that are important but were *omitted due to feasibility considerations* such as missing data.

The choice of dimensions is interconnected with the choice of weights *between* dimensions (addressed later). For example, dimensions might be chosen such that they are of relatively equal weight. This, indeed, is the recommendation given by Atkinson et al (2002, p25) in their work on social indicators in Europe: 'the interpretation of the set of indicators is greatly eased where the individual components have degrees of importance that, while not necessarily exactly equal, are not grossly different'.

Choice of variables/indicator(s) for dimensions

Once the selection of dimensions has been accomplished, it is necessary to select the variables or indicators within each dimension that are appropriate to the purpose of the measure. One consideration is whether to choose indicators of resources, functionings, utility or (where possible) capability. For example, if the underlying framework is that of the capability approach, the researcher might seek indicators of *functionings* rather than resources or *basic needs*. '[B]asic needs are usually defined in terms of means rather than outcomes, for instance, as living in the proximity of providers of health care services (but not necessarily being in good health), as the number of years of achieved schooling (but not necessarily being literate), as living in a democracy (but not necessarily participating in the life of the community), and so on' (Duclos and Araar, 2006, Part I). Other things being equal, one will select indicators that are a strong proxy for the dimension and are not highly correlated with other indicators in the measure. If we select more than one indicator per dimension, we must decide whether to combine them into a dimensional index, or use each indicator directly.

Choice of poverty lines

As in the uni-dimensional case, poverty lines need to be selected. A desirable method is to set a poverty line for each indicator or dimension. In the multi-dimensional context, absolute lines have typically been used. They reflect a value judgement about poverty – but are often based on some national or international consensus. Examples of these are the thresholds set by the MDGs. However they are set, it is important to make explicit the process through which the values of the poverty lines were decided. Analysis of the sensitivity and robustness of rankings to changes in one or more poverty line are also essential.

Choice of the identification criterion

In the uni-dimensional case, identification was easy: anyone who earned less than the poverty line was poor; anyone who did not was not poor. In the multi-dimensional case, we have to decide the *range* or number of dimensions used to identify a poor person. If a person is deprived in *any* one dimension, do we consider them multi-dimensionally poor? If we say yes we take the *union approach*. If a person must instead be deprived in *all* dimensions before we consider them poor, we are taking the *intersection approach*. It is also possible to take an intermediary *counting approach* – for example everyone who is deprived in any 3 of 7 dimensions. If the dimensions are not equally weighted, we use the weighted sum of dimensions instead (Alkire and Foster, 2007).

Choice of weights

In the capability approach, because capabilities are of intrinsic value, the relative weights on different capabilities or dimensions are value judgements. Weights can be applied in three ways in multi-dimensional poverty measures: (i) *between* capabilities and dimensions (the relative weight of nutrition and education for example), (ii) *within* dimensions (if more than one indicator of mobility is used for example), and (iii) *among* people in the distribution (to give greater priority to the most disadvantaged, for example).[30]

Weights between dimensions can represent:

1   the enduring *importance* of a capability relative to other capabilities (long term) or
2   the *priority* of expanding one capability relative to others in planning and policy.

In practice, weights on indicators that are aggregated *within* dimensions are often set as equal (which is a value judgement), or else are generated by a statistical process. Weights *among* people are often accomplished through the choice of aggregation such as the FGT-2 in income space, rather than through explicit distributional weights.

Weights are also implicitly influenced by technical issues, such as the number and choice of dimensions/indicators, the poverty line and, where relevant, the transformation function. For example, the use of a very low poverty line for one dimension (few people are deprived) and a high poverty line for another (many are deprived) will implicitly give more weight to the dimension in which many people are deprived.

In summary, 'since any choice of weights should be open to public debate, it is crucial that the judgements that are implicit in such weighting be made as clear and comprehensible as possible and thus be open to public scrutiny' (Anand and Sen, 1997, p6).[31]

Choice of the poverty measure

When these decisions have been made, it is possible to select the methodology by which a composite index will be created. The next section introduces two measures – the HPI, as an example of a measure that aggregates first across people, and the Alkire and Foster (2007), which aggregates first across deprivations for each person or household.

> **Box 6.10** A multi-dimensional poverty measure
>
> Many new multi-dimensional poverty measures are being developed, and are likely to emerge in the next few years. For example Alkire and Foster (2007) have developed a new set of measures that are simple, flexible for different contexts, easy to use, and academically robust. They construct four measures:

H – this is the headcount ratio of all persons who are identified as multi-dimensionally poor.

$M_0 = HA$ – this is the headcount ratio times A, the average *breadth* of dimensions poor people suffer.

$M_1 = HAG$ – this also considers the *depth* of deprivation in each dimension.

$M_2 = HAS$ – this also considers *inequality* among the poor. It prioritizes the poorest of the poor.

The main features of all this class of measures are:

- **The choice of dimensions and indicators is flexible**, and can be chosen locally.
- **Equal or variable weights** can be used. Policy-makers can choose what weights to set.
- **The data can be cardinal, ordinal or categorical**. Most measures require cardinal data.
- **The measure reflects the breadth of poverty** – the multiplicity of deprivations every household faces.
- **The identification of 'who is poor' is transparent**. The headcount ratio builds on the 'counting method' used widely by NGOs – a household is considered poor if it is deprived – for example – in any 3 of 9 dimensions, with the dimensions being equally weighted. As the number of dimensions goes up, it is like a magnifying glass, and focuses more and more acutely on the poorest of the poor.
- The final measure is one number. But what will be most interesting to policy-makers is that **the measure can be decomposed and compared** for example by state, by ethnic group, or (if the unit of analysis is the person) by gender or age.
- The M_0, M_1 and M_2 measures **can be broken down by dimension**, so policy-makers can see immediately what components of poverty are the biggest in different states or regions. Often this varies a great deal.

Measures of multi-dimensional poverty

Measures using aggregate data: The Human Poverty Index (HPI)

The Human Poverty Index (HPI), the fourth companion to the HDI, was introduced in the 1997 *Human Development Report*. Although very limited, it is a measure of multi-dimensional poverty that can be calculated in the absence of disaggregated data. The HPI looks at the same three dimensions as the HDI: health, education and standard of living. It differs from the HDI in that it focuses on deprivations, not achievements. There are two versions of the HPI, one for developing countries (HPI-1), the other for developed countries (HPI-2).

The indicators used for the HPI-1 are, the probability at birth of not surviving to the age of 40, the adult literacy rate, and the equally weighted average of (1) the percentage of population without access to an improved water source and (2) the percentage of children under weight for their age. The three indicators are deprivation indicators, name them DH, DE and DY (as in the HDI, the indicators are normalized to range between 0 and 1). Analogously to the case of the HDI, if dh, de and dy represent the distribution of deprivation among the population in each of the three dimensions, the indicators can be seen as the average deprivation across the population: $DH = \mu(dh)$, $DH = \mu(de)$, $DH = \mu(dy)$. However, the aggregation uses general means. The HPI-1 is obtained as the β-mean of these three average deprivations, using a value of $\beta = 3$, which emphasizes inequality and the condition of the poorest.

(9) $HPI - 1 = [(DH^3 + DE^3 + DY^3)/3]^{1/3} = \mu_3(\mu(dh),\mu(de),\mu(dy))$

Because the elements of the index are deprivation indicators rather than indicators of achievements, $\beta = 3$ is used to penalize countries for inequality across dimensions giving a higher weight to the dimensions that present higher levels of deprivations.

More demanding thresholds are used in HPI-2, and the HPI-2 includes a fourth dimension, 'social exclusion'.

The indicators of deprivation are: the probability at birth of not living to the age of 60, the percentage of adults (between 15 and 65 years) lacking functional literacy skills, the percentage of the population below the income poverty line (defined as 50 per cent of the median household income) and, for the social exclusion dimension, the rate of long-term unemployment (12 months or more). These indicators also correspond to the mean deprivation in each dimension, and the aggregation for the HPI-2 also uses the β-mean of order 3.

Both versions of the HPI provide summary information on aggregate deprivation, which is mainly helpful for constructing rankings between countries and regions. However, when designing policies, one may wish to identify the groups to target more specifically as well as the dimensions with the highest deprivation incidences and depths. For this reason one much newer and less established measure is introduced, because it is user friendly, robust and can be implemented with existing data.

Measures using disaggregate data: Alkire and Foster (2007)
In this sub-section we present one family of measures of multi-dimensional poverty developed at the Oxford Poverty and Human Development Initiative (OPHI) by Alkire and Foster (2007) (AF measure). It looks at all the deprivations that batter a person or household together. The family of measures is a multi-dimensional extension of the uni-dimensional FGT class of poverty indices, introduced above. It is important to remark that other measures of multi-dimensional poverty have been proposed in the literature as by Tsui (2002), Bourguignon and Chakravarty (2003 – this is also a multi-dimensional extension of the FGT class) and Maasoumi and Lugo (2008), and counting-based measures are widely used in policy. We have chosen to present

the AF measure because (1) it can be used with ordinal data, and (2) it uses a new identification criterion for the multi-dimensionally poor (most of the others use the *union* approach to identification), and (3) it can be decomposed by group and broken down by dimension, which brings a great deal of insight to policy.

As in the unidimensional case, there is a set of desirable properties for a multi-dimensional poverty measure. Most of them are natural extensions from the uni-dimensional case, which were introduced in the second section. For simplicity, we avoid its enumeration here, but mention them when describing the different members of the family of measures presented here.[32]

The raw information for this family of measures is a matrix which gives the achievements of each person i, with $i = 1,...,n$, in each dimension $j = 1,...,d$. For simplicity, assume for the moment, that each dimension has one indicator, that each dimension is equally weighted and that we have data for individuals. Name such matrix X:

Dimensions

$$\text{Achievement Matrix } X = \begin{bmatrix} x_{11} & x_{12} & \cdots & x_{1d} \\ \cdot & \cdot & & \\ \cdot & & \cdot & \cdot \\ x_{n1} & x_{n2} & \cdots & x_{nd} \end{bmatrix} \text{Persons}$$

Poverty lines $z = [z_1 \ z_2 \ ... \ z_d]$

Each entry of the matrix x_i indicates the achievement of person i in dimension j. Each row of the matrix indicates the achievements of individual i in the d dimensions, whereas each column indicates the distribution of achievements in a specific dimension across the population. For each dimension, a poverty line is defined. The poverty lines can be presented in vector $z = (z_1, z_2,...,z_d)$, where z_j is the poverty line of dimension j. Similarly to the procedure followed in the uni-dimensional case (described in the third section), one can define a normalized gap for each individual in each dimension. For achievements that are below the poverty line, this gap is given by the distance between the poverty line in that dimension and the achievement, measured in poverty line units. If the person's achievement is at or above the corresponding poverty line, the normalized gap is zero.

(10)   Normalized gap
        for each person

$$g_{ij} = \begin{cases} \left(\dfrac{z_j - x_{ij}}{z_j} \right) & x_{ij} < z_j \\ 0 & x_{ij} \geq z_j \end{cases}$$

Now, we can create matrix G^{α}, which contains each normalized gap raised to the power α (with $\alpha \geq 0$):

$$G^{\alpha} = \begin{bmatrix} g_{11}^{\alpha} & g_{12}^{\alpha} & \cdots & g_{1d}^{\alpha} \\ \cdot & \cdot & & \cdot \\ \cdot & & \cdot & \cdot \\ g_{n1}^{\alpha} & g_{n2}^{\alpha} & \cdots & g_{nd}^{\alpha} \end{bmatrix} \qquad \text{'count' vector } c = \begin{bmatrix} c_1 \\ \cdot \\ \cdot \\ c_n \end{bmatrix}$$

At this point one needs to define an identification criterion of the multi-dimensionally poor. The authors propose the following. Consider the matrix G^0, in which all entries are 1 if the individual is deprived in that dimension, or 0 if she is not. With such matrix one can 'count' the number of deprivations that each individual in the distribution has, and construct a vector $c = (c_1,...,c_n)'$ where each element c_i indicates on how many dimensions person i is deprived. Then, it is a matter of deciding on how many dimensions should someone be deprived so as to be considered multi-dimensionally poor. That is equivalent to setting a second poverty line, which the authors call the 'dimension cutoff', and name it k. A person i is considered multi-dimensionally poor if $c_i \geq k$.

This is why the approach is said to use a *dual cutoff*, first the *within* dimension cutoffs z_j and second, the *across* dimensions cutoff k. The decision on the value of k is left to the researcher, and several different values can be tested. One could set k = 1, requiring an individual to be deprived in at least one dimension to be considered multi-dimensionally poor, and this would correspond to the *union approach*. Others would set k = d, requiring an individual to be deprived in all the considered dimensions so as to be multi-dimensionally poor, the *intersection approach*. Clearly, other intermediate values for k may be more appropriate.

Once the multi-dimensionally poor have been identified, one wants to focus only on them. To do that, the normalized gaps of people who have not been identified as multi-dimensionally poor are replaced by zero. Name this censored normalized gaps as $g_{ij}(k)$. These are given by:

(11)
$$g_{ij}^{\alpha}(k) = \begin{cases} g_{ij}^{\alpha} & c_i \geq k \\ 0 & c_i < k \end{cases}$$

With these censored gaps, one can construct the censored matrix :

$$G^{\alpha}(k) = \begin{bmatrix} g_{11}^{\alpha}(k) & g_{12}^{\alpha}(k) & \cdots & g_{1d}^{\alpha}(k) \\ \cdot & \cdot & & \cdot \\ \cdot & & \cdot & \cdot \\ g_{n1}^{\alpha}(k) & g_{n2}^{\alpha}(k) & \cdots & g_{nd}^{\alpha}(k) \end{bmatrix}$$

The multi-dimensional poverty measure of AF is simply obtained as the mean of this matrix:

(12) $$M_\alpha(X;z) = \mu(G^\alpha(k)) \qquad \alpha \geq 0$$

Example: An example will help to clarify the computation of the measures and some of the salient members of this family. Suppose that there are four people and four considered dimensions, say, consumption, years of education, empowerment and access to health care. For the purpose of a numerical example the dimensions itself could be any. The matrix of achievements and the vector of poverty lines are given by:

$$X = \begin{bmatrix} 13.1 & 14 & 4 & 1 \\ 15.2 & 7 & 5 & 0 \\ 12.5 & 10 & 1 & 0 \\ 20 & 11 & 3 & 1 \end{bmatrix}$$

$$z = (\ 13 \quad 12 \quad 3 \quad 1)$$

Then, the G^0 matrix, and the vector of deprivation counts c, are given by:

$$G^0 = \begin{bmatrix} 0 & 0 & 0 & 0 \\ 0 & 1 & 0 & 1 \\ 1 & 1 & 1 & 1 \\ 0 & 1 & 0 & 0 \end{bmatrix} \qquad c = \begin{bmatrix} 0 \\ 2 \\ 4 \\ 1 \end{bmatrix}$$

Suppose that a cutoff of $k = 2$ is selected. The second and third person will be considered multi-dimensionally poor, but not the fourth person. The $G^\alpha(k)$ matrix is therefore given by:

$$G^\alpha(k) = \begin{bmatrix} 0 & 0 & 0 & 0 \\ 0 & 0.42^\alpha & 0 & 1^\alpha \\ 0.04^\alpha & 0.17^\alpha & 0.67^\alpha & 1^\alpha \\ 0 & 0 & 0 & 0 \end{bmatrix}$$

The Multidimensional Headcount Ratio H

One first intuitive measure, which is not a member of the $M\alpha$ family, is the multi-dimensional headcount ratio. That is, the fraction of the population that is multi-dimensionally poor $H = q/n$, where q is the number of multi-dimensionally poor. In this example, $H = 1/2$. In the uni-dimensional case, we noted that the headcount ratio is insensitive to the depth and distribution of poverty, and that remains true in the multi-dimensional case. Moreover, the multi-dimensional headcount ratio is not sensitive to the number of deprivations the poor experience. For example, if the second person becomes deprived in three dimensions rather than two, the multi-dimensional headcount ratio would not change.[33] For this reason, the multi-dimensional H is said not to satisfy *dimensional monotonicity*.

The Adjusted Headcount Ratio M_0

The first member of the $M\alpha$ family is the adjusted headcount ratio M_0, obtained as the mean of the $G^0(k)$ matrix. In this case, $M_0 = HA = (0.5)(0.75) = 0.375$. Note that M_0 is lower than H, and that is precisely why it is called the 'adjusted' headcount ratio: it is the multi-dimensional headcount ratio (H) multiplied by the average deprivation share among the poor (A). The average deprivation share among the poor can be obtained adding the number of deprivations of the multi-dimensionally poor and dividing them by the total number of deprivations and poor people. In this case: $A = (2 + 4)/(4*2) = 3/4$. Now it is clear that $M_0 = HA = (0.5)(0.75) = 0.375$ – which is, again, the mean of the matrix. Note that if the second person became deprived in the first dimension – consumption, the M_0 measure would increase to $M_0 = 7/16 = 0.437$, because the average deprivation share among the poor would increase, satisfying dimensional monotonicity. However, if any of the multi-dimensionally poor became more deprived in one dimension, M_0 would not change, violating monotonicity. (For example, if the third person had 9 years of education rather than 10, M_0 would be the same).

The Adjusted Poverty Gap M_1

Consider now the actual value of each normalized gap – just as we did for the poverty gap earlier. In other words, we have $\alpha = 1$. Immediately we can see that the mean of the matrix is $M_1 = 3.3/16 = 0.206$. But what does that mean? This measure is the product of three informative partial indices. In addition to HA, it considers the average poverty gap G across all instances in which poor persons are deprived. Here, $G = (0.04 + 0.42 + 0.17 + 0.67 + 1 + 1)/6 = 0.55$. So the formula is $M_1 = HAG = (0.5)(0.75)(0.55) = 0.206$. It is worth noting that, because M1 is based on the poverty gaps that individuals experience, if a poor person becomes more deprived in one dimension, the M_1 measure will increase, satisfying monotonicity (as well as all members of the family with $\alpha > 0$). (If the third person had 9 years of education rather than 10, $M_1 = 3.38/16 = 0.211$). However, as in the poverty gap, an increase in deprivation counts the same for the barely poor and for the extreme poor. To favour the poorest of the poor we turn to the M_2 measure.

The Adjusted Squared Poverty Gap M_2

Now we consider the matrix of squared gaps, just like we considered the squared gaps for the FGT-2 index earlier. Here $\alpha = 2$. The mean of the matrix is now $M_2 = 2.66/16 = 0.166$. As with the previous members of the family, this measure is also the product of other informative partial indices. We replace the average gap G, by the average squared gap, which represents the severity of deprivations S across all instances in which poor persons are deprived. Here $S = (0.04^2 + 0.42^2 + 0.17^2 + 0.67^2 + 1^2 + 1^2)/6 = 0.44$. So the formula for $M_2 = HAS = (0.5)(0.75)(0.44) = 0.166$. This measure satisfies monotonicity and, moreover, favours the extreme poor. For example, if the third person had 9 years of education rather than 10, then M_2 would increase to $M_2 = 0.168$, whereas if the second person had 6 years of education rather than 7, this would increase M_2 to $M_2 = 0.170$. This measure (and all members of the family with $\alpha > 1$ satisfies the multi-dimensional transfer principle).

All members of the $M\alpha$ measures satisfy a very useful property for designing policy: they are decomposable in subgroups of people, and – after the identification step has been completed – they can also be broken down by dimensions. In this way, it is possible to identify the percentage contribution of a particular group to overall multi-dimensional poverty, as well as the percentage contribution of deprivation in each particular dimension to overall multi-dimensional poverty.

This presentation of the $M\alpha$ family of measures used equal weights for simplicity. However, any weighting structure can be used. Let $w = (w_1, w_2, \ldots, w_d)$ be a d dimensional row vector, where each element w_j is the weight associated with dimension j. The weights must add to the total number of dimensions ($\sum_{j=1}^{d} w_j = d$). One can define the matrix G^α, where the typical element is the weighted normalized gap $g_{ij}^\alpha = w_j((z_j - x_{ij})/z_j)^\alpha$, when $x_{ij} < z_j$, while $g_{ij}^\alpha = 0$ otherwise. As before, one can obtain a vector of deprivation counts c_i, which indicates for each individual the *weighted* number of dimensions in which she is deprived (for example if an individual is deprived in consumption and health, and consumption has a weight of 2, while health has a weight of 0.5, then $c_i = 2.5$ and not 2, as it would be with equal weights). The dimensional cutoff for the identification step of the multi-dimensionally poor k, now ranges between the minimum weight ($k = \min\{w_j\}$, which corresponds to the union approach) and the total number of dimensions ($k = d$, which corresponds to the intersection approach). As before, once the multi-dimensionally poor have been identified, the censored matrix $G^\alpha(k)$ can be defined, and $M\alpha$ be calculated as the mean of such matrix.[34]

As a last comment on these measures, it should be noted that they treat dimensions as independent rather than assuming all are substitutes or all are complements. The issue on how to account for interactions across dimensions (either substitutability or complementarity) is a much discussed topic in multi-dimensional poverty measurement and although some proposals have been made (such as Bourguignon and Chakravarty's (2003) measures – which however cannot be broken down by dimension), no consensus has been achieved yet.

Measuring freedom

Most frequently, when trying to measure multi-dimensional poverty or inequality from the capability approach, researchers measure functionings rather than capabilities. This might seem disappointing, given the importance the human development approach places on freedom. However, as an increasing number of researchers have become interested in the capability approach, understanding it as the appropriate space in which well-being, inequality and poverty should be assessed, more creative ways of measuring freedoms (that is, obtaining information on the capability sets) are being devised. Some methods at the research stage include the following:

- If multi-dimensional measures aggregate functionings that nearly everyone reasonably values, and if these functionings are not coercively imposed, then multi-dimensional measures of functionings poverty might be interpreted to reflect unfreedoms directly.
- Drawing on functioning-specific data on whether a person's actions are coerced or are motivated by their own values, a capability measure could summarize the ordered pairs representing the achieved functionings and the respective agencies of each person.
- It may be possible to map capabilities onto 'equivalent incomes' which would usefully connect the capability approach and other economic analyses.
- Some researchers use subjective data regarding people's perceptions of their opportunities in different domains as direct measures of capabilities.
- It may be possible theoretically and/or empirically to estimate the size of the capability set associated with certain discrete functioning choices.
- Even if it is not possible to map the capability set directly, data on income and time use (at least) could be used to map the binding constraints on the capability set.

In any case, as we said at the start of this chapter, quantitative measurement is only one part of the set of activities that comprise human development. Whether or not user friendly and accurate direct measures of capabilities emerge, people's freedoms and agency can be advanced by the human development approach in other ways.

Questions

6.1 If you were responsible for the Statistical Office of your government, how would you measure income inequality in your country?

6.2 Without doing any calculations, which of these two income distributions do you think has a higher Gini coefficient: $X = (6,3,13,8)$ or $Y = (7,3,7,13)$? Why? Which one has a higher Atkinson's measure with $\beta = -1$? Why? What do the Lorenz curves of these two distributions look like? Now verify your 'informed guesses' by doing the calculations.

6.3 If you had to advise your government on which income poverty measure to use to guide policy, which one would you recommend? Why?

6.4 If your organization was interested in measuring multi-dimensional poverty, which dimensions and indicators would you use – or by what process would you decide? Why?

6.4 Suppose that you have data from your country at the regional level. Suppose that there are three regions, and that evaluation is being done in three dimensions: health, education and income. Suppose that you have the information on the achievements in these areas, already normalized, given by:

$$D = \begin{bmatrix} 0.5 & 0.6 & 0.4 \\ 0.7 & 0.7 & 0.7 \\ 0.9 & 0.7 & 0.5 \end{bmatrix}.$$

Each row of this matrix indicates the achievements of each region in the three development dimensions. According to FLS' index of human development HDI_β, and using a value of $\beta = -1$, what is the value of this index for the country? What is the value for each of the regions? What are the aggregate and regional values of human development using the traditional HDI? Compare the aggregate country values as well as the regions' ranking obtained with the two indices. Why are they different?

6.5 What happens to the value of M_0 as k increases? In terms of policy implication, what do you think would be some of the drawbacks of using the union approach to identify the multi-dimensionally poor, and what would be the drawbacks of using the intersection approach?

6.6 Discuss the statistics and graphs available at http://www.gapminder.org/ (a non-profit venture promoting sustainable global development and achievement of the MDGs by increased use and understanding of statistics and other information about social, economic and environmental development at local, national and global levels). What strikes you?

Notes

1   Many resources for the integrated analyses of poverty can be found on the Q-squared website, http://www.q-squared.ca/

2   In fact, there have been proposals of ways in which the most commonly used inequality indices (originated in the personal distribution approach) can be decomposed by income source, such as by Shorrocks (1999).

3   This goes beyond the usual incorporation of 'adult equivalent scales', which is merely based on nutritional aspects according to age and gender.

4   For more discussion on these issues see Ravallion (1996).

5   Shorrocks and Foster (1987) provide additional conditions by which two distributions can be ranked when their Lorenz curves cross once. Still this does not eliminate all the incompleteness.

6   Three well known additional properties are *transfer sensitivity* (when the measure is more sensitive to transfers at the lower end of the distribution), *subgroup consistency* (so that whenever inequality rises in a population subgroup, overall inequality also increases) and *additive decomposability* (such that total inequality can be expressed as the sum of a *within*-group inequality and a *between*-group inequality). For an in-depth discussion of these additional properties, see Foster and Sen (1997).

7   'Bad' measures of inequality include the range, the Kuznets ratio, the relative mean deviation and the variance of logarithms, all of which violate the transfer property, and also the variance, which violates scale invariance. For further discussion on these measures, see Sen (1973) and Foster and Sen (1997).

8   More precisely, the decomposition of the Gini coefficient into an inequality between and an inequality within groups *is* possible when the distributions of the groups do not overlap. When they overlap, a residual term needs to be added to the equation. For details on this, see Foster and Sen (1997, p153).

9   This draws on Prof. James E. Foster's class notes of his course *Distribution and Development* at Vanderbilt University, available in the teaching section of www.ophi.org.uk.

10   Foster and Sen (1997, pp125–127) provide a useful graphical representation of the EDE income and the associated inequality measure.

11   Note that incomes need to be strictly positive, that is why we refer to $A_\beta = 1$ as a limiting case.

12   This presentation of the generalized entropy measures follows Foster and Sen (1997, pp140–141).

13   Foster and Shneyerov (1999) noted that for $\beta < 1$, the generalized entropy measures are (as Atkinson's measures) a decreasing function of (μ_β/μ), with $\mu_\beta \leq \mu$, whereas for $\beta > 1$ they are an increasing function of (μ_β/μ), with $\mu_\beta \geq \mu$. Foster (2006a) presents a unifying framework for measures of inequality in which he highlights that virtually all relative inequality measures are a function of a ratio between two income standards (such as the β-means and the arithmetic mean).

14   For in-depth discussion of this property, see Foster and Sen (1997, pp149–163) as well as Shorrocks (1980).

15   This is usually done by multiplying the cost of the food basket by the inverse of the Engel Coefficient (which is the ratio between food expenditure and total expenditure) calculated for people with incomes just above the food poverty line.

16   The need of a linen shirt and leather shoes in the England of the late 17th century remarked by Adam Smith (1776) is an example of context-specific needs.

17   For example, Foster (1998) suggests a possible hybrid line given by a weighted geometric average of a relative threshold (z_r) and an absolute threshold (z_{aa}): $z = z_r^\rho z_a^{1-\rho}$, with $0 < \rho < 1$. By selecting the value of ρ, one can choose the weight to be attached to each component to the hybrid line (with $\rho = 0$ making it all absolute, and $\rho = 1$ making it all relative). Provided z_r is a fraction of a living standard, ρ is the elasticity of the poverty line to the living standard (p339). Atkinson and Bourguignon (2001) and Ravallion and Chen (2009) provide alternative approaches and further discussion on hybrid poverty lines.

18   This sort of discussion has fostered the fuzzy sets approach to poverty

measurement (Cerioli and Zani, 1990; Cheli and Lemmi, 1995, among others), as well as the development of dominance analysis in poverty measurement (Atkinson 1987; Foster and Shorrocks 1988; Foster and Jin 1998, among others). It also suggests the need to do sensitivity analysis in empirical applications.

19   Foster (2006b) provides a recent and thorough review on properties of poverty measures and the different indices proposed in the literature.

20   Watts (1969) and Sen (1976) initiated the discussion on the desirable properties for a poverty measure.

21   This implies that each income in the distribution can be measured 'in poverty line units'. Poverty measures that are scale invariant are called relative measures, as opposed to absolute poverty measures, which are invariant to translations or additions of the same absolute amount to each income and to the poverty line. For distinction between the two, see Blackorby and Donaldson (1980), and Foster and Shorrocks (1991).

22   To avoid further technicalities, we have omitted the continuity property, which is also usually required in poverty measurement, demanding the measure not to abruptly change as incomes approach (and cross) the poverty line.

23   For more discussion on the subgroup axioms, see Foster and Sen (1997), as well as Foster and Shorrocks (1991).

24   For discussion on other poverty measures, we refer the reader to Foster (2006b), Foster and Sen (1997) or Atkinson (1987).

25   The P_2 measure has a neat relation with the squared coefficient of variation among the poor. Measures with $\alpha > 2$ not only satisfy transfer, but are also 'transfer sensitive' stressing transfers at low income levels.

26   For each indicator, normalization is done subtracting the minimum value from the observed value and dividing it by the difference between the maximum and the minimum values. The minimum and maximum values for life expectancy at birth are 25 and 85 years correspondingly; for the adult literacy rate and for the combined enrolment ratio are 0 and 100 correspondingly, and for GDP per capita (in PPPUS$) are 100 and 40,000. Once the adult literacy rate and the gross enrolment rate have been normalized, the composite indicator is obtained as a weighted average between the two, with a weight of 2/3 for the normalized literacy rate and of 1/3 for the normalized gross enrolment rate.

27   Formally, the distribution of health, education and income across the population is given by vectors $h = (h_1, h_2, ..., h_n)$, $e = (e_1, e_2, ..., e_n)$ and $y = (y_1, y_2, ..., y_n)$ respectively.

28   For an analysis on this issue see Seth (2008). For criticisms of the normalization process of the HDI indicators (which implicitly affects the weights of the variables), see Kelley (1991) and Srinivasan (1994).

29   In this way, the index reflects that while there is some substitutability between the dimensions of development, this is not infinite, as it is implicitly assumed when $\beta = 1$.

30   As noted by Tsui (2002, p72), it is worth noticing that in the unidimensional measurement of poverty the weights used are the prices, assuming implicitly that these prices are 'right'. Clearly this position is no less value-free than using other sets of weights.

31   For more discussion on weights in multi-dimensional measures, see Decanq and Lugo (2008).

32   The reader interested in formal statements of the properties in multi-dimensional poverty measurement can find them in Tsui (2002), Bourguignon

and Chakravarty (2003), Alkire and Foster (2007) among others.
33 Only when the intersection approach is used for identifying the multi-dimensionally poor (k = d), is the multi-dimensional headcount ratio sensitive to the number of deprivations that the poor experience.
34 If there is more than one indicator per dimension, a structure of 'nested' weights can be used. For further explanation of this option, see Alkire and Foster (2007).

Readings

Alkire, S. (2008) 'Choosing dimensions: The capability approach and multidimensional poverty', in N. Kakwani and J. Silber (eds) *The Many Dimensions of Poverty*, Palgrave Macmillan, Basingstoke
Alkire, S. and Foster, J. E. (2007) 'Counting and multidimensional poverty measurement', OPHI Working Paper No. 07, OPHI. www.ophi.org.uk
Atkinson, A. B., Cantillon, B., Marlier, E. and Nolan, B. (2002) *Social Indicators: The EU and Social Inclusion*, Oxford University Press, Oxford
Duclos, J.-Y. and Araar, A. (2006) *Poverty and Equity Measurement, Policy, and Estimation with DAD*, Berlin and Ottawa, Springer and IDRC
Foster, J. E. (2006b) 'Poverty indices' in A. de Janvry and R. Kanbur (eds) *Poverty, Inequality and Development: Essays in Honor to Erik Thorbecke*, Springer Science & Business Media Inc., New York
Foster, J. E. and Sen, A. (1997) 'On economic inequality: After a quarter century'. Annex to the expanded edition, A. Sen *On Economic Inequality*, Clarendon Press, Oxford
Foster, J. E., Calva, L. F. and Székely, M. (2005) 'Measuring the distribution of human development: Methodology and application to Mexico', *Journal of Human Development*, vol 6, pp5–30
Human Development Report Office (2007) *Measuring Human Development: A Primer*, UNDP, New York. Available at http://hdr.undp.org/en/nhdr/support/primer/
Ranis, G., Stewart, F. and Samman, E. (2006) 'Human development: Beyond the human development index', *Journal of Human Development*, vol 7, no3, pp323–358

Further Readings

Alkire, S. (2002) 'Dimensions of human development', *World Development*, vol 30, no 2, pp181–205
Alkire, S. (2007) 'The missing dimensions of poverty data: Introduction to the special issue', *Oxford Development Studies*, vol 35, no 4, pp347–359
Anand, S. and Sen, A. (1997) 'Concepts of human development and poverty: A multidimensional perspective', *Human Development Papers*, UNDP, New York
Atkinson, A. B. (1970) 'On the measurement of inequality', *Journal of Economic Theory*, vol 2, pp244–263
Atkinson, A. B. (1987) 'On the measurement of poverty', *Econometrica*, vol 55, pp749–764
Atkinson, A. B. and Bourguignon, F. (2001) 'Poverty and inclusion from a world perspective', in J. Stiglitz and P.-A. Muet (eds) *Governance, Equity and Global Markets*, Oxford University Press, Oxford
Blackorby, C. and Donaldson, D. (1980) 'Ethical indices for the measurement of poverty', *Econometrica*, vol 48, pp1053–1060

Bourguignon, F. and Chakravarty, S. R. (2003) 'The measurement of multidimensional poverty', *Journal of Economic Inequality*, vol 1, pp25–19

Cerioli, A. and Zani, S. (1990) 'A fuzzy approach to the measurement of poverty', in C. Dagum and M. Zenga (eds) *Income and Wealth Distribution, Inequality and Poverty*, Springer Verlag, Berlin

Cheli, B. and Lemmi, A. (1995) 'A totally fuzzy and relative approach to the multidimensional analysis of poverty', *Economic Notes*, vol 24, pp115–133

Dalton, H. (1920) 'The measurement of the inequality of incomes', *Economic Journal*, vol 30, pp348–361

Deaton, A. and Grosh, M. (2000) 'Consumption', in M. Grosh and P. Glewwe (eds) *Designing Household Survey Questionnaires for Developing Countries: Lessons from Ten Years of LSMS Experience*, vol I, ch 5, pp91–133. Full text available online at http://siteresources.worldbank.org/INTPOVRES/Resources/477227-1142020443961/2311843-1197996479165/part1_DesigningHHS.pdf, accessed 14 March 2009

Decanq, K. and Lugo, M. A. (2008) 'Setting weights in multidimensional indices of well-being', OPHI Working Paper No. 18, OPHI. www.ophi.org.uk

Foster, J. E. (2006a) 'Inequality Measurement', in D. Clark (ed.) *The Elgar Companion to Development Studies*, Edward Elgar, Cheltenham

Foster, J. E. (1985) 'Inequality measurement', in H. Peyton Young (ed.) *Fair Allocation*, American Mathematical Society, Providence, RI

Foster, J. E. (1998) 'Absolute versus relative poverty', *American Economic Review, Papers and Proceedings*, vol 88, pp335–341

Foster, J. E. and Jin, Y. (1998) 'Poverty orderings for the Dalton utility-gap measures', in S. P. Jenkins, A. Kapteyn and B. M. S. van Praag (eds) *The Distribution of Welfare and Households Production*, Cambridge University Press, Cambridge

Foster, J. and Shneyerov, A. (1999) 'A general class of additively decomposable inequality measures', *Economic Theory*, vol 14, pp89–111

Foster, J. E. and Shorrocks, A. (1988) 'Poverty orderings and welfare dominance', *Social Choice and Welfare*, vol 5, pp179–198

Foster, J. E. and Shorrocks, A. (1991) 'Subgroup consistent poverty indices', *Econometrica*, vol 59, pp687–709

Foster, J. E., Greer, J. and Thorbecke, E. (1984) 'A class of decomposable poverty indices', *Econometrica*, vol 52, pp761–766

Fukuda-Parr, S. (2000) 'Rescuing the human development concept from the HDI: Reflections on a new agenda', in A. K. S. Kumar and S. Fukuda-Parr (eds) *Readings in Human Development*, Oxford University Press, New Delhi

Gini, C. (1912) *Variabilità e mutabilità*, reprinted in E. Pizetti and T. Salvemini (eds) (1955) *Memorie di Metodologica Statistica*, Libreria Eredi Virgilio Veschi, Rome

Green, M. and Hulme, D. (2005) 'From correlates and characteristics to causes: Thinking about poverty from a chronic poverty perspective', *World Development*, vol 33, no 6, pp867–879

Grimm, M., Harttgen, K., Klasen, S. and Misselhorn, M. (2006) 'A human development index by income groups', background paper for *Human Development Report 2006*, UNDP Human Development Report Office, New York

Grosh, M. and Glewwe, P. (eds) (2000) *Designing Household Survey Questionnaires for Developing Countries: Lessons from 15 years of the Living Standards Measurement Study*, vol 1–3, World Bank, Washington, DC

Harris, J. (2007) 'Bringing politics back into poverty analysis', Q-Square Working Paper 34, April. Available at http://www.q-squared.ca

Ibrahim, S. and Alkire, S. (2007) 'Agency and empowerment: A proposal for internationally comparable indicators', *Oxford Development Studies*, vol 35, no 4, pp379–403

Kelley, A.C. (1991) 'The human development index: Handle with care', *Population and Development Review*, vol 17, pp315–324

Lorenz, M. O. (1905) 'Methods for measuring concentration of wealth', *Journal of the American Statistical Association*, vol 9, no 70, pp209–219

Maasoumi, E. and Lugo, M. A. (2008) 'The information basis of multivariate poverty assessments', in N. Kakwani and J. Silber (eds) *Quantitative Approaches to Multidimensional Poverty Measurement*. Palgrave Macmillan, Basingstoke

McGillivray, M. (2005) 'Measuring non-economic wellbeing achievement', *Review of Income and Wealth*, vol 51, pp337–364

Marx, K. (1867) *Capital*, J. M. Dent, London (1933 edn)

Nussbaum, M. (2003) 'Capabilities as fundamental entitlements: Sen and social justice', *Feminist Economics*, vol 9, no 2/3, pp33–59

Pigou, A. C. (1912) *Wealth and Welfare*, Macmillan, London

Ravallion, M. (1996) 'Issues in measuring and modelling poverty', *Economic Journal*, vol 106, pp1328–1343

Ravallion, M. and Chen, S. (2009) 'Weakly relative poverty' *Policy Research Working Paper 4844*, World Bank, http://papers.ssrn.com/sol3/papers.cfm?abstract_id=1348985

Ricardo, D. (1817) *Principles of Political Economy and Taxation*, G. Bell, London (1891 edn)

Robeyns, I. (2005) 'Selecting capabilities for quality of life measurement.' *Social Indicators Research*, vol 74, no 1, pp191–215

Robeyns, I. (2006) 'The capability approach in practice', *Journal of Political Philosophy*, vol 14, no 3, pp351–376

Sen, A. K. (1973) *On Economic Inequality*, Oxford University Press, Oxford

Sen, A. K. (1976) 'Poverty: An ordinal approach to measurement', *Econometrica*, vol 44, pp219–231

Sen, A. K. (1987) 'The standard of living: lectures I and II', in G. Hawthorn (ed.) *The Standard of Living*, Cambridge University Press, Cambridge

Sen, A. K. (1996) 'On the foundations of welfare economics: Utility, capability and practical reason', in F. Farina, F. Hahn and S. Vanucci (eds) *Ethics, Rationality and Economic Behaviour*, Clarendon Press, Oxford

Sen, A. K. (2004) 'Capabilities, lists and public reason: Continuing the conversation', *Feminist Economics*, vol 10, no 3, pp77–80

Seth, S. (2008) 'A class of association sensitive multidimensional welfare indices', OPHI Working Paper No. 27, OPHI. www.ophi.org.uk

Shorrocks, A. F. (1980) 'The class of additively decomposable inequality measures', *Econometrica*, vol 48, no 3, pp613–625

Shorrocks, A. F. (1999) 'Decomposition procedures for distributional analysis: A unified framework based on the Shapley value', mimeo. Department of Economics, University of Essex

Shorrocks, A. F. and Foster, J. E. (1987) 'Transfer sensitive inequality measures', *Review of Economic Studies*, vol 54, pp485–497

Smith, A. (1776) *An Inquiry into the Nature and Consequences of the Wealth of Nations*, Clarendon, Oxford

Srinivasan, T. N. (1994) 'Human development: A new paradigm or reinvention of the wheel?', *American Economic Review, Papers and Proceedings*, vol 84, pp238–243

Székely, M. (ed.) (2006) *Números que mueven al mundo: La medición de la pobreza en México*, ANUIES-CIDE-Sedesol (Miguel Ángel Porrúa, México)

Tsui, K. (2002) 'Multidimensional poverty indices', *Social Choice and Welfare*, vol 19, pp69–93
United Nations Development Programme (2007) *Human Development Report 2007/2008: Fighting climate change: Human solidarity in a divided world*, UNDP, Washington, DC
Watts, H. W. (1969) 'An economic definition of poverty', in D. P. Moynihan (ed.) *On Understanding Poverty*, Basic Books, New York

7

Institutions, Markets and Economic Development

Susan Johnson

Aims of the chapter

- To understand the role of institutions, both formal and informal, in promoting economic development and human flourishing.
- To analyse markets as institutions in themselves and as regulated by social institutions.
- To draw the policy implications of this institutionalist view of markets.
- To assess the relationship between the human development approach and the role of institutions in development in general, and in markets in particular.

Key Points

- Institutions are rules and norms that enable human interaction to take place. How they operate is critical if economic development is to be achieved. 'Getting institutions right' has become a key priority in development policy. Thus the main focus of mainstream economists has been on particular rules, such as property rights, regulatory institutions, macroeconomic stability and social insurance as the main institutions enabling the economy – especially markets – to work well.
- There are also social conventions, moral rules and informal norms that underpin how people interact and influence how the economy works. These rules and norms may often be discriminatory. Social identities and differences based on gender, age, ethnicity, race, religion, caste and so on affect how people engage with institutions and markets.
- Mainstream economics has neglected to analyse the ways in which actual markets operate. Its support for markets as the best mechanism for delivering the greatest welfare is based on unrealistic assumptions that do not always take into account the actual institutions markets involve. Other economic approaches demonstrate that social identity and power relations matter and that markets are 'socially regulated.'

- The human development approach recognizes that valuable capabilities can be expanded through institutions but also that institutions can constrain the achievement of capabilities, particularly in contexts where social norms discriminate between people.
- The human development approach is not for or against markets but recognizes that they may assist in promoting freedom and equity. However, markets are affected by deeply-rooted social norms and social identities that may enable some people to do well while discriminating against others. Addressing such inequities requires not only rules and regulations agreed through democratic processes but also a sustained effort to reverse the underlying power relations, as well as the attitudes and beliefs, based on the informal norms from which they arise.

The core argument of this book is that the objective of development is to promote human flourishing. Chapter 4 discussed economic growth as an important means for achieving that very objective. This chapter examines two other key means for promoting human flourishing: institutions and markets. Institutions are the rules and norms that enable human interaction to take place in all spheres of social, economic, political and cultural life. Thus the institutions of society range from formal rules, such as a national constitution, which may define the specific rights and obligations of citizens to representation and voice, to national laws, such as those of property rights, criminal law and so on. The informal institutions encompass social norms of interaction, such as what is moral, good or bad behaviour, or what are acceptable ways of undertaking certain activities, such as what side of the road to drive on, how to queue, or what it is an appropriate tip in a restaurant.

The idea that it is necessary to 'get institutions right for development' has become a critical component of contemporary development discourse. This focus strongly converges with the concerns for good governance in the political sphere and encompasses, for example, the need to define and enforce property rights so the economy can function effectively. In the economy itself, markets in most countries play a key role in the allocation of resources, along with the state and other mechanisms within families and communities for the management and sharing of resources. From the 1980s onwards, development policy was focused on 'getting prices right' in markets as a means to jump-start economic growth. At the time, it was thought that the de-regulation of markets from government control would enable everyone to seek the highest returns for their goods. The broad failure of these policies to produce the expected increases in production and income led to the identification of key institutions that were deficient, particularly those pertaining to the ownership of private property and the rule of law that would enforce these rights. These specific concerns were framed more broadly within the general need for improvements in transparency and accountability in government.

From the point of view of economic analysis, institutions are seen as important because of their role in supporting markets. However, markets can also be seen as institutions in themselves, which operate within a wide set of formal and informal rules and norms. Hence we can also examine ways in which markets can contribute, because of their intrinsic ability to enhance freedoms, to human flourishing. In order to command higher wages, people need to be able to have access to labour markets that are non-discriminatory and non-exploitative. Labour markets that discriminate against women or ethnic minorities or that pay below minimum wage enhance human flourishing inadequately. Similarly, access to commodity markets are a crucial means for poor people to sell their produce and to buy the goods necessary for their lives. But when markets function in a macroeconomic climate of hyper-inflation, or when they do not rely on the basic norms of trust that guarantee a fair transaction, they are not conducive to promoting greater well-being.

This chapter begins by exploring the role of institutions in economic development in greater depth, reviewing the dominant approach developed by the economist Douglass North. We then discuss the view that markets in themselves can be considered as institutions and use this to question the idea of 'free' or 'self-regulating' markets. Once markets are understood to be institutions connected to a whole range of formal and informal institutions – including being embedded in deeper social and cultural norms and networks – the importance of enabling them to enhance human freedoms and well-being, however difficult, becomes apparent. We conclude with analysing the specific contribution of the human development and capability approach to the analysis of institutions and markets.

Institutions in economic development

The institutional turn

In the 1990s, the role of institutions in understanding the functioning of the economy became prominent, signalling what has been described as 'the institutional turn' in development policy (Evans, 2007). The recognition of the role of institutions in the economy came to the forefront of economic thinking with the work of Nobel Prize-winning economist Douglass North. In his book *Institutions, Institutional Change and Economic Performance* (1990), he argued that institutions are a key factor in determining a country's economic performance.

North defines institutions as 'the rules of the game in society, or the humanly devised constraints that shape human interaction' (1990, p3). North goes on to elaborate that institutions provide structure to everyday life, limiting the nature of exchange and determining the forms incentives take. It is this effect on incentives that is critical from the point of view of economics. Depending on how institutions work, they can affect the way in which incentives to produce are structured. This can therefore determine the nature and speed of economic development. 'Good' institutions are seen as those that enable actors, such as entrepreneurs, to make profits, work hard and continue to invest. This arises when contracts can be easily enforced, property rights are secure and governments pursue growth-promoting policies that encourage a virtuous circle of innovation, capital accumulation and increased economic output. If, on the other hand, states extract these surpluses from their citizens and do not use them productively, a vicious cycle of exploitation and low or negative growth can occur.

For North, the underlying institutions are endogenous to (i.e. determined within) the system being studied. Institutions can change as a result of groups within the system perceiving the possibility of gains through, for example, changes to property rights or mechanisms that enforce such rights and related contracts. They may act politically to change property rights and other regulations in order to be able to capture greater benefits. Putting this in historical perspective, this dynamic occurs in relationships between organizations and institutions. Organizations, such as firms or political groups, who are what North calls the 'players of the game', are formed out of the incentives inherent in any underlying institutional context. Once formed, they produce new knowledge and ideas through which they identify how to improve their respective contexts and act to change the rules in order to achieve this. This means that change is what is called a 'path-dependent' process, i.e. the past has a strong influence, with changes happening only slowly and gradually. But, at the same time, the organizations that have sought to change the rules to their benefit will seek to defend and maintain them, leading to a significant degree of inertia. In analysing trajectories of economic development in different countries, North argues that these ideas can be applied to examine how specific economies have developed.

That institutions matter for economic development is not new in economics – there is a long tradition of studying them by economists such as John Commons and Clarence Ayres – known as (old) 'institutional economics'. Where mainstream economics is primarily concerned with resource allocation, the distribution of income and how output and prices are determined, institutional economics is concerned with how the economic system as a whole is organized and controlled, and hence with the power structures within it. Where for mainstream economists the market (and this includes the sale and purchase of goods and services by the public sector) is the sole means through which economic activity takes place, institutional economists argue that the market is itself an institution that is supported by, and interacts with, a wide range of subsidiary institutions in society. The economy is therefore more than the market and it is this larger organizational complex that allocates resources. However, institutional economists – in contrast to North – tend to see underlying institutions as immutable, exogenous and impervious to change.

The recent emphasis on the role of institutions in development has not, however, primarily drawn from this heritage. Instead, it has been based on what is called the 'new institutional economics'. This approach, developed by Ronald Coase, responded to problems related to certain core assumptions in neoclassical economics about the costless and perfect information on which actors make their utility-maximizing decisions. Before making decisions, actors must search for information and may incur a range of costs when finding out about the products or services they happen to be interested in. This leads to the so-called problem of imperfect information (when information is not easily accessible) and asymmetric information (when one party in an exchange may have information that they are unwilling to reveal to the other party). These in turn generate a range of other problems relating to the 'principal's' ability to assess and/or monitor a contract with an 'agent'. 'Moral hazard' is one such problem and arises when an agent is not fully exposed to the risk of a situation and therefore acts in a different way. For example, suppose that a lender (principal) has lent funds to a borrower (agent) for a specific project. There is a risk that the entrepreneur will not invest all of the funds in the proposed project or that she may not adequately manage and supervise the project because the funds invested are not hers, thus leading to low returns and to the lender not recouping her funds. In this case, the lender may decide to closely monitor the borrower to overcome the problem, but this tends to incur additional costs for the lender.

Recognizing problems such as these at the micro level has led mainstream economics to explain a number of forms of contracts and economic arrangements with the use of concepts of asymmetric information and transactions costs incurred. Previously, many types of behaviour in markets, such as the use of collateral in credit markets, could not be theorized, and were found to be inefficient or sub-optimal, but could be understood once they were seen to help protect against moral hazard. Another example is the practice of share-cropping in many agrarian societies. Landlords often needed to find ways to incentivize tenants to optimize production, since the costs of supervision would otherwise be too high. Share-cropping is thus an institutional solution, i.e. a set of rules effectively addressing information problems. More generally, then, North suggested that economic development would be constrained without the presence of institutions that effectively solve information problems at a sufficiently low cost.

Testing the theory

This view, which suggests that economic development is determined in part by the ways in which institutions are organized, has led to a body of work examining the relationship between economic growth and institutions in the form of particular rules and laws. This contrasts with previous views that saw geographical location, natural resource endowments or cultural factors as key determinants of economic development. Analysis can indeed quickly show that there is a strong correlation between economic performance and the existence of 'good' institutions, such as effective property rights. But this does not always tell us whether the causes of better performance lie in the institutions themselves or in other underlying economic, social, geographical or cultural factors.

It is difficult to investigate this causality by using the techniques of regression analysis – a favourite among economists – because it is not easy to find variables that can capture the quality of institutions independently of these other underlying factors. As is apparent from the discussion on North's work above, the quality of institutions is the outcome of a long historical process. If economic growth is thought to be both dependent on those institutions and a cause of their continuation, then it is not very easy to isolate variables that can capture each of these factors independently. This has therefore led to a methodological endeavour to find ways of separating causes and effects. The main approach considers colonization as a process in which institutions were imposed upon many different countries, but in some of these they were set up primarily to extract resources, while in others effective systems for property rights protection were established, which benefited a 'broad cross-section' of the society, including the European settlers. This availability of rights to a significant proportion of the population appears to have made a big difference to subsequent patterns of development. A factor determining whether or not Europeans settled in greater numbers was mortality rates due to diseases, such as yellow fever and malaria. Acemoglu et al (2007) have therefore used this variable (settler mortality rates) in their analysis because it is related to the type of institutions established at the outset, but is independent of their subsequent effects on growth. As a result, they have been able to conclude that these broad institutional differences – European settlements and the wide availability of property rights – are important in explaining differences in economic growth.

Rodrik et al (2004) have also used this methodological approach to assess whether differences in income are due to either: (1) geography determining climate, natural resource endowments, diseases, transport costs and so on; (2) integration, that is, the extent to which economies are integrated into the world economy through openness to trade; or (3) institutions, such as the protection of property rights and the rule of law. They find that institutions are by far the most significant and positive determinants of income levels. Once this is taken into account, integration is seen as having no direct effect and geography only a weak direct effect.

While this research leads to broad conclusions about the importance of institutions, it does not help to identify which specific institutions are the most important for specific contexts. The focus in the empirical analysis has primarily been on property rights and their enforcement. It is evident that there are many other types of institutions that enable economic growth to take place. Rodrik and Subramanian (2003) highlight three categories of institutions: those that are (1) market stabilizing: institutions that manage the economy to produce stable conditions for growth by minimizing volatility, producing low inflation and averting crises (this is done through fiscal rules, budgets and exchange rate regimes); (2) market legitimizing: institutions that promote redistribution through social protection, insurance and welfare systems; (3) market regulating: institutions that deal with externalities, economies of scale and imperfect information, e.g. regulatory agencies for specific sectors, such as utilities, telecommunications or financial services.

This institutional literature has therefore tended to focus on property rights and institutions for regulation, macroeconomic stabilization and social insurance. However, this has been criticized because it is not clear *why* these particular institutions are the ones that are most focused on or, in other words, it is not clear how this focus is theoretically informed (Chang 2005). Moreover, the *function* that institutions deliver within the economy may be similar, but the institutions themselves can take on many *forms*. Hence, legal systems can be organized in very different ways to secure property rights, as can competition or regulatory agencies dealing with externalities or other market failures. More work therefore needs to be done to properly conceptualize the contribution of institutions to economic development.

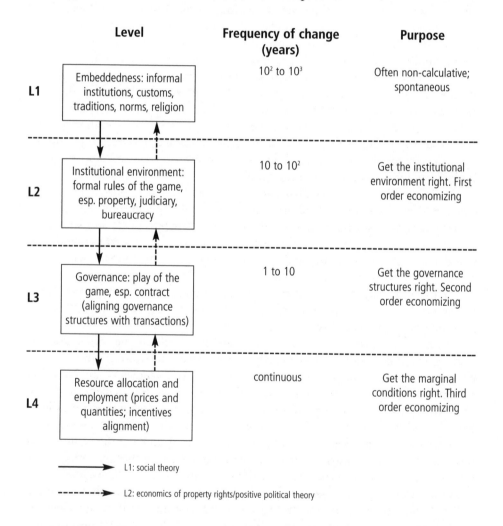

Figure 7.1 Categorization of institutions in the economy by level

Source: Williamson (2000, p597)

Williamson (2000) has described a categorization of institutions consisting of four levels (Figure 7.1): the first level is those institutions that relate to the underlying social structures. This is not a level that other theorists have considered greatly, while the other three levels relate more clearly to the institutional aspects suggested above. The second level relates to the rules of the game, such as property rights and the judiciary, which define the overall (formal) institutional environment or what can be exchanged (in the context of markets). The third level is about rules that relate to the playing of the game, such as contracts; and the fourth about rules that relate to resource-allocation mechanisms, such as social security systems. This certainly helps us to consider the nature of institutions, and in particular which underlying social institutions underpin which different levels. We further explore the idea that institutions are embedded in informal institutions, customs and norms below.

All the institutional levels described in Figure 7.1 determine the way the economy operates and the way economic development therefore occurs. This implies that 'getting institutions right' is not as straightforward as transplanting formal rules and regulations seen to operate well in some contexts to other countries. Indeed, it becomes apparent that the functions of institutions may arise from a range of forms. Moreover, this situation becomes even more complex when we appreciate how formal rules are underpinned by informal rules and norms.

From formal rules to informal norms

So far, our discussion of institutions has suggested that there are some key rules in society that matter for economic development and that most attention has been paid in the literature to rules around property rights and their enforcement. But there have also been other areas of focus around the wider range of ways in which regulations are enacted, such as regulations surrounding the registration of businesses.

However, North highlights the key distinction between institutions as *formal* rules and regulations, on the one hand, and *informal* institutions (such as conventions, moral rules and social norms), on the other. Conventions are social rules that are commonly accepted in society. For example, countries have conventions about which side of the road people should drive on. Similarly, there are conventions that guide book-keeping practice and accounting. There are also conventions in legal practice. The purpose of these conventions is to guide the behaviour of members in society and to make their transactions and exchanges easier. Through these conventions, people know what to expect in terms of documents, behaviour on the road or accounting formats. This obviates the need to learn and assess a situation from scratch every time and to go through a lengthy process of decision-making about how to respond accordingly in any given context.

Moral rules or norms are those such as 'do not steal', 'do not break your promise', 'respect the elderly.'[1] These rules are imparted during one's socialization process in all societies, and they are reinforced in different ways, for example, through the education system, children's literature or religious instruction. Economists would also argue that there are solid economic reasons for these moral rules to be instilled in the minds of individuals. For example, when people are generally truthful and honest, it is easier to undertake contracts and conclude transactions because it is simply not possible to commit oneself to a written agreement every time one makes a transaction. These observations are in line with the views of the sociologist Emile Durkheim, who noted that there is a basic sociality that is 'pre-contractual' and without which it would be hard to undertake transactions. The transaction costs incurred would be enormous if it was necessary to pin down every possible aspect of a transaction every time it was made.

This 'basic sociality' includes a wide range of social norms that society expects of individuals. Social norms are patterns of behaviour that reflect the customs, traditions, values or ways of life of a particular society or group, the transgression of which generally leads to social ostracism. Jon Elster (1989, p105) defines a social norm as 'the propensity to feel shame and to anticipate sanction by others at the thought of behaving in a certain, forbidden way. This propensity becomes a social norm when and to the extent that it is shared with other people.' Given this definition, it should be noted that norms are not necessarily explained by the efficiency of their outcome. People would sometimes be better off without norms, and are sometimes better off with norms. Although social norms are shared with others, this does not necessarily mean that they are equitable in their impact – as Elster's definition suggests, ostracism is often the result of breaching them. Thus social norms around the role of women in the economy, for example, have been a critical reason for their inability to gain access to particular jobs or leadership roles in society. It therefore becomes necessary to recognize how key social differences between people, such as gender, age, ethnicity, race, class, religion and so on create social discrimination.

Institutions as a 'grand' theory of development

North's major contribution was to recognize the underlying role of institutions in processes of economic development and to suggest how they might be studied. He recognized that actors – in the form of organizations – might seek to change the rules but that the incentives enabling them to do so are themselves determined by these institutions, and hence constrain their actions. As a consequence, when actors seek to innovate and create new opportunities, what they are ultimately able to achieve is constrained by existing institutions – both formal and informal – and economic development is therefore 'path-dependent'.

As we have pointed out, North's approach identifies the problems of imperfect and asymmetrical information. This entails two limitations: the first is that, when considered at a society-wide level and used to explain economic development, institutions continue to evolve in their efforts to address particular problems in the economy. North proposes that those involved in organizations act to further their own interests by changing the rules and regulations to enable them to perform better. This creates a 'functionalist' view of institutions, that is, institutions exist and change to solve particular *economic* problems (Toye, 1995). However, as we have seen, institutions, defined as rules and norms, operate at many levels of the economy and are deeply-rooted within an array of informal norms, conventions and moral rules. We therefore need to understand these social sources and non-economic dimensions of institutions. Do institutions exist only to solve economic problems? Moreover, how can economists know if they have actually solved the underlying problems efficiently if there are no alternatives to compare them with? From the point of view of the human development approach, we would want to know whether they exist and evolve to promote human flourishing, since discrimination can be economically efficient, for example, while detracting from these goals at the same time.

A second limitation relates to the role of politics. North recognizes that it is important to have polities that enable the rules of the game to be enforced, but this leaves unanswered the question of whether the prevailing institutional set up arises because of the structure of transactions costs or because of political structures. 'New institutional economics' as outlined above is a theory about agents possessing different levels of information but still assumes that they have equal power. This is clearly not the case in most (if not all) societies. Some have greater opportunities and abilities to promote changes to the institutional frameworks that favour them over others. The issue of political power is therefore not adequately resolved by institutional analysis. A wider political economy analysis is required.

Thus, while these 'new' institutional approaches were heralded in the early 1990s as a bridge between political economy analysis and mainstream economics, and while the institutional focus has certainly widened the analysis of economic development to encompass history, it also begins to highlight the need for sociological and political analysis, and especially for careful attention to power relations (Bardhan, 1989).

Markets

Markets as institutions

Historically, markets emerged in particular locations as places where goods and services were exchanged. Over centuries, markets have developed to become more diffuse in their physical forms with greater volumes of exchange operating at great distances and, more recently, via technology such as the internet directly linking buyers and sellers in distant locations. It is therefore not location that defines a market. So what defines it then? In contemporary usage, the term refers to supply and demand, buyers and sellers, and competition and exchange. But, surprisingly, the definition of 'market' itself has not been much discussed by economists. Indeed, it is notable how little attention mainstream economics has devoted to either defining markets or studying how they work. As North (1977, p710) observes, 'It is a peculiar fact that the literature on economics ... contains so little discussion of the central institution that underlies neo-classical economics – the market.'

As we have indicated above, the 1990s saw a transition in the dominant development discourse from 'getting prices right' to 'getting institutions right'. Under the Washington Consensus (see endnote 13, Chapter 1), it was expected that significant liberalization and de-regulation of the economy would enable markets to operate. Prices would become effective incentives and lead to efficient resource allocation and eventually improved productivity and economic growth. The failure of governments to allocate resources effectively through either planning systems or state intervention in developing countries led to the unexamined view that markets would be effective where governments and planning had failed. There was little real thought or policy on how exactly markets would be developed, simply because mainstream economics did not have the analytical tools with which to examine them. Indeed, markets were expected to emerge spontaneously or, as Williamson (1983, p20) puts it, 'in the beginning there were markets'. In some contexts, especially the transition economies of the socialist bloc, this belief caused widespread problems since the mechanisms through which markets could work effectively did not 'spontaneously' emerge, and the vacuum left by planning failures allowed opportunism to fill the gap. This inadvertently led to the emergence of markets, but markets that were turbulent and chaotic and not those anticipated by the proponents of market reform.

This episode of failed policy led to the re-examination of a few underlying assumptions about markets. Specifically, it led to the recognition that markets require a wide variety of institutions in order to work effectively. Hence, the transition to 'getting institutions right' is significantly related to the view that markets can work to allocate resources effectively if they have the 'right' institutional framework.

Markets in mainstream economic theory

Mainstream neoclassical economic theory suggests that markets exist in which prices arise from the interaction of supply and demand, and that prices thus generated lead to the efficient allocation of resources in the economy as a whole and hence to maximum welfare. However, this happens under a very restrictive set of conditions which are rarely found in reality. For example, markets have to be perfectly competitive, which suggests that no individual agent is able to exert any form of market power over another agent; also, all agents must have complete and perfect information about the goods or services that are being traded. Under these conditions, neoclassical theory can demonstrate that the economy will arrive at an equilibrium set of prices that allows for the efficient allocation of resources, or what is otherwise called 'Pareto efficiency'. This is a situation where, given the initial allocation of resources, no one can be made any better off through trading without making another worse off.

This theory has been extremely powerful because it suggests that markets are the most efficient way of allocating resources, and it was this theory that underscored the view that 'getting prices right' would enable economic development to take place. The assumptions under which the theory arrives at these conclusions never actually exist in the economy. This observation is at the heart of North's comment quoted above. The idea that markets can bring about a Pareto-efficient solution is therefore very detached from identifying the way markets actually operate in practice. Policies which proposed that markets should be the key mechanism for resource allocation have thus not been based on a real understanding of how markets work but rather on the somewhat naïve belief that the right types of markets could and would emerge if allowed to do so. So why has such a huge gap between reality and the dominant neoclassical economic model been able to survive, persist and even thrive, despite its unrealistic assumptions about the market?

In his book *The Great Transformation*, Karl Polanyi (1944) offers an explanation and critique of the way the idea of the spontaneously emerging 'self-regulating' market came about. He argues that it arose in the 18th century from thinkers of the time – Malthus and Ricardo among them – who related the economy to nature: 'essentially, economic society was founded on the grim realities of Nature; if man disobeyed the laws that ruled that society, the fell executioner would strangle the offspring of the improvident' (Polanyi, 2001, p131). Thus, it was necessary to follow the 'inexorable laws of Nature' and, as a result, 'the unshackling of the market [came] to be an ineluctable necessity' (Polanyi, 2001, p132). This, he argued, was the reason for the reform of the 'poor laws' that existed in England at the time and which provided safety-nets for poor people through a system of parish-based welfare. These laws were regarded as inefficient because they stopped people from moving in response to demand for labour in the economy since, if they moved, they would lose their entitlement to support. Polanyi's argument went further to say that the thinkers of the 18th century took the normative view that 'natural laws' were unavoidable and therefore assumed that these laws should form the basis for organizing the economy. Because of this, they set about creating policies which they thought would enable these natural laws to work. But the fact that they had to create 'self-regulating markets' suggests that there is nothing 'natural' about markets in the first place.

Polanyi's analysis went on to show that this attempt to construct 'self-regulating' markets did not happen without a reaction from society at large. He argued that people resisted these changes in all sorts of ways in order to preserve their preferred ways of doing things, i.e. their rules and norms. He noted that this resistance was varied and specific and not the result solely of specific organizations, such as unions or class-based organizations. Rather, this reaction was what he called a 'double movement' in the face of the attempt by policy-makers to transform society through the creation of an economy based on the 'self-regulating market'. Thus, Polanyi recognized that the idea of a self-regulating market was the product of a school of thought in economics rather than an analysis of the actual ways in which the economy, and markets, operated. In practice, he could see that there were a myriad of ways in which social practices affected the way markets actually worked. This he described as the 'embeddedness' of the economy in society itself.

Institutionalist definitions of markets

While mainstream economics has spent little time defining markets and developing the analytical tools with which to examine them, a few economists from the 'old' institutionalist school have given the issue some thought. G. M. Hodgson reviewed the conceptual framework of markets, including that of Ludwig von Mises, whose definition relates to all forms of exchange that involve private property, which in turn is defined as assets under private control. Hodgson (2008) points out that the problem with this definition is that the market is dependent on what we understand to be 'exchange' and 'property', since all sorts of gift-giving and reciprocal exchanges could be included in such a definition. Problems also arise if exchange is not voluntary as it tends to overlook underlying legal requirements. A further problem with von Mises's definition is that many transactions involve ongoing relationships between buyers and sellers that do not take place on a competitive basis. This is often called relational exchange or contracting. Hodgson proposes that these transactions be excluded from a definition of markets because of their uniqueness.

Hodgson's preference is therefore for a narrower definition of markets, which suggests that they should be organized and institutionalized. Markets:

> involve multiple exchanges, multiple buyers and multiple sellers and thereby a degree of competition. A market is defined as an institution through which multiple buyers or multiple sellers recurrently exchange a substantial number of similar commodities of a particular type. Exchanges themselves take place in a framework of law and contract enforceability. Markets involve legal and other rules that help to structure, organize and legitimize exchange transactions. They involve pricing and trading routines that help to establish consensus over prices, and often help by communicating information regarding products, prices, quantities, potential buyers and possible sellers'. (Hodgson 2008, electronic source)

This definition is helpful in clarifying that markets are both underpinned by wider institutions in the economy and in its clear recognition that they have their own structure of rules and norms that enable them to operate. As we have pointed out above, institutions as rules and norms are based on social practices and systems. Polanyi recognized this, as did Hodgson, who described the market as 'a set of social institutions in which a large number of commodity exchanges of a specific type regularly take place and to some extent are facilitated and structured by those institutions' (Hodgson 1988, p176). Having discussed above the focus of institutional analysis on property rights, the rule of law and wider governance, the next section turns to examining in greater depth how markets may be 'embedded' in social institutions and structures.

From 'self-regulated' to 'socially regulated' markets

We introduced above Williamson's idea of the levels of institutions in which the economy operates. In applying them more specifically to markets, we can recognize that institutions at all of these levels affect the way transactions are carried out. Hence, we can see that the purchase of a commodity, say rice, in a market depends on many institutions. It depends on how the macroeconomy is operating in terms of inflation, interest rate, exchange rate, etc. The purchase of the rice is also based on the rules that regulate exchange in that particular market (rules may be about the way different varieties and qualities of rice are signalled and labelled). Underlying this, then, are the property rights which indicate that, once payment has been made, exclusive control of the rice passes to the buyer (i.e. the existence of private property rights over the rice).[2] Finally, the exchange may be affected by *who* is involved in the transaction and the ability of the buyer or seller to discriminate for or against another person. Thus, we can see that a wide range of institutions affect the way in which the exchange takes place.

That *the actors* involved might matter in the exchange is not a point mainstream economics generally considers. This goes back to Polanyi's idea that the economy is embedded in social institutions, and hence that relations such as gender, age, race, ethnicity, class and religion affect the way they work. These are means by which people are often discriminated against and this discrimination therefore affects the way they are able to engage in markets. Even if many countries have legislation that outlaws discrimination on such grounds in all spheres of life, discrimination often remains deeply-rooted in social practices and its specific and long-term effects are often very hard to identify and reverse. One example is labour markets, where women are often paid less for a day's work than men. This practice can persist despite the existence of equal pay legislation. This type of discrimination can be pervasive in markets, as in other areas of social life, because of the multiple ways it affects people's interactions with one other, without being overt. Hence, as is well known, women's property rights in marriage are often insecure and are often not recognized at all. This in turn affects their ability to enter financial markets as they may be prevented from using their assets as collateral for loans, for example. This can then affect their ability to develop businesses and compete in the economy.

This has led Harriss-White (2003a, 2004) to identify these forms of embeddedness in markets and to see them as sources of power derived from both social and political influences (e.g. the state). She describes the means through which these influences operate as 'social regulation'. She argues that social institutions operate both inside the economy to regulate it while also operating outside it in other domains of social life. As she points out, institutions such as those of gender, class, religion and ethnicity are rarely those that (even) institutional economists have focused on.

Her study of the Indian economy demonstrates that social relations in the workforce and social class, gender, religion, caste and space interact in complex ways with each other to create a 'socially regulated' economy. She shows that such structures of social regulation do not end with these institutions but extend and emanate into more formal structures of regulation, that is, those imposed by the state. Her study also directs attention to the formal institutions that operate to govern inputs, labour, consumption and demand, which can be found in the legal constitution of firms, labour law and banking.

Moreover, the politics of markets does not solely arise from the role of the state. Harriss-White outlines four dimensions of power in markets: first, the state has the ability to both intervene directly and regulate politically. Second, associations of market actors form to pursue collective interests. Third, economic structures also confer power, depending on the underlying endowments of different groups operating within it and which can allow for the extraction of surplus. Finally, social authority and status can be derived outside the economy through social embeddedness and this also enables the exercise of power in the market – e.g. gender relations allow the operation of patriarchy (White, 1993; Harriss-White, 2003b).

The analysis of markets as socially regulated offers a particularly important perspective on the role of markets in development because it directs our attention to the underlying inequalities that arise from social identity. It also calls for a better understanding of how such inequalities pervade markets directly and indirectly through their influence on the way formal institutions in turn influence markets and therefore perpetuate their effects in the long term.

Box 7.1 The embeddedness of a microfinance market in gender relations in Kenya

Informal financial services are an important feature of local financial markets in many parts of the world. Research into the financial services used by people in and around the small town of Karatina in central Kenya showed that one of the most widely-used services was informal group systems, especially the Rotating Savings and Credit Association (ROSCA). ROSCAs are systems in which a number of people form a group and contribute an agreed amount on a regular basis. At each meeting, the fund is usually given to one person, who takes all of the money, until everyone in the group has received the money in turn. The order of rotation may be determined by ballot, age, seniority or other social systems of preferment. In Karatina, these were used more by women than by men. Why was this? In some parts of the world, such as Taiwan, it is men who use ROSCAs more extensively than women.

The explanation is to be found in underlying gender relations. First, it is necessary to understand the division of labour and control of income in the household and how this influences the type of savings and loans services men and women need. While women contribute important labour to agricultural activities, it is usually the case that men control the income from activities with the highest financial returns. This enables them to make large and lumpy expenditures for which they have prime responsibility, such as asset purchase, school fees and farm inputs. Women are likely to be given control of smaller income streams from particular activities, which enable them to pay for food and other household items that are needed on a regular basis. These different flows of income result in men and women having different needs (demand) for financial services to manage these flows. Women have regular but small amounts to manage and ROSCAs are an ideal way of saving regularly to turn these into a larger amount over a number of weeks in order to make purchases of goods, such as household utensils or clothes. ROSCAs do not suit men's needs in the same way. Their income, from the sale of such cash crop products like coffee, is often irregular. They can hence not make regular ROSCA contributions. Moreover, their need for loans (ROSCA payouts) can be strongly seasonal to buy farm inputs or pay for school fees. Hence, many men in a ROSCA would want to have access to the payout at the same time, so it is not such a useful mechanism for meeting their credit needs.

Second, we can look at the supply side, in the sense of what enables men and women to engage in ROSCA-type activities. One of the key reasons men and women explained their differential use of ROSCAs was the social consequences of non-payment. Women said they could not attend the group and experience the embarrassment and shame of not being able to pay the contribution or 'spoiling' the group. On the other hand, men were not ashamed of not paying, did not trust each other to make it work, did not like the strictness of the rules and realized that little could be done to them if they did not pay – so their groups had a history of failure.

These differences reflect gender norms that are deeply-rooted in society. Women's groups have a long history in Kikuyu society and serve to socialize women in how they should act and behave. To be seen as being able to participate effectively in a group is an important social skill. At the same time, participation in the group enables the woman to provide some of the essentials in the household, like cooking utensils and blankets, that it is her responsibility to provide. In contrast, socialization processes for men were traditionally in the form of age-sets which did not promote solidarity after men settled down in a household. Now that these traditions have ended, there is no alternative process that promotes cross-lineage collaboration.

This story shows us how analysing underlying gender norms helps to explain the operation of certain types of financial services or, in other words, how these norms affect financial markets. Other better known features of the way gender norms affect differential participation of men and women in financial markets relates to their ability to access banks for loans since property, especially land, is rarely exclusively under women's control. However, in Kenya it is not exclusively under men's control either and its use as collateral requires that family members agree. Women can thus refuse to agree if they think the loan may be misused. There are also, more generally, deep social concerns about the potential loss of land. A further gender norm is that men usually hold the licences for the production of cash crops (tea, coffee) and hence it is they who can open accounts with crop-based savings and credit cooperatives while their wives will usually simply be co-signatories.

Adapted from Susan Johnson (2004a, 2004b).

Institutions and markets in the human development approach

The human development and capability approach brings the 'institutionalist' school's analysis of institutions into line with its overall objective of development. Institutions, and the functionings of markets, should ultimately be seen in terms of the expansion of valuable freedoms. Like institutional economics, it stresses the interdependence of institutions, formal and informal, market and non-market related:

> Individuals live and operate in a world of institutions. Our opportunities and prospects depend crucially on what institutions exist and how they function. Not only do institutions contribute to our freedoms, their roles can be sensibly evaluated in the light of their contributions to our freedom... Even though different commentators have chosen to focus on particular institutions (such as market, or the democratic system, or the media, or the public distribution system), we have to view them together, to be able to see what they can or cannot do in combination with other institutions. It is in this integrated perspective that the different institutions can be reasonably assessed and examined. (Sen, 1999, p142)
>
> Development calls for the use of many different institutions – the market, the public services, the judiciary, the political parties, the media and so on. These institutions can often supplement and also complement each other. Since freedoms of different kinds contribute to one another, a freedom-centred view calls for an institutionally-integrated approach. [There is a] need for thinking in terms of a multi-institution format. (Drèze and Sen, 2002, p20).

Development and the expansion of freedoms can therefore not occur without the presence of multiple institutions. For example, the capability of women to read and write can often be deeply hindered by social norms that are hostile to gender equality. The capability of indigenous people to maintain their language and traditions cannot exist without an adequate legal framework that fully protects and implements the rights of cultural minorities. The capability to be healthy and educated is greatly enhanced by the institution of social security and other key welfare institutions.

In Chapters 2 and 5, we argued that one of the reasons why higher incomes were not automatically translated into higher well-being was because of variations in institutional arrangements. Institutional analysis provides a wider framework for analysing which institutions constrain or enhance people's capabilities and helps us to theorize how change takes place. The specific contribution of the human development and capability approach to this framework is the recognition of the critical importance of political participation in creating and reforming institutions, whether market or non-market, so they can provide opportunities for people to live the lives they have reason to value.

The overall objective of expanding people's freedoms is ultimately the benchmark through which institutions and markets should be seen. For example, Sen (1999, p112) emphasizes the value of the freedom to participate in markets: 'We have good reasons to buy and sell, to exchange, and to seek lives that can flourish on the basis of transactions. To deny that freedom would in itself (be) a major failing of society.' But this has to be seen not as an endorsement of the allocation mechanisms of markets but in terms of the agency and well-being aspects of the approach (see Chapter 2). One can think here of feudal societies where people are denied the freedom to buy and sell goods to whomever they wish, or peasants who have to give their harvest to landlords because they have been forced to borrow from them at very high interest rates in order to survive. Similarly, denying people the freedom to transact in labour markets may be another violation of human freedom. When they are forced to work in unfavourable contexts or unable to seek employment of their choice, or when women are forbidden, in certain cultures, to work and receive a salary, their human freedom is violated. That market freedom is valuable does not of course mean that other forms of material provision are necessarily less valuable – i.e. via the state, community and family, with their respective forms of redistribution and reciprocity. What the capability approach emphasizes here is the agency and well-being of people. When the economic system, whatever it is, functions in a way that does not enable people to be agents of their own lives, the system is viewed as unjust. In certain contexts, well-functioning markets can indeed be more just and more conducive to promoting valuable freedoms than traditional forms of material provision, such as feudal or clientelistic relations.

Another reason the human development and capability approach values market freedom is because of its long-term consequences. When markets function well, they can be a good mechanism for allocating resources efficiently – efficiency being understood here as a state in which it is impossible to increase a person's well-being without decreasing someone else's.[3] If, in some contexts, market provisioning is more efficient in enhancing valuable capabilities than state provisioning, it follows that the former is a better choice than the latter. In that sense, the human development and capability approach is neither pro-state nor pro-market, nor does it favour any particular economic system of material provisioning. The essence of the approach is that the success of social and economic processes should be assessed according to whether they expand valuable freedoms. That these processes are state or market-led does not matter, provided that two conditions are met: people's agency and well-being (of current and future generations) should be both promoted and respected.

However, it is clear from the above discussion that the way markets work is complex because of the many levels of institutions that are involved. It can therefore not be assumed that introducing a market will necessarily promote and expand valuable freedoms because this all depends on the rules and norms that operate in a given context. Indeed, since the ways in which they are socially regulated arise from a wide range of inequalities in society itself, markets are, on the contrary, likely to perpetuate these deep-rooted unfreedoms even further. While the basic freedom to participate in markets should not be denied, the question of whether the terms and conditions of people's access to and participation in markets are in fact equitable must still be carefully examined.

When markets do not promote equity, the human development and capability approach advocates political participation as a way of reforming market mechanisms. The remedy to correct the unfreedoms that market freedoms might generate 'has to lie in more freedom – including that of public discussion and participatory political decisions' (Sen, 1999, p123). This demonstrates, however, that the ways in which markets create unfreedoms out of underlying inequalities can have both subtle and far-reaching consequences. While political participation may be a route to making markets equitable, it can sometimes be difficult. This route requires that those who experience market discrimination are able to identify the source of their disadvantage and are able to articulate and mobilize around this in effective ways – or that others are prepared to do so on their behalf. As we have seen, gender inequalities, for example, can be deeply-rooted and multi-layered, which means that it is not always easy to identify their origins and effects since doing so tends to require plentiful resources. While deliberative democracy may appropriately implement laws and regulations to redress these inequalities, the latter may be so deeply-rooted that a change in rules alone remains ultimately ineffective in reversing their effect. Instead, it can take many years – even decades – and requires an investment of resources and a concerted attempt to create strategies that can influence the underlying attitudes and beliefs in a given society.

Box 7.2 summarizes how political participation can influence the functioning of markets when reforms are seen to conflict with the core principles of equity and participation.

Box 7.2 Water privatization and political participation in Bolivia

The privatization of public utilities was a key feature of economic reform programmes in the 1990s. The expectation was that private sector companies would be more efficient in running these services than governments or local authorities. The privatization of such services has taken many forms, such as the outright sale of utilities, including the underlying infrastructure or, alternatively, franchise contracts that allow the company to run services throughout the infrastructure for a period of years, usually under a regulatory framework. The expectation was that the privatized service would be run more efficiently because of the introduction of market incentives into their provision: private investors would have incentives to invest in the infrastructure and provide good services in order to make profits.

In Bolivia, attempts to reform water resource management had been going on since the 1970s, culminating, in 1999, in Law 2029. This created concessions in which private enterprise could take over water supplies in major towns and cities, with the principle caveat that they be run on a financially self-sustaining basis. In the third largest city of

Cochabamba, the municipal water service was not performing well. It served only 57 per cent of the urban population, with permanent rationing caused by high levels of leakage. As a result of this, many people had resorted to sinking their own wells or building their own water tanks. The unserved population was dependent on wells and private vendors, and often ended up paying more. The concession was put up for bids, but only one international company, Aguas del Tunari (AdT), submitted a tender. The contract included increased prices but these were socially progressive, charging high-income households more than low-income ones, and the scheme planned for the gradual extension of services to areas that remained hitherto unserved.

When the company began to operate the concession in November 1999, protests and riots broke out and, by April 2000, the concession was withdrawn. The causes were multiple. First, there was general unrest regarding the neoliberal reforms being implemented nationally and the negative impact these were having on growth and employment and, more specifically, the concern that such privatization epitomized a preference for foreign capital (with its imperialist implications). Second, although price increases and progressive tariffs had been agreed, when they were implemented, some households experienced very high increases (because their consumption had been rationed earlier by leaks). Third, farmers in the surrounding area operated their own mechanisms of water management, and they feared their rights were threatened even though these had been recognized in the agreement. Moreover, the apparently now exclusive control of water resources by AdT also threatened the richer consumers, who had developed their own resources through wells and tanks. Likewise, it threatened the situation of poorer consumers, who were dependent on water vendors and other sources, and these were expected to disappear as the network was expanded to cover their areas. Fourth, local political interests were at stake. While local politicians had been involved in the contract negotiations and had agreed to the price rises, they opposed them once they were implemented. The municipal elections in December 1999 brought tensions between central and local government. Moreover, local pressure groups and professional associations had not been involved in the negotiations and perceived it to be against the public interest. Fifth, the regulator had not carried out a public awareness campaign on the terms of the concession in advance. It also lacked regulatory capacity and could not operate at arm's length from local politics.

Utility privatization presents a good example of how markets are constructed since the abrupt shift from public to private enterprise operations demonstrates the array of factors that underlie the construction of any market. This case shows that norms about what is acceptable matter: for example, the role of foreign investment was not acceptable, nor was the fact that their private water resources (wells and tanks) could be owned by a company. Politics, both at local and national levels, is therefore critical to the way interests are pursued. While the protests in Bolivia have been claimed as an example of people power by some, the coalitions of interests mobilized were not clearly representing the interests of the poorest water users, who may have benefited from improved provision of services and lower prices. It also points out the need for inclusive debate and deliberation prior to the implementation of such major reforms, and for information to be well-publicized and easily available.

Adapted from Assies (2003) and Nickson and Vargas (2002).

Questions

7.1 Take one specific capability and examine the institutions, both formal and informal, which are promoting or constraining it. Identify a particular group of people who have difficulty achieving this capability and identify the specific ways in which these formal and informal institutions are involved in producing this outcome.

7.2 To what extent is access to markets crucial for people to achieve a certain level of human flourishing? Illustrate with examples.

7.3 Think of a market with which you are familiar. Identify the formal rules and regulations that affect this market. Try to identify the informal institutions which support the operation of this market. Examine whether women and men engage differently with it and, if so, why? What formal and informal institutions create or affect these differences?

7.4 Consider a change in institutional environment in a particular context you are familiar with – this could be a reform of rules around markets (e.g. privatization) or around other resources (such as land or water). Consider how the change came about and the politics surrounding it. How did political interests affect the way the reform was eventually worked out? Who gained and who lost out from this change in rules?

Notes

1 This paragraph has been written by Shankaran Nambiar.
2 This may seem obvious but it is possible to think of traded goods which may not have such straightforward exchanges, such as land or trees. Land is a particularly complicated case. In many countries, the emergence of a land market is hugely constrained by the fact that many people may have claims over it or its products.
3 Sen (1993) has demonstrated that such efficiency results can be obtained when well-being is conceived in the space of individual freedoms and not utility.

Readings

Acemoglu, D., Johnson, S. and Robinson, J. (2007) 'Institutions as the fundamental cause of long-run growth', in P. Aghion and S. Durlauf (eds) *Handbook of Economic Growth*, Elsevier, North Holland

Chang, H.-J. (2005) 'Understanding the relationship between institutions and economic development – Some key theoretical issues', WIDER Jubilee Conference, Helsinki, available at www.rrojasdatabank.info/widerconf/Chang.pdf

Drèze, J. and Sen, A. K. (2002) *India: Development and Participation*, Oxford University Press, Delhi

Elster J. (1989) 'Social norms and economic theory', *Journal of Economic Perspectives*, vol 3, no 4, pp99–117

Evans, P. B. (2007) 'Extending the "institutional" turn: Property, politics and development trajectories', in H.-J. Chang (ed.) *Institutional Change and Economic Development*, Anthem Press, London

Harriss-White, B. (2003a) *India Working: Essays on Society and Economy*, Cambridge University Press, Cambridge

Harriss-White, B. (2003b) 'On understanding markets as social and political institutions in developing economies', in H.-J. Chang (ed.) *Rethinking Development Economics*, Anthem Press, London

Harriss-White, B. (2004) 'India's socially-regulated economy', *Indian Journal of Labour Economics*, vol 47, no 1, also available at www.qeh.ox.ac.uk/dissemination/conference-papers/harriss-white.pdf/

Hodgson, G. M. (1988) *Economics and Institutions: A Manifesto for a Modern Institutional Economics*, Polity Press, Cambridge

Hodgson, G. M. (2008) 'Markets', in S. N. Durlauf and L. E. Blume (eds) *The New Palgrave Dictionary of Economics*, Palgrave Macmillan, Basingstoke (electronic version)

Johnson, S. (2004b) 'Gender norms in financial markets: Evidence from Kenya', *World Development*, vol 32, no 8, pp1355–1374

North, D. (1977) 'Markets and other allocation systems in history: The challenge of Karl Polanyi', *Journal of European Economic History*, vol 6, no 3, pp703–716

North, D. (1990) *Institutions, Institutional Change and Economic Performance*, Cambridge University Press, Cambridge

Polanyi, K. (2001) *The Great Transformation: The Political and Economic Origins of Our Time*, Beacon Press, Boston (1st edition, 1944)

Rodrik, D. and Subramanian, A. (2003) 'The primacy of institutions (and what this does and does not mean)', *Finance and Development*, June, pp31–34

Sen, A. K. (1999) *Development as Freedom*, Oxford University Press, Oxford

Toye, J. (1995) 'The new institutional economics and its implications for development theory', in J. Harriss, J. Hunter and C. M. Lewis (eds) *The New Institutional Economics and Third World Development*, Routledge, London

White, G. (1993) 'Towards a political analysis of markets', *IDS Bulletin*, vol 24, no 3, pp4–11

Williamson, O. (1983) *Markets and Hierarchies: Analysis and Antitrust Implications*, Macmillan, New York

Williamson, O. E. (2000) 'The new institutional economics: Taking stock, looking ahead', *Journal of Economic Literature*, vol 38, no 3, pp595–613

Further Readings

Assies, W. (2003) 'David versus Goliath in Cochabamba', *Latin American Perspectives*, vol 30, no 3, pp14–36

Bardhan, P. K. (1989) *The Economic Theory of Agrarian Institutions*, Oxford University Press, Oxford

Johnson, S. (2004a) '"Milking the elephant": Financial markets as real markets in Kenya', *Development and Change*, vol 35, no 2, pp249–275

Kregel, J. (2007) 'Financial markets and economic development: Myth and institutional reality', in G. M. Hodgson (ed.), *The Evolution of Economic Institutions: A Critical Reader*, Edward Elgar, Cheltenham

Mantzavinos, C. (2001) *Individuals, Institutions and the Market*, Cambridge University Press, Cambridge

Nickson, A. and Vargas, C. (2002) 'The limitations of water regulation', *Bulletin of Latin American Research*, vol 21, no 1, pp99–120

Platteau, J.-P. (1994a) 'Behind the market stage where real societies exist – Part I: The role of public and private order institutions', *Journal of Development Studies*, vol 30, no 3, pp533–577

Platteau, J.-P. (1994b) 'Behind the market stage where real societies exist – Part II:

The role of moral norms', *Journal of Development Studies*, vol 30, no 4, pp386–422

Platteau, J.-P. (2000) *Institutions, Social Norms, and Economic Development*, Harwood, Amsterdam

Rodrik, D., Subramanian, A. and Trebbi, F. (2004) 'Institutions rule: The primacy of institutions over geography and integration in economic development', *Journal of Economic Growth*, vol 9, no 2, pp131–165

Rosenbaum, E. F. (2000) 'What is a market? On the methodology of a contested concept', *Review of Social Economy*, vol 58, no 4, pp455–482

Sen, A. K. (1993) 'Markets and freedoms: Achievements and limitations of the market mechanism in promoting individual freedoms', *Oxford Economic Papers*, vol 45, no 4, pp519–541

8

Democracy and Political Participation

Séverine Deneulin

Aims of the chapter

- To analyse various mechanisms through which people exercise their agency in the public space.
- To examine the complexity of democratic decision-making and its consequences for development outcomes.
- To understand the intricate relationship between economic, social and political processes.

Key points

- An effective democracy requires more than free and fair elections and majority rule. It also requires key political institutions and basic political and civil rights, such as freedom of speech, association and information.
- Democracy has intrinsic, instrumental and constructive value.
- Economic and social rights, on the one hand, and political and civil rights, on the other, are intimately related.
- Political equality is a basic requirement for democracy. Economic, social and political inequality tend to reinforce one another.
- Careful attention must be paid to the *quality* of the democratic process, particularly with respect to the inclusion of all voices in the exercise of public reasoning.

Agency is a core concept of the human development and capability approach. People are not passive patients of social welfare institutions, but are active subjects of their own destiny. A benevolent dictator who ensures that his people have the capability to be healthy, educated and live in a peaceful environment still fails to recognize them as subjects of their own development. This is because the process of development ultimately rests on 'the ability of people to help themselves and to influence the world' (Sen, 1999, p18). In the modern world, this ability is specifically expressed through political participation and democratic decision-making.

Tragically, there is no dearth of countries where this ability is being denied to the majority every day. Perhaps the most disturbing example of how autocratic rule has led a country into chaos and despair in recent times is Zimbabwe. But we will never know the exact number of casualties exacerbated by military inaction during the 2008 cyclone in Burma, in view of an earlier crackdown on peaceful protests against price inflation. As long as Kim Jong-Il rules over North Korea, we will also never know the number of people who starved to death under the misguided policies of his autocratic regime. In contrast, some might argue that the lack of agency among Cubans is precisely the reason why everyone in the country has the opportunity to be healthy and educated, unlike those in other Latin American countries.

This chapter does not examine the relationship between democracy and human development in a consequential way, as if democracy were not an integral component of human development but merely an external variable. Rather, it discusses democracy and political participation as a fundamental dimension of the human development and capability approach. As detailed in Chapter 2, the capability approach contains three key terms: capabilities, functionings and agency. This chapter relates to the latter and its practice in the public sphere.

We start by discussing democracy as a mechanism through which people exercise their agency in the public space. We highlight that democracy is much more than free and fair elections. It requires fundamental political and civil rights and basic political institutions. We also highlight that political participation is a necessary component of electoral democracies. We then discuss the universal value of democracy, which Sen has split into three components: intrinsic, instrumental and constructive. We further underscore that civil and political rights are closely connected to economic and social rights, and vice versa. In addition, we examine how these democratic ideals are translated into the practice of politics and policy-making. We illustrate that democracy is not confined to the realm of politics but also has socio-economic roots. We discuss the relationship between political equality – the foundation of democracy – and social and economic equality. Furthermore, we briefly discuss the deliberative aspect of democracy and how public reasoning constitutes its essence. We stress in this respect the close links between education and democracy. Finally, we examine democracy at the global level and ask whether global civil society can be an answer to the so-called global democratic deficit.

A mechanism for exercising agency in the public sphere

Democracy literally means 'rule by the people' (from the Ancient Greek *demos*, people, and *kratos*, rule). Essentially, democracy is nothing more than a mechanism that people have designed to rule themselves. In a small book entitled *Democracy*, which summarizes his substantial scholarship on the issue, the American political scientist Robert Dahl defines democratic decision-making by five criteria (2000, pp37–38). First, democracy requires effective participation. Before a policy is adopted, all members must have equal and effective opportunities for making their views known to others as to what the policy should be. Second, it is based on voting equality. When the moment arrives for the final policy decision to be made, every member should have an equal and effective opportunity to vote, and all votes should be counted as equal. Third, it rests on 'enlightened understanding'. Within reasonable limits, each member should have equal and effective opportunities for learning about alternative policies and their likely consequences. Fourth, each member should have control of the agenda, that is, members should have the exclusive opportunity to decide upon the agenda and change it. Fifth, democratic decision-making should include all adults. All (or at least most) adult permanent residents should have the full rights of citizens that are implied by the first four criteria.

The idea of political equality lies at the core of democratic decision-making. A violation of one of the above criteria leads to political inequality between people, and hence disrupts the democratic process. A democratic government is one which strives to meet as many of these criteria as possible. These criteria do not however exist in an institutional vacuum. Dahl outlines the following institutions necessary for a well-functioning democracy (2000, p86):

1 *Elected officials*: control over government decisions about policy is constitutionally vested in elected officials.
2 *Free and fair elections*: elected officials are chosen in frequent and fairly-conducted elections in which coercion is comparatively uncommon.
3 *Inclusive suffrage*: practically all adults have the right to vote in the election of officials.
4 *Right to run for office*: practically all adults have the right to run for elective offices in the government, though age limits may be higher for holding office than for the suffrage.
5 *Freedom of expression*: citizens have a right to express themselves without the danger of severe punishment on political matters broadly defined, including criticism of officials, the government, the regime, the socio-economic order and the prevailing ideology.
6 *Alternative information*: citizens have a right to seek out alternative sources of information. Moreover, alternative sources of information (should) exist that are not under the control of the government or any other single political group attempting to influence public political beliefs and attitudes, and these alternative sources are effectively protected by law.

7 *Associational autonomy*: to achieve their various rights, including those listed above, citizens also have a right to form relatively independent associations or organizations, including independent political parties and interest groups.

Dahl uses the word 'polyarchy' (meaning 'rule by the many') to refer to a government that possesses all of the above institutions. Polyarchy is thus a modern representative democracy which rests on fundamental civil and political rights, such as the right to vote, the right of association and the right to freedom of expression.

As should be obvious from the above, democracy is much more than majority rule obtained at elections, a theme that runs throughout the literature on democracy found in the human development and capability approach:

> We must not identify democracy with majority rule. Democracy has complex demands, which certainly include voting and respect for election results, but it also requires the protection of liberties and freedoms, respect for legal entitlements, and the guaranteeing of free discussion and uncensored distribution of news and fair comment. Even elections can be deeply defective if they occur without the different sides getting an adequate opportunity to present their respective cases, or without the electorate enjoying the freedom to obtain news and to consider the views of the competing protagonists. (Sen, 1999, p10)

Free and fair elections are fundamental, as Box 8.1 discusses, but they make a mockery of democracy if they are not accompanied by the other fundamental civil and political rights. This is echoed in Drèze and Sen (2002, p24), who list other elements that are essential to democratic decision-making beyond the existence of free and fair elections, such as a respect for legal entitlements; the right to free expression (and uncensored media); the right to associate freely and hold public discussions; and the right to organize political movements or protests.

Box 8.1 Beyond free and fair elections

The past three decades have seen the global expansion of democracy, which has led to an extraordinary focus on the institution of elections. In countries around the world, elections have served to help resolve long-standing conflicts and to initiate or consolidate transitions to democracy. For states recovering from recent conflict, elections have often been central to peace agreements. Fair elections have become an increasingly critical requirement if governments hope to have legitimacy in the eyes of the international community and their own citizens. Electoral legitimacy and outcomes, in turn, greatly affect the prospects for effective governance.

International declarations, agreements and norms unambiguously establish democratic elections as the basis of legitimate government. The Universal Declaration of Human Rights provides that the 'will of the people shall be the basis of the authority of government' as 'expressed in periodic and genuine elections'. Incorporating this principle into a binding international treaty, the International Covenant on Civil and Political Rights (ICCPR), provides that 'Every citizen shall have the right and the opportunity … to vote and to be elected at genuine periodic elections'. Other international agreements and declarations, including declarations by regional organizations in Africa, Europe and the Americas, recognize the right to participate in government through elected representatives.

Elections remain central to broader strategies for promoting democracy. First, competitive elections can catalyse profound political change in a society. Elections in societies in transition or crisis can be seminal events that, if successful, not only confer legitimacy on governments but can also profoundly influence institutions, power arrangements and citizens' expectations. Second, elections provide significant new opportunities for citizen involvement in public affairs. They are an opportunity to engage civic organizations and citizens in democratic politics through voter education, election monitoring, policy research and advocacy. They can provide an avenue for the participation of women, minorities and disadvantaged groups, who traditionally have had less access to politics and governance. Finally, competitive elections offer a means of establishing accountability, channelling political competition and determining leadership succession.

Genuine democracy, of course, requires substantially more than democratic elections. Even countries that hold reasonably competitive elections may lack constitutional limits on governmental power, deprive citizens of basic rights, or lack tolerance of religious or ethnic minorities. Indeed, in some circumstances, elections can sharpen ethnic differences or exacerbate communal tensions. To build genuine democracy, societies must foster a democratic culture and the rule of law in addition to holding democratic elections. But elections are essential to democracy and to legitimate government.

Extract from Eric Bjornlund 'Free and Fair Elections', published on the website of Democracy International at www.democracyinternational.com, and based on his book *Beyond Free and Fair Elections: Monitoring Elections and Building Democracy* (John Hopkins University Press, 2004).

In development circles, the term 'democratic governance' is widely used. The *Human Development Report* (UNDP, 2002) on 'Deepening Democracy in a Fragmented World', defines democratic governance as a 'set of principles and core values that allow poor people to gain power through participation while protecting them from arbitrary, unaccountable actions in their lives by governments, multinational corporations and other forces' (2002, pvi). The *Report* highlights some key institutions of democratic governance, which are reminiscent of Dahl's classification. These include (UNDP, 2002, p4): a system of representation with well-functioning political parties and interest associations; an electoral system that guarantees free and fair elections, as well as universal suffrage; a system of checks and balances based on the separation of powers, with independent judicial and legislative branches; a vibrant civil society, able to monitor government and private business – and provide alternative forms of political participation; a free, independent media; and effective civilian control over the military and other security forces.

Democratic governance contains at its core not only a well-functioning representative democracy but also participatory mechanisms that enable people to voice their concerns outside normal electoral processes, such as direct protests against a government's policies.[1] The case of the Mabira forest in Chapter 1 is a good example of political participation beyond elections – the section below relates further examples.

The language of 'participation' to refer to the ability of people to be agents of their own lives entered mainstream development discourse in the 1970s through 'Rapid Rural Appraisal', a method aimed at enabling outsiders to design agricultural projects that responded to local contexts. Rapid Rural Appraisal became 'Participatory Rural Appraisal' in the 1980s, a methodology that enables local people to decide for themselves about what should be done and changed in their lives (Chambers 1998).

This focus on 'participation' has come under critical scrutiny in the development literature. In *Participation: The New Tyranny*, Cooke and Kothari (2001) argue that participatory development inherently implies the danger of tyranny and 'unjustified exercise of power'. Participation, including political activism, can sometimes reinforce injustices if sufficient attention is not paid to the complexities of power – a point we shall return to in greater detail below. Cooke and Kothari warn against a blanket endorsement of participatory mechanisms of decision-making:

> [The fundamental problems of participation] that are most apparent to us are the naïveté of assumptions about the authen-ticity of motivations and behaviour in participatory processes; how the language of empowerment masks a real concern for managerialist effectiveness; the quasi-religious associations of participatory rhetoric and practice; and how an emphasis on the micro-level of intervention can obscure, and indeed sustain, broader macro-level inequalities and injustice. (Cooke and Kothari, 2001, pp13–14)

In *Participation: From Tyranny to Transformation?* Hickey and Mohan (2004) address the critique that participation can often ignore power relationships. They argue that participation discourses have to be embedded into coherent theories of development and brought beyond the individual and local level to the institutional and structural level. Participatory development is not only about implementing local projects, but is also about people ruling themselves through representation. In other words, political participation is the necessary companion to representative democracy. And this includes addressing the biases of power imbalances.

Before addressing the disruptive effects of power imbalances in participatory and democratic mechanisms, we must address another question:

why should people be agents of their own development? Why should they be able to rule themselves, either directly through participation or indirectly through representation?

The value of democracy

Robert Dahl justifies the desirability of democracy by invoking its alternative. Democracy is desirable because it is ultimately better than authoritarianism and fares better on a number of issues (2000, pp60–61): it prevents cruel and megalomaniac autocrats from coming to power and harming citizens; it guarantees fundamental human rights, such as the freedom of expression that autocratic governments cannot grant; it better serves people's interests than an autocratic government; it gives people the right to self-determination; it is better at guaranteeing peace between nations; and citizens are generally more prosperous under a democratic government than under an autocratic one. Dahl concludes that, 'with all these advantages, democracy is, for most of us, a far better gamble than any attainable alternative to it' (2000, p61).

Intrinsic value

The human development and capability approach justifies the desirability of democracy as a form of government and mechanism for people to rule themselves on three fronts: first, democracy and political participation is a value in itself. As Sen (1999, p10) puts it: 'Political freedom is a part of human freedom in general, and exercising civil and political rights is a crucial part of good lives of individuals as social beings'. To deny people the freedom to participate in political life, either through direct or indirect forms of political participation, is a violation of their human dignity. Drèze and Sen (2002) push the argument further by affirming that this intrinsically valuable freedom does not have to rest on the fulfilment of other freedoms. For example, not being able to be adequately nourished does not entail that people should not be able to participate as political agents: 'being able to do something through political action – for oneself and for others – is one of the elementary freedoms that people have reason to value. The popular appeal of many social movements in India confirms that this basic capability is highly valued even among people who lead very deprived lives in material terms' (2002, p359).

One has to note here that this intrinsic value of democracy does not mean that democratic institutions will be the same everywhere and at any time. Democracy, this mechanism that allows people to rule themselves, need not be exercised in the same way across time and space. The democratic institutions that were outlined earlier are not universally identical but are always embedded into local cultures and practices. Box 8.2 illustrates how the universal aspiration of people to rule themselves may take different forms in different cultures. Thus, democratic rule does not necessarily have to be modelled on Western liberal democracies.

Box 8.2 Local forms of democratic institutions in Afghanistan

With the formal justice system fragmented, ineffective and lacking in resources, reach and legitimacy, informal justice institutions serve as important alternative mechanisms of dispute resolution in Afghanistan. These informal systems of justice are, by and large, based on indigenous tribal practices and local religious traditions. One of the most important institutions of informal justice in Afghanistan is the *jirga* (or its approximate equivalent *shura*). In the cultural and political context of Afghanistan, *jirga* is most closely associated with the rituals and processes of traditional Pashtun dispute settlement, where people sit in a large circle in order to resolve a dispute, and/or make collective decisions about important communal issues and problems.

In the context of the resolution of disputes and crimes, *jirga* are much more often an ad hoc body rather than a standing institution with a fixed membership or, in some cases, a combination of these two forms – a standing body with additional members chosen according to the issue at hand. In the south and east of Afghanistan, the traditional *jirga* is more strongly institutionalized and structured. In this context, the *jirga* at the local community level is a tribal institution of dispute settlement that incorporates the prevailing unwritten, centuries-old body of customary laws and the views of tribal elders who are respected for their expertise and social influence in the community. Their *prikra* (judgment) is binding (morally and socially) on the parties involved.

Jirgas deal with issues ranging from relatively minor problems, such as disputes over the boundaries of farms and minor bodily harm, to more serious offences, including murder and disputes over personal property and inheritance. The survey commissioned for this study [i.e. the *National Human Development Report*] reveals that Afghans tend to take non-public land and other property disputes to *jirga* for settlement. An important feature of the *jirga* is that its outcome commands a morally- and socially-binding effect only when it is arrived at fairly, and is so perceived by the accused offender, the victim and the village. Should any of these stakeholders, especially the immediate protagonists, see a *prikra* as unfair, the affected party is entitled to appeal. This often happens when customary laws are wrongly applied and/or misinterpreted, or when corruption and favouritism by the mediators are noticed. Unlike state courts, the outcome of which usually result in finding losers and winners (the guilty and the non-guilty), *jirga* brings disputants and the village together to find collective solutions to problems.

Despite their appeal, *jirgas* have nonetheless very negative features. Among the most serious of these are the lack of participation by, and the treatment of, women in the process of dispute settlement. Normally all-male or male-dominated local councils, *jirgas* exclude women and young people from participation and decision-making. Like other rule of law institutions, *jirgas* need to be held accountable on various fronts. The Afghan Independent Human Rights Commission, as an independent government institution funded primarily by external donors, monitors the compliance of *jirgas* to human rights principles. Reforming and monitoring *jirgas* and creating a framework in which they can act as complementary dispute resolution mechanisms, will give them an even wider appeal and will make justice in Afghanistan more accessible.

Edited excerpts from the 2007 *National Human Development Report* of Afghanistan, on 'The Rule of Law: Bridging Modernity and Tradition', pp90–94, with comments by Khwaga Kakar.

Instrumental value

The intrinsic value of democracy, that the ability of people to take part in decisions that affect their lives is a good in itself, does not detract from its instrumental value. Democracy is good because it leads to good consequences. Because democracy is a mechanism through which people can voice their concerns in the public space – concerns, for example, about receiving adequate health care, about preserving the environment for future generations, about care of immigrants and asylum seekers, etc. – it means that people's demands are generally met.

This means that securing civil and political rights should be allied with securing economic and social rights at the same time. In fact, the human development and capability approach firmly maintains that there can be no dichotomy between the economic and political spheres, and that both are deeply intertwined. Ensuring economic and social security is a matter of politics. This links to what has been said in Chapter 1: ethics – and politics – lies at the heart of economics. This insight has had a critical impact on the understanding of famines. Sen was possibly the first author to attribute the cause of famines to the failure of democracy and not to food shortages:

> Political and civil rights give people the opportunity to draw attention forcefully to general needs and to demand appropriate public action. The response of a government to the acute suffering of its people often depends on the pressure that is put on it. The exercise of political rights (such as voting, criticizing, protesting and the like) can make a real difference to the political incentives that operate on a government. I have discussed elsewhere the remarkable fact that, in the terrible history of famines in the world, no substantial famine has ever occurred in any independent and democratic country with a relatively free press. We cannot find exceptions to this rule, no matter where we look: the recent famines of Ethiopia, Somalia or other dictatorial regimes; famines in the Soviet Union in the 1930s; China's 1958–1961 famine with the failure of the Great Leap Forward; or, earlier still, the famines in Ireland or India under alien rule. China, although it was in many ways doing much better economically than India, still managed (unlike India) to have a famine, indeed the largest recorded famine in world history: nearly 30 million people died in the famine of 1958–1961, while faulty governmental policies remained uncorrected for three full years. The policies went uncriticized because there were no opposition parties in parliament, no free press and no multiparty elections. Indeed, it is precisely this lack of challenge that allowed the deeply-defective policies to continue even though they were killing millions each year. (Sen, 1999, p7)

While citizens may have the power to challenge policies that do not promote their well-being, the relationship between the latter and democracy itself nonetheless remains a complex one.[2] Many democratic countries live with high levels of poverty and inequality: to begin with, look at the case of the biggest democracy in the world, India. Moreover, because people have different concerns about what matters, democracy cannot guarantee the fulfilment of *everyone*'s demands since they might be in conflict with one another. For example, the demands of a particular group to live in an ethnically homogenous country conflict with the demands of other groups, who welcome economic and political refugees, or the demands of a landed elite to keep their assets conflict with the demands of landless farmers who would like a claim to the same land.

It is beyond the scope of this textbook to proceed with a careful examination of the conditions under which democracy can lead to better conditions of life for the general population. But one condition that can be stressed here is the importance of the political inclusion of marginalized groups. As we will discuss in the next section, political equality is a requirement of democracy. Without a minimum level of equality, democratic decision-making risks furthering injustices and inequalities. This does not suggest that authoritarianism becomes a better option when it is more instrumental to promoting basic freedoms than democracy. Land reform may be better achieved in a communist dictatorship than in a democracy with conflicting interests, and Cuba is often cited as an example of a country with much higher social achievements than its democratic neighbours in Latin America. But rejecting democracy on the basis of its lower instrumental value also means rejecting its intrinsic value. If an authoritarian government performs better socially or economically than a democratic one, it would still undoubtedly be denying people their most elementary freedoms.

Constructive value

Finally, the third value that the human development and capability approach attributes to democracy is that of its contribution to the construction of values around which a society is arranged. Democracies construct collective values, such as the values of tolerance and social equity, and establishing the priority of helping those in need first – but it is noteworthy that some democratically-constructed values might be negative, like racism. Political parties are based on certain sets of values. Democrats in the US traditionally endorse the value of solidarity and social justice, while Republicans tend to endorse more the values of individual freedom as non-interference. In Britain, similar values divide the Labour and Conservative parties. Depending on which party wins the elections, the policies implemented reflect the winning party's values. In turn, these policies may socialize people into adopting certain values, which then lead them to support these policies even further. Not that democracy is the only place where values are constructed – social values are similarly constructed by the advertising industry, the media, or religious organizations, for example.

Nevertheless, democracy is the mechanism through which these different sets of values are debated in the public space so that a consensus can be built around a government's policy priorities. Box 8.3 illustrates this in the case of the establishment of the welfare state in Costa Rica during the early 1940s.

Box 8.3 The democratic construction of social welfare-related values in Costa Rica

In 1940, Rafael Calderón won the presidential elections. In 1941, he introduced a social security scheme, which incorporated social insurance and social welfare programmes for the poorest. He also introduced other social guarantees, such as an eight-hour working day, a minimum wage, protection against arbitrary dismissal, and the right for workers to organize themselves. In 1942, the Constitution was amended in order to incorporate a new social security law and a Labour Code.

In 1949, another President, José Figueres, instituted universal suffrage for both men and women, and introduced compulsory secondary education, making both primary and secondary education free and state-financed. Food and clothing was state-provided to poor students and adult education programmes were organized for those left out by the educational system. He also introduced a law that allocated each year 6 per cent of GDP to public expenditures in education. He nationalized the banking system, abolished the army and imposed a wealth tax. These measures allowed the state to plan economic development, and they also led to a political weakening of the coffee elite, which had hitherto dominated the ownership of financial capital. By weakening the power of the coffee elite, and building the 'state entrepreneur', Figueres determined the subsequent conditions for the economic and social development of the country. His party, the *Partido de Liberación Nacional*, became the majority party that Costa Ricans voted for during the entire post-war period until the mid-1980s.

Among the policies implemented were education policies, which further improved child and adult education and increased rural educational coverage, and an expansion of the health system. In 1960, the social security system covered 15 per cent of the total population. A constitutional amendment in 1961 gave the government 10 years to provide full coverage to all the population. The percentage of the general population covered by health insurance increased from 15 to 78 per cent between 1960 and 1980. A special health programme, involving a network of health centres and mobile clinics, was established for those living in rural areas. This strong emphasis on primary healthcare (vaccination, hygiene and nutrition education, sanitation, nutrition programmes, child and maternal care and family planning, etc.) led to a strong improvement in health outcomes (infant mortality rates decreased by more than a third during the 1970s).

By the beginning of the 1980s, Costa Rica had become an exemplary social democracy with levels of human well-being rivalling those of industrial countries, despite much more modest economic resources. Life expectancy had increased by nearly 30 years in half a century. Between 1940 and 1990, the proportion of illiterate people had been reduced from 27 to 7 per cent. Infant mortality rates had decreased from 137 to 15 per thousand. Health insurance coverage had expanded from zero to 84 per cent in 1990, and the coverage of basic services, such as water and sanitation facilities, was almost complete in both rural and urban areas.

In sum, the value that these social policies contained – solidarity – and the consensus that the state was the best keeper of this value – not private initiative – was constructed through democratic processes. The success of the social policies in responding to people's claims (e.g. for better health and education) led Costa Ricans to further endorse the value of state-provided solidarity by continually electing the same political party, until the debt crisis of the 1980s introduced a new set of values, which questioned the democratic consensus centred around the value of state-provided solidarity, and favoured the value of freedom seen as non-state interference.

Adapted from Séverine Deneulin (2005) 'Development as freedom and the Costa Rican human development story', *Oxford Development Studies*, vol 33, no 3/4, pp493–510.

As a concluding note on the value of democracy, one has to bear in mind that, by recognizing the intrinsic, instrumental and constructive values of democracy, the human development and capability approach does not advocate whether a democracy should endorse either liberalism or socialism. It precludes any ideological presupposition regarding the appropriate function of democracy, whether to safeguard capitalism or signal its demise. Democracy does not serve any other purpose than being a mechanism enabling people to express their ability to be agents in their own lives. Whether the outcome of that process leads to a social democratic government which interferes in markets and generates generous welfare institutions or to a neoliberal government which lets markets function, it is ultimately a matter of the demands of *all* people being *fairly* represented through democratic institutions.

From democratic theory to practice

So far, we have discussed what democracy and political participation are in theory. We saw that, ideally, a democracy functions on the basis of the formal exercise of political and civic rights (freedom of expression, of association, etc.), the full political participation of people (i.e. every citizen should have a say in matters that affect his/her life), an accountable and transparent government and well-functioning electoral institutions, etc. In practice, however, these democratic ideals are never fully observed. Contrasting the *practice* of democracy with its *ideal*, Drèze and Sen (2002, p347) observe that the actual practice of democratic ideals in a given society critically depends on a large array of factors. They cite the following: first, the practice of democracy depends on the extent of political participation, like election turnouts, the number of political parties, and the number of people who present themselves in elections. If a leader is elected with only 30 per cent of the electorate voting, his or her decisions can hardly been seen as representative of the wishes of the population. Or if citizens can only vote for two, and indeed perhaps only one, candidate, one cannot argue that the holding of elections was an entirely democratic practice. Another factor that Drèze and Sen single out is public awareness of political processes, as well as policy decisions and implications. For example, the public should have access to complete information about the social consequences of a certain policy decision. If a government makes the case for, say, a certain type of trade policy, the public should have access to the information about the consequences of that policy. If the democratically-elected government hides crucial information, such as the impact assessment of the trade policy on the livelihoods of poor farmers but publicizes widely the impact of the policy on large-scale producers, that government could not be said to be 'democratic'. Also, democratic practice depends on the vigour of the opposition to the ruling political party. An elected government may eliminate by intimidation members of the opposition – by threatening voters that, for example, their house might be demolished if they are seen to be supporting the opposition. Linked to this is the nature of popular organizations at the grassroots level. Democratic practice depends on lively civil society organizations, which are accountable to the people they serve. Finally, Drèze and Sen stress the distribution of power in the country as a major factor impeding democratic ideals, a point we shall examine in greater detail later.

Among other factors that disrupt democratic institutions are inefficiency, corruption, incompetency of the bureaucracy and lack of motivation (Drèze and Sen, 2002, p352). In some countries, some legal cases might take years to receive a hearing in courts. Some might never be heard at all. Corruption, which Transparency International defines as 'the misuse of entrusted power for private gain',[3] may dramatically affect the depth of democratic institutions and their ability to respond to people's claims in some contexts. When bribes largely dwindle the public resources available for the financing of public goods, or when people have to bribe their doctor in order to receive health treatment, or bribe the teacher in order for their children to receive education, this certainly undermines the quality of democracy, even if the country may guarantee 'free and fair elections', freedom of information, association and other civil and political rights. Another democratic dysfunction that Drèze and Sen highlight is the lack of skill among civil servants who work in democratic institutions – an electoral commissioner might not be familiar with electoral law, for example. Moreover, civil servants might lack motivation to conduct their work, creating a significant backlog of demands unmet – often typical in legal services.

At a more basic level, a frequent cause for the lack of translation of democratic ideals into practice, or even the democratic functioning of democratic institutions, is the lack of an appropriate democratic political culture – political culture being defined as the attitudes, beliefs and values that underlie a political system itself (Burnell and Randall, 2008, p278). Democracy is not just a matter of writing a new constitution or establishing democratic institutions. Mentalities have to be prepared as well. As the *Human Development Report* 2002 put it, in relation to the lasting influence of the military in some democratic countries, 'Old habits die hard' (p88). The report gives the example of Nigeria, where the armed forces overturned democratically-elected leaders in the 1990s, and continue to hold strategic political and economic positions, such as in the oil industry. When a country has known a dictatorship, military or civilian, it is difficult to break the authoritarian political culture or to suddenly curb the power of the military.

In a study on democratization, Whitehead (2002) insightfully pointed out that it is one thing to design democratic institutions and quite another to educate or persuade citizens to live by democratic precepts. In the Dominican Republic, for example, where the dictator Trujillo ruled for 31 years until 1961, the country continues to struggle to transform its clientelist political culture into a democratic one to this day. In a political survey conducted in 2001, 86 per cent of Dominicans still identified the role of a good president with a paternalist figure who should solve the problems directly affecting their lives. Clientelism can certainly survive within democratic institutions. Democracy requires a political culture where people have attitudes that express democratic practices and values, such as the attitude of considering oneself as a citizen with rights and not the client of a patron. Box 8.4 provides a further illustration of clientelistic political practices – sometimes violent ones – which are able to survive within democratic institutions.

Box 8.4 Democracy and the politics of violence in Bangladesh

Since the re-introduction of democracy in 1990, Bangladesh has held three parliamentary elections organized under caretaker governments, and recording very high voter participation. All three elections resulted in the transition of power from one party to another, and this was managed peacefully. Successive governments have introduced important administrative changes aimed at promoting a more inclusive political culture. Currently, there are four levels of elected government (village, Union, Thana and District), which are entrusted with a wide range of development and welfare responsibilities. Finally, Bangladesh has a vibrant civil society sector and one of the largest NGO communities in the world today, all of which have assumed important roles in public life.

Since 1990, the main political parties have actively sought to increase their support base by extending their presence to the grassroots of rural and urban communities. One of the ways they have managed to accomplish this has been to establish party-affiliated, interest-based organizations such as trade unions, farmers' cooperatives, youth and women's groups among communities, and to use these to recruit new members. However, despite not having formal roles in local government, party leaders have increasingly exerted considerable influence on decisions related to key activities, including the distribution of relief, the delivery of key public services and the implementation of development projects. In seeking access to these public benefits or goods, people reported that the support of party activists was more important than that of those elected to carry out local government responsibilities.

Politics in Bengali – *rajniti* – literally translates as the rule or custom of the king. Today, it is the rule or custom of the network linked to the party in power that imposes itself locally. For citizens, therefore, having the correct political affiliation or connection significantly strengthens entitlement claims or increases the chance of well-being needs being met. Equally, for those with the wrong political connections, the possibility of exclusion is high.

In Bengali, the term *mastaan* refers to a person involved in organized crime and with the criminal underworld. Mastaans are feared because of their use of violence and intimidation in pursuit of their own interests. While researching the dynamics of people's access to government services, the term 'mastaan' frequently came up in interviews. There is considerable overlap and interaction between mastaans and local party leaders. Thus, political activists deployed mastaans in order to capture or retain control over populations in their constituencies. Mastaans, on the other hand, used the relationship to political parties to promote their own political careers, or protect and extend their different 'enterprises'. This relationship effectively allowed mastaans to manipulate important aspects of the state and governance. The support of mastaans is also sought to deal with everyday events, such as accessing health and education services, dealing with law enforcement and judicial systems, and protecting business interests.

In seeking to improve their lives, poor people have to negotiate their way through this political terrain on a daily basis. This is the terrain of 'real' governance, a terrain that is as harsh as it is uncertain. While some poor people can benefit from the system, they do so on terms that they know ultimately will reinforce their dependence on those helping them. This is because the political terrain is organized to serve private or partisan interests, and to distribute favours instead of responding to rights or entitlements. Clientelism has long been recognized as a problem for development in Bangladesh and in many other developing countries. The irony of this case is that, while superficially governance has improved, clientelism has become more of a problem. Poor people in Bangladesh have not moved towards a status of greater citizenship, but instead have moved to a position of being even more tightly-controlled clients. For the majority (including those fortunate enough to benefit), therefore, the world of politics is a contaminated, exclusionary and potentially violent reality.

Edited extract from Joseph Devine, 'Well-being and the rotten foundations of a development success', WeD Briefing Paper 3, February 2008, available at: http://www.welldev.org.uk

A basic assumption of democratic theory is that respecting the principle of 'one person, one vote', and the respect of all civil and political rights, is a sufficient condition for meeting the requirement of political equality and for democracy itself to function effectively. However, this does not guarantee that all citizens will be granted equal participation in the decision-making process. Political equality is not only determined by political conditions, but also economic and social ones, as has already been alluded to above. One of the hallmarks of the human development perspective on democracy is to go beyond the political boundaries and emphasize the importance of social and economic conditions in determining how democratic political institutions function. These social conditions range 'from educational levels and political traditions to the nature of social inequalities and popular organizations' (Drèze and Sen, 2002, p350).

They illustrate this with the right to vote. When people are not well-informed about different political parties and their programmes or when they do not have the educational level to understand their programmes or the policy issues that concern them, their vote may not reflect their best interests. They may vote for the politician that talked nicely to them during a political visit to the area where they live while not fully understanding the political programme of the party that the politician represents. Or they may vote for the politician that gave favours to a member of their family, or vote out of fear of sanction if they do not support the patron that protects their family. Drèze and Sen (2002, p351) also give the example of the Indian legal system to illustrate this lack of correspondence between the ideal of democracy and its actual practice. The legal system may theoretically be based on democratic principles, such as equality of all before the law but, in practice, those who are from lower castes tend to have their cases delayed, and cases that relate to domestic violence – rape is condemned by law – do not often lead to legal punishment.

The failure of democratic practice to meet its ideals thus has economic and social roots. Another important mechanism that leads to severe dysfunction in democratic institutions is that of the unequal exercise of power based on economic and social inequalities. Even if elections are free and fair, those who command more money have a large capacity to finance the political campaigns that will best serve their interests – such as the National Rifle Association, the American Israeli Public Affairs Committee or the oil lobby in the US. Those who are better off economically will also tend to be better off in educational terms, and hence have a better grasp of political issues than less educated people, and will be better able to influence policies according to their own interests – for example, public resources destined to education going to the furthering of technology and science for a few at the expense of basic elementary schooling for the general population. In the case of India, Drèze and Sen (2002, p29) observe that the issues discussed in parliament tend to represent the concerns of corporate chambers and the defence establishment, in contrast to basic social issues such as primary education, health care and rural employment, which receive little attention in parliamentary debate. Those who command more economic resources also have a better control of the media and of what kind of 'news' goes into major national newspapers and television channels.

We therefore seem to reach a perverse situation: political equality is undermined by social and economic inequality, resulting in political decisions favouring those already enjoying an economically- and socially-privileged position, thereby deepening social and economic inequality, and ultimately political inequality itself. If economic, social and political inequalities reinforce one other, what hope is there of breaking this vicious circle through democratic practice? Here, again, the human development approach re-affirms the intrinsic value of democracy. After all, the unequal socio-economic outcomes of democracy do not justify authoritarianism. Rather, the solution lies in the strengthening of democratic practice. Drèze and Sen (2002) suggest two concrete ways for 'overcoming this association between social privilege and political power' (p10) and 'enhancing the political power of the underprivileged' (p29). First, the capability of the underprivileged for self-assertion must be enhanced by offering the marginalized incentives to organize in political organizations through which they can gain sufficient power to counteract the power of the privileged. The best example of this is probably the formation of the political party, Partido dos Trabalhadores (or Worker's Party) in Brazil, which was created in the early 1980s and elected to power in 2002. Since the PT obtained the majority in parliament and took the reins of the country, Brazil has made considerable progress in reducing its levels of poverty and inequality. The second option that Drèze and Sen propose to break the vicious circle of economic, social and political inequality is to create a sense of solidarity between the most privileged and the underprivileged (e.g. intellectuals and higher social classes speaking on behalf of the underprivileged and defending their interests). Drèze himself is one of the best examples of this, a sharp and bright intellectual with in-depth experience of life at the grassroots and who is entirely committed to fighting injustices of all kinds in India – he has, for example, been a key player in the Employment Guarantee Act, which seeks to give the legal right to work for people in rural areas, and in the campaign 'The Right to Food'.

Public reasoning

The two routes proposed above to overcome the disruptive influences of inequality on democratic decision-making are based on the fundamental assumption that, at the core of the democratic process, lies public reasoning. Decisions are reached not through force of violence, but through the force of argument and debate in the public space. For the human development and capability approach, democracy is first and foremost 'government by discussion' (Drèze and Sen 2002, p379).

Seeing public reasoning as central to the democratic experience requires that one pay particular attention to the way and the context in which this public debate takes place. This has been one of the major contributions of the literature on deliberative democracy. In a book on *Public Reasoning*, Henry Richardson (2002) argues that deliberation is the essence of democracy, because democracy is nothing else but an exercise in reasoning about what ought to be done in the public space, which policies should be undertaken, and what priorities should be pursued. The ends of policy-making are not given, neither are the means to achieve them, and policies have thus to be decided by the citizens themselves. Because decisions are not made following a pre-established rule or by 'flipping a coin' (2002, p76), but following a search for the 'best' decisions according to what ought to be done given a certain conception of truth and what is good, Richardson argues that reasoning is the mechanism in a democracy through which people rule themselves.

Understanding democracy as 'self-rule by reasoning' allows us to understand better why the idea of political equality is closely connected to social and economic equality, for economically and socially disadvantaged people often lack the reasoning and persuasive skills to participate fully as citizens. This point has been made strongly by deliberative democracy theorist James Bohman (1996, 1997). He introduces the concept of 'political functioning' to convey the idea that political equality requires economic and social conditions. In order for the democratic process to be fair, those who participate in the process need the capability to function politically, that is, they need to have the capability to participate in public reasoning. This requires that people have certain cognitive and communication skills in order to engage in the public debate. Among the skills required for effective political functioning are: the skill of initiating public dialogue or making proposals about an issue; the ability to engage in argument and counter-argument; skills in framing and reframing a debate, and finding ways to harmonize proposals and deal with conflicting views; and an ability for persuasive but not manipulative rhetoric (Bohman, 1996).

A just and legitimate democratic process is one in which citizens are endowed with a certain threshold level of adequate political functioning. If citizens are below the threshold, they lack the cognitive and communication skills necessary to engage in public deliberation, and will therefore not be able to participate and influence the outcome of these deliberations. They are in a situation of what Bohman describes as 'political poverty', which he defines simply as 'the inability of groups of citizens to participate effectively in the democratic process' (Bohman, 1997, p332). Conversely, if some citizens are above the threshold, they will have too much power in influencing the outcome of deliberations.

In other words, full political participation entails not only including everyone in a discussion but ensuring that every person included is equipped with an adequate level of political functioning and adequate cognitive and communication skills to advance her claims, so that 'the silence [of the uneducated] is [not] turned into consent by the more powerful deliberators who are able to ignore them' (Bohman, 1997, p333). This requires a strong educational system guaranteeing equal educational opportunities, with adequate public spending. Education is crucial for a healthy democracy, a point that will be developed more extensively in the next chapter. Those who lack these skills, even though they are formally and physically included in the democratic process, will most likely remain excluded from it.

Political participation at global level

The discussion above focused on democratic decision-making at the national level, as elections always take place within the boundaries of a nation-state. However, matters that affect people's lives are increasingly of a global nature – climate change, food production, terrorist threats, to name a few.

Unfortunately, there is no global government to address these issues in a democratic way. The current institutions of global governance, such as the World Bank, IMF and World Trade Organization, are perceived to be minimally accountable to the general public. This situation is often perceived to be one of global democratic deficit. Given the unrealistic feasibility of a democratically-elected government at the global level, political participation takes the place of involvement with civil society organizations that transcend national boundaries and affect democratic processes beyond their border. Or in other words, political participation becomes 'global public action'.

Public action is not to be understood solely as actions taken by elected governments, but also by direct efforts undertaken by the public at large to determine their lives. This can be done through collaborative actions – such as the participation of a group of citizens in the design and spending of a municipal budget – or adversarial action – such as demonstrations against the privatization of public services (Drèze and Sen, 2002, pv). The direct involvement of citizens in political processes, not through indirect representation, is crucial for a thriving democracy.

The term civil society refers broadly to the space between markets and states. It is:

> a political space where voluntary associations deliberately seek to shape the rules that govern one or the other aspect of social life. 'Rules' in this conception encompass specific policies, more general norms, and deeper social structures. ... Civil society exists whenever and wherever voluntary organizations try deliberately to mould certain governing rules of society. (Scholte, 2002, pp283–284)

It has been argued that civil society, taken in its global dimensions, is essential to making the global decision-making architecture more democratic. Scholte (2002, pp293–294) highlights six contributions of global civil society to making the economic and political system more democratic at a global level. First, global civil society gives voice to stakeholders. Civil society associations can open political space for social circles, like the poor and women who tend to get a limited hearing through other channels. For example, the organization 'Shack/Slum Dwellers International' plays a pivotal role in providing adequate housing for those living in slum conditions.[4] Second, global civil society engages in public education activities and an effective democracy depends on an informed citizenry, and civic associations can raise public awareness and understanding of transnational laws and regulatory institutions. In this respect, we can cite Transparency International, a global civil society organization that provides information about corruption and helps tackle the problem at national level. Third, global civil society fuels debate in and about global governance. For example, international NGOs like Oxfam, Action Aid and many others, and the campaign 'Make Poverty History', were influential in mobilizing public opinion and press for trade reforms at the World Trade Organizations that were less detrimental to developing countries. Fourth, global civil society increases the public transparency of global governance. Pressure from civil society can help bring regulatory frameworks and operations into the open, where they become susceptible to public scrutiny, as witnessed at the Doha trade rounds, for example. Fifth, global civil society increases the public accountability of regulatory agencies; and, sixth, it provides legitimacy to global governance institutions.

Despite global civil society's contribution to addressing the global democratic deficit, Scholte warns that strengthening and giving it more power is not necessarily the panacea to end all ills. He argues that global civil society organizations are often dominated by white middle-class Westerner 'do-gooders', that they can also function in a non-transparent way with secretive practices and leaders appointed rather than elected by members, and that their campaigns to change public opinion and contribution to global public reasoning might indeed carry biased information. For all these reasons, he concludes that one must be cautious in seeing global civil society as a way forward in addressing global problems democratically. The answer lies rather in deepening democracy at the national level itself, so that it can better design policies dealing with global problems in the long term. As is obvious from the arguments presented in this chapter, democracy is not a state that is reached, nor is it ever a completed process. Democracy is always in the making.

Questions

8.1. How would you describe the state of democratic institutions in your country?

8.2. Is democracy in your country responding to people's needs? Briefly outline and discuss how this is being achieved.

8.3. What are the values constructed by democratic decision-making in your country?

8.4 Critically discuss how the political power of marginalized groups might be enhanced in the context of military repression.

8.5 Give examples of civil society actions, at either the national or global level, that have changed a policy decision.

Notes

1   For more information on democratic governance, see the resources on the UNDP Oslo Governance Centre at www.undp.org/governance/about.htm. See also the Governance and Social Development Resource Centre at www.gsdrc.org.

2   See, for example, the UNRISD research project on 'Democracy, Governance and Wellbeing' at www.unrisd.org.

3   See www.transparency.org. Transparency International further differentiates between corruption 'according to rule' – when a bribe is paid to receive preferential treatment for something that the bribe receiver is required to do by

law – and corruption 'against the rule' – where a bribe is paid to obtain services the bribe receiver is prohibited from providing.

4   See www.sdinet.co.za. The success of this organization has been widely documented in Arjun Appadurai's article 'Capability to Aspire', which will be discussed further in Chapter 11.

Readings

Bohman, J. (1996) *Public Deliberation: Pluralism, Complexity and Democracy*, MIT Press, Cambridge, MA

Bohman, J. (1997) 'Deliberative democracy and effective social freedom', in J. Bohman and W. Regh (eds) *Deliberative Democracy: Essays on Reason and Politics*, MIT Press, Cambridge, MA

Burnell, P. and Randall, V. (eds.) (2008), *Politics in the Developing World*, Oxford University Press, Oxford

Chambers, R. (1998) 'Foreword', in J. Blackburn with J. Holland (eds) *Who Changes? Institutionalizing Participation in Development*, Intermediate Technology Publications, London

Cooke, B. and U. Kothari (eds) (2001) *Participation: The New Tyranny*, Zed, London

Dahl, R. (2000) *On Democracy*, Yale University Press, New Haven, CT

Drèze, J. and A. K. Sen (2002) *India: Development and Participation*, Oxford University Press, Delhi

Hickey, S. and G. Mohan (eds) (2004) *Participation: From Tyranny to Transformation?* Zed, London

Richardson, H. S. (2002) *Democratic Autonomy: Public Reasoning about the Ends of Policy*, Oxford University Press, Oxford

Scholte, J. (2002) 'Civil society and democracy in global governance', *Global Governance*, vol 8, no 3, pp281–304

Sen, A. K. (1999) 'Democracy as universal value,' *Journal of Democracy*, vol 10, no 3, pp3–17

UNDP (2002) *Human Development Report*, Oxford University Press, New York

Whitehead, L. (2002) *Democratization and Experience*, Oxford University Press, Oxford

Further readings

Boix, C. (2002) *Democracy and Redistribution*, Cambridge University Press, Cambridge

Crocker, D. (2006) 'Sen and deliberative democracy', in A. Kaufman (ed.) *Capabilities Equality: Basic Issues and Problems*, Routledge, New York

Dahl, R. (1989) *Democracy and its Critics*, Yale University Press, New Haven, CT

Diamond, L. (1999) *Developing Democracy*, Johns Hopkins University Press, Baltimore, MD

Dryzek, J. (2000) *Deliberative Democracy and Beyond*, Oxford University Press, Oxford

Fung, A. and Wright, E. O. (2001) *Deepening Democracy: Institutional Innovations in Empowered Participatory Governance*, Verso, London

Gutmann, A. and Thompson, D. (1996) *Democracy and Disagreement*, Harvard University Press, Cambridge, MA

Held, D. (1995) *Democracy and the Global Order*, Polity Press, Oxford

Przeworski, A. et al (1995) *Sustainable Democracy*, Cambridge University Press, Cambridge

Przeworski, A. et al (2000) *Democracy and Development: Political Institutions and Well-Being in the World, 1950–1990*, Cambridge University Press, Cambridge

UNDP (2004) *Democracy in Latin America*, UNDP, New York

Young, I. M. (2000) *Inclusion and Democracy*, Oxford University Press, Oxford

Welzel, C. and Inglehart, R. (2008), 'The role of ordinary people in democratization', *Journal of Democracy*, vol 19, no 1, pp126–140

9

Education

Elaine Unterhalter

Aims of the chapter

- To analyse what the key concepts of the capability approach – capability, functioning and agency – imply for educational theory and practice.
- To examine education as a human development dimension and in its role in promoting other valuable dimensions.
- To understand the differences between the human capital and human development approach to education.

Key Points

- Human capital theory sees the role of education as being instrumental to economic growth. Education provides people with the necessary productive skills that an industrialized economy requires. Education is an investment that yields economic returns.
- In contrast, the human development and capability approach sees education as fulfilling three roles: it is instrumental, empowering and redistributive.
- Education nurtures critical reflection and has crucial links with a healthy democracy.
- Applying the capability approach to the field of education puts the emphasis on capabilities and not only on functionings. It stresses the importance of conversion factors and diverse institutional arrangements for educational inputs to be translated into valuable outputs.
- Education has critical links to social justice.

Previous chapters have examined the human development and capability approach and how these ideas affect our understanding of central development topics, such as economic growth, equality, measurement, markets and democracy. Ideas are central to shaping policies and, indeed, 'changing history', as Chapter 3 has discussed.[1]

But no new ideas can emerge without educated minds. Education is the driving force of change in the world. Education (which is not always the same as schooling) brings empowerment. Without education, people can be subject to abuses by the most powerful. For example, illiterate peasants can be driven off their land by those who have access to legal instruments which they cannot influence. A woman, who does not have access to other points of view, may never come to question the arbitrary authority her husband has over her. Without education, people may be constrained to find menial jobs that do not fulfil them and others will look down on those who perform these jobs. Without education, those who are marginalized or oppressed may not have the resources to denounce the injustices they suffer from and to claim their rights.

Education is thus central to human flourishing. It not only opens the mind to further horizons, it also opens the way to acquire other valuable capabilities. The *Human Development Reports* accounted for the central importance of education by incorporating an education indicator – literacy rates – into the first Human Development Index; later versions have included education indicators based on enrolment rates. There is, however, much more to education than a literacy or school enrolment statistic. This chapter analyses education as a key dimension of human development. It starts by examining how education became a concern for development in the 1960s. Education was seen as an instrument for economic productivity. This approach – known as human capital – is still prevalent today. The chapter then contrasts human capital with the human development and capability approach to education. It describes how its key concepts of agency and capability introduce new ways of considering the role of education in development.

Human capital

Like other ideas, ideas about education policy are closely connected to their historical context and the narratives that inform them. In the 1960s, ideas about the economic value of schooling were expanded upon and they have had considerable impact ever since. The idea of 'human capital' originates from the observation that schooling develops certain qualities in people, and that these qualities enhance economic productivity and economic growth, just as an increase in physical capital or investment does. This idea has been particularly compelling in policy circles, as it points to how and why governments should intervene in social policy to connect the social and economic aspirations of individuals, families and nations.

Gary Becker's classic work, *Human Capital* (1964), elaborates on the notion of human capital in the context of neoclassical economics. It registers that investment in humans could be viewed as similar to investment in other means of production, like factories or mines. Investment in human capital, just like investment in physical infrastructure, would yield a rate of return, which could be calculated. Becker's study set out to estimate the return to college and high school education in the US, but he was able to show that it was not only schooling per se that was significant for growth, but that it was influential in a range of other educational investments, such as scientific and technological knowledge. Becker's findings found a receptive ear in capitalist, communist and developing countries alike. Box 9.1 reproduces an extract from his seminal study.

Box 9.1 Education and human capital

Economic analysis has no trouble explaining why, throughout history, few countries have experienced very long periods of persistent growth in income per person. For if per capita income growth is caused by the growth of land and physical capital per worker, diminishing returns from additional capital and land eventually eliminate further growth. The puzzle, therefore, is not the lack of growth, but the fact that the US, Japan and many European countries have had continuing growth in per capita income during the past 100 years or more. Presumably, the answer lies in the expansion of scientific and technical knowledge that raises the productivity of labour and other inputs in production. The systematic application of scientific knowledge to production of goods has greatly increased the value of education, technical schooling and on-the-job training, as the growth of knowledge has become embodied in people – in scientists, scholars, technicians, managers and other contributors to output. However, even economists know the difference between correlation and causation, and have developed rather straightforward methods for determining how much of income growth is caused by growth in human capital. In an excellent study for the US, Edward Denison (1985) finds that the increase in schooling of the average worker between 1929 and 1982 explains about one fourth of the rise in per capita income during this period. He is unable to explain much of the remaining growth, I like to believe, because he cannot measure the effects on earnings and improvements over time in health, on-the-job training and other kinds of human capital.

Extract from Gary Becker, *Human Capital*, University of Chicago Press, 3rd edn, 1993, pp23–24.

This extract expresses some of Becker's key ideas regarding the ways in which investment in schooling was associated with levels of growth, and the ways in which he distinguished between different forms of investment – i.e. in school, higher education and training – suggesting that these might have different rates of return to people and countries.

Developing Becker's work further, another economist, Theodore Schultz, set out to map how rates of return from education could be calculated in countries with different levels of income, different variables concerning wage patterns, and different human attitudes to forgoing earnings to develop human capital. His argument is that education has an important economic value and that economic thinking has thus far tended to ignore the productive returns that education has had on economies.

Box 9.2 The economic value of education

In thinking about economic growth, one does not ask the traditional query: what is the area of land, the size of the labour force, and the number of machines and structures? In allocating investment, one asks: what is the marginal increase in production from a particular additional investment? The productive services of land can be augmented by investment; investment in man can increase both his satisfactions and the productive services he contributes when he works; and the productive services of machines and structures can also be augmented in this manner. In addition, and to an increasing extent, there is the investment in organized research to acquire new information, a source of new skills and new materials (techniques), which can significantly alter the investment opportunities in land, man and machines. In line with this approach, there is no assumption of a rate of technical change but a search to determine the rate of return to organized research; no assumption with regard to population growth to account for the rate of increase in the labour force but a search to determine the rate of return to children (child capital) and to the acquisition of useful skills; no assumption of a fixed supply of natural resources but a search to determine the rate of return to investment in land improvements and in discovering and developing other natural resources; and similarly there is the analytical task of determining the rate of return to investment that changes the composition of the reproducible forms of material capital as new and better forms become available from the production activities of organized research. It is my contention that economic thinking has neglected two classes of investment that are of critical importance under modern circumstances. They are investment in man and in research, both private and public.

Extract from Theodore Schultz, *The Economic Value of Education*, Colombia University Press, 1963, pp22–23.

It can be seen that Schultz's hypothesis was that calculating rates of return from investment in human capital would confirm the importance of investment in schooling and research for the productivity of the labour force and the economy's capacity to grow.

Detailed work investigating rates of return from education to families and national economies was undertaken by George Psacharopoulos in the 1970s and 1980s. In his *Returns to Education* (1973), he brought together data from many countries on the role of education in economic growth and set out to examine how the profitability of investment in education compared with profits from investment in physical capital, symbolized in the rhetorical question about whether it was more profitable to invest in schools or steel mills. He was also interested in whether inter-country differences in human capital could explain differences in per capita income, what the rate of return by level of education was across countries, whether there were differences with regards to the level of public subsidies in education, and whether subsidies reduced or increased incentives in the long-term. Psacharopoulos' findings, as detailed in Box 9.3, were to have a profound significance on international policy with regards to investment in education.

Box 9.3 Returns to education

[R]ates of return decline by the level of education. Looking first at the social rates of return, the average for primary education is 19.4 per cent, for secondary 13.5 per cent and for higher 11.3 per cent. This pattern proved to be statistically significant when tested by means of individual country observations. Private rates show a similar pattern between the primary and secondary level (23.7 per cent and 16.3 per cent respectively), while the rate of return to the university level is 17.5 per cent. The second pattern in our data shows that the private returns to investment in education are about 3 to 6 percentage points higher than the social returns. The difference between private and social rates is even more pronounced in developing than in advanced countries, showing that the former group of countries subsidize their educational sector more heavily. ... On the question of whether investment in the education of men is more profitable than that in the education of women, the examination of 8 case studies where the returns for males and females are reported separately shows that, on average, males show higher return by about 2 percentage points at both the higher and the secondary levels. The average return for males for primary school is 16.3 per cent while that for females is 9.8 per cent.... The widely debated issue about whether a country should emphasize technical secondary rather than general education was not resolved.

Extract from George Psacharopoulos, *Returns to Education. An International Comparison*, Amsterdam, Elsevier, 1973, pp5–6.

Although there was considerable criticism of the way Psacharopoulos calculated rates of return and reached these conclusions, the policy implications of his work were enormous. It led the World Bank and other major institutions to engage in development assistance and many governments to emphasize the importance of investing in basic education because of these high rates of return.

Before turning to look at the ways in which writers working within the capability approach paradigm have posed questions about the notion of human capital, it is useful to ask some questions about these canonical works in human capital theory. How do they conceptualize the nature of the labour market and estimate the value of an economy? What assumptions do they make about the nature of schooling and its outcomes? To what extent do they take note of different social groups and relationships based on social division? What are the implications of analysis based on human capital for government policy in education?

Generally, work within a human capital framework assumes that labour markets work rationally and efficiently and that, once schooling has developed certain aspects of human capital, the labour market will allocate people to occupations that are appropriate for their level of skills. The framework does not take into account segregated labour markets where people, irrespective of their level of education, are allocated to particular jobs on the grounds of race, gender, or assumptions about class or caste. The framework tends to view schooling as something like a machine, which children enter and exit with their human capital appropriately topped up. The ways in which different schools provide different learning environments for different children with very diverse outcomes is not considered. Thus, writers interested in human capital will generally consider whether the school is efficient. In other words, how many hours of instruction are provided? In addition, what is the level of teacher qualification? Can children pass? These writers are generally not interested in debates about the content or cultural dynamics of schooling, the social lives of teachers or learning processes. The ways in which inequalities in education are associated with race, class or gender and persist over generations are not a key focus. Social division is only a matter of concern with regards to whether it supports or impedes the development of human capital appropriate for economic growth. While some of the writing on human capital noted differential rates of return for women and men, and for those in communities that experienced segregation, their general conclusion was not that the institutional structures of gender or race inequality in schooling and the labour market should be considered. Human capital theorists concluded instead that more education should be provided for these groups to improve levels of economic growth. It can therefore be seen that what is important for human capital theorists is to understand the economy as a system that will support growth. In this framework, schooling assists growth, and a major social obligation is thus to increase access to schooling so as to facilitate this very growth.

Human capital and the capability approach compared

Seen from the perspective of the human development and capability approach, the value of an economy does not lie in economic growth but in its capacity to provide opportunities for human flourishing, i.e. for each human being to live a life he has 'reason to choose and value'. Comparing the two perspectives, Sen (1997) argues that human capital 'concentrates on the agency of human beings – through skill and knowledge as well as effort – in augmenting production possibilities'. In contrast, a capability approach to education 'focuses on the ability of human beings to lead lives they have reason to value and to enhance the substantive choices they have'. He highlights, however, that the two approaches are connected because they 'both are concerned with the role of human beings, and in particular with the actual abilities that they achieve and acquire' (Sen, 1997, p1959). However, the idea of human capabilities is a more expansive notion than human capital because education encourages aspects of human flourishing that are wider than those associated with merely increasing productivity or economic growth, as Box 9.4 summarizes.

Box 9.4 Human capital and capabilities

Given her personal characteristics, social background, economic circumstances, etc., a person has the ability to do (or be) certain things that she has reason to value. The reason for valuation can be *direct* (the functioning involved may directly enrich her life, such as being well nourished or healthy) or *indirect* (the functioning involved may contribute to further production or command a price in the market). The human capital perspective can – in principle – be defined very broadly to cover both types of valuation, but it is typically defined – by convention – primarily in terms of indirect value: human qualities that can be employed as 'capital' in production in the way physical capital is. In this sense, the narrower view of the human capital approach fits into the more inclusive perspective of human capability, which can cover both direct and indirect consequences of human abilities.

Consider an example. If education makes a person more efficient in commodity production, then this is clearly an enhancement of human capital. This can add to the value of production in the economy and also to the income of the person who has been educated. But even with the same level of income, a person may benefit from education, in reading, communicating, arguing, being able to choose in a more informed way, in being taken more seriously by others and so on. The benefits of education thus exceed its role as human capital in commodity production. The broader human capability perspective would record – and value – these additional roles. The two perspectives are thus closely related.

There is, however, also a crucial difference between the two approaches – a difference that relates to some extent to the distinction between means and ends. The acknowledgement of the role of human qualities in promoting and sustaining economic growth – momentous as it is – tells us nothing about *why* economic growth is sought in the first place. If, instead, the focus is, ultimately, on the expansion of human freedom to live the kinds of lives that people have reason to value, then the role of economic growth in expanding these opportunities has to be integrated into that more foundational understanding of the process of development as the expansion of the human capability to lead freer and more worthwhile lives.

The distinction has a significant practical bearing on public policy. While economic prosperity helps people to lead freer and more fulfilling lives, so do more education, health care, medical attention and other factors that causally influence the effective freedoms that people actually enjoy. These 'social developments' must directly count as 'developmental' since they help us to lead longer, freer and more fruitful lives, in addition to the role they have in promoting productivity and economic growth or individual incomes.

Extract from Amartya Sen (1997) 'Human capital and human capability,' *World Development*, vol 25, no 12, pp1959–1961.

In contrast with the arguments made by key writers on human capital above, the human development and capability approach places the quality of human life – and not economic growth – at the centre of its concerns. Concern for human capital should not be neglected as it is alert to the ways in which people develop skills and enhance their income, but earning power and economic values are ultimately not the only dimensions of human flourishing that are important. Education has wider values for individuals beyond enabling them to contribute to economic growth or enhance their own or their families' earning power.

Human development goes much further than the human capital approach in thinking about the ways in which education enhances freedom. Education might contribute to overcoming inequalities, and facilitating participation in processes that redress injustice. Sen (1992) has identified three distinct ways in which we can link the importance of education to the expansion of valuable capabilities: first, education fulfils an *instrumental social role*. Literacy can foster public debate and dialogue about social and political arrangements, for example. Education also has an *instrumental process role* in facilitating our capacity to participate in decision-making processes at the household, community or national level. Finally, it has an *empowering and distributive role* in facilitating the ability of disadvantaged, marginalized and excluded groups to organize politically since, without education, these groups would be unable to gain access to centres of power and make a case for redistribution to begin with. Indeed, education has *redistributive* effects between social groups, households and within families. Overall, education has an *interpersonal* impact because people are able to use the benefits of education to help others as well as themselves and can therefore contribute to democratic freedoms and the overall good of society as a whole.

It is not easy to translate these broad ideas into simple policies that governments and communities can advocate for and act upon. Nonetheless, attempts have been made to go beyond the simple human capital concerns in international declarations such as the Millennium Development Goals (MDGs), Education for All (EFA), the Decade of Education for Sustainable Development (DESD) and the Beijing Declaration on Women. For example, the MDG targets have indicators not just for access to schooling, but for improved gender equality ratios in earning and political representation, eradicating hunger, support for sustainable development, and improved access to health and water. In comparison, the EFA goals express a vision for quality education, gender equality, adult literacy and early childhood education. A number of governments have also used the expansion of education provision to think about redressing race, gender, class and caste divisions. In addition, a number of large NGO education programmes draw upon ideas about capabilities and rights.[2]

The concern with education as a way of developing capabilities for 'freer and more fruitful lives', to paraphrase Sen, requires careful analysis of its modalities of provision. It entails dealing with the content of schooling, efficiency in organization and some of the problems encountered by learners with diverse needs. Regrettably, there is not much emphasis on these issues in the human development and capability approach literature. Nevertheless, by emphasizing education as a way of enabling people to live more freely and fully, the approach still makes a significant contribution to the field of education. Namely, it stresses the importance of the ability to exercise critical reasoning about their lives and the societies in which they live – something the human capital theory ignored almost entirely. In two recent works, Sen (2005, 2006) emphasizes the importance of education that specifically encourages critical reflection, the ability to debate, public reasoning and the inclusion of traditionally excluded voices.

There is a clear contrast between the emphasis on the value of argument and understanding history, literature and mathematics, on the one hand, and the narrow interpretations of human capital, on the other. For the human development and capability approach, what is important for children is not just developing particular skills that have economic value, but the reflective capacities that would lead to 'examined lives' (Saito, 2003).

This more philosophical concern with the nature of human flourishing (and how education helps develop it) has also been discussed by Martha Nussbaum. In a lecture given at the fifth international conference of the Human Development and Capability Association held in Paris at UNESCO, Nussbaum (2006a) argues that education is crucial to the health of democracy itself. She criticizes an education that is narrowly focused on science and technology at the expense of the arts and humanities. She emphasizes the role of education in forming the student's critical and imaginative capacities. Nussbaum is interested in the content of what is taught and the process of teaching, stressing the importance not just of marshalling facts, but of understanding the worlds of others and critically reflecting on the appearances of things, including one's own experience (see Box 9.5). This substantive notion of what education should be about is associated with her list of ten central capabilities (see Chapter 2). Education in its widest sense is an important component of nearly all the capabilities on the list. Nussbaum also places a high premium on compassion for people in other cultures, signalling the role of education in expanding the notion of social justice beyond national boundaries (Nussbaum, 2006b). She highlights important content for higher education, noting how it can help to develop global understanding, critical perspectives on one's own society and the capacity to see the world with the eyes of others (Nussbaum, 1997). She is thus particularly attentive to the complexities of cultural discussion and the educational processes that result from it.

Box 9.5 Two descriptions of education in Bihar, India

First, a typical example of education for the rural poor, as conducted by one of the countless NGOs that work on this issue. Infrastructure in Bihar is generally so bad that it took us two days, even in a jeep, to get to this district near the Nepalese border. When we arrived, we found very meagre facilities. Teaching mostly went on outside on the ground, or under the shade of a barn (in which rats ran around, occasionally across our feet). Students had very little paper, and only a few slates that were passed from hand to hand.

Nonetheless, it was creative education. The literacy programme for adult women, called 'Reflect', began the day by asking the 20 or so women to draw (on a large sheet of rough wrapping paper) a map of the power structure of their village. We then discussed the map together, as the women identified possible points of intervention that might change the deal they have with the landlords, for whom they currently work as sharecroppers. Everyone was animated; the prospect of criticizing entrenched structures of power had obviously led these women to attach great importance to the associated task of learning to read and write. At the end of the meeting, we all joined in a song that is a staple of the women's movement here. It began, 'In every house there is fear. Let's do away with that fear. Let's build a women's organization'. It went on to sing the virtues of education as an antidote to fear.

Next, I visited the literacy programme for girls, housed in a shed next door. The girls of the village, goatherds by day, were beginning their school day around 4 pm. About 15 girls in all, age six to fifteen, come to this single 'classroom' for three hours of after-work learning. There are no desks, no chairs, no blackboard and only a few slates and bits of chalk. Nonetheless, it all seemed to work, through the resourcefulness and passion of the teachers, themselves poor rural women who have been assisted by Adithi's programmes. Proudly the girls brought in the goats that they had been able to buy from the savings account they have jointly established in their group. Math is taught in part by focusing on such practical issues. After that, the girls performed for us a play that they had recently performed for their village. It was about dowry, and the way this institution makes female lives seem to be of lower value to parents than male lives. Playing both male and female roles themselves, the girls told a story of how one young woman refused to be given in marriage with dowry. Her parents were shocked, and the father of the prospective groom became extremely angry. After much discussion, however, including a description of the way in which dowry is linked to the malnutrition and death of girls and the murders of adult women, the groom himself decided to refuse a dowry. He stood up proudly against his father — and the tall girl playing the groom stood up all the more proudly. Eventually, even the two sets of parents agreed that the new way was better. The marriage took place, and no money changed hands. Teachers told us that the whole village came to the play, and they think it did some good. Meanwhile, the girls giggled with pleasure at the subversive entertainment they had cooked up.

Extract from Martha Nussbaum (2006a), 'Education and democratic citizenship: Capabilities and quality education', *Journal of Human Development*, vol 7, no 3, p385–6.

The human development perspective thus considers the purpose of education to be much wider than simply developing the skills that will enhance economic growth. Education nurtures processes of critical reflection and connection with others that are intrinsically ethical and not merely instrumental.

Both the human capital and the capability approaches to education have strengths and weaknesses. Human capital writers have a clearly marked-off area of work, which is supported by research data on how, for example, growth links with specific levels of investment in education. This in turn generates clear policy messages. But this is both a strength and a weakness. The approach does not respond to concerns about different learning needs, nor does it explain why some educational content might be valuable even if it does not necessarily generate economic growth. It is also not particularly interested in social inequalities that cannot be 'fixed' by merely completing school. In contrast, writers on the capability approach do not always have the 'hard' empirical data to substantiate rates of return, although they do observe certain correlations associated with human development, as we will discuss below. Policy messages about the capability approach are also somewhat more diffuse because they encompass a broader idea of connecting human development together. However, the capability approach emphasizes what kinds of learning are valuable, and is particularly concerned with inequalities and developing capabilities through education. It does not dismiss human capital concerns about the economy, skills and growth, but seeks instead to add to these a wider remit for education and social justice.

Applying the capability approach to education

The work of a number of writers on the capability approach and education can be loosely grouped into three categories: (1) those who have adopted the language of capabilities, functionings and conversion factors – how resources are translated into capabilities, and have applied it to education by throwing new light on old discussions regarding the value of education and the processes for evaluating it; (2) those who have looked at the ways in which the capability approach intersects with other discussions about human rights, equality and social justice in education, looking closely at particular areas of education, such as curriculum, higher education pedagogy, disability and special educational needs, and gender inequality; (3) those who use the capability approach to analyse data on children's or adults' views of learning, the value of education and of measurement.

Using the language of the capability approach

The capability approach provides a useful language with which to articulate both the learning processes and social value of education. The distinction between capabilities and functionings is very useful in education. The concept of capability stresses the real freedoms a learner has to make informed choices in order to achieve a life she has reason to value. Capabilities are the real opportunities and options learners have to strive for certain educational achievements. For example, being literate and numerate or well-regarded as an educated person, being knowledgeable about history, being able to take part in a discussion with other learners, and being respected by teachers and peers in school are important achievements that the capability approach stresses. But evaluating only functionings or outcomes can give too little information on how well people are doing. Some cases may appear to have achieved the same functionings but, behind these equal outcomes, very different stories may in fact be hidden.

Let us take the example of two 13-year old girls in Kenya. They have both participated in an international study of learning achievements and have both failed mathematics. One attended a well-equipped school in Nairobi with qualified and motivated teachers offering adequate learning support and a safe learning environment. Despite this, she failed. A major reason for her failing the maths exam was her decision to spend less time on studying and more with friends in the drama club and other leisure activities. The other girl attended a school in Wajir, one of the poorest districts, and showed great interest in mathematics and school work generally. Despite this, she failed her exam simply because of the lack of a proper mathematics teacher at her school. The subject was taught by an English specialist. Private lessons after school were available, but her parents could not afford this for all their children. So they decided to give priority to their son and required their daughter to perform housework and childcare. She therefore had little time to prepare for her exams.

This case illustrates how evaluating capabilities or functionings will mean that one will tend to see situations differently. If one looks only at functionings – performance in examinations – one sees equal (if regrettable) outcomes. But while the functionings of the students are the same, their capabilities are different. The capability approach requires that we do not simply evaluate the functionings – the actual achievements – but the real freedom or opportunities each student has to choose and achieve what she values. Our evaluation of equality must therefore take account of freedom in opportunities as much as in observed choices. Capabilities to undertake valued and valuable activities should thus constitute an indispensable and central aspect of the relevant basis for evaluation.

Using the capability approach as a method to evaluate educational advantage, and equally to identify disadvantage, marginalization and exclusion, entails another perspective on public policy in education. It requires that educational policy pay attention to the transition from capabilities to functionings, and to the conversion factors that affect them (see Chapter 2). From the perspective of the human development and capability approach, educational policy focuses on the freedoms individuals and social groups have to achieve valued functionings (the capability set) and the ways in which conversion works to limit or expand these capabilities. Conversion might work both internally (with regard to how individuals learn or understand the value of education) and externally (with a bearing on the quality of school provision, the level of teacher knowledge and capacity to put this into practice, forms of discrimination, such as education privileges some learners might have, and so on).

Current evaluations of education systems only look at inputs (such as expenditure and level of teacher qualification) and outputs (such as what grades students get or whether they pass tests in particular skills). There is no current standardized means of evaluating education in terms of capabilities, although capability-informed methods of evaluating education are currently being developed (see below).

Another approach to evaluating education is based on what people say they want from their schooling – this approach is reminiscent of the 'revealed preference approach' detailed in Chapter 2. If children from low-income groups receive only primary education, and children from high-earning families attend primary and secondary school, both groups may say they are satisfied, because this is what each has come to expect. So, when their educational opportunities are assessed from the viewpoint of what people want, there is no problem as both groups are apparently equally content and satisfied. Yet there is something disconcerting about this type of conclusion, which ultimately suggests the problem of 'adaptive preference'. A focus on capabilities requires us not only to evaluate our satisfaction with individual learning outcomes, but to question the range of real educational choices that have been available to people: whether they have the genuine capability to achieve a valued educational functioning. We would need to ask whether people's educational aspirations had become adapted to their respective circumstances, and whether the low-income group had a range of valued learning opportunities to choose from, out of which they then selected just minimal primary education. The capability approach therefore invites a range of more searching questions about equality that go well beyond a narrow focus on desire satisfaction.[3]

Thinking in terms of capabilities raises a wider range of issues than simply looking at the amount of resources or commodities people have. Because of interpersonal diversity, people need a different amount of resources in order to transform them into the functioning 'being educated' – thus a dyslexic child might require more inputs in order to be able to read and write, for example. One might argue that the education provided by one type of school may not be suitable or accessible for all children because some children necessarily have different needs. Thus, for example, five years of basic schooling in a class with a 40:1 pupil/teacher ratio and with lessons delivered in the majority language of a region might suit quick and confident learners, who speak the majority language at home, always sit in the front of the class and have high levels of concentration because of their good nutrition (see Chapter 10). The same level of resources may be woefully inadequate for children who are shy, hungry, have poor concentration skills, always sit at the back of the class and only speak a minority language. The capability approach therefore alerts us to the fact that we cannot simply evaluate resources and inputs (such as teachers or years of schooling) and that we must look at whether learners are able to actually *convert* resources into capabilities, and thereafter into functionings.

Another example of the importance of conversion factors relates to how formal schooling can provide literacy – the capability to read and write – which can then be used to convert a resource, such as a newspaper, into a source of information for an individual. If we only evaluate inputs, each child in the class appears to have access to equal amounts of resources. If we evaluate the link between resources and capabilities, we would need to take into account critical issues like the availability of newspapers, the amount of free time for children to read, the acceptability of even reading a newspaper for some types of children (particularly girls and those living in poverty) in certain societies, and the actual accuracy of investigative methods being employed. There could be certain social processes that form inequalities and limitations on capabilities or, alternately, sometimes close inequality gaps and promote capabilities – both types of which standard evaluation methodologies might tend to overlook. Box 9.6 describes an example from non-formal education in Uganda, which demonstrates how standard education evaluations – such as attendance in schools – could miss out on important information since children might be receiving their education through non-formal networks outside the school system.

Box 9.6 Reducing inequalities in education in an isolated community

Kalyakooti is a hard-to-reach community located at the periphery of Nakasongola District in Uganda. Because some children have limited access to the structured education system offered in government schools, the community has devised alternative resources for providing education for its orphans and vulnerable children, such as those belonging to child-headed households or living with members of an extended family network. In order to identify the children who fall under this category, the community draws a village map and finds out which households contain children who do not go to school.

With the help of NGO funding, the community has built a resource centre with classrooms made of mud and grass-thatched roofs. It has also established leisure facilities that encourage ease of communication and interaction between children and their 'parents' – parents are community members who have volunteered to take on the responsibility of addressing the learning needs of these orphans and vulnerable children. The NGO trains parents in psycho-social support skills so that their interaction with the children leads to appropriate child development. The interaction involves reading books, poems and stories that prepare them to become responsible adults. The leisure centre is also being used to provide immunization, to monitor child growth and for educating parents about the importance of child nutrition.

The community members identify trained teachers (also recruiting them with the support of the NGO) who can teach children during specific times. Teachers are paid and looked after by the community, while the NGO assists with basic commodities such as grain and soap. Children are taught a different curriculum from the one in the normal school system. Girls and boys are equally treated, and the learning takes into consideration the community's peak seasons, such as harvesting and planting, and other household activities. For instance, when the children have to help with certain activities, classes start a little later, thereby allowing everyone to participate. Throughout the learning process, children are assessed but are not given formal reports. This is done to minimize inequalities within the group so that some pupils do not feel more or less intelligent than others. At the end of each year, the community organizes a party to mark the children's promotion to the next level. At the end of their primary education, the children sit for the same examination as all the children in the district (it is noteworthy, however, that the community had to negotiate with the district education office so the children could do this).

The Kalyakooti example is one of several local initiatives that provide different resources to disadvantaged groups so that they can have the same 'capability to be educated' as those who come from more privileged backgrounds. It also reflects the creativity of a community to offer educational opportunities that take into account the specificities of different learning needs and environments.

This box was written by Saidah Najjuma.

Learners differ along intersecting dimensions: personal (e.g. gender, race, class), environmental (wealth, climate, etc.) and inter-individual. These intersections critically determine when a difference becomes an inequality. The key point for education is that resources are very important, but what then matters are the opportunities each person has for converting their bundle of resources into valued doings and beings. Conversion factors link diverse individual biographies to social arrangements, further underscoring the difficulty of focusing solely on the subjective wants of learners, since these might be adapted in ways that do not necessarily serve their best interests. For example, girls might adapt their educational ambitions in a culture where maleness has more relative prestige and cultural power. In this case, gender difference becomes inequality. What and who students are learning to be, and how they are learning to be good choosers, ultimately affects equality in education.

Thus, the capability approach offers a useful perspective on education by teaching us to evaluate learning opportunities, processes and outcomes. It asks questions such as: are valued capabilities distributed fairly and equally in and through education? Do some people get more opportunities to convert their resources into capabilities than others? Which capabilities matter most when it comes to developing agency and autonomy for educational opportunities, social connection and valued dimensions of living?

Equality and justice

A second group of writers have linked discussions on the capability approach with wider questions concerning equality and social justice in education. They are concerned with distinguishing capabilities from human rights, assessing different forms of equality in education, and addressing how education can affect and influence our thinking about social justice.

The distinctions between the human capital, human rights and capability approaches have been used to analyse gender equality in education. While the human capital model mainly stresses the instrumental economic role of education, and the rights-based approach the intrinsic personal role of education, the capability approach acknowledges these different roles of education, as Box 9.7 explains.

Box 9.7 Gender equality in education: Human capital, human rights and capabilities

The assumption in the human capital model is that decisions, for example whether to educate a son or a daughter, are taken only on the grounds of economic efficiency, and not also based on structural power relations in families, which are in part sustained by the local nature of gender relations. In rights-based approaches, men and women are entitled to equal rights but, once these equal rights are granted, no further claims for social change can be made. For example, if citizenship rights grant equal access to schooling for boys and girls, then governments might be satisfied under such a rights-based approach, even if the outcomes display significant gender inequalities. Gender inequalities are often reproduced in very subtle ways. Moreover, gender inequalities affect men's and women's identities, which lead to behaviours, choices and judgements that tend to 'normalize' gender inequalities.

Human capital is always only instrumental; it should therefore only enter our normative analysis when thinking about efficiency concerns and some of the content of education but, for the reasons pointed out earlier, it should never function as the overarching theoretical framework used to guide educational policies, fiscal policies and budgetary decisions. Rights clearly are important in daily discourse. However, at the theoretical level, rights always need a prior moral criterion. Rights are always rights *to something*. Capabilities, on the other hand, are always things that must matter intrinsically, whether or not they additionally also matter instrumentally.

Thus, our ultimate aim is to expand people's capabilities, including the capability of education. Rights can be an instrument in reaching that goal. In some contexts, however, there might be more useful instruments, such as creating a new language that will allow new forms of association and collaboration between groups that are now using different languages or instruments to challenge social norms, such as street theatre or other art forms. Moreover, if the right to education is interpreted too narrowly and does not deliver the capability of education, then concerned children, parents and other citizens should argue that more needs to be done to expand the educational capability. We should thus deal with rights strategically: in some political contexts, this might be a useful instrument; in other political contexts, we need other instruments. But it might always be good to keep in mind that what ultimately matters is not just the proclamation that we all have a right to education, or the effective protection of that right, but whatever it takes policy-makers, and others who are in a position to contribute, to work towards a high quality education for all, as part of a more comprehensive view on what we owe each other, and especially to children, in a just society and a just world.

Edited extracts from Ingrid Robeyns (2006), 'Three models of education: rights, capabilities and human capital', *Theory and Research in Education*, vol 4, no 1, pp80–83.

In addition to issues of gender equality, the capability approach has been applied to address justice and equality in the provision of education for children with disabilities (Terzi, 2008). The distinction between functionings and capabilities has considerable implications for policy and the provision of resources. Educational equality to support capabilities and functionings requires additional resources for children with special educational needs, such as dyslexia, deafness, autism and other issues. As has been emphasized earlier, the capability approach stresses the importance of conversion factors: given interpersonal heterogeneity, it should be understood that similar educational resources do not necessarily lead to similar learning outcomes.

Another application of the capability approach has been in the area of pedagogy in higher education (Walker, 2006, 2008a, 2008b; see also Appendix). The approach becomes an ethically informed process in which we become alert to questions of equitability, humane justice, how we would like students to be, and what we would like them to become. Such a project is not a simple matter of organizing higher education institutions to respond to requirements for a knowledge society, whether these are imperatives couched in terms of efficiency, human capital or cost–benefit. Higher education pedagogies have to be transformative and stretch beyond the bounded spaces in which teaching and learning take place. This involves a critical engagement with knowledge, interwoven with the processes of freedom entailed in student and staff identity formation, institutional change and support for the well-being and agency of students. These insights echo a pedagogical framework pioneered in the 1970s by Paulo Freire in *Pedagogy of the Oppressed*, which is discussed further in the Appendix on teaching human development written by Melanie Walker.

Box 9.8 Problem-solving education or education as the practice of freedom

In the banking concept of education, knowledge is a gift bestowed by those who consider themselves knowledgeable upon those whom they consider to know nothing. Projecting an absolute ignorance onto others, a characteristic of the ideology of oppression, negates education and knowledge as processes of inquiry. The teacher presents himself to his students as their necessary opposite. Banking education maintains and even stimulates the contradiction through the following attitudes and practices, which mirror oppressive society as a whole. The teacher teaches and the students are taught; knows everything and the students know nothing; thinks and the students are thought about; talks and the students listen; the teacher disciplines and the students are disciplined; chooses and the students comply; acts and the students have the illusion of acting through the action of the teacher; the teacher chooses the programme content and the students adapt to it; confuses the authority of knowledge with his or her own professional authority; is the subject of the learning process, while the pupils are mere objects.

It is not surprising that the banking concept of education regards men as adaptable, manageable beings. The more students work at storing the deposits entrusted to them, the less they develop the critical consciousness which would result from their intervention in the world as transformers of that world. The more completely they accept the passive role imposed on them, the more they tend simply to adapt to the world as it is and to the fragmented view of reality deposited in them.

Authentic liberation – the process of humanization – is not another deposit to be made in men. Liberation is a praxis: the action and reflection of men and women upon their world in order to transform it. Those truly committed to liberation must reject the banking concept in its entirety, adopting instead a concept of women and men as conscious beings, and consciousness as consciousness intent upon the world. They must abandon the educational goal of deposit-making and replace it with the posing of the problems of human beings in their relations with the world.

Problem-posing education can fulfil its function as the practice of freedom only if it can overcome the teacher–student contradiction. The teacher is no longer merely the-one-who-teaches, but one who is himself taught in dialogue with the students, who in turn while being taught also teach. They become jointly responsible for a process in which all grow. In this process, arguments based on 'authority' are no longer valid; in order to function, authority must be *on the side of* freedom, not against it.

Extracts from Freire's *Pedagogy of the Oppressed*, London: Continuum, ch 2, taken from an on-line version of the book available at www.marxists.org/subject/education/freire/pedagogy/index.htm

Data and measurement

A third group of writers explore how people discuss and collect data on educational capabilities. For example, literacy has conventionally been used as an indicator of the capability to read and write, but people might express the view that they have that capability even if they do not pass standard literacy tests. There are different degrees of literacy, such as being able to read and write in the context of making accounts for one's small rickshaw business, which can already be very empowering for many (Maddox, 2008). Other studies highlight important points about understanding the social context of capabilities, their relational dynamic and the difficulties of focusing solely on individuals and particular capabilities (Biggeri, 2007; Raynor, 2007).

The discussion on educational capabilities data takes two forms: on the one hand, there is an emerging literature on some of the distinctions that need to be made in order to improve current measures for education quality. In looking at the missing dimensions of poverty data (Chapter 6), we have already highlighted the significance of inadequate dimensions for measuring empowerment, which has a particular bearing on education. There is also the question of what is measured in assessing educational development and why we need to distinguish between different ways of understanding education in measuring progress between and within countries (Unterhalter and Brighouse, 2007).

On the other hand, in contrast to these exploratory and clarifying works on measurement, there are a number of practical studies that have attempted to develop capability-informed methods for measuring education. The UNESCO Global Monitoring Report drew on the methodology of the Human Development Index and the Gender Development Index (see Chapter 6) to develop an index of education for all, the Education Development Index, and an index for gender parity in education, the Gender Parity Index. However, these measures of gender equality in education remain too narrow, in that they focus solely on gender in terms of enrolment rates. The Beyond Access project sponsored by Oxfam has developed an index of gender equality in education, which tries to capture the ability of girls to convert educational resources into educational capabilities (Unterhalter et al, 2005).[4]

Questions

9.1   In measuring educational achievements, are there better indicators than enrolment rates or success in examinations? What might those indicators be? How easy would it be to collect data on them?

9.2   Think about your own learning experience, concentrating on one particular phase (primary, secondary, tertiary, training). How would you assess this education from a human development and capability perspective? Write a specific commentary of the curriculum, approach to learning, teaching and assessment, distribution and management of resources, and student participation in decision-making.

9.3   What would the human capital approach say about addressing the education of children with disabilities?

9.4   What are the ways in which education can be a bridge to social justice?

9.5   Comment on this African proverb: 'If you educate a boy, you educate an individual. If you educate a girl, you educate a community'.

9.6   Drawing a distinction between a right-based and capability-based approach to education, make a critical assessment of the UNESCO campaign 'Education for All' (www.unesco.org/education/efa/).

Notes

1   This chapter draws from Walker and Unterhalter (2007), and Unterhalter, Vaughan and Walker (2007), and from many other discussions with the members of the HDCA education thematic group.

2   See, for example, the reports of the ActionAid projects TEGINT (Transforming education for girls in Nigeria and Tanzania) and SVAG (Stop Violence against Girls), see www.actionaid.org ('what we do' section, and then 'education' section).

3   Watts and Bridges (2006) have discussed questions about adaptive preference in education and some of the challenges they raise for the capability approach.

4   See www.ioe.ac.uk/efps/beyondaccess.

Readings

Becker, G (1993) *Human Capital*, 3rd edn, University of Chicago Press, Chicago, IL

Biggeri, M. (2007) 'Children's valued capabilities', in M. Walker and E. Unterhalter (eds) *Amartya Sen's Capability Approach and Social Justice in Education*, Palgrave, New York

Chiapero-Martinetti, E. and Moroni, S. (2007) 'An analytical framework for conceptualising poverty and re-examining the capability approach', *Journal of Socio-economics*, vol 36, no 3, pp360–375

Denison, E. (1985) *Trends in American Economic Growth 1929–1982*, Brookings Institution, Washington DC

Freire, P. (2000) *A Pedagogy of the Oppressed*, 30th anniversary ed., Continuum, London

Lanzi, D. (2007) 'Capabilities, human capital and education', *Journal of Socio-economics*, vol 36, no 3, pp424–435

Maddox, B. (2008) 'What good is literacy? Insights and implications of the capabilities approach', *Journal of Human Development*, vol 9, no 2, pp185–206

Nussbaum, M. (1997) *Cultivating Humanity*, Harvard University Press, Cambridge, MA

Nussbaum, M. (2000) *Women and Human Development*, Cambridge University Press, Cambridge

Nussbaum, M. (2006a) 'Education and democratic citizenship: Capabilities and quality education', *Journal of Human Development*, vol 7, no 3, pp385–395

Nussbaum, M. (2006b) *Frontiers of Justice*, Harvard University Press, Cambridge, MA

Psacharopoulos, G. (1973) *Returns to Education. An International Comparison*, Amsterdam, Elsevier

Robeyns, I. (2006) 'Three models of education: Rights, capabilities and human capital', *Theory and Research in Education*, vol 4, no 1, pp69–84

Saito, M. (2003) 'Amartya Sen's capability approach to education: A critical exploration', *Journal of Philosophy of Education*, vol 37, no 1, pp17–33

Sen, A. (1992) *Inequality Re-examined*, Oxford University Press, Oxford

Sen, A. (1997) 'Human capital and human capability', *World Development*, vol 25, no 12, pp1959–1961

Sen, A. (2005) *The Argumentative Indian*, Penguin Books, London

Sen, A. (2006) *Identity and Violence*, W. Norton, New York

UNESCO (2003 Walker, M. 2008) *The Global Monitoring Report*, UNESCO, Paris, available at: www.efareport.unesco.org/

Unterhalter, E. (2007) *Gender, Schooling and Global Social Justice*, Routledge, London

Unterhalter, E. (2008) 'Cosmopolitanism, global social justice and gender equality in education', *Compare*, vol 38, no 5

Unterhalter, E., Challender, C. and Rajagopalan, R. (2005) 'Measuring gender equality in education', in S. Aikman and E. Unterhalter (eds) *Beyond Access: Transforming Policy and Practice for Gender Equality in Education*, Oxfam Publications. Each chapter is available online at http://publications.oxfam.org.uk/oxfam/add_info_010.asp

Unterhalter, E., Vaughan, R. and Walker, M. (2007) 'The capability approach and education', *Prospero*, vol 13, no 3, pp13–21

Walker, M. (2005) 'The capability approach and social justice in education', *Maitreyee* e-bulletin of HDCA, October.

Walker, M. (2006) *Higher Education Pedagogies*, Open University Press, Buckingham

Walker, M. (2008a) 'Human capability, mild perfectionism and thickened educational praxis', *Pedagogy, Culture & Society*, vol 16, no 2, pp149–162

Walker, M. (2008b) 'A human capabilities framework for evaluating student learning', *Teaching in Higher Education*, vol 13, no 4, pp477–487

Walker, M. and Unterhalter, E. (eds) (2007) *Amartya Sen's Capability Approach and Social Justice in Education*, Palgrave, New York

Further Readings

Brighouse, H. and Unterhalter, E. (2009) 'Education, primary goods and capabilities', in H. Brighouse and I. Robeyns (eds) *Measuring Justice: Primary Goods and Capabilities*, Cambridge University Press, Cambridge

Gemmell, N. (1996) 'Evaluating the impacts of human capital stocks and accumulation on economic growth: Some new evidence', *Oxford Bulletin of Economics and Statistics*, vol 58, no 1, pp9–28

Glewwe, P. (2002) 'Schools and skills in developing countries: Education policies and socioeconomic outcomes', *Journal of Economic Literature*, vol 40, no 2, pp436–482

Hanushek, E. and Welch, F. (eds) (2006) *Handbook on the Economics of Education*, Elsevier, Amsterdam

Kingdon, G. (2006) 'The return to education', in David A. Clark (ed.) *The Elgar Companion to Development Studies*, Edward Elgar, London

McMahon, W. (1999) *Education and Development: Measuring the Social Benefits*, Oxford University Press, Oxford

Psacharopoulos, G. and Patrinos, P. (2004) 'Returns to investment in education: A further update', *Education Economics*, vol 12, no 2, pp111–134

Raynor, J. (2007) 'Schooling girls: An intergenerational study of women's burdens in rural Bangladesh', in S. Fennell and M. Arnot (eds) *Gender, Education and Equality in a Global Context*, Routledge, London

Terzi, L. (2008) *Justice and Equality in Education*, Continuum, London

Unterhalter, E. and Brighouse, H. (2007) 'Distribution of what for social justice in education? The case of Education for All by 2015', in M. Walker and E. Unterhalter (eds) *Sen's Capability Approach and Social Justice in Education*, Palgrave, New York

Watts, M. and Bridges, D. (2006) 'Enhancing students' capabilities? UK higher education and the widening participation agenda', in S. Deneulin, M. Nebel and N. Sagovsky (eds) *Transforming Unjust Structures*, Springer, Dordrecht

10
Health

Proochista Ariana and Arif Naveed

Aims of the chapter

- To recognize the shortcomings of conventional approaches to health.
- To understand the advantages of the capability framework for assessing health.
- To realize the challenges in applying the capability approach to health.

Key Points

- Health is a complex, multi-dimensional phenomenon that is not readily measured by any single indicator.
- Health is an intrinsic, as well as instrumental, element of human development.
- Health gains can facilitate numerous achievements in various aspects of life, while losses in health can exacerbate deprivations in other dimensions.
- Looking beyond resource inputs and utilitarian outputs facilitates our ability to appreciate a more holistic notion of health, as well as the individual, social and contextual factors which facilitate the translation of given inputs into valued outputs.
- Choices in health are important to consider in contexts where health is readily seen as a commodity and health-related preferences are manufactured to suit commercial interests.

Few would argue with the intrinsic importance of health to nearly all aspects of our lives. How we conceive of health and measure its success, however, has implications for the policies we adopt and the programmes we implement in the long term. By looking at health from the perspective of the human development and capability approach, this chapter presents a new perspective on the many factors that contribute to healthy living.

Like education (Chapter 9), health is often viewed from a human capital perspective, where the value of health lies in its ability to ensure productive inputs to achieve economic ends. While it is true that health can ensure a reliable and hardy workforce, there are other values of health that may not contribute in any meaningful way to economic outputs. Indeed, if we were to rely solely on its economic value, health status would effectively be one of several factors that are prioritized because of their critical contribution to the economy (i.e., thus, those of working age would be prioritized over the elderly and, in certain contexts, men over women). If, on the other hand, we reconsider the value of health from the perspective of the people whose health we want to improve, and if we look beyond utilitarian outputs to factors that expand people's capabilities to achieve valued states of health, we would make very different recommendations altogether. We will use several examples to illustrate how utilitarian approaches to health lead to resource inputs that may not effectively address health problems and may even exacerbate inequities in individual capabilities to achieve health.

The chapter begins by considering what is meant by health and how it can be effectively measured. It then examines some conventional approaches to achieving health before illustrating the advantages of the capability approach. The chapter concludes by acknowledging some of the weaknesses in the capability framework and other health challenges facing us today.

What is health?

According to the World Health Organization (WHO), 'the enjoyment of the highest attainable standard of health is one of the fundamental rights of every human being.'[1] As Sen observes, 'health is among the most important conditions of human life and a critically significant constituent of human capabilities which we have reason to value' (2002, p660). In addition to its intrinsic value, it is also agreed that health is instrumental to economic growth, educational achievements and cognitive development, employment opportunities, income earning potential, as well as the more amorphous aspects of dignity, safety, security and empowerment. But what is health? According to the constitutional preamble of the WHO (1946), 'health is a state of complete physical, mental and social well-being and not merely the absence of disease or infirmity.'[2] Although holistic and indisputable, this definition is far from operational. All too often, we rely on a common set of readily-available variables to proxy health more broadly. At a population level, the conventional indicators adopted are infant mortality rate or life expectancy (which is derived from demographic models using age-standardized death rates of a particular cohort, with expected variations). While life expectancy and mortality are undoubtedly important, they do not adequately convey aspects related to the 'quality' of life. For example, an individual can be alive while living with an unbearably painful disease, which leaves her bed-ridden and unable to function to her fullest capacities.

Similarly, many economists resort to measures of anthropometry to proxy health, that is, the measure of height-for-age, weight-for-height or body-mass-index (BMI). While such measures are meant to convey aspects of nutritional deficiency and/or over-nutrition, they are general proxies that fail to convey precise micronutrient circumstances. Moreover, the standards that are used to draw cut-offs – similar to poverty lines to indicate over- or under-nutrition – are highly contested in the international literature.[3] Nevertheless, while nutritional circumstances may have contributed to current anthropometries (i.e. measures of an individual's height and weight for their given age and gender), they do not necessarily reflect a poor quality of life. Does an individual who is exceptionally short for their age (i.e. stunted) have fewer opportunities or a compromised intellectual capacity? It is assumed that an individual who is stunted has become that way because of nutritional deprivations that also have an effect on cognitive development, educational attendance and subsequent opportunities and potential. However, despite the obvious correlations, such assertions merit further scientific scrutiny since there is considerable debate within the medical and psychological literature on such causal relationships.

What is important here is that the measures we often use for health convey a very limited aspect of health. Moreover, if we were to consider health from the perspective of the human development and capability approach, we would consider what matters most to individuals concerned and not what researchers or policy-makers deem to be most relevant.

If, as is often the case, we use infant mortality as a measure of population health and the utility which we seek to maximize, we could focus on the factors that most effectively prevent infant deaths. Our resource inputs would include an arsenal of vaccinations, trained birth attendants, oral-rehydration therapy or even baby formula. We would fail to see how such inputs get *converted* to a set of capabilities that people themselves value. What are the contextual, individual or cultural factors that intervene?

Similarly, if we decide that a reduction in stunting is most necessary for improving the health of a population, we would naturally focus on maximizing food inputs – especially protein, which is particularly relevant for linear growth (i.e. height). However, does that input necessarily get translated into health or the capability to achieve health? If not, why not? This chapter argues that, by failing to account for relevant conversion factors and by disregarding individual choices and constraints, we may not, in actuality, be efficient in our efforts to improve health.

In addition, it is important to recognize that health is multi-dimensional, and individuals make choices between and within these dimensions every day. For example, an individual may choose to live a short but full life rather than suffer from a painful and debilitating, but non-lethal, disease. Or, they may choose to risk a heart disease for the pleasures of a rich diet.

Conventional approaches to health

Human capital or health as input

Many of the conventional approaches to health consider the need to justify expenditures on health through the advantages it can bring to the economy.

For example, the World Bank's 1993 World Development Report *Investing in Health* focused on the benefits that improved health would have on economic growth. More recently, a report by the Commission on Macroeconomics and Health (2001), *Investing in Health for Economic Development*, draws on similar types of arguments made by such authors as David Bloom et al (2004), whose human capital and 'quality of labour' persuasions are well-known. The commission reports that a 10 per cent improvement in Life Expectancy at Birth (LEB) is associated with a rise in economic growth of at least 0.3–0.4 percentage points per year, controlling for other growth factors (Bloom et al 2004, p24). The difference in annual growth between a high-income country (having an LEB of 77 years) and a low-income country (LEB 49 years) is about 1.6 percentage points per year. The cumulative effect over a period of time becomes quite substantial. Similarly, based on the findings of Gallup and Sachs (2001), the same report attributes a short-run effect of malaria on growth of −1.3 per cent per year. In the long term, the report observes that the per capita income of a malaria-infected economy is only 52 per cent of that of a non-malaria infected country, when controlling for other determinants of growth (Gallup and Sachs, 2001, p117).

Box 10.1 Health as human capital

Since 1950, life expectancy has increased much more modestly [than that in previous decades] by 11 years in the US, 8.5 years in Scandinavian countries, 8 years in the UK, and 12.5 years in France, but by 24 years in Japan. Along with the 'quality' of health, American expenditures on health care have increased faster than in any developed country. Between 1960 and 1998, real per capita expenditures on US health care increased from $679 to $4,030, or at an annual rate of 4.9 per cent. Over the same period, per capita incomes grew at 2 per cent annually. By 1998, US health expenditure accounted for 12.9 per cent of national income – far more than any other country and roughly 60 per cent more than all other Organization for Economic Co-operation and Development (OECD) countries. The US is also spending much more on medical research than any other country or all European Union (EU) countries combined.

From 1970 to 1998, the reduction in death rates is concentrated at ages 55+ for men and 65+ for women. Using data for vital statistics on death rates from all causes by age and sex (National Centre for Health Statistics), we compute the economic value of the observed improvements in life expectancy from all sources over 1970–1980. Improvements totalled $200,000 for males at birth – $100,000 for 1970–1980, and $50,000 each for 1980–1990 and 1990–1998. Because these health improvements were concentrated late in life and we are using a discount rate of 3.5 per cent, the value peaks at approximately 50 years of age and not at birth. For example, at 50, the value of the 1970–1980 health improvements is roughly $150,000; 1980–1990 health improvements, $12,000; and 1990–1998 is roughly $100,000 for a cumulative total value of about $370,000. Comparable valuations for women are smaller but show similar patterns.

The aggregate gain in wealth due to reduced mortality over 1970–1998 is $45.6 trillion for men and $26 trillion for women. The mortality gains in 1970s are the largest, totalling $21 trillion for men and $15.8 trillion for women. The total gain across both sexes and all years is $72 trillion, which translates into a gain of about $2.6 trillion per year. By comparison, real GDP over this period averaged about $5.7 trillion. If we include the increased value of life as generated by greater longevity from 1970 and 1998 into national income measures, it would increase real output over this period by roughly 50 per cent.

Although expenditure on human health (including medical R&D) is large, a key question is whether we are spending too little or too much. The numbers given above for the US from the point of view of enhanced longevity greatly exceed medical costs. But let us take a world perspective on health benefits and costs by examining the potential loss of life due to pandemics. In the 1918–1919 world flu pandemic, 2.8 per cent of the world population died. If there was a world avian flu epidemic of a similar scale, roughly 168 million people would die. The ratio of world GDP per capita to per capita US GDP in 2004 was 0.22. Using the $3 million lives lost based on US data, a rough estimate of a world avian flu pandemic is $3 million × 0.22 × 168 million people or $111 trillion. Thus, the potential wealth loss of an avian flu pandemic is staggering. One can conclude that we are most likely under-investing in R&D to reduce this probability from occurring.

In conclusion, what is the answer to the question of why we spend so much on medical knowledge, medical care and change in lifestyles? It is mainly because saved lives are so valuable.

Edited extract from Gary S. Becker (2006) 'Health and human capital: The inaugural T. W. Schultz Lecture,' *Review of Agricultural Economics*, vol 28, no 3, pp323–325.

The approach adopted here is that healthier is wealthier: we should care about health, not only because it is an intrinsic good, but also because it contributes to economic growth. It is argued that health, through its contribution to the quality of human capital, as well as increases in savings and investment that correspond to longer lives, has a strong and significant effect on economic growth. This approach puts economic growth as an end and health as a means of achieving this end.

Health as output

The reverse has also been argued, where wealth is seen to be a necessary input for the achievement of health (specifically infant mortality) outcomes. Indeed, Pritchett and Summers (1996) argue that 'wealthier nations are healthier nations', as demonstrated by the strong and consistent association between per capita income and child mortality. They suggest that the effect of income on health is *causal* (not accounted for by reverse causation or a third variable) and that, for every unit change in per capita income, there is a 0.2–0.4 drop in child mortality rates. So, they conclude, if we focus on economic growth, we will ultimately save children's lives. Thus, economic growth assumes a central role in development objectives.

However, many have contested the centrality of economic growth to health. Sudhir Anand and Martin Ravallion (1993), for example, find the relationship between GNP per capita and health to operate mainly through the impact of GNP on private incomes (particularly of the poor) and public expenditure on health care. When both factors are included in their statistical analysis, GNP alone explains very little about the relationship. While it is true that increased economic growth provides the resource base to develop and strengthen health systems, increases in GNP are not always translated into health improvements. Health improvements have more to do with public, as well as individual, resource allocation and priority setting. In other words, it is not only the absolute availability of resources, but rather how these resources are distributed and used.

Sen (1999, p620) describes GNP-induced health improvement as 'growth-mediated' health development. This takes place, he argues, when fast economic growth is broad and highly employment-oriented, as well as when economic growth results in the expansion of social services, including health care, education and social security. This argument has been empirically verified by Ranis et al (2000). By cross-country regression analysis, they find that economic growth contributes to human flourishing (improved health and education) only if it is followed by a shift in resource-allocation towards health and education, equitable distribution of income, and extensive employment programmes for the unemployed (see Chapter 4 for a lengthier discussion on their study). Recently, Angus Deaton (2006) has also concluded that many contributions to health do not depend on economic growth or income. Indeed, there are numerous cases where health achievements have been made without high incomes (e.g. Sri Lanka, Cuba, Costa Rica), as well as reverse cases, where the expected level of health outcomes are not realized despite high levels of economic growth (e.g. Saudi Arabia). Deaton argues that there is likely a third factor relating both to economic growth and health, which explains the relationship (e.g. education, governance). Moreover, he emphasizes the need to recognize that health measures used for such macro level analysis often come from incomplete or inaccurate vital registries, particularly in poor countries, and life-expectancy figures come from model life tables which, by design, give more weight to infant and child death.

It is therefore clear from the discussion above that economic growth does not automatically translate into improved health. Instead, there is a set of social policies required to promote health; in the absence of such policies, fast economic growth may only benefit a few. The so-called 'trickle-down effect' never quite happened in much of the developing world, despite occasionally impressive cases of economic growth (see Chapter 4).

Whether we consider wealth to be the input and health the output – or the reverse, where health is the input for economic growth outputs – we are confined by our own conventional conceptions of inputs and outputs that relate to one another in a predictable and reliable fashion. Health necessarily improves wealth and wealth invariably improves health. Such approaches lead us to the critical question of whether economic growth is necessary for improving health. Sen (1999) asserts that this is not always the case. It is not always necessary to wait for high economic growth to take place before focusing on improving health. Indeed, the success of pre-reform China, Costa Rica, Sri Lanka and the Indian state of Kerala in improving the health and life expectancy of their citizens without substantial increases in income, supports the claim that economic growth is not a pre-condition for health improvement. Sen describes this health improvement as 'support-led' processes of health development, which result from priority being given to the provision of social services, particularly health care and basic education. These support-led processes, he argues, are economically viable since the required social services (i.e. health care and basic education) are labour-intensive and developing countries have cheap labour. Thus, low wages provide opportunities for improving health without requiring economic growth.

Health in the context of the human development and capability approach

Resource inputs and conversion factors

One of the distinguishing features of the human development and capability approach is its focus on the *process* of generating health. This stands in contrast to conventional approaches, which are mainly concerned with outputs we can measure and the commodities/resource inputs needed to achieve these outputs. Moreover, the capability approach recognizes that different people may have different values in terms of health and often weigh these against other dimensions in life. In acknowledging human diversity and agency, the capability approach suggests that people may require different kinds of resources to achieve the outcomes they value and have reason to value (i.e. functionings). It suggests that there are numerous factors influencing how different individuals convert resource inputs into valued functionings. These 'conversion factors' occur at the individual, social, institutional (formal or informal) and environmental level. Individual factors that determine how a given resource will be used include, for example, age, gender, metabolic rate, pregnancy, illness and knowledge. Social or family dynamics are also relevant in converting resource inputs to health outputs of value. Formal rules or informal regulations similarly intervene in our ability to use resource inputs to achieve desired functionings. And, lastly, our natural or man-made environment can facilitate the efficient (or inefficient) use of given inputs (see Chapter 2). As Sen writes (2002, p660):

> The factors that can contribute to health achievements and failures go well beyond health care, and include many influences of very different kinds, varying from (genetic) propensities, individual incomes, food habits and lifestyles, on the one hand, to the epidemiological environment and work conditions, on the other... We have to go well beyond the delivery and distribution

of health care to get an adequate understanding of health achievement and capability.

Before examining conversion factors in greater detail, let us consider what resource inputs are to be converted. Conventionally, the choice of inputs is determined by identified outputs. For example, if we focus on addressing under-nutrition as our output of interest, we would of course resort to the provision of food. In comparison, if we are specifically concerned with a particular micro-nutrient deficiency, we would concoct ways of supplementing existing food with this particular micro-nutrient. If, on the other hand, we are concerned with reducing infant mortality, we would ensure access to health facilities and medi-cines, as well as the provision of preventive interventions (such as vaccines). If we are specifically focused on preventing deaths from diarrhoea, we would make oral-rehydration therapy available. If it is the incidence of malaria we want to reduce, we would provide bed-nets impregnated with insecticide. The list can go on. In general, health resource inputs can be categorized to include food or food supplements, preventive interventions (e.g. immunization), and access to medicines and health-care personnel. Inputs might also include the provision of health education or information on particular aspects of health disseminated in a particular format (e.g. pamphlets, radio programmes, bill-boards, etc.). In the conventional approach, it is generally assumed that such inputs would necessarily result in the identified outputs (i.e. improvements in nutrition or reductions in morbidity and mortality). However, there is a broad heterogeneity in the effectiveness of such inputs, much of which can be explained by the variation in existing conversion factors. Accounting for such factors and focusing more on the process by which inputs are (or are not) trans-lated into health outputs facilitates the development of more effective and efficient health programmes.

Considerable empirical evidence exists to substantiate the importance of conversion factors in translating health inputs into valued health outputs. With respect to individual conversion factors, the evidence is largely physiological. For example, there are distinct physiological differences between men and women that render female infants with higher survival rates and longer life expectancies. Likewise, there are physiological changes that take place in the process of ageing that alter the immune systems of individuals and their respective susceptibilities to ill health. Moreover, even those of the same age and gender can differ genetically such that one individual is more susceptible to particular diseases than another. In addition, there are acquired differences between individuals that can affect their ability to use resources. For example, an individual who has intestinal infections will receive less nutritional value from the same amount of food consumed by an individual who is uninfected (since intestinal infections can disrupt one's absorptive capacity).

Conversion factors also include a number of external conditions, such as the natural or man-made environment in which we operate, formal or informal rules and regulations to which we subscribe, and the social or family dynamics that determine our daily lives (which may result in part from existing rules and regulations). The WHO Commission on Social Determinants of Health has called attention to some of these factors: what they refer to as 'social determinants' effectively encompass a variety of conversion factors that differ between social groupings. As the commission states in its final report, 'inequities in health ... arise because of the circumstances in which people grow, live, work and age, and the systems put in place to deal with illness. The conditions in which people live and die are, in turn, shaped by political, social, and economic forces' (Commission on Social Determinants of Health, 2008, pi.). This, however, includes both the differentials in resource inputs as well as factors that influence how these inputs might effectively be used.

One clear example of a conversion factor in health is education. Numerous studies have demonstrated that educated individuals tend to have lower mortality and morbidity than their less educated counterparts. For example, evidence from Sweden suggests that adults with doctorates have lower mortality rates than adults with professional degrees or master's degrees, and those with professional or master's degrees have lower mortality rates than those with bachelor's degrees (Erikson, 2001). Moreover, children of educated mothers fare better in terms of health than those whose mothers have less education. For example, evidence from El Salvador indicates that, if mothers have no education, their babies have a one in ten chance of dying in the first year of their life. The infant death rate falls to a quarter of that if mothers have at least secondary education (World Bank, 2006).

Another kind of conversion factor may be social status or occupational hierarchy. For example, Marmot (2006) assessed differences in mortality (specifically the 25-year mortality rates of men, aged 40–69, at death) between British civil servants in Whitehall on the basis of their occupational hierarchy (divided in order of hierarchy: top administration, professional/executive, clerical and others). He found that, despite having access to clean water and sanitation, a surplus of calories and adequate shelter, the professionals/executives had higher death rates than top administration, and the clerical staff had higher death rates than the professional/executive staff. Marmot speculates that the observed mortality differential relates to the relative lack of control those in lower positions in the occupational hierarchy had over their own respective lives. In other words, despite the fact that all civil servants have almost equal access to resource inputs, their occupational ranks (or degree of control over their lives) provide them with different conversion factors, affecting their respective health functionings in the long term.

Yet another conversion factor may involve the authority an individual has within their household or community to access or convert a particular resource into a valued health outcome. For example, the provision of anti-retrovirals (resource inputs) to HIV-positive women in contexts where women are unequal participants in the political process, and where they have unequal rights to (and control over) property, unequal access to economic assets, or even unequal restrictions on physical mobility, reproduction and sexuality – is not likely to increase their health functioning in general. Instead, a focus on their empowerment might address not only their HIV-status but also improve their health outcomes in a broader sense.

The importance of conversion factors indicates that, in order to achieve health equity, health policy cannot be isolated from the overall set of public policies pertaining to the distribution of the 'social determinants of health'. Thus, health policy is not only about providing treatment for people with diabetes but about dealing with the social and economic drivers of the obesity epidemic; it is not only about providing health treatment for children but about educating women who will become mothers; and it is not only about treating their stress-related illnesses medically but also about improving the conditions in which they live and work (Marmot, 2007).

Capabilities and functionings

We have thus far discussed resource inputs and conversion factors at length. But what is it that we are converting the resources to? In other words, what does the capability set for health look like? What 'we value and have reason to value' in terms of health is often related to nutrition (i.e. the ability to be well-nourished), morbidity (i.e. the ability to be free from illness) and mortality (i.e. the ability to live long lives). *Health capabilities* would then include the set of vectors which our resource inputs and conversion factors would allow, and *health functionings* would refer to the particular capability we choose (i.e. the one we identify to be of value).

There has been a dearth of discussion in the academic literature as to what constitutes health capabilities. Is it having access to a wide range of nutrition-rich foods that are socially and culturally acceptable; having a wide set of health-care options without financial, physical or cultural barriers; or a range of safe living and working environments free from harmful exposures or threats of injury? Despite discussions suggesting the contrary, the capability approach itself does not spell out a universal set of health capabilities. As with capabilities more broadly, health capabilities are determined by the population within which the capabilities are being assessed. How do they define health and what aspects of that conception of health can be achieved through available resources and conversion factors? For example, many communities may value psychological or social health above physical health. They may therefore find the resources pool to achieve this type of health to be quite different from what is needed to achieve physical health; similarly, the conversion factors required may also differ. Indeed, there may be inconsistencies between the capability to be well-nourished or free from illness and the capability to have good psychological or social health.

It is also important to consider the possible distinction between *functionings* more broadly and *achieved functionings*, which can be readily observed and measured. Being well-nourished and free from illness are good examples of achieved functionings that have a high likelihood of reflecting *valued states of being*. There are, however, other valuable health states, which may not be as easily observed or measured (e.g. psychological or social well-being). By focusing on achieved functionings, therefore, we may be misguided in assessing only a subset of valued health outcomes.

In sum, given available resources and conversion factors, an individual may secure a set of possible vectors of functionings (i.e. capabilities). From this set, an individual has the choice of realizing the functioning he values or has reason to value (in that particular space and at that particular time). Or, to put it in simpler terms, these functionings can be 'elementary functioning', to paraphrase Sen, such as escaping from morbidity and mortality or being adequately nourished or mobile. They can also represent more 'complex functionings', such as achieving self-respect, taking part in the life of the community, or appearing in public without shame. However, as we have discussed, different conceptions and values of health will affect not only how resources are converted into capabilities but also *which* functionings are actually achieved.

An important factor in considering health from a capability perspective is the importance of choice, which depends on information and individual values, as well as social, cultural and religious norms. It must be recognized that such choices, and the information upon which they are based, can be manipulated and modified, depending on the nature of the norms that inform them. Indeed, given the highly profitable nature of health issues, information pertaining to health or health-related consumables is highly influenced by commercial interests and economic motives. Moreover, people are not always rational when it comes to health matters. This has to do in part with the multi-dimensional nature of health but also with the fact that health values are weighted against other values. For example, there is a multitude of people who continue to smoke despite an awareness of the physical dangers of smoking. The same can be said of high fat diets and sedentary lifestyles. There is considerable literature on social choice and the complex manner in which individuals and societies go about making decisions. With respect to health, there is the added complication that individuals often have incomplete (e.g. subclinical pathologies) or biased (e.g. influenced by the pharmaceutical industry) information.

Health at the heart of inter-locking deprivations

Health is a fundamental capability that is instrumental in the achievement of other capabilities. The unfair distribution of health capabilities may therefore affect social justice in several ways (Sen, 2002). Based on evidence from South Asia, Osmani and Sen (2003) conclude that gender bias results in high maternal under-nutrition, which leads to intra-uterine growth retardation of the foetus. This leads to a very high prevalence of low birth weights, which in turn contributes to a high prevalence of both child under-nutrition and adult ailments. Thus, women's deprivation in terms of nutrition and health attainment has serious repercussions for society as a whole.

The occurrence of multiple deprivations is usually complex and interconnected; deprivation in one dimension often induces and reinforces deprivation in other aspects of life. Such a continuous inter-play between various capabilities produces (and reproduces) the vicious cycle of poverty. As we have argued earlier, health capabilities have both an intrinsic and instrumental role in enhancing human well-being. Deprivation in health can potentially cause deprivations in a number of other dimensions, such as education, employment, subjective well-being and participation in socio-economic spheres. When people are ill, malnourished, have mental disorders or life-debilitating disabilities, their overall capabilities are greatly reduced. Lack of health can therefore be at the heart of inter-locking deprivations.

To elaborate further, let us consider Nussbaum's list of fundamental capabilities (see Chapter 2) and how health can potentially affect them:

1   *life*: lack of health reduces life expectancy and therefore people die younger;
2   *bodily health*: lack of health greatly reduces all aspects of bodily health capability;
3   *bodily integrity*: people suffering from severe illness and life-debilitating disabilities may face serious problems in their ability to move freely from place to place; there might also be legal restrictions on the free movement of people with severe mental disorders; a lack of reproductive health (such as in the case of HIV/AIDS) may greatly reduce sexual satisfaction; similarly, stigma associated with various infectious and chronic diseases, disabilities and mental disorders may severely limit the opportunities to have sexual satisfaction (e.g. by limiting their opportunities for marriage which in turn may affect their social acceptance within a community);
4   *senses, imagination and thought*: certain health problems lead to the mental impairment of individuals (e.g. lack of iodine or neural tube defects), which in turn affect their ability to use sense, imagination and thought; lack of health in childhood may also reduce individual chances of acquiring education;
5   *emotions*: mental and psychological disorders can greatly affect the emotional health of individuals, therefore stunting their emotional development;
6   *affiliation*: the stigma associated with various diseases (such as HIV/AIDS), disabilities and mental disorders may greatly affect an individual's sense of self-respect; chronic diseases may also affect one's professional opportunities and also a person's sense of self-esteem;
7   *play*: people with physical and mental disorders may not be able to play and enjoy recreational activities in the ways that healthy people do.

The impact of health on education is one of the main channels affecting overall well-being and individual health. By using longitudinal data of a large sample of Filipino children, Glewwe et al (2001) found that well-nourished children perform better in school than under-nourished ones, mainly because their learning productivity per year was higher. Malnutrition not only lowers the learning productivity of school children; it also reduces their intellectual capacities. Iodine deficiency, for example, lowers IQ scores by as much as 10–15 percentage points (UNICEF 2005). In a randomized experiment with 30,000 school children in 75 primary schools in rural Kenya, Miguel and Kremer (2004) noted the adverse affects of worming (intestinal helminths infect one in four individuals worldwide) on education. They demonstrated that deworming results in a 7.5 per cent gain in primary school participation and a 25 per cent reduction in absenteeism, and generates positive externalities for untreated children.

The World Bank's study *Voices of the Poor* (Narayan et al, 2000) suggests that death, injury or severe illness in the family is considered to be one of the major causes of poverty in developing countries. The 2005 WHO Report finds a very close link between chronic diseases and poverty. While acknowledging that poverty is a causal factor of chronic diseases, the report argues that the incidence of chronic diseases also causes poverty. Furthermore, there are huge costs involved in the medical care of individuals suffering from chronic diseases. As the report puts it:

> Chronic diseases have an indirect impact on people's economic status and employment opportunities in the long term. Indirect costs include: reduction in income owing to lost productivity from illness or death; the cost of adult household members caring for those who are ill; reduction in future earnings by the selling of assets to cope with direct costs and unpredictable expenditures; and lost opportunities for young members of the household, who leave school in order to care for adults who are ill or to help the household economy (WHO, 2005, p67).

Thus, it is clear that poor health is not just suffering from illness, for those living in contexts of poverty. It pushes individuals and households towards losses in productivity, incomes assets and education – further entrenching the cycle of poverty. Health deprivations thus reinforce deprivations in other dimensions, which in turn reinforce deprivations in health. Box 10.2 describes the way that poor health results in deprivations in many aspects of life, and vice versa, for a household in rural Pakistan.

Box 10.2 Fatima's story: The coincidence of health deprivation, illiteracy and material deprivation[4]

Fatima, aged 39, lives with her family in a remote village in the southern part of Punjab, in Pakistan. She and her husband have two daughters and three sons. Her husband Rafiq, 40, is a mason, who earns his livelihood from irregular construction work in nearby villages. Both Fatima and Rafiq never attended school. When they married in 1987, Fatima was only 18. After one year of marriage, she gave birth to a girl, Maria, and one year later, to another one, Razia. As there was no health facility nearby, she did not have access to medical care during and after her pregnancy. Both births were attended by a traditional birth attendant. No vaccines were provided to mother and daughters to protect them from disease.

After one year, Fatima gave birth to another child. However, the baby died on the same day. At that point, Fatima had become weak and anaemic after three close pregnancies. In the absence of education and access to family-planning facilities, she was expecting soon thereafter and gave birth to another child who died on the same day. In the meantime, the two girls were experiencing frequent episodes of illness, sometimes treated by the local *hakim* (traditional healer). Yet another baby was born. When the newborn fell ill, the family took it to a private clinic at the first sign of illness. The doctor diagnosed that Fatima was suffering from a metabolic disorder – caused mainly by close pregnancies – in which babies have less chances of survival. That baby also died, but Fatima started medical treatment. At the next pregnancy, Jaffer was born: a healthy child, he eventually survived. The household, though very poor, was happy because one child had survived after three consecutive infant deaths.

In 1998, Maria, then 10 years old, fell seriously ill. Initially, her parents took her to the local *hakim.* She had developed symptoms of meningitis. As she did not recover, her parents went to the basic health-care unit and were then referred to the district hospital. Maria's situation continued to worsen. To finance her medical treatment, they sold some assets and borrowed money from their relatives. They took Maria to the tertiary care hospital in the nearby big city, but she died. The household ended up losing their eldest child, selling their small assets, incurring debts and losing income, since Rafiq could not work for an entire month while he was taking care of his daughter.

One birth after the other, life kept on moving, though miserably for Fatima because of physical weakness and her overwhelming sense of grief over the death of her four children. She gave birth to another son and a daughter. One morning, her elder son Jaffer was bitten by a rabid dog on his way to school. Disillusioned by the health facilities around them, they took him to a private clinic. He was given an expensive vaccination that they paid for by borrowing money from their relatives. The treatment proved to be ineffective and the boy began to develop the symptoms of rabies. Following a relative's advice, they borrowed more money and finally took him to the largest provincial hospital in Lahore. Jaffer died on the bus on the way to Lahore. Once again, Fatima and Rafiq ended up losing a child, incurring more debts for the treatment and funeral of their son.

They now have two daughters and three sons, all of them apparently anaemic and frequently suffering from illness. None of them is enrolled in school. In the past two years, Rafiq began to lose his eyesight. He visited 'eye camps' and hospitals run by various charities. Every time, he was given some medicine, but did not recover. Now he has completely lost sight in one eye. This has significantly affected his work, resulting in major income losses. Thanks to the family-planning programme Fatima learned about during her visit to the city, she is now using contraception. Previously, she used to earn some money by doing embroidery work, along with childcare. Now she complains of eyesight problems as well and can no longer perform her income-generating activities.

This box was written by Arif Naveed and is a true story.[4]

The paragraphs above detail how health interacts with other capabilities. There is yet another reason why health deserves a central place in development policy. In other deprivations, individuals who have been deprived in one dimension of their lives might be able to offset their deprivations at some other stage: for example, individuals who were not educated during childhood might benefit from adult literacy programmes, which could train them to be functionally literate. They could also profit from distance learning programmes. Those who are poor at the age of 25 might still be able to command a decent income later in life, once they have found gainful employment. Similarly, individuals who are unempowered at one point in their lives may become so at a different point through institutional reforms. In other words, it is still possible to reverse these deprivations over a period of time. We are not arguing here that this reversal fully compensates past deprivations. Clearly, an individual who is not deprived in any aspect of her life today but spends ten years of her life with deprivation in terms of income, education and empowerment, has had a lower overall quality of life than others who never faced such deprivations in the first place. But there always remains the possibility of partial compensation for such deprivations.

In contrast, deprivations in health may be irreversible. Once individuals have suffered from incurable diseases, they do not necessarily regain their health over a period of time. Such irreversible health losses may occur at any age. In the case of the elderly, irreversible dementia (the progressive decline in cognitive functions due to damage or disease), neural hearing loss and visual impairment are examples of irreversible health losses. Neural tube defects provide an example of irreversible health losses for children, which are often associated with maternal malnutrition. There are also various congenital disorders and genetic predispositions which cause irreversible health losses. Certain infectious diseases such as HIV/AIDS and congenital syphilis also cause similar losses. There are numerous other diseases that, despite the existence of a cure, remain incurable for the poor because of the fragile health-care systems in much of the developing world. Individuals suffering from such health losses cannot recover from them but can be compensated by other means, given a supportive context and adequate resources and conversion factors. The health and nutritional status of children can potentially determine their achievements in the social, psychological and economic spheres of their lives. Given the interactions between health and other capabilities, the incidence of irreversible health loss may indicate irreversible deprivation in multiple capabilities. There is thus an urgent need for appropriate social arrangements to tackle diseases before they occur. Public policy should therefore emphasize the importance of preventive health care, so that individuals are protected from the types of multi-faceted deprivations that could potentially threaten their overall well-being.

Questions

10.1 Take the example of any country where sufficient data are available and determine how adopting different indicators for health could influence policy decisions.

10.2 Trace the effects compromised mental health (or other compromised health-related capabilities) could have on various dimensions of human development.

10.3 Take a community of your choice and illustrate the various conversion factors that could influence how a given resource (e.g. food) is translated into outputs of value.

10.4 The conventional approach to the problem of undernutrition is the provision of food. Reconsider how undernutrition would be addressed were it to be framed in the capability approach. Use an example to illustrate your point.

10.5 Health related choices are particularly susceptible to manipulation by market interests. Consider in your own life the factors that influence your choice of the foods you eat, the activities you undertake, and the medicines you seek when ill.

Notes

1   Constitution of the World health Organization, 1946 can be found in the Official Records of the world Health Organization, no 2, p100.

2   The Preamble to the Constitution of the World Health Organization, 1946, can be found in the Official Records of the world Health Organization, no 2, p100 www.searo.who.int/LinkFiles/About_SEARO_const.pdf accessed January 2009.

3   International anthropometric standards and cut-offs have recently been revised to reflect a more international cohort. However, the debates continue and the applicability of the new standards is still under investigation.

4   Thanks to Shabana Saleem for providing and verifying Fatima's medical history.

Readings

Anand, P. and Hees, M. V. (2006) 'Capabilities and achievement: An empirical study', *The Journal of Socio-Economics*, vol 35, pp268–284

Anand, S. and Ravallion, M. (1993) 'Human development in poor countries: On the role of private incomes and public services', *Journal of Economic Perspectives*, vol 7, no 1, pp133–150

Bloom, D. E., Canning, D. and Sevilla, J. (2004) 'The effect of health on economic growth: A production function approach', *World Development*, vol 32, no 1, pp1–13

Commission on Social Determinants of Health (2008) *Closing the gap in a generation: health equity through action on the social determinants of health. Final Report of the Commission on Social Determinants of Health*, World Health Organization, Geneva

Deaton, A. (2006), 'Global patterns of income and health: Facts, interpretations, and policies', *NBER Working Paper* 12735, National Bureau of Economic Research, Cambridge, MA

Erikson, I., Undén, A. L. and Elofsson, S. (2001) 'Self-rated health. Comparisons between three different measures. Results from a population study', *International Journal of Epidemiology*, vol 30, no 2, pp326–333

Gallup, J. L. and Sachs, J. D. (2001) 'The economic burden of malaria', *American Journal of Tropical Medicine and Hygiene*, vol 64, no 1, suppl, pp85–96

Marmot, M. (2006) 'Health in an unequal world: Social circumstances, biology and disease', *Clinical Medicine*, vol 6, no 6, pp559–572

Marmot, M. (2007) 'Achieving health equity: From root causes to fair outcomes', *The Lancet*, vol 370, 29 September, pp1153–1163

Narayan, D., Chamber, R., Shah, M. and Petesch, P. (2000) *Voices of the Poor*, Oxford University Press for the World Bank, New York

Osmani, S. and Sen, A. K. (2003) 'The hidden penalties of gender inequality: Foetal origins of ill-health', *Economics and Human Biology*, vol. 1, pp105–121

Pritchett, L. and Summers, L. H. (1996) 'Wealthier is healthier', *Journal of Human Resources*, vol 31, no 4, pp841–868

Ranis, G., Stewart, F. and Ramirez, A. (2000) 'Economic growth and human development', *World Development*, vol 28, no 2, pp197–219

Ruger, J. P. (2006) 'Health, capability, and justice: Towards a new paradigm of health ethics, policy and law', *Cornell Journal of Law and Public Policy*, vol 53, no 2, pp403–482

Sen, A. K. (1999) 'Health in development', *Bulletin of the World Health Organization*, vol 77, no 8, pp619–623

Sen, A. K. (2002) 'Why health equity?' *Health Economics*, vol 11, pp659–666

UNICEF and Micronutrient Initiative (2005) *Vitamin and Mineral Deficiency: A global progress report*, http://www.unicef.org/nutrition/index_hidden_hunger.html

WHO (2005) *Preventing Chronic Diseases: A vital investment*, WHO Global Report, www.who.int/chp/chronic_disease_report/full_report.pdf

World Bank (2006) *World Development Report: Equity and Development*, Oxford University Press, New York

Further Readings

Anand, P. and Dolan, P. (2005) 'Equity, capabilities and health', *Social Science & Medicine*, vol 60, pp219–222

Coast J., Smith, R. and Lorgelly, P. (2008) 'Should the capability approach be applied in health economics?' *Health Economics*, vol 17, pp667–670

Gandjour, A. (2008) 'Mutual dependency between capabilities and functionings in Amartya Sen's capability approach', *Social Choice Welfare*, vol 31, pp345–350

Glewwe, P., Jacoby, H. G. and King, E. M. (2001) 'Early childhood nutrition and academic achievement: a longitudinal analysis', *Journal of Public Economics*, vol 81, pp345–368

Miguel, E. and Kremer, M. (2004) 'Worms: Identifying impacts on education and health in the presence of treatment externalities', *Econometrica*, vol 72, no 1, pp159–217

Smith, J. P. and Kington, R. S. (1997) 'Demographic and economic correlates of health in old age', *Demography*, vol 34, no 1, pp159–170

Stephens, C., Porter, J., Nettleton, C. and Willis, R. (2006) 'Disappearing, displaced, and undervalued: A call to action for indigenous health worldwide,' *The Lancet*, vol 367, pp2019–2028

11
Culture and Religion

Aims of the chapter

- To understand how culture and religion affect how people understand and seek to achieve development.
- To critically assess different perspectives on culture and religion.
- To explore the contribution of the human development approach to our understanding of culture and religion.

Key points

- From a position of relative neglect, culture and religion are now recognized as being important factors in development.
- Culture is not just about ideas or values, but is deeply embedded in material life and power relations.
- Culture is not set: instead it is porous, contested and always capable of change.
- Religion is often seen as a form of culture but can also be understood as being in tension with it, as major religious traditions are found in all kinds of cultural contexts and take on different forms depending on socio-political realities locally.

Part I Culture

Sarah White

> Culture .... however important it may be as an instrument of
> development (or obstacle to development), cannot ultimately be
> reduced to a subsidiary position as a mere promoter of (or
> impediment to) economic growth. Culture's role is not exhausted
> as a servant of ends – though in a narrower sense of the concept
> this is one of its roles – but is *the social basis of the ends themselves.*
> Development and the economy are part of a people's culture.
>
> Javier Pérez de Cuéllar (UNESCO 1995, p15, emphasis added)

From a position of relative neglect, there has been a recent explosion of
attention to 'culture' in international development. The period 1988–1997 saw
the United Nations World Decade for Cultural Development, culminating in
the report of the World Commission on Culture and Development led by Javier
Pérez de Cuéllar (UNESCO 1995). Interest within the World Bank in the
significance of culture was promoted under the presidency of James
Wolfensohn, and is expressed in the collection *Culture and Public Action*
(2004), which was edited by two of the Bank's economists (Rao and Walton
2004) and includes a chapter by Amartya Sen. In the human development and
capability approach, a similar pattern can be observed: 1995 saw the first
explicit engagement with culture with the publication of *Women, Culture and
Development*, a collection of essays edited by Martha Nussbaum and Jonathan
Glover. This was followed by the 2004 *Human Development Report* on
cultural liberty, and a later book by Sen (2006), in part paralleling ideas in the
report, entitled *Identity and Violence*.

The growth of interest in culture has also marked a shift in the way it has
been positioned in development debates. The oppositions between tradition
(or culture), on the one hand, and development, on the other, once a central
preoccupation of modernization theory, while by no means absent in
contemporary writings, have now been joined by a different voice. Rather than
inhibiting progress, culture is now being celebrated as a resource for
development. Religious institutions such as churches, mosques and temples,
formerly seen to be diverting investment into 'unproductive' activities, are now
welcomed as potential partners in development. Moreover, understanding
(other) people's cultures is seen as being critical if development effectiveness is
to be enhanced (Rao and Walton 2004). While this 'rehabilitation' in the
perception of culture is in many ways very welcome, it should not simply be

taken at face value. It reflects the more general tendency within globalization to re-inscribe the value of the 'local'. It is also part of a broader disillusionment with (and ideological opposition to) state-led development, combined with the aim of fostering more 'participatory' forms of development intervention. Finally one could also read against the grain of development discourse itself, observing in this new celebration of culture the shadow of a perceived threat that still needs to be neutralized. Depicted by Samuel Huntington as a 'clash of civilizations', embodied in street protests against globalization and in the destruction of the Twin Towers – culture has become a major site of struggle for those who wish to preserve (or challenge) the hegemony of the present international order.

The first part of this chapter explores how the relations between culture and development have been enunciated and how the human development approach has contributed to this discourse; this part concludes by offering a few principles that bear further scrutiny.

Development perspectives

Writings on international development use the notion of culture in a number of different ways. At root, the term simply means 'cultivation' – of land, crops, animals, bacteria. This led to: the cultivation of the mind and representation in art and literature; characterizing elite conduct and lifestyles as being 'cultured'; and, more recently, a more democratized perspective in the current preoccupation with 'popular culture'. Traditionally a matter for personal or national investment, this has long been an area of concern for UNESCO (the United Nations Educational Scientific and Cultural Organization), and its place has been consolidated in international policy with recent World Bank interest in supporting sites of 'cultural heritage', such as the walled city in Lahore or the Medina in Fez (Serageldin and Martin-Brown 1999).[1]

The predominant use of 'culture' in development, however, tends to be more general. Talk is usually of 'other cultures' or 'a people's culture'. 'Cross-cultural' is often used interchangeably with 'cross-national'. Culture thus appears as shorthand for group identity, often coterminous with a nation state, or (increasingly) language-based or ethnic groups within it. This runs counter to many theorizations of identity, which stress the multiple dimensions and scope for variation and change within and between them. Sen's contributions to the debate press for a vigorous acknowledgement of this diversity, and are central to the advocacy of 'cultural freedom', which is discussed in greater detail below. This reflects in part the priority given to the individual in the human development approach (see Chapter 2). It also, however, has a political intention. (Cross)cultural generalizations serve as a fertile breeding ground for the bigotry and identity-based conflict that Sen, especially in *Identity and Violence*, is at pains to counter. The danger of a renewed emphasis on culture is that it be used to seal off debate, rather than open an additional point of entry into further discussion.

To use culture as an explanation is to view it as a factor whose presence or absence is responsible for development itself. The earliest example of this is Max Weber's *The Protestant Ethic and the Spirit of Capitalism*, which maintained that the cultural and religious beliefs of early capitalist entrepreneurs were significant to the development of capitalism in Europe. It is noteworthy, however, that Weber saw 'culture' as being only one part of the explanation, which came into play only because of the presence of appropriate material factors. More recent authors have been less scrupulous, however: Samuel Huntington (2000) uses 'culture' to explain the developmental differences between Ghana and South Korea since the 1960s. This is strongly rejected by Sen (2004), who pointed out that differences during this period also existed in terms of class structures, politics and government, relations with major capitalist economies and levels of literacy. Such 'cultural determinism' (to use Sen's term) tends to fix entire nations within certain cultural coordinates, ignoring many forms of interaction with the wider world and changes in culture over time.

Huntington's approach echoes the dominant way in which culture has been conceived in relation to international development – as an obstacle. Modernization theories in the 1960s were built on the contrast between 'tradition' and 'modernity', using culture as a marker of the otherness of peoples who were prevented by primordial bonds from joining the rational pursuit of progress. Psychologists demonstrated how, in the process of 'making men [sic] modern' cultural difference (indexed by nation) would eventually slip away (Inkeles, 1969). This form of cultural chauvinism, and the very tangible relations of power over which it was draped, continues to be a significant aspect of the development enterprise, within countries as well as between them. Stacey Leigh Pigg (1992) shows how manuals for health development workers in Nepal reproduced stereotypes by caste and class in their depiction of 'more' and 'less' developed people, for example. Such stereotypes are not always negative, of course. Since colonial times the relationship has also been seen in the reverse, with development as the threat and 'indigenous cultures' as endangered, needing protection if they were to retain their local values and integrity. Such images predominate, for example, in representations of contemporary clashes over the construction of dams or extractive industries in areas where indigenous people live.[2] Tanya Li (1996) helpfully reminds us that the cultural unity even of such communities is not merely given, but may be represented differentially depending upon the making of claims on specific resources.

Another strong trend in the development literature is to identify culture cognitively, that is, with ideas, beliefs and values. This is a step forward from the simple opposition between subjective perceptions (of individual actors?) and objective measures (of outsiders?), since it recognizes that perceptions do not belong simply to isolated individuals, but are conditioned by societal norms and expectations. Nevertheless, to use Marxist terminology, this still situates 'culture' at the level of superstructure, rather than seeing it as structuring society itself in more fundamental ways. A good example of this approach can be found in Vijayendra Rao and Michael Walton's introduction to *Culture and Public Action* (2004, p9), which was sponsored by the World Bank:

> A culturally-informed perspective is thus not so much a prescription as it is a lens – a way of seeing. It sees individuals as (being) driven by a culturally-influenced set of motives, incentives, beliefs and identities that interact with economic incentives to affect outcomes.... We believe that incorporating this lens into more conventional economic ways of understanding will, in many situations, lead to more effective policy.

This approach has much to recommend it over the simplistic notion that beliefs and values are somehow fixed or given for any nation or social group as a whole. Instead, culture is viewed more flexibly, as a prism that offers people particular ways of seeing the world. However, the move is not perhaps as welcome as it might at first appear. Seeing culture as a 'lens' does not undermine the 'analytic primacy of the rational, value-maximizing individual' (Good, 1994, p39, after Sahlins, 1976), which is so foundational to Western economic thought. Individuals and the economic incentives to which they respond remain, it would seem, outside culture, and even motives, beliefs and identities are only 'influenced' by them. Similarly, the confidence that such a lens might be 'incorporated' within existing approaches suggests that there is no need for a fundamental shift in existing institutions of international development. This rationale for taking culture into account is in fact highly reminiscent of arguments for increasing people's participation in development projects: the more people are involved, the more effective projects are likely to be. As many critics have pointed out, however, instituting participation in public projects does not necessarily signal any real shift in power relations. It may simply neutralize and de-politicize potential threats (Cooke and Kothari, 2001; Selznick, 1949; White, 1996). If a 'cultural lens' is to be used to enhance policy effectiveness, this leaves the bigger question open: who owns the policy or the development intervention?

Anthropological perspectives

In contrast to this 'bird's eye view' of culture and development, anthropological debates on culture take us, as one might expect, somewhat closer to people's lives and to their everyday social practice. In his discussion on 'the capacity to aspire', Arjun Appadurai discusses how development 'needs' are always grounded in culture. Aspirations, he claims, 'form parts of wider ethical and metaphysical ideas which derive from larger cultural norms' (Appadurai, 2004, pp67–68).

Appadurai identifies three levels that ground people's aspirations in culture.

The first and most immediate level consists of a 'visible inventory of wants'. These contain the specific wants and choices for this piece of land or that marriage partner that people consciously identify and seek to pursue. It is this level that commonly appears – though usually in a rather more generalized way – when people are asked to itemize their goals or needs by development agents. At the next level are the 'intermediate norms', which may not be explicitly expressed but nevertheless structure specific wants through local ideas about marriage, family, work, virtue, health and so on. These in turn relate to 'higher order normative contexts', which comprise a larger 'map' of ideas and beliefs concerning such matters as life and death, the value of material goods versus social relationships, this world and other worlds, peace and conflict, etc. 'Culture' is thus not something separable from everyday life, but instead structures material and relational desires through a cascade of associations that make them meaningful and even, at times, pressing and urgent.

The relationship between culture and materiality in human welfare is discussed at length by Marshall Sahlins in his *Culture and Practical Reason* (1976). For Sahlins, the construction of meaning is the key distinguishing characteristic of humankind. It is not that materiality does not matter, he argues, but that social and cultural life are in fact shaped by 'nature' and the economy rather than the other way around: 'No society can live on miracles...None can fail to provide for the biological continuity of the population in determining it culturally...Yet men do not merely "survive". They survive in a definite way' (Sahlins, 1976, p168).

That 'definite way' – the aspiration, as Appadurai might put it – not just for shelter but for a particular kind of house, not just for calories but for a particular kind of food, is mediated by culture. The material and cultural are thus not separable, such that one can separate 'objective reality' from 'cultural values', but are in fact inextricably linked:

> It is not that the material forces and constraints are left out of account, or that they have no real effects on the cultural order. It is that the nature of the effects cannot be read from the nature of the forces, for the material effects depend on their cultural encompassment. The very form of social existence of material force is determined by its integration in the cultural system. (Sahlins, 1976, pp205–206)

As an example, he offers the fact that, in the US, dogs are considered inedible, unlike cattle, which is considered to be 'food' (1976, p169). The fondness for beef in the North American diet has major material outcomes, in terms of prices of meat, land use, agricultural subsidies, health issues and so on, with effects that tend to ricochet around the world. But the basis for choosing cattle over dog meat – the root cause of all these different effects – is neither 'nature' nor 'utility' but culture.

Veena Das (2000) explores how culture and agency interact at the individual level. She describes how a Punjabi woman, named Asha, responds to the disasters that the partition of India and Pakistan wrought on her family life. She shows the practical *work* that Asha conducts in building a sense of self and a life worth living out of a context of violence and subjugation, 'not through an ascent into transcendence but through a descent into the everyday' (2000, p208). Culture, in this reading, can be deeply imbued with power: the overall cultural terms that have defined Asha's identity were patriarchal ones, and even in pursuing the relationships that were important to her (with her dead husband's sister and her son), she had to adopt a patriarchal idiom. At the same time, Das stresses how Asha did not allow her life to be simply defined by the power of patriarchy, but actively worked instead to achieve a positive way of being in the world. This involved careful repair work over many years of damaged relations with her first husband's family, guided by her love for key individuals and the way in which she saw her relationships as being fixed in the long term. The meaning of this was inscribed by culture, since she saw in her first marriage the connections that she would carry into eternity. But the settled cultural world to which these meanings belonged was smashed by the disaster of Partition and the fracturing of family relations that followed. Critically, therefore, this cultural meaning and these relations were also re-claimed by her, and re-inhabited as a long act of witnessing to the hurt she had suffered through them. The cultural 'work' that she took on was transformative – not sweet and easy, but hard and painful – not simply an inflection of goals, but rather a lived experience achieved through a lifetime of struggle.

Building on Das's approach, it may be useful to consider culture not so much as a lens but a form of 'work'. The idea of 'the work of culture' was first proposed by Obeyesekere (1990). Writing at the boundary between psychoanalysis and anthropology, he saw the 'work of culture' as the process whereby the deep and often darkly painful sides of human existence rooted in the unconscious could be symbolically transformed into publicly shared meanings and imagery. In terms of development, approaching culture as a form of work has four main advantages: first, it sees people as agents of culture, who use the resources culture has given them and reproduce or transform them through their actions. In addition to bringing culture to the ground, this emphasizes its flexibility and capacity to change over time. Second, it recognizes that culture is at once material and symbolic. As Pierre Bourdieu (1977) has recognized in the notion of 'habitus', it is expressed in how we hold our bodies, how we decorate our houses, how we bring up our children – all parts of life, not limited to ideas, values or meaning. Third, it puts power into the picture. The work of culture, like other kinds of work, is clearly conditioned by broader social and cultural structures of class and patriarchy. As Roger Keesing remarks, criticizing the widely used and somewhat idealist formulation of culture by Clifford Geertz: 'Cultures do not simply constitute webs of significance, systems of meaning that orient humans to one another and their world. They constitute ideologies, disguising human political and economic realities ... Cultures are webs of mystification as well as significance' (Keesing, 1987, p161). Finally, viewing culture as a form of work recognizes that it is not free-floating, but is shaped by the specific institutional context in which each encounter takes place. 'Culture' can thus be seen to be affected as much by institutional setting – legal, therapeutic or educational – as by national or religious contexts (e.g. Spencer, 1997).

Taking culture seriously means analysing it always in the context of social structure and political economy. Without due attention to material resources and the power relations that govern them, a focus on 'culture' could obscure as much as it enlightens. For those not driven by ideology, simple declarations about 'culture' as a homogenous entity shared by large collectivities of people are no longer available. Appadurai (2004, p61) helpfully summarizes the current points of consensus on culture in anthropology: relationality – cultural meaning lies in the relationship between different elements, rather than inhering intrinsically within a particular item considered in isolation; dissensus – culture is non-unitary, subject to considerable internal negotiation and dispute; and leakiness – the boundaries of culture are highly porous, such that flows, borrowings and interactions across borders are the norm rather than the exception.

Does this complexity suggest that culture is no longer a useful analytic category? Attractive though such an option might appear to be, it does not do justice to much that can be gleaned from cultural readings. But, just as explanations of 'culture' make no sense in the absence of an awareness of the social structures and political economy that inform them, cultural analysis cannot be done in abstract terms. While class, gender, ethnicity, disability and age may be common axes of differential advantage, they do not always and everywhere mean the same things. This links back to Sahlins's statement above – that people do not only survive but do so 'in a particular way'. But it also goes beyond this because the making of social difference is not simply coloured by culture: culture, in fact, lies at the heart of social difference. The current enthusiasm for cultural celebration in development circles notwithstanding, it should be noted that the creation of differing value, the affirmation of some and the debasement of others are absolutely central to the work of culture itself. As Sahlins (1976, p102) puts it: 'the creation of meaning is the distinguishing and constituting quality of men – the "human essence" of an older discourse – such that by processes of differential valuation and signification, relations among men, as well as between themselves and nature, are organized.'

Human development perspectives

Three significant 'moments' are noteworthy in the human development approach to culture. The first, in 1991, discusses culture but does not explicitly acknowledge it: this is Sen's analysis of the 'cooperative conflicts' involved in intra-household bargaining in India. The second is the edited collection on women and culture noted above, in which Martha Nussbaum has a prominent voice. The third is the 2004 *Human Development Report* on 'cultural liberty' and Sen's (2004) linked paper in the *Culture and Public Action* volume, also mentioned above.

Cooperative conflicts

In 'cooperative conflicts', Sen (1991) builds on the work of feminist scholars on intra-household divisions to propose a model for gender-based bargaining at the household level. Here he notes that there is a contrast between women's real interests as individuals and their perceptions that they should put their families first – a theme that permeates his work on adaptive preferences (see Chapter 2). Perceptions cannot be taken, he argues, as real indicators of well-being, which are given by a person's capabilities. Subjective perceptions of utility, in contrast, 'can be moulded by social conditioning and a resigned acceptance of misfortune' (Sen, 1991, p133). Perceptions are significant, however, because they affect the bargaining positions of the parties in terms of how they perceive their interests and how they perceive their relative contributions. 'Perception biases unfavourable to women' (1991, p137) combined with a sexual division of labour that strongly favours men leads to a worse breakdown position for women (i.e. what would happen if the marriage were to fail) and thus a significantly weakened voice in intra-household conflicts.

While culture is not mentioned here, it is clearly lurking behind discussions of 'perception'. The approach is straightforward: the perception is wrong (ideological, though this is not Sen's language) and an individual-based capability approach would yield the 'true' (or 'truer') picture. The paper by Das (2000) discussed above might caution us to seek a rather more nuanced analysis, in which women do not simply accept what is given but work with (and on) it to achieve the aims they have reason to value. It is also important to recognize that men's understanding of their interests is equally socially constructed, and should be subjected to similar analytic scrutiny in terms of whether or not it reflects their 'true' well-being. Following Das, this might open the question of whether the pursuit of individual advantage is the whole story in assessing well-being. However, Sen's analysis is valuable in introducing into an economics-dominated discourse the social construction of 'preferences,' firmly placing power asymmetries at the centre of analytic thinking.

Culture in Nussbaum's capabilities approach

Nussbaum's version of the capability approach takes a broader, philosophical approach, which is 'frankly universalist and "essentialist"' (Nussbaum 2000, p63). Her attention focuses on women in developing countries and her starting point is that culture itself is a problem. As Nussbaum and Glover state on the first page of *Women, Culture and Development*: 'Cultural traditions pose obstacles to women's health and flourishing'. And, even more strongly, they continue on page 3: 'Customs, in short, are important causes of women's misery and death'.

The primary response to culture is thus conceived in moral terms, and concerns 'the relationship between culture and justice' (Nussbaum and Glover 1995, p6), especially as a riposte to cultural relativists who appear to value cultural continuity above human life chances. Nussbaum takes as her starting point the (pre-cultural) human being and 'the capacities and needs that join all humans, across barriers of gender and class and race and nation' (Nussbaum, 2000, p61). Her project is then to define the set of functionings that are essential for a human life, and to identify a further threshold, beyond which that life may be said to be 'good'. She sets out a list of central human capabilities to construct a universal measure against which to assess the lives of women in developing countries 'who are currently being deprived of their full "human development"', and to launch claims for justice on their behalf (see Chapter 2).

A fundamental problem with this is discussed in Chapter 2: the objection, by Sen and others, that such lists are inherently problematic because they are far from universal and represent a very particular point of view. Still, they can serve as a basis for dialogue about what constitutes a 'good life'. This draws attention to the list's particular cultural assumptions and values (rather than denying them) in a way that has opened them up to further debate. Nussbaum's approach is somewhat different. She deliberately makes the list general, allowing 'for the possibility of multiple specifications of each of the components' (2000, p93). In theory, then, there is considerable scope for accommodating cultural difference. In practice, however, there may be relatively little room for manoeuvre. For example, as a liberal feminist, she rejects the possibility of gender-differentiated norms in functionings, even though all human societies and virtually all species have some distinction of function on the basis of gender. This suggests that the range of cultural forms she would deem acceptable as a means to express these capabilities could be rather limited.

A further concern is with the politics of the thresholds themselves. Nussbaum's 'minimum' threshold of functioning, below which a life is not seen as a human life, seems to open rather wider questions than are necessary to address the ethical questions that she raises concerning severe disability and the beginning and end of life. The politics of the second threshold are even more problematic, as it appears to say that a whole set of people – in practice the vast majority of the global population – are not living 'a good human life'. Without glorifying struggle or minimizing hardship, it is essential to recognize that people often achieve meaningful, valuable lives under even the most difficult circumstances. One cannot read off the quality of a life lived simply on the basis of the constraints people face – or indeed the apparent advantages they enjoy.

This relates to a third point: the politics of agency. One of the foundational criticisms of cultural imperialism in colonialism and in development as a whole concerns its codification of agency and subjectivity. This deploys a series of binary tropes to specify the subjects and objects of agency: the 'developed' and the 'underdeveloped'; those who do and those who need development; those who 'give' and those who 'receive'. Work on the 'status of women' since colonial times has offered a paradigmatic instance of this, with its highly coloured imagery of downtrodden women needing the salvific intervention of colonial powers to protect them from male oppression (Shehabuddin 2008). While this is far from Nussbaum's intention, the morally-charged generalizations she makes raise uncomfortable resonances of this. The positioning of subject and object is brought into focus by her invocation of two impoverished women from India and Bangladesh, whose stories she narrates, but who have no opportunity to respond with their own respective points of view.

In sum, then, we would agree with Susan Wolf, the discussant of Nussbaum's chapter in *Women, Culture and Development*, that her capabilities approach could be tempered with considerably more modesty and openness to other points of view. It is equally important to note that all available options are not exhausted by the two modes offered by Nussbaum: the cultural relativism of 'anything goes' so long as the 'local culture' endorses it; and universalist essentialism – both advocated, incidentally, by empowered external observers of 'other' lives. Rather, as the discussion above suggests, culture (at 'home' as well as 'abroad') is a primary bearer of power, which always needs to be analysed critically for its implications on political economy. Also, insiders are typically much more adept agents than many stereotypes allow us to see.

Cultural freedom

The 2004 *Human Development Report* asserts the importance of culture as a serious part of life and entitlements, the denial of which leads to 'significant deprivations' (p13). With its emphasis on 'freedom in cultural spheres', the report is a blast of liberalism in a field in which group rights have predominated over individual rights and concerns for cultural conservation over advocacy for change. As the report states, 'cultural liberty is an important aspect of human freedom, central to the capability of people to live as they would like and to have the opportunity to choose from the options they have – or can have' (p13). The fundamentals of a particular vision of the human development approach are thus re-stated: secular states are apparently the most likely to expand human freedom and human rights, and to recognize democracy.

The report is very clear that the recognition of culture derives from, but is ultimately of secondary importance to, the ultimate value of freedom. As the overview observes, cultural liberty is about defending individual choices, not about preserving values or tradition as an end in itself. Cultural liberty is about 'being able to choose one's identity – who one is – without losing the respect of others or being excluded from other choices ...' (UNDP, 2004, p10).

Much of this is familiar from the 'cultural rights' enshrined in the United Nations Declaration on Human Rights: the right to nationality (article 15); to freedom of thought, conscience and religion (article 18); to participate freely in community cultural life (article 27); and duties to the community, including to respect the rights and freedoms of others. What is distinctive is the overwhelming emphasis on choice and the individual, and the tendency to elide 'culture' with 'lifestyle'. This needs to be subjected to far more critical discussion. While the power relations of cultural conservatism do gain some recognition, there is no general examination of 'individual choice' (and, for example, its implication in global marketing) in the way that Sen cautioned against taking 'subjective preferences' in intra-household bargaining on their own terms.

There is partial recognition of the materiality of culture, in discussions of its impact on poverty and in leading to the relative deprivation of being unable to participate in social life in accordance with local norms (UNDP, 2004, p14). The language of exclusion also links it to the social and political. Cultural exclusion is said to take two forms: 'participation exclusion' – discrimination in education, employment, politics, etc; and 'living mode exclusion', which 'denies recognition of a lifestyle that a group chooses to have' (ibid.).

As mentioned above, the report's analysis of 'culture' owes much to recent theorizing of identity. It usefully draws attention to the multiplicity of identities that any individual has, thereby contesting approaches that apply a single label to an entire national, ethnic, cultural or religious group:

> Typically, each individual can identify with many different groups.
> A person may have an identity of citizenship (for example, being French), gender (being a woman), race (being of Chinese origin), regional ancestry (having come from Thailand), language (being fluent in Thai, Chinese and English, in addition to French), politics (having left-wing views), religion (being a Buddhist), profession (being a lawyer), location (being a resident of Paris), sports-affiliation (being a badminton player and a golf fanatic), musical taste (loving jazz and hip-hop), literary preference (enjoying detective stories), food habits (being a vegetarian) and so on. (UNDP, 2004, p17)

The problem with this list is that it mixes up the socially significant (class, gender, ethnicity) with the trivial (liking badminton or hip-hop). This takes away from the serious points it could potentially make. The report admits that the choices are limited – you cannot choose to be a Sumo wrestler if you are not one – but goes on: 'Within the range of the memberships that you actually have, you can choose what priority to give to one membership or another, in a particular context' (UNDP, 2004, p17).

In reality, however, there are some aspects of our identity – such as, for most of us, gender, age, ethnicity and perhaps class – which we cannot change. We may be able to choose how we represent them by how we dress, use make-up, style our hair, etc., but we do not, crucially, have power over how others read them, and how they act towards us as a result. While, for privileged people in particular, these basic identifiers may not appear to be of particular importance much of the time, when caught on the wrong side of town at the wrong time of day, they can suddenly become *all* that you are seen to be. Even in ordinary times, as West and Fenstermaker (1995) argue in their paper 'Doing difference', women *may* be treated equally but are always 'at the risk of' a gender assessment, just as people of colour are always 'at the risk of' racial assessment. These basic forms of social difference may affect the way that you play badminton or how your choice of music is perceived, but they operate at a very different level, and should not be equated with such contingent preferences. The critical issues concern freedom from discrimination or victimization and the right to respect and equality of opportunity, regardless of one's gender, age, sexuality, disability or racial/ethnic/religious community. And while this affects the life chances of individuals, it cannot simply be analysed at an individual level.

Other parts of the report are more useful. Recognition of the plural histories of tolerance and democracy is an important ballast against Eurocentric views. The discussion of multicultural institutions is valuable, although it would be good to see more discussion of the Indian experience of caste reservation, and the ways in which policies to address disadvantage can often end up re-enforcing the very identities they recognize. However, as the closing statement of the overview makes clear, the main thrust of the report is a robust assertion of liberalism: 'Individuals have to shed rigid identities if they are to become part of diverse societies and uphold cosmopolitan values of tolerance and respect for human rights'(UNDP, 2004, p23).

In closing, it may be helpful to reflect upon Inga-Britt Krause's (1998, p2) description of how, when beginning psychotherapy with clients from different cultural backgrounds, there is a common experience of paradox. At first, there is an easy personal connection, but then this is followed by a gulf of unknowing. It is perhaps this sense of unknowing that development academics and practitioners need to rediscover. Rather than thinking of the culture of others as a lens, it may be equally useful to become more aware of how 'our' higher order, intermediate norms, positions within social structure and political economy, institutional cultures, disciplinary persuasions and professional techniques themselves act as lenses, condition us and, in turn, pre-shape our understanding of other lives.

Questions

11.1 How, as a development worker, would you respond to a context in which most men claim that it is inappropriate for them to share household tasks with women?

11.2 Is the human development and capability approach, with its focus on freedom, a culturally embedded approach to development?

11.3 How do you see globalization as reducing and/or emphasizing cultural difference?

Notes

1   See the topic of 'Cultural Heritage in Sustainable Development' under the heading 'Urban Development' in the 'Topics' section of the World Bank website at www.worldbank.org.

2   See for example www.survival-international.org.

Readings

Appadurai, A. (2004) 'The capacity to aspire: Culture and the terms of recognition', in V. Rao and M. Walton (eds) *Culture and Public Action*, Stanford University Press, Palo Alto, CA

Bourdieu, P. (1977) *Outline of a Theory of Practice*, Cambridge University Press, Cambridge

Cooke, B. and U. Kothari (eds) (2001) *Participation: The New Tyranny?*, Macmillan, London

Das, V. (2000) 'The act of witnessing: Violence, poisonous knowledge, and subjectivity', in V. Das, A. Kleinman, M. Ramphele and P. Reynolds (eds), *Violence and Subjectivity*, University of California Press, Berkeley

Good, B. J. (1994) *Medicine, Rationality and Experience: An Anthropological Perspective*, Cambridge University Press, Cambridge

Huntington, S. P. (2000) 'Foreword: Cultures count', in L. E. Harrison and S. P. Huntington (eds) *Culture matters: How values shape human progress*, Basic Books, New York

Inkeles, A. (1969) 'Making men modern: On the causes and consequences of individual change in six developing countries', *American Journal of Sociology*, vol 75, no 2, pp208–225

Krauss, I. B. (1998) *Therapy Across Culture*, Sage, London

Leigh Pigg, S. (1992) 'Inventing social categories through place: Social representations and development in Nepal', *Comparative Studies in Society and History*, vol 34, no 3, pp491–521

Li, T. Murray (1996) 'Images of community: Discourse and strategy in property relations', *Development and Change*, vol 27, no 3, pp501–528

Nussbaum, M. (2000) *Women and Human Development: The Capabilities Approach*, Cambridge University Press, Cambridge

Nussbaum, M. and Glover, J. (eds) (1995) *Women, Culture and Development*, Oxford University Press, Oxford

Obeyesekere, G. (1990) *The Work of Culture: Symbolic Transformation in Psychoanalysis and Anthropology*, University of Chicago Press, Chicago, IL

Rao, V. and Walton, M. (eds) (2004), *Culture and Public Action*, Stanford University Press, Palo Alto, CA; see also www.cultureandpublicaction.org/

Sahlins, M. (1976) *Culture and Practical Reason*, University of Chicago Press, Chicago, IL

Selznick, P. (1949) *TVA and the Grass Roots: A Study in the Sociology of Formal Organisation*, University of California Press, Berkeley

Sen, A. K. (1991) 'Gender and co-operative conflicts', in I. Tinker (ed.) *Persistent Inequalities*, Oxford University Press, Oxford

Sen, A. K. (2004) 'How does culture matter' in V. Rao and M. Walton (eds), *Culture and Public Action*, Stanford University Press, Palo Alto, CA

Sen, A. (2006) *Identity and Violence*, W. Norton, New York

Seralgeldin, I. and Martin-Brown, J. (1999) *Culture in Sustainable Development: Investing in Cultural and Natural Endowments*, The World Bank, Washington, DC

Shehabuddin, E. (2008) *Reshaping the Holy. Democracy, Development and Muslim Women in Bangladesh*, Columbia University Press, New York
UNDP (2004) *Human Development Report: Cultural Liberty in Today's Diverse World*, UNDP, New York; available at http://hdr.undp.org/en/
UNESCO (1995) *Our Creative Diversity*, Report of the World Commission on Culture and Development, UNESCO, Paris
UNESCO (2000) *World Culture Report*, UNICEF, Paris
West, C. and Fenstermaker, S. (1995) 'Doing difference', *Gender and Society*, vol 9, no 1, pp8–37
White, S. C. (1996) 'Depoliticising development: The uses and abuses of participation', *Development in Practice*, vol 6, no 1, pp6–15

Further Readings

Cooper, F. and Randall, P. (eds) (1997) *International Development and the Social Sciences: Essays on the History and Politics of Knowledge*, University of California Press, Berkeley
Crush, J. (ed.) (1995) *Power of Development*, Routledge, London
Geertz, C. (1973) *The Interpretation of Culture*, Basic Books, New York
Hall, S. and du Gay, P. (eds) (1996) *Questions of Cultural Identity*, Sage, London
Keesing, R. (1987) 'Anthropology as interpretive quest', *Current Anthropology*, vol 28, no 2, pp161–168
Kuper, A. (1999), *Culture: The Anthropologists' Account*, Harvard University Press, Cambridge, MA
Marglin, F. and Marglin, S. (eds) (1990) *Dominating Knowledge: Development, Culture and Resistance*, Clarendon Press, Oxford
Marglin, F. and Marglin, S. (1996) *Decolonizing Knowledge: From Development to Dialogue*, Clarendon Press, Oxford
Nederveen Pieterse, J. (2005) 'The *Human Development Report* and cultural liberty: Tough liberalism', *Development and Change*, vol 36, no 6, pp1267–1273
Nussbaum, M. and Sen, A. K. (1989) 'Internal criticism and Indian rationalist traditions', in M. Krausz (ed.) *Relativism: Interpretation and Confrontation*, University of Notre Dame Press, Notre Dame, IN
Schech, S. and Haggis, J. (2002) *Culture and Development*, Blackwell, Oxford
Spencer, J. (1997) 'Fatima and the enchanted toffees: An essay on contingency, narrative and therapy', *Journal of the Royal Anthropological Institute*, vol 3, no 4, pp693–710

Part II Religion

Séverine Deneulin

Religion is inextricably linked to culture. It relates to beliefs and practices about the Transcendent, about a realm beyond earthy realities. Many religions rely on a set of teachings derived from Sacred Texts.[3] However, how these teachings are interpreted and the ways in which they are practised are always time- and space-dependent, i.e. culturally embedded. In Christianity, for example, the Bible affirms the fundamental equality of all human beings before God. This teaching arguably gives rise to a so-called 'Christian culture' that fosters a sense of respect for all members of society. But how that equality is interpreted is in turn culturally dependent. Equality between men and women, between slaves and non-slaves, and between people of different religions is conceived differently by Christianity depending on the socio-historical and cultural context of each experience. Thus the interpretation of equality during the Inquisition was certainly different from the way it is interpreted today. Religion and culture, then, influence each other in ways that are both profound and subtle. Like cultures, religions are dynamic and ever-changing, responding to specific realities and the wider political economies and power relations that inform them. How equality is understood in Christianity has a lot to do with who has authority within the Church at any given time and the type of power they wield; in other words, like culture, religion cannot be separated from power and politics.

In this chapter, we identify five dominant (and non-mutually exclusive) modes of conceiving religion in development thinking: (1) religion is instrumental to development goals (such as economic growth and the Millennium Development Goals); (2) religion influences people's values and what they consider to be legitimate development; (3) religious freedom and worship is a fundamental human right that has to be respected; (4) religion is a constitutive part of people's well-being; and (5) religion is a political force that shapes a society's economic, social and political structures. We conclude by discussing how the human development and capability approach includes each of these modes of engagement, paying particular attention to religion as a source of moral values that shapes our interpretation of what constitutes 'good' social change or development, and allows us to analyse them within the context of public reasoning.

The Protestant ethic approach

Max Weber's pioneering study (*Protestant Ethic and the Spirit of Capitalism*) on the role of religious ideas in economic development has deeply influenced the treatment of religion in the social sciences. Weber begins with the observation that Protestants are more involved in industrial, trade and business activities than any other Christian denominations or religions. Based on this empirical observation, he puts forward the hypothesis that the underlying beliefs informing the more puritan forms of Protestantism (as can be found in Calvinism, for example) explain why capitalistic expansion occurred in Western Europe and not in other parts of the world.[4]

The features of Protestantism[5] were the precise ingredients required for capitalistic development: hard work, high labour productivity, high rates of saving (and investment) and the production of goods beyond the mere satisfaction of material needs for biological survival. According to Weber, it is this 'this-worldly asceticism' of Protestantism that led to capitalist expansion.

Certainly, while some religious beliefs are highly conducive to development, others can in fact hinder it. In *The Theory of Economic Growth*, Arthur Lewis's *Theory of Economic Growth*, published in 1955 exemplifies this. In this canonical text, he argues that economic growth depends on certain attitudes towards variables, such as the social value placed on material goods, work, wealth-creation, thrift, invention, population growth and the treatment of strangers. Countries have different levels of economic growth because they have different attitudes in relation to these key variables, and religion accounts for these critical differences. Religion may be a hindrance to economic growth if it preaches asceticism and the virtuous benefits of consuming less rather than more. Religion becomes an obstacle to economic growth, Lewis argues, when it imbues people with certain negative attitudes towards wealth- accumulation and economic growth. A religious society that fails to see wealth as a means to social status or condemns the search for higher status as being sinful may not have favourable conditions for economic growth. Population expansion, which growth theories have long considered to be a significant hindrance to economic growth, can also be negatively affected by religious attitudes towards contraception and family planning.

This instrumental approach to religion tends to prevail not only in contemporary studies of the variables affecting economic growth,[6] but also in the context of the MDGs. Religion is often taken into account when looking at the impact of its teachings, whether positive or negative, on a set of development goals or indicators. For instance, religious attitudes to women could have a detrimental effect on achieving gender equality in primary education, or religious attitudes towards the environment could be a springboard for catalysing social action against climate change. Given the respect they command within their respective religious communities, religious leaders are increasingly called upon by the development community to fight poverty and meet the MDGs.

Religion as a moral base

A special issue of *World Development* on the relationship between religion and development, published in 1980, roundly criticized this instrumental approach to religion. In their opening article, the editors, Charles Wilber and Kenneth

Jameson, argued that the limitations of development (as economic growth) and fundamental concerns about redistribution required that the Weberian approach to religion in (economic) development be revisited entirely. Equally, the secular view of religion – that religion is a purely private matter which has no place in the public sphere, and that religion can be neglected because when societies develop and become more modern, religion disappears from people's lives[7] – also required re-examination.

Wilber and Jameson warn that these views ignore what they deem to be an essential aspect of religion: as the moral fabric of society, it also provides the set of norms within which the legitimacy and validity of the development process can be assessed. Viewing religious values solely as a means to achieve development goals derived from sources outside the social mores of a given society could, they argue, put the enterprise of development itself in jeopardy:

> In most cases, the moral base of society has religious roots, and that moral base has been undermined during the process of capitalist development since 1945. But, unless this tension between moral base and development is resolved, the process of development will be self-limiting, and it is likely in many cases to engender major instability, which can radically transform the entire experience...This conclusion supports the claim that development must build on indigenous religious values because the preservation or growth of the moral base of the society is central to development...Religion is more than a mere instrument for development. A broad definition as meeting basic human needs would include religious values as one of those needs that are ends in themselves. (Wilber and Jameson, 1980, p475)

Thus, ignoring religion as the moral base of society may lead to a situation in which the development process, characterized by goals generated outside the country's value system, alienates people and makes them reject the entire process. Wilber and Jameson conclude that, if the development process fails to rest on indigenous (religious) values, it risks being alienating and becoming a source of conflict, thereby distorting policy outcomes. One has to note here, of course, that their conclusion does not recognize the heterogeneity of a 'society's values', as discussed in the section on culture above. Whose value system is a development process to be based on?

As we will see, the view that the development process has to rest on values originating from a given society was only fully taken on board – at least in theory[8] – during the 1990s, with the introduction of the human development and capability approach and its explicit recognition of development as a value-laden process. Basing development initiatives on the values that people have clearly entails, then, including religious values. If, for example, a community devastated by an earthquake values building a church, temple or mosque more than building a school, their values should be taken into account and not dismissed prima facie by aid donors with other views. A discussion and consensus-building process is required rather than the imposition of values and priorities over others – bringing us back to the importance of recognizing power differentials in any given context.

Religion as a human right

Another treatment of religion in development thinking is enunciated in the Declaration of Human Rights. Although written as early as 1948, the 'rights-based' approach to development only became prominent in the 1990s. The Declaration states in article 18 that 'everyone has the right to freedom of thought, conscience and religion; this right includes freedom to change his religion or belief, and freedom, either alone or in community with others and in public or private, to manifest his religion or belief in teaching, practice, worship and observance.'[9]

The 2004 *Human Development Report* takes the same approach to religious rights as it does to cultural rights and cultural liberty. The report emphasizes that the right to freedom of religion has to be critically examined in light of other basic human rights. Religions, like other cultural traditions, are not static and homogenous, but are instead dynamic and heterogeneous. Taking religions seriously also means taking seriously the possibility that religious authority may be captured by particular factions, who could mobilize politically to impose their own interpretation of sacred texts. Given these dangers of power and domination, the report argues that religious groups need to abide by democratic principles. This is why there need not be a trade-off between the right to religious freedom and other basic human rights, as long as active participation in decision-making processes within the religious community is guaranteed (this will be discussed in greater detail in the final section).

The report concludes that democracy is the best way to ensure harmony between the different human rights within religious communities and providing an environment in which people can fully exercise their religious liberties. It notes that, all too often, movements asserting religious superiority and seeking to impose their vision of the world on others disrespect their freedom to live lives they value. It argues that these movements often stem from legitimate grievances and that, therefore, seeking to suppress them risks strengthening and radicalizing their base, as was the case in Algeria when the military cancelled elections in 1991 and banned the winning political party, the Islamist Salvation Front, which resulted in years of bloody civil war. The report proposes instead to deal with these movements in a democratic fashion, encouraging the expression of a range of different views. This democratic route would involve prosecuting hate crimes, paying attention to school curricula, and helping communities come to terms with past hatred and violence (UNDP, 2004, p81).

Religion as a dimension of well-being

The World Bank study *Voices of the Poor* (Narayan et al, 2000) gathered the voices of thousands of 'poor' people throughout the world in order to understand how they themselves understood their own respective poverty and well-being. One of its major findings was that religion permeates people's conception of well-being:

> For many, a spiritual life and religious observance are woven in with other aspects of well-being. Poverty itself could get in the way. An old woman in Bower Bank, Jamaica says, 'I got up this morning and all I want to do is read my Bible, but I share a room with my son and my grandchildren and all they do is make noise, I can't even get a little peace and quiet.' In Padamukti, Indonesia, being able to make the pilgrimage to Mecca means much, as does having *sholeh* (dutiful and respectful) children who will look after their parents in old age and pray for them after they are dead. In Chittagong, Bangladesh, part of well-being is 'always [being] able to perform religious activities properly'. For older women in Cassava Piece, Jamaica, their church gives them a spiritual uplift and physical support. The importance to poor people of their sacred place – holy tree, stone, lake, ground, church, mosque, temple or pagoda – is repeatedly evident from their comparisons of institutions in which these frequently ranked high, if not highest. (Narayan et al, 2000, p38)

Another empirical finding of the study's participatory exercises was that poor people trusted religious leaders more than politicians because they listened to them, unlike the latter. Also, poor people rated faith-based organizations much higher than state institutions. In rural areas, religious institutions were often valued as the most important ones in people's lives. Given the prominence of religion, then, *Voices of the Poor* includes a section entitled 'churches, mosques, temples, shrines, trees, stones and rivers'.

The study argues that this finding about people's valuation of religion as a central part of their lives has considerable consequences for the way development has been conceived and practised thus far:

> Reflecting on poor people's perception of poverty has driven us to revisit the meaning of development. What is significant change, and what is good? And which changes, for whom, matter most? Answers to these questions involve material, physical, social, psychological and spiritual dimensions. [...] The increments in well-being that would mean much to the poor widow in Bangladesh – a full stomach, time for prayer, and a bamboo platform to sleep on – challenge us to change how we measure development. (Narayan et al, 2000, p234)

Voices of the Poor presents a challenging conclusion. If religion is central to how people conceive of a 'good life', along with health, education, shelter, material security and other needs, then conventional development practices which have hitherto ignored religious dimensions will necessarily have to be transformed. Alkire (2002) describes a case study of a development project in rural Pakistan that fully integrates such values, including religious ones. A group of women had to decide between a goat-rearing and a rose-cultivation project. Although the goat project yielded more income, the women opted for rose cultivation because this enabled them to do more things they valued, such as the ability to use the roses in their religious ceremonies, and the ability to walk in the rose fields and experience peace of mind and unity with their Maker. The spiritual dimension of well-being was seen by the women as being as important as the material dimension.

Faith-based organizations

In the development literature, the role of religion in development has been widely documented by 'faith-based organizations' (FBOs). In an edited volume entitled *Development, Civil Society and Faith-Based Organizations*, Clarke et al (2007) give a broad overview of the role of FBOs in development. They use the term FBO 'in reference to any organization that derives inspiration and guidance for its activities from the teachings and principles of the faith or from a particular interpretation or school of thought within the faith' (p6). Clarke (2006, Clarke et al, 2007) offers a five-fold classification of FBOs: (1) faith-based representative organizations that govern the faithful; (2) faith-based charitable or development organizations which run projects and provide services for marginalized groups; (3) faith-based socio-political organizations that politically mobilize the faithful; (4) faith-based missionary organizations which promote the faith; and (5) faith-based illegal or terrorist organizations engaging in armed struggles in the name of religion. The volume gathers information regarding a wide range of FBOs representing different regions and religious persuasions.

It is beyond the scope of this chapter to review the different instances in which religious organizations and religious traditions themselves (through their missionary work, for example) have influenced political processes (and hence development outcomes), for better or worse. For example, a study of the emergence of the welfare state in Europe would be intellectually impoverished if it did not include an analysis of how Christianity led to the emergence of social democratic parties and influenced their agenda. Even the creation of the European Union owes a great deal to the faith of its main initiator, Jean Monnet. In developing countries, the reality of political life also abounds with examples illustrating the presence of religion in the public sphere and politics itself, such as the Muslim Brotherhood in Egypt and Jama'at-i-Islami in Pakistan and Bangladesh.[10]

In terms of the provision of social services and political involvement in the interests of social justice, religious organizations have become increasingly prominent. Faith-based organizations often play an important role in providing health and education services for the poor, particularly in the context of fragile or weak states. According to World Bank estimates, 50 per cent of health and education services in sub-Saharan Africa were provided by faith-based organizations in 2000 (Clarke et al, 2007). Religious organizations can also be powerful mobilizing forces when it comes to social reforms. The Movemiento Sim Terra, the organization demanding land rights for landless peasants in Brazil, was begun by Catholic churches that had mobilized peasants to press the government on land reform. In Britain, the Citizens Organisation Foundation is another example of how faith communities mobilize for social action. One successful campaign was to demand that the mayor of London secure a minimum wage adjusted to the cost of living in London. A large number of churches and religious-based organizations have participated in advocacy campaigns, such as Make Poverty History and the Jubilee Campaign for debt relief. The role of churches in apartheid South Africa, against the dictatorship in El Salvador, Brazil and Chile in the 1980s,[11] is also an illustration of how religious organizations can be countervailing powers when a government violates human rights and deepens inequalities and injustices. The Buddhist-inspired Sardovaya movement in Sri Lanka has also been well analysed as a striking example of the transformative power of religion in development (Tyndale, 2007).

The possibility of reasoning

The human development and capability approach encompasses the five modes of engagement with religion and development described above, but it also adds another dimension: that of reasoning and deliberation. Development is not about promoting whatever people value but what they have *reason* to value. The values that guide the development process have to be critically examined with a thorough process of reasoning in the public space, allowing the views of all the members of a society to be heard. There is obviously the risk that democratic decision-making might be disrupted by some groups imposing their views on others or manipulating them, as has been pointed out earlier. But what is important is that public debate continues, and that efforts are made to level off the disruptive effects of power relations on participatory and democratic processes.

In her chapter on religion in *Women and Human Development*, Nussbaum (2000) details how this type of critical reasoning and deliberation can take place within a religion itself. She describes the apparent dilemma that may sometimes arise when respecting the right to religious liberty, on the one hand, and other rights, on the other. For example, respecting religious liberty might entail that women are denied equality in inheritance, or that women are denied protection in the case of divorce. Nussbaum argues that the secular humanist route (that the right to religious liberty can never trump rights to non-discrimination and equality) and the traditionalist route (that religious liberty always overrides any other rights) are both impasses. A society can indeed never be ruled by values external to it, but this does not mean that values internal to a society cannot be changed from within. If a certain religion denies women equality in front of the law, this can be challenged by elements within (and outside) the society's own religious tradition. Because of the diversity inherent in each religious tradition, such conflicts can be solved by actively engaging with those who accept the legitimacy of fundamental human rights within the tradition. This is what Nussbaum calls the 'principle of moral restraint', that is, religion is recognized as a basic influence on people's actions but its influence should also be restricted by the moral claims of the religion itself.

The importance of reasoning is also a recurrent theme in Sen's *Identity and Violence*.[12] He expresses considerable concern about the fact that religions are in increasing danger of becoming rigid political identities. First, he contends, a division must be drawn between discussions of Islam as a religion and of people who happen to be Muslim.[13] This draws in part on the notion of multiple identities – that it is illegitimate to define a set of people simply on the basis of their religious identity, rather than recognizing the many factors that may comprise it: although they may be Muslim, they are also highly heterogeneous. More specifically, Sen argues against the political energies that some political leaders such as George W. Bush and Tony Blair have put into (re)defining Islam – as a 'peaceful religion', for example, thereby attempting to recruit religion to 'our side' in the war on terror. This confuses the *religious* criteria of orthodoxy and belonging (issues of belief and religious practice) with social and political principles and behaviour, which are other matters entirely. The danger of this 'religion-centred political approach' is that its effect will be 'to bolster and strengthen the voice of religious authorities, while downgrading the importance of nonreligious institutions and movements' (Sen, 2006, p77).

This risks giving a commanding voice to figures of the religious establishment and downplaying the importance of civic initiatives by ordinary people who happen to be Muslim. Emphasizing religious identity also places 'community leaders' between Muslim citizens and the government, thus placing them at a relative disadvantage to members of other groups. As Sen asks: 'Should a British citizen who happens to be Muslim have to rely on clerics or other leaders of the religious community to communicate with the prime minister of his country?' (2006, p78). The point that people of Muslim faith – or any other – should not have their civic and political participation perpetually packaged within a religious wrapping is an important one.

The immanent presence of religion in development processes cannot be swept under the carpet. Religion is often a significant, if not the most foundational part, of people's lives which infuse what they value, who they are and what they do. However, as this chapter has shown, religion is never immune from power and is always embedded in social structure and political economy. Therefore, religion bears close association with culture, which structures human life itself in particular ways. The topics of 'culture and religion' remain a challenge for development for they expose the fragility of any conception of development with universalist aspirations, and the complexities of the strive for human flourishing.

Questions

11.4 Does it make sense to use religion to challenge certain cultural practices?

11.5 How do the values of your religious tradition speak to those who appear to dominate in development interventions?

11.6 How would you describe the nature of FBOs in your country? How do they influence development processes and outcomes?

Notes

3   Given the scope of this textbook, this chapter only presents an analysis of monotheistic religions and leaves out indigenous forms of belief systems like animism. The analysis is taken from Deneulin with Bano (2009).

4   For a critical discussion of Weber's work, see Giddens (1987).

5   The Calvinist doctrine of predestination placed an emphasis on attaining personal salvation through grace and faith. Calvinists expressed the belief that one would be saved by being industrious and devoting one's life to doing good work in this world. Wealth-creation was thus an activity blessed by God but the wealth produced by one's labour could not be used for a lavish and ostentatious lifestyle; instead, it had to be re-invested in productive activities.

6   See Jackson and Fleischer (2007) for a literature review of the role of religion in economic development.

7   For more information on the secularization process, see Casanova (1994).

8   Some critics would undoubtedly argue that the human development approach remains deeply embedded in a Eurocentric and liberal humanist understanding of such notions as 'freedom' and 'agency', and that there is still some way to go before such a freedom-based view of development can be truly culturally sensitive and respectful of the values and visions of the world that other societies might hold.

9   Taken from the Declaration that can be accessed in full at www.un.org/Overview/rights.html.

10 For a study about the growing support for Islamic political parties and the factors underpinning it, see Kepel (2000).

11 For a summary of the literature of the relationship between religion and democracy with reference to Christianity and Islam, see Deneulin with Bano (2009).

12 This discussion on *Identity and Violence* was written by Sarah White.

13 This is also a point made by Scott Appleby (2000) – that there is no such thing as 'Christianity' or 'Islam' but that there are Christians and Muslims who embody their faith depending upon the social, political, cultural and economic contexts in which they live.

Readings

Alkire, S. (2002) *Valuing Freedoms*, Oxford University Press, Oxford

Appleby, S. (2000) *The Ambivalence of the Sacred: Religion, Violence and Reconciliation*, Rowan and Littlefield, London

Casanova, J. (1994) *Public Religions in the Modern World*, University of Chicago Press, Chicago, IL

Clarke, G. (2006) 'Faith matters: Faith-based organisations, civil society and international development', *Journal of International Development*, vol 18, no 6, pp835–848

Clarke, G., Jennings, M. and Shaw, T. (eds) (2007) *Development, Civil Society and Faith-Based Organisations*, Palgrave Macmillan, Basingstoke

Deneulin, S. with Bano, M. (2009) *Religion in Development: Rewriting the Secular Script*, Zed Books, London

Giddens, A. (1987) *Capitalism and Modern Social Theory: An Analysis of the Writings of Marx, Durkheim and Max Weber*, Cambridge University Press, Cambridge

Jackson, P. and Fleischer, C. (2007) 'Religion and economics: A literature review', Working Paper 3, DFID Religions and Development Research Programme, Birmingham, www.rad.bham.ac.uk

Kepel, G. (2006) *Jihad: The Trail of Political Islam*, transl. by Anthony F. Roberts, 4th edn, I.B. Tauris, London

Narayan, D., Chambers, R., Shah, M. and Petesch, P. (2000) *Voices of the Poor*, Oxford University Press for the World Bank, New York

Nussbaum, M. (2000) *Women and Human Development*, Cambridge University Press, Cambridge

Sen, A. K. (2006) *Identity and Violence*, London, Allen

Tyndale, W. (ed.) (2007) *Visions of Development: Faith-Based Initiatives*, Ashgate, Aldershot

Wilber, C. and Jameson, K. (1980) 'Religious values and the social limits to development', *World Development*, vol 8, no 7/8, pp467–479

Further Readings

Alkire, S. (2006) 'Religion and development', in D. A. Clark (ed.) *The Elgar Companion to Development Studies*, Edward Elgar, Cheltenham

Armstrong, K. (2000) *The Battle for God: Fundamentalism in Judaism, Christianity and Islam*, Harper Collins, London

Asad, T. (1993) *Genealogies of Religion: Discipline and Reasons of Power in Christianity and Islam*, John Hopkins University Press, Baltimore

Bradley, T. (2006) *Challenging the NGOs: Women, Religion and Western Dialogues in India*, I.B. Tauris, London

Giddens, A. (1987) *Capitalism and Modern Social Theory: An Analysis of the Writings of Marx, Durheim and Max Weber*, Cambridge University Press, Cambridge

Hastings, A. (1997), *The Construction of Nationhood: Ethnicity, Nationalism and Religion*, Cambridge University Press, Cambridge

Lincoln, B. (2003) *Holy Terrors: Thinking about Religion after September 11*, University of Chicago Press, Chicago, IL

Marshall, K. and Van Saanen, M. (2007) *Development and Faith: Where Mind, Heart and Soul Work Together*, World Bank, Washington, DC

Ter Haar, G. and Ellis, S. (2006) 'The role of religion in development: Towards a new relationship between the European Union and Africa', *European Journal of Development Research*, vol 18, no 3, pp351–367

Thomas, S. (2005) *The Global Resurgence of Religion and the Transformation of International Relations*, Palgrave, Basingstoke

Part III
Policy

12

Human Development
Policy Analysis

Randy Spence and Séverine Deneulin

Aims of the Chapter

- To analyse the different areas of public policy.
- To provide tools for analysing public policy from a human development perspective.
- To outline the policy implications of the human development and capability approach.

Key Points

- Public policy involves a course of action and a web of decisions, and cannot be associated with only one moment, one actor, one decision and one action.
- Policy is political: the policy process is closely connected to the nature of power itself.
- Policy analysis contains both 'analysis of policy' and 'analysis for policy'; both contribute to ongoing policy development and implementation through the monitoring and evaluation functions that connect them.
- A human development approach to policy analysis is based on the notion that *all* areas of public policy promote human freedom and flourishing, and that the policy process itself should respect people's agency.
- From the perspective of the human development and capability approach, some areas of public policy are more researched than others. Aggregate economic performance continues to dominate other policy paradigms in international, goals and practice although alternative views continue to grow.

This textbook has analysed many topics in relation to the human development and capability approach: economic growth, equality and justice, measurement, institutions and markets, democracy, education, health and nutrition, culture and religion. But there is a central piece that is still missing: an examination of the policy implications of the approach itself. Policy permeates our daily living and what options are available to us. Educational policies, health policies, transportation policies, environmental policies or macroeconomic policies, to name a few, ultimately affect what we are able to do. Studying can be very difficult in contexts where governments have no appropriate education policy enabling students to access higher education independently of their parents' income, or have no macroeconomic policy to ensure relative price stability. One can think of additional examples where 'policy' affects one's daily life. Analysing policy and how it impacts our lives is therefore a cornerstone of the human development and capability approach. Indeed, given that the approach is an evaluative framework for assessing states of affairs, the exercise of analysing the impact of policies upon human flourishing is particularly critical.

Although individuals have policies, policy is generally conceived as being what organizations do. A stated policy is what an organization plans to do or officially says it is doing. A revealed or actual policy is what it is actually doing. Policy occupies a large middle-ground between mission and strategy at the 'top' end, and specific programmes, products or services at the detailed implementation end. Policy is made and implemented by government, corporate and non-profit organizations. Combinations of organizations have varying degrees of combined or coordinated policies. For example, coalitions of non-governmental organizations, corporate conglomerates and governments (local, regional, national) are themselves combinations of many organizations and agencies.

This chapter is mainly concerned with public policy, that is, what governments do, although it touches briefly on the policy of other organizations. It starts by examining various areas of public policy which are particularly important for human flourishing. It then looks at the fundamental political nature of the public policy process, from its design to its implementation. It concludes by giving some tools for policy analysis from the perspective of the human development and capability approach.

Main areas of public policy

Public policy covers hundreds, if not thousands, of areas of activity: economic, social, scientific and technological. Governments essentially operate by legislating, taxing and spending. A national government handles a range of policy processes and services from macro to micro, from broader policy and legislation to sectoral policy and regulation, and to building and operating schools and health clinics. Table 12.1 provides a listing of the main areas of public policy. This section looks at each area of the listing, and analyses how policy and policy processes appear when viewed from a human development perspective in relation to other perspectives. Given the hundreds of important public policy areas facing all governments at any given moment, developing the skills and capacities of people and processes involved in public policy is a primary determinant of successful policy development and implementation.

Table 12.1 *Areas of public policy*

Macro-policy (framework)	
Constitution and legal system	Constitution (rights and freedoms), criminal law, civil rights
Economic law	Covering formal and informal sectors, business law, informal sector regulatory and tax framework
Macroeconomic policy	Overall fiscal policy (budget deficit/surplus, borrowing/debt)
	Monetary policy (money supply, inflation, financial management)
	Exchange rate policy and management
IP and competition policy	Intellectual property (IP) policy and law, competition policy and law
Trade policy	(Overall) levels of tariff and non-tariff barriers, international negotiations and commitments (WTO, regional, bilateral)
Tax and revenue policy	Levels of direct and indirect taxes, tax collection, borrowing
Innovation policy	(Overall) education, research, science and technology policies (from high tech to grass roots innovation)
Sector policy and regulation – private sectors	
Resource sectors	Agriculture, forestry, fisheries, mining, energy (mining)
Manufacturing sectors	Food and beverage, textile and apparel
	Wood, paper, petroleum, chemicals, rubber and plastic, metals
	Machinery/equipment: heavy, electrical, electronic, medical
	Vehicles, transportation, furniture, other consumer goods
Services sectors	Financial (banking, insurance), business and professional
	Construction, wholesale and retail trade, tourism
	Defence, justice and legal services
	Research and development services/activities
	Entertainment, recreational, cultural, sporting, personal
Sector policy, regulation and delivery – mixed public/private sectors	
Economic services	Financial sector management, financial intermediation
	Economic and business law, enforcement, courts
	R&D/innovation support/investment
	Energy, water, refuse/recycling, posts and telecom/information and communication technology (ICT)
Social services	Education (primary, secondary, tertiary)
	Health (preventive, curative, research)
	Personal security (defence, justice, courts, police)
	Social equity, dignity, empowerment
	Social security (pensions, social insurance, welfare)

These categories derive from the International Standard Industrial Classification at www.ilo.org/public/english/bureau/stat/class/isic.htm. Most governments are structured around these areas: ministries of defence, justice, finance, trade, industry, agriculture, energy, environment, education, health, social security, science and technology and culture and sports.

Macro-policy

Constitution and legal system

This area of policy is of particularly high priority. The way political processes are structured and enforced are fundamental to policy-making processes and outcomes. Processes of informed public discourse based on clear rights and freedoms are essential to expanding political participation and providing the conditions amenable to human flourishing. Current international discussion and investment places too little emphasis on this policy area in many countries. It neglects the building of political and governance capacities and prefers instead to focus on governance per se. This contrasts with a prevalent emphasis on building capacities for engaging in market activity. It also neglects the capacities necessary for effective and accountable political processes. The human costs of political failures of all kinds are high, as the enormous suffering of people living in such so-called 'failed states' as the Democratic Republic of Congo or Haiti demonstrates all too well. There are always sets of internal, regional and international interests – business, government and often military – with the power to support failed regimes or to do little to oppose them. Current processes in several countries – Kenya, Zimbabwe, Myanmar, Tibet, to name a few – offer some hope that the 'right' kinds of regional and international involvement can be helpful and effective, and that strategic and geopolitical interests may shift to greater support of international cooperation in the interests of political renewal. In many cases, the key ingredients are progressive internal opposition supported by key bilateral and regional partners, with sufficient consensus in the broader international community, particularly from the UN and the Security Council.

Economic law

We could make many points here. However, we are more interested in highlighting the importance, from the perspective of the human development and capability approach, of laws and policies that facilitate the expansion of informal economic activity and the quality of informal employment. These policies are critical in many developing countries where percentages of employment in the informal sectors (especially agriculture) range up to more than 80 per cent, as is the case in India. Internal political advocacy has brought about significant changes, which is one reason why international organizations such as the International Labour Organization (ILO) have been monitoring and advocating improved informal sector financing, licensing, regulation and taxation since the 1980s.

Macroeconomic policy

Many argue that, in today's global economy, there is not much room for manoeuvre when it comes to deciding what constitutes good macro-policy and management – fiscal deficits have to amount to a certain percentage of GDP, inflation cannot go above a certain rate, the exchange rate has to be on a 'managed float'. While these conservative macro-policies are 'tried and true', additional human development dimensions need to be considered. A society needs to adopt the macro-policies that best expand human freedoms, both material and non-material. China – given a combination of low labour costs, high productivity and innovation, and a fairly open international trade environment – has been financing the movement of some 400 million people from low productivity agriculture to higher productivity/wage manufacturing in large part by maintaining a low exchange rate, exporting heavily and lending foreign exchange earnings back to importing countries to buy even more. So far, this has been a very effective macro-strategy and policy framework under the circumstances but serious challenges face other areas of public policy, including redistribution, environmental management and human rights – and these may in turn require adjustments to macroeconomic policies.

Not everyone can achieve rapid growth in this way, but pursuing all areas of human and economic potential – given country conditions – should be a macroeconomic policy priority. Periods of intensive structural adjustment are particular challenges to macroeconomic policy. The current global economy is experiencing structural adjustment to a degree at least matching the 1980s, in response to positive forces of overall economic growth and technology advancement, and negative ones including global warming, HIV/AIDS, energy and food prices and financial boom and bust (see Chapter 4).

An important aspect of macroeconomic policy is setting the fiscal framework each year, notably the size of the public budget, based on analysis and projections of economic and financial activity, tax revenues and prudent borrowing. Ministries of finance, economics and planning are typically crucial here, and different forms of economic modelling are also important tools.

Intellectual property (IP) and competition policy

Societies strike a balance between protection of IP for business purposes and accessibility for public interests. In general, genuine competition is largely positive. Competition policy is essential in this respect by countering excessive market power – monopoly and oligopoly interests that tend to arise in most sectors and markets. The principal IP policy instruments are patents, copyright, trademarks, geographical indications and industrial designs. The principal aims of competition policy are reducing excessive concentrations of market power in different industries, or directing their behaviour to be more competitive.

Many developing countries lack capacity in IP and competition policy. In addition, policies have been substantially dictated by international accords such as the TRIPS (Trade-Related Aspects of Intellectual Property Rights) and even more market-friendly provisions in bilateral FTAs (Free Trade Agreements). Other central institutions include: WIPO (World Intellectual Property Organization) and UN agencies such as UNCTAD (UN Commission on Trade and Development), UNIDO (UN Industrial Development Organization) and WHO (World Health Organization). There are other sectoral or issue-area accords and institutions in plant genetic resources, health, biological resources and traditional knowledge. These international issues have increasingly become a source of contention between developed and developing countries, and within international organizations.[1]

The human development perspective on policy, in focusing on human flourishing, does not elude the question of balances between private and public interests, but would instead advocate informed public processes in deciding issues, such as the rights of countries to introduce compulsory licensing and parallel trade, where there are no feasible or affordable alternatives for obtaining essential medicines and other public goods. It would also focus on all dimensions of human flourishing, rather than on the more narrow focus on economic consequences, in analysing and deciding a host of specific IP and competition policy issues.

Trade policy

Trade policy and its impacts have arguably been studied more than almost any other area of economic policy. Trade liberalization is principally the reduction of tariffs (import taxes) and non-tariff barriers such as quantitative restrictions and quotas. Some areas of agreement on the economic results of trade liberalization include the following:

- The initial impacts of across-the-board trade liberalization have been small (relative to GDP) but, in most cases, quite positive. There are initial winners and losers among the poor, as well as among wealthier segments of the population, suggesting that trade liberalization is difficult to tie directly to equity and poverty reduction objectives.[2]
- Tariff reductions usually imply significant falls in government revenues, requiring increases in other revenues or expenditure cuts altogether. Compensating tax or revenue changes often have a bigger short-term impact on equity and income poverty than tariff changes. Hence, progressive tax policy is a key affiliate of trade liberalization.
- Longer-term potential benefits of trade liberalization are widely believed to be positive and large in terms of productivity and income growth. However, benefits do not come automatically and need accompanying public policies and investment (notably in infrastructure), which enable or assist producers to realize export opportunities, and assist those who lose to retrain, relocate or find new sources of livelihood.

As noted in Chapter 4, one of the primary reasons for the growth *and* distributional (poverty reduction) success of the initial price reforms in agriculture in Vietnam was that the de-collectivization process was generally done equitably, resulting in a fairly reasonable distribution of land. This fact, coupled with a supporting public environment and the establishment of networks between factories (public, private or mixed), producers and local governments proved to be crucial for the uptake of new crops and technologies. This example illustrates that policy analysis, from the perspective of the human development and capability approach, involves assessing alternative country-specific policy sets in terms of their impact on a full range of human freedoms, and addressing the political interests which can constrain or support their expansion.[3] We will return in detail to these issues later.

Trade policy is a complex and specialized field which includes, in addition to import barriers, subsidies; equal treatment of foreign and domestic service suppliers; government (local/foreign) procurement practices; dumping or anti-dumping practices; dispute settlement mechanisms; and health, environmental and labour conditions, etc. Trade liberalization is done unilaterally (although rarely), bilaterally, regionally and internationally (WTO) where the most favoured nation principle extends the treatment of a country's best-treated partner to all countries. Trade policy is closely related to foreign investment policy and incentives. Foreign direct investment (foreigners investing in plants and equipment), unlike portfolio investment (foreigners buying bonds and stocks), can bring skills, knowledge and technology with it.

Tax and revenue policy

The configuration of tax systems is important to economic efficiency, equity and stabilization. Indirect taxes, that is, taxes on transactions like sales, are preferred for reasons of efficiency. They do not change relative prices and valuations of goods and services if applied to all relevant transactions. Direct taxes apply to income (personal and corporate) and are progressive (the higher the income, the higher the tax rate). Direct taxes, along with the incidence of the public spending system, are thus a key public policy instrument for equity and redistribution. Tax administration and collection challenges are present in all countries, but prominent in less advanced countries in determining tax system structure. Indirect taxes are usually easier to administer, and import taxes are particularly easy – a main reason for trade protection in many countries. Building and improving tax systems is important and challenging. This involves designing taxes in ways that are as efficient, workable and equitable as possible. This is a particular challenge in economies that are predominantly informal. Corruption may need to be ended and, on the collection side, voluntary compliance by tax payers is also a major factor. Building understanding and consensus on taxes and the services they finance is therefore essential.

Borrowing is typically a small percentage of total revenue, and therefore the tax system, along with the growth of the tax base (that is, the growth of the economy), primarily determines annual levels of public spending on economic and social services. In other words, economic growth determines the public budget. Foreign borrowing is particularly risky where a country's exchange rate is likely to depreciate. There are also limits to how much borrowing governments can or should do domestically, but government bonds are both staples in government revenue systems and important financial market instruments.

Innovation policy

A system of innovation can be defined as 'a set of functioning institutions, organizations and policies which interact constructively in the pursuit of a common set of social and economic goals and objectives, and which use the introduction of innovations as the key promoter of change.'[4] One major international programme adds the following:

> Working with (and re-working) existing knowledge, rather than simply generating new knowledge through research, is a predominant activity in innovation. The actors that comprise innovation systems are not limited to scientific elites working in research and higher education organizations. People in banks, in companies, on farms, in business associations and in non-government civil society organizations contribute extensively to innovation. Interactions between the actors and organizations that comprise innovation systems can be technical, commercial, legal, social and financial. Innovation systems in poorer countries are much smaller in comparison with advanced countries and have weak links between different types of STI capabilities. Formally organized R&D activities undertaken in most developing countries, moreover, do not tend to align or overlap with the activities of private sector or 'productive' enterprises to any significant extent. These structural, organizational and linkage deficiencies in developing country innovation systems are compounded by a number of other factors – policies, political leadership, laws, rules, cultural practices and infrastructure are all vital to the functioning of innovation systems. (International Development Research Centre 2006, p3)

The main levers and issues of innovation policy include:

- public research funding: basic or applied, sectoral, balance between high-tech and local or grassroots;
- public funding of primary, secondary and tertiary education, pursuit of social equity goals, especially access and gender equality;
- the system of support for innovation in business, non-profit and public (including university) sectors: tax incentives, venture capital connections, public funding for business commercialization and community extension;
- the nature of the decision-making processes: openness and inclusiveness.

Box 12.1 Local systems of innovation in Thailand

EU countries use innovation systems as development drivers, but Thailand (and others) cannot just copy their systems. We have been mistaken in the past in trying to plant Western models; hence the need to establish our own innovation system. Thailand has all the pieces, but manages them poorly.

The education system in Thailand has deteriorated over the past three decades. Teachers pay less attention to students given other demands, and are not trained to encourage creativity. Student performance on national and international standard exams has declined noticeably. One main point is that policy-makers tend to think only about the modern sector, not the whole society. Innovation is present at the grassroots but is suppressed by Thai culture and governance. How to 'open the lid' is a key question. Western societies are much more equal and less dual. In Thailand, effort is needed to allow local innovation to prosper.

One example is in organic rice farming: by giving up chemicals, farmers have realized substantial increases in production, reduction in costs and reduction in labour time. They seek and use micro-organisms from forests for the best decomposition of biomass, control of insects and propagation of these organisms. In some areas, this has been initiated by farmers, but in many, it has been helped by researchers from the universities who can engage research and lab support and some degree of technical assistance for the farmers (who by culture will generally not themselves request it).

Innovation at the local level gets too little consistent attention. The modern sector innovation system managers overlook local innovations and the potential linkages in research and business development (e.g. national food supply chain and export). Organic rice is a perfect example of the potential of local development for export. Continuing failure to connect the modern system with the traditional rural system, and giving priority to the modern one, results in a widening gap which becomes at some point almost dangerous. One needs therefore to focus on the integration of the two systems, the modern and the local. It does not take much to foster local innovation and, in doing so, links between research and business enterprises are forged.

Based on the *Report on Science, Technology and Innovation Systems in Indonesia, Vietnam, Philippines, Thailand, Malaysia and Singapore*, IDRC (2008), led by R. Spence.

Sector policy

Sector policies are a host of special fields of public policy and regulation. In general, these are more oriented towards private sector services, where regulation should be as light and as enabling as possible of private and non-profit sector development, while insisting on competition and the rule of law. Resource and service sectors dominate the economies of less advanced developing countries. Within resource sectors, the development of agriculture and food processing are particularly important, and are constrained by many factors that challenge public policy and action, such as a capacity for agricultural research and effective extension, local and global market concentrations, and developed country protection of its agricultural markets.

Other readily exportable resources, like timber, diamonds and precious stones or metals, petroleum or uranium, are a boon when managed well, but a curse when mismanaged, since resource revenue pushes up a country's exchange rate and undermines other exports. Principles of good resource revenue management include: establishing a transparent public royalty at a level that is low enough to stimulate production and export but keeps enough for the public purse; using public royalty for public investment, particularly in infrastructure, education and health; and 'sterilizing' revenues as needed – parking them in good financial instruments offshore and bringing them in gradually as good investment projects are developed. This kind of policy set minimizes exchange rate appreciation while building market capital, infra- structure and skills. The major challenge remains moving from governance by theft to a serious development path, and realigning domestic and foreign interests involved in revenue mismanagement.

In the manufacturing and service sectors, it has become common wisdom that governments are not good at 'picking winners' in terms of particular goods and services and companies. Governments do, however, finance production inputs such as labour (education or human capital), knowledge (R&D activities) and infrastructure. Industrial policy is therefore more than just the innovation policy described above (measures to put new ideas into practice in both the private and public sectors). The emphasis of public support for private innovation in most countries is on areas of economic growth, particularly where export-led economic growth is strong. Chile's industrial policy has, for example, focused on the export sectors of mining, forestry, salmon, horticulture and wines. In contrast, a human development perspective emphasizes the need for public policy to pay attention to innovation possibi- lities among people whose economic prosperity and other freedoms are particularly limited.

As we will examine later, many of the sectors (resources, manufacturing and services) are mixed in terms of investment, spending or management. The share of public and private involvement varies among countries. The next sub- section elaborates more on the public participation in the service sector.

Economic and social services

Economic and social services are the primary sectors of public economic activity and spending. Countries have annual decision-making processes on budget allocations within the country's current fiscal framework. Policy and spending issues come together on broad allocations (defence and security, economic infrastructure and social services) and on more detailed within- sector decisions, such as health spending on hospitals, clinics, clean water, vaccinations, maternal and child health, education and other preventive measures. At each level, these are political decisions where discussion among those involved and even advocacy is typically needed (see below).

Social services are recognized as being critical for human development, particularly education, health, personal and economic security, and those that provide equity, dignity and empowerment. Economic services are also very critical for attaining human development objectives. Financial sector management has received considerable policy attention in most countries in this era of volatile international capital markets and flows. Thus reducing the real impact of such volatility as much as possible can lead to high returns.

Utilities, such as energy, water, refuse and recycling, posts and telecom and transport (such as airports) are fundamental bases of an economy, requiring efficient delivery and equitable access. As utilities are often and increasingly private companies, public policy tends to focus both on regulation and on the public goods components of infrastructure and R&D investment. The roles and functions of regulators are well-analysed, particularly for the Information, Communication and Technology (ICT) sector. ICT-related policies are particularly important since ICT is a key component of national innovation systems and a major enabler and re-shaper of capacities, systems and institutions in economic, political and social activity. Box 12.2 illustrates the importance of ICT policies for enhancing people's freedoms.

Box 12.2 Policy and regulation in ICT

In the mid-1990s, most countries had public telecom utilities and fixed-line telephones were the only type available. Privatizations were pushed hard by the World Bank and the Washington Consensus in many developing countries, without much thought to competition, resulting initially in many private monopolies. Proponents of these international policies argue with some justification that privatizations had to happen to break the patterns of vested interests and inefficiency.

But the lack of competition with the new privatized monopolies meant in practice that the stagnation in the growth of fixed lines continued. In many developing countries, there has been no recent growth, or indeed shrinkage, in fixed-line connectivity at exactly the time when the internet was becoming prominent in more advanced countries. In contrast, mobile phone providers were numerous, and escaped being trapped in the poor regulation of vested interests. Mobile connectivity has expanded rapidly since the 1990s, particularly in this decade, and has extended to the 'bottom of the pyramid' through low-cost handsets and business plans based on large volumes and very low margins. This has enabled many other services and activities and has also been instrumental in expanding political freedoms and empowerment. Here are some examples of the impact of ICT in several sectors:

- Market-based services and activities:
  - finance: (micro-)credit, banking, (micro-)insurance, remittances;
  - trade: getting market information, advertising/marketing/selling goods or services;
  - agriculture and fisheries: reducing middle margins, selling directly to multiple markets
  - employment: learning about jobs, getting jobs, making jobs better;

- personal services: arranging household services (e.g. child care, family and other);
- skills: farming know-how, other employment or income-related skills, and other life skills.
- Civil activities and public services:
  - understanding: knowledge of government agencies and services, knowledge of rights;
  - organization and action to increase political and civil service transparency and performance;
  - health: receiving tele-health services or medical/health information, arranging medical care;
  - education: distance learning courses, receiving other useful information;
  - security: contacting police, family or friends in emergencies;
  - disaster warning and relief: advanced warning, getting relief and rebuilding assistance.
- Other impacts and benefits:
  - dignity and empowerment: mobilizing support, expressing views in communities or politics; family and social relations, sense of value or opportunities, music and entertainment.

In short, ICTs facilitate the expansion of economic, political and social activity, and are instrumental to human flourishing. The main job of public policy is to expand access and lower its cost. More specifically, the broad functions of ICT/telecom regulators are to ensure low-cost interconnectivity among providers, ensure competition in the market, facilitate cost reduction and organize universal service mechanisms. As all these functions are typically political, regulators are given independence from politicians in many countries, and are governed by processes involving stakeholders.

Regulators are now more regularly assessed using quantitative and qualitative data, and this comparative cross-country policy analysis has helped policy analysts and advocates bring pressure on countries performing poorly. At this moment, for example, Pakistan leads South Asia in terms of its Telecom Regulatory Environment.[5]

This box was written by Randy Spence.

Policy in the private, non-profit and international sectors

While this chapter is concerned with the public policy of countries, we would like to briefly sketch here how this policy and experience intersects with policy in the private and non-profit sectors and with international policy debates.

Private enterprises, by structure and ownership, have the overarching objective of making profits for their owners. In providing typically 75 per cent of the jobs and incomes in an economy, they contribute heavily to providing the conditions for people to pursue what they value. There is also a long history of corporate philanthropy and corporate social responsibility. For example, annual surveys indicate that corporate philanthropy is primarily in education and health initiatives. Corporate foundations also support building capacities in the public sector, with a growing (though still minority) share in total financing. One can cite the Nike Foundation as an example of this. It was created in part because the corporation saw limits to what it could do through social responsibility policies such as improved working conditions and paying employees above local wages. The foundation's focus is now on girl's education through funding and partnerships with communities, stakeholders and international development organizations.

The private part of the informal sector is, in many ways, a different world, with as many faces as there are informal sectors. Micro-enterprises are the form of livelihood for sometimes large majorities of people in developing countries, who typically make little profit, but are responsible for philanthropic activity organized through family and social networks. There are several public policy concerns when assisting informal sector activity, as described above, but 'policy' (in the case of individual, family and small businesses themselves) is typically made on the fly.

The non-profit sector represents both national and international organizations, usually called non-governmental organizations (NGOs). They have a substantial developmental impact in generating economic activity and livelihoods, and in social services activity – accounting for typically 5–10 per cent of measured economic activity, and a much higher share of the total (including informal) economy. Discussions around NGO policies generally include issues of what individual NGOs are responsible or accountable to and for. NGOs tend, like corporations, to have structured policy analysis and decision-making, by and for their board or governance structure. Large NGOs, and NGO umbrella groups, play prominent economic and social roles in many countries, and there are strong proponents of the growth of new business models (essentially non-profit) serving poor communities. Certainly, international NGOs often play the key operational roles in international crisis and humanitarian assistance.

Scrutiny of both corporate and non-profit policies in any country is essential. Our focus on public policy in this chapter reflects a particular concern with the close relationships between public policy and human development priorities.

Finally, there are major development policy analyses and debates in international spheres, in all areas of public policy – rights, intellectual property, food, health, finance, trade, energy, environment and climate change, etc. International policy is often specified in international agreements and institutions. The WTO, UN Charter and Universal Declaration of Human Rights are only some of hundreds of examples. They interact at national and local levels, presenting complex policy analysis challenges. Box 12.3, written by Amartya Sen, on the global food crisis, illustrates several of these points, including the multi-disciplinary nature of policy, and the urgent challenge of aligning international and national policies.

Box 12.3 The rich get hungrier

Will the food crisis that is menacing the lives of millions ease up – or grow worse over time? The answer may be both. The recent rise in food prices has largely been caused by temporary problems like drought in Australia, Ukraine and elsewhere. Though the need for huge rescue operations is urgent, the present acute crisis will eventually end. But underlying it is a basic problem that will only intensify unless we recognize it and try to remedy it.

It is a tale of two peoples. In one version of the story, a country with a lot of poor people suddenly experiences fast economic expansion, but only half of the people share in the new prosperity. The favoured ones spend a lot of their new income on food, and unless supply expands very quickly, prices shoot up. The rest of the poor now face higher food prices but no greater income, and begin to starve. Tragedies like this happen repeatedly in the world.

A stark example is the Bengal famine of 1943, during the last days of the British rule in India. The poor who lived in cities experienced rapidly rising incomes, especially in Calcutta, where huge expenditures for the war against Japan caused a boom that quadrupled food prices. The rural poor faced these skyrocketing prices with little increase in income.

Misdirected government policy worsened the division. The British rulers were determined to prevent urban discontent during the war, so the government bought food in the villages and sold it, heavily subsidised, in the cities, a move that increased rural food prices even further. Low earners in the villages starved. Two to three million people died in that famine and its aftermath.

Much discussion is rightly devoted to the division between haves and have-nots in the global economy, but the world's poor are themselves divided between those who are experiencing high growth and those who are not. The rapid economic expansion in countries like China, India and Vietnam tends to sharply increase the demand for food. This is, of course, an excellent thing in itself, and if these countries could manage to reduce their unequal internal sharing of growth, even those left behind there would eat much better.

But the same growth also puts pressure on global food markets – sometimes through increased imports, but also through restrictions or bans on exports to moderate the rise in food prices at home, as has happened recently in countries like India, China, Vietnam and Argentina. Those hit particularly hard have been the poor, especially in Africa.

There is also a high-tech version of the tale of two peoples. Agricultural crops like corn and soybeans can be used for making ethanol for motor fuel. So the stomachs of the hungry must also compete with fuel tanks.

Misdirected government policy plays a part here too. In 2005, the US Congress began to require widespread use of ethanol in motor fuels. This law combined with a subsidy for this use has created a flourishing corn market in the US, but has also diverted agricultural resources from food to fuel. This makes it even harder for the hungry stomachs to compete.

Ethanol use does little to prevent global warming and environmental deterioration, and clear-headed policy reforms could be urgently carried out, if American politics would permit it. Ethanol use could be curtailed, rather than being subsidized and enforced.

The global food problem is not being caused by a falling trend in world production, or for that matter in food output per person (this is often asserted without much evidence). It is the result of accelerating demand. However, a demand-induced problem also calls for rapid expansion in food production, which can be done through more global cooperation.

While population growth accounts for only a modest part of the growing demand for food, it can contribute to global warming, and long-term climate change can threaten agriculture. Happily, population growth is already slowing and there is overwhelming evidence that women's empowerment (including the expansion of schooling for girls) can rapidly reduce it even further.

What is most challenging is to find effective policies to deal with the consequences of the extremely asymmetric expansion of the global economy. Domestic economic reforms are badly needed in many slow-growth countries, but there is also a big need for more global cooperation and assistance. The first task is to understand the nature of the problem.

OpEd written by Amartya Sen, published in the *New York Times*, 28 May 2008, available at www.nytimes.com/2008/05/ 28/opinion/28sen.html

Politics and power

In the above section, we reviewed different areas of public policy; we now look more closely at how public policy is decided and implemented. The first characteristic of public policy is that it cannot be associated with a single moment, policy-maker, decision or action, as we mentioned earlier. Public policy involves a course of action and a web of decisions (Hill, 2005). There is no unique 'policy-maker' but a multiple set of agents who make policy. For instance, it is not easy to identify who exactly crafts an educational policy. Is it the Minister for Education? Or schools that put pressure on the government to make certain decisions? Or international organizations that determine the education agenda of a country? Who exactly decides on the budget allocated to education? These questions reveal that it is not easy to identify 'policy-makers' or policy moments. Public policy is, more than anything else, a *process*.

Another feature is that policy-making cannot be easily distinguished from implementation. It is difficult to ascertain exactly when a policy was made. Is it at the time when a law is passed in Parliament? If, say, the UK introduces a new employment policy that encourages low-skilled workers to access the labour market by giving tax incentives to their employers, is that policy tantamount to being a law in Parliament? Or does the policy also include its actual implementation? The policy is eventually what actors on the ground are doing, whether or not businesses have made use of the law in order to boost low-skilled employment. By separating policy-making from implementation, one risks ignoring the deeply political nature of policy itself. It is easy to attribute the failure of a policy to a 'lack of political will', as if policy were a technical matter that did not depend upon the implementation of those responsible for it.

Separating policy-making from policy implementation also ignores the principle that effective implementation planning is part of good policy-making, and that there are policy processes organizations continuously cycle through – policy analysis and design, decision-making, implementation, monitoring and evaluation, and new analysis and design, etc.

Development policy has sometimes fallen into the trap of seeing policy as a technical issue the implementation of which is separate from its crafting. In an anthropological study of the actions of various development agencies in Lesotho during the 1980s, Ferguson (1990) highlights the dangers of such a depoliticized use of the notion of policy. In such a depoliticized context, he argues that poverty is seen as something that requires technical action from 'experts' attached to the government, as opposed to being a larger political problem that could be resolved through politics and negotiating conflicting interests. His study led him to conclude that, 'development is an "anti-politics machine", depoliticizing everything it touches' (1990, pxiv). Politics, along with history, has been swept aside by development actors. In this aseptic universe, the state has become, as Ferguson argues, 'a machine for implementing "development" programmes (and) an apolitical tool for delivering social services and engineering economic growth.' The state is a 'machinery (with) policies, but no politics (1990, pp65–66),' referring to certain groups and interests controlling government action.

That policy is political suggests that the policy process is closely connected to the nature of power itself. A policy is a chaotic process dominated by political, practical and socio-cultural forces. In his pioneering study on power, Stephen Lukes (2004) describes three dimensions of power at play in the policy process (see also Hill, 2005, pp27–34). First, there is the single dimension of power: 'A has power over B to the extent that s/he can get B to do something that B would not choose to do.' By virtue of A's power, B will modify his/her behaviour despite the knowledge that this may be contrary to his/her interests. This entails asking the question: who made B do what s/he would otherwise not have chosen to do? The second dimension of power that Lukes highlights is when 'A can limit the scope of the political process to considerations of issues that are innocuous to A (and possibly against the interests of B)'. In other words, power is exercised in 'setting the agenda' for decision-making, and excluding people from it. This non-decision-making entails two processes: 'mobilization of bias' (ensuring that issues of significance to group A never enter the decision-making process, in other words, it is a process which confines decisions to safe issues) and 'organizing out' (excluding opposing interest groups from decision-making).

In the two examples above, power is overt. There is however a third, more insidious, face of power. Even when there is no observable conflict of interest or consensus, this does not mean that power has not in fact been exercised. Power can be manifested in the form of (unconscious) preference shaping. Not only could A exercise power over B by prevailing in the resolution of key issues or by preventing B from effectively raising those issues, but A could influence

B's conception of the issues altogether. Consensus could be an indication of the exercise of unequal power relations. For example, when there seems to be a consensus about consumerism as a way of life in the West, and no opposition to the economic policies that encourage it, this does not preclude the possibility that power has been exercised in the form of preference-shaping on the part of the retail industry or capitalist market forces.

Tools for policy analysis

Given its political, dynamic and often chaotic nature, policy resists general attempts at modelling or theorizing. There is no policy model or theory to follow and, as a consequence, no blueprint for analysing policy. However, there are some conceptual frameworks that guide governments' roles and policies. The most dominant in the past 70 years has been that of market economics plus public finance – welfare economics. Here it should be noted that the human development and capability approach provides a broader framework that includes welfare economics. While there are human development and other principles for policy-making and implementation (such as equity, efficiency, empowerment and sustainability), there is no good alternative to clear political and policy analysis (and action) in each specific case.

The public administration literature gives us some indicative policy guidelines on how to analyse and understand the actions of governments. Michael Hill begins by distinguishing 'analysis of policy' from 'analysis for policy' (2005, p5). The analysis of policy consists, he argues, of the following:

- *Studies of policy content*: description and explanation of the genesis and development of particular policies: how a policy emerged, how it was implemented and what the results were.
- *Studies of policy outputs*: explanation of the levels of expenditure or service provision.
- *Studies of the policy process*: how policy decisions are made and how policies are shaped in action.

'Analysis for policy' consists of:

- *Evaluation*: analysis of the impact that policies have on the population (this is a distinguishing feature of analysis for policy and analysis of policy).
- *Information*: collection of data in order to assist policy-makers to reach their decisions. This relates to 'evidence-based' policy-making.
- *Process advocacy*: improving the nature of policy-making systems.
- *Policy advocacy*: pressing specific options and ideas in the policy process.

In reality, the two are often linked and it is not easy to separate analysis of and for policy. In its analysis of water and sanitation policy (Box 12.4), the *Human Development Report* 2006 deployed a combination of the above.

Box 12.4 Water and sanitation policy in 19th century Great Britain

'Parliament was all but compelled to legislate upon the great London nuisance by the force of sheer stench.' Thus commented the London *Times* on an episode known as the 'Great Stink'. So severe was the stench of sewage emanating from the Thames River in the long hot summer of 1858 that parliament was forced to close temporarily. Beyond parliament, the problems were more serious.

As industrialization and urbanization accelerated in the 19th century, fast-growing cities like Birmingham, London and Manchester became centres of infectious disease. Sewage overflowed and leaked from the limited number of cesspools into neighbourhoods of the poor and ultimately into rivers like the Thames, the source of drinking water.

Parliamentary nostrils were offended – while poor people died. In the late 1890s, the infant mortality rate in Great Britain was 160 deaths for every 1000 live births – roughly the same as Nigeria today. Children died mainly from diarrhoea and dysentery. They died for the same reason that so many children still die in developing countries: sewage was not separated from drinking water. Between 1840 and the mid-1890s, average income doubled while child mortality increased slightly – a powerful demonstration of the gap between wealth generation and human development.

Growing awareness of the human costs of urban industrial life forced water onto the political agenda. In 1834, the Office of the Registrar General was formed, producing a steady stream of mortality figures that generated public concern. Social investigation became another powerful tool for reform. Edwin Chadwick's *Report on the Sanitary Condition of the Labouring Population of Great Britain* provided an account of a crisis on a grand scale, documenting in graphic detail the consequences of the water and sanitation problem: 'The annual loss of life from filth and bad ventilation is greater than the loss from death or wounds from any war in which the country has been engaged in modern times' (p369). Chadwick's recommendations: a private tap and a latrine connected to a sewer for every household and municipal responsibility for providing clean water.

Reform came in two great waves. The first focused on water and began in the 1840s with the Public Health Act (1848) and the Metropolitan Water Act (1852), which expanded public provision of clean water. The discovery by John Snow in 1854 that cholera was a waterborne infection and that its spread could be halted by access to uncontaminated water supplies added to the impetus. By 1880, municipalities had displaced private water operators as the main providers of water in towns and cities.

The second great wave of reform shifted the locus of the public action from water to sanitation. This wave gathered momentum after 1880 and was reflected in a surge of public investment. Between the mid-1880s and mid-1890s, capital spending per capita on sanitation more than doubled in constant prices. It then doubled again over the next decade.

After 1840, life expectancy began to increase partly because of the first wave of reforms in water. It then came to a standstill, to resume after the great sanitation reforms came into play in the 1880s. In the space of little more than a decade (since) 1900, the infant mortality rate fell from 160 deaths per 1000 live births to 100 – one of the steepest declines in history. Public investment in sanitation, not rising private income, was the catalyst. Average incomes rose by only 6 per cent between 1900 and 1912.

New approaches to financing played a critical role in the second wave of reform. Mounting political pressure for public action generated an active search for new fiscal mechanisms to address a dilemma familiar in developing countries today: how to finance large upfront payments from a limited revenue base without raising taxes or charges to politically-unfeasible levels. Cities supplemented low-interest loans from the central government with municipal borrowing on bond markets. Water and sanitation accounted for about a quarter of local government debt at the end of the 19th century.

This huge mobilization of public finances reflected the changing place of water and sanitation in political priorities. Sanitation reform became a rallying point for social reformers, municipal leaders and public health bodies, who increasingly viewed inadequate sanitation as a constraint not just on human progress but on economic prosperity. The public voice of civil society played a key role in driving the sanitation reform that made advances in public health possible.

But why the lag between the two great waves of reform? One of the major reform coalition partners in the first wave were the industrialists, who wanted water for factories but who were reluctant to pay higher taxes for extending sanitation to the poor. Politically powerful segments of society remained more interested in insulating themselves from the effects of poor sanitation among the poor than in universal provision. It was not until the electoral reform that extended voting rights beyond propertied classes that the voice of the poor became a more telling factor.

Edited extract from Box 1.1 of the *Human Development Report*, 2006, pp29–30.

This analysis of sanitation policy in Victorian Britain illustrates how analysis *of* policy is intertwined with analysis *for* policy. First, there is analysis of the content of the sanitation policy, and how it originated – Parliament could not function because of the smell from the Thames. The 'policy-making' stage is described in terms of its output, the mobilization of public finances to provide sanitation facilities. This policy content is however not alien from 'analysis for policy' in the form of evaluation. Chadwick's study on the sanitary condition of the British labouring population had a lot to do with the passing of acts expanding the provision of clean water in the 1840s. And the discovery that cholera thrived in dirty water provided a final impetus to raise public awareness of the importance of water and sanitation. These conditions – the earlier advances in water provision, the scientific evidence, the evaluation of the health consequences of a lack of sanitation, and the Great Stink of 1858 which affected Parliamentarians themselves – led to public provisions for sanitation. The policy did not struggle against powerful interests because the Great Stink affected both rich and poor Londoners. Another significant factor in the policy process is that workers had acquired voting rights and were able to challenge the power of the rich to block taxation reform that would enable the financing of sanitation. Last but not least, the policy of sanitation provision in Victorian Britain discussed above is at the same time an 'analysis for policy'. It contains a strong evaluative component: it reports the substantial impact that the introduction of the sanitation policy had on public health. It further demonstrates that providing public health is not necessarily rocket science. A well-functioning sanitation system is all that is needed, and this does not always have to cost huge amounts of money. And, finally, the policy analysis is not done for its own sake but for the sake of advocacy. It presses others to develop similar policies.

Analysis of policy and for policy, whether ex-ante or ex-post, is extremely complex. There are no precise guidelines on how to do it. In an influential book entitled *A Practical Guide for Policy Analysis*, Eugene Bardach (2005) proposes eights steps in policy analysis:[6]

1   *Describe the problem* (without diagnosing its causes or proposing a solution).
2   *Assemble the evidence*: gather information in the form of factual data which has meaning.
3   *Construct the alternatives*: each alternative must address not only the basic intervention strategy, but also indicate how the strategy will be financed and implemented.
4   *Select the criteria*: evaluative criteria are used to judge the best outcomes.
5   *Project the outcomes*: determine as far as possible the benefits and costs of the policy options. Indicate the values and dimensions of the indicator to assess the outcomes.
6   *Confront the trade-offs*: measure trade-offs across outcomes rather than alternatives.
7   *Decide*: select the best alternatives given the analysis.
8   *Tell your story.*

Other basic questions arise when doing policy analysis, depending in part on who is doing the analysis – the organization(s) that will implement it, other stakeholders, other interested parties, etc. These questions include: what is the policy environment, international as well as national? Who are the political actors? How do the political actors interact with one other? What power do they command? How do they influence the policy process?

A human development perspective

A human development perspective on policy analysis begins with the observation that policies are deeply political. Therefore, policy analysis cannot ignore the political forces that shape policy. As Sen noted in *Hunger and Public Action* (1981), policy-making 'depends on a number of influences, going beyond the prevalent notion of what should be done, ... there are political issues in policy-making' (1981, p19). A human development perspective requires a political analysis of the forces that shape public policy itself. It especially demands a detailed analysis of the power relations at stake.

In addition to careful attention to power relations and politics, a human development perspective on policy analysis holds that: (1) the success of policies should be assessed according to whether they promote people's freedoms, and (2) policies should respect people's agency and be specifically based on their ability to participate (giving particular voice to marginalized groups). These reflect the 'evaluation' and 'agency' aspects of human development discussed in Chapter 1. Practically speaking, this means that the 'evaluation stage' of policy analysis has to include considerations about people's freedom, both in its opportunity and process aspect. The use of statistics and other forms of well-being measurement is crucial here. What is the impact of liberalization policies on the freedom of people to be nourished, educated and healthy? To what extent have poor people been able to have a voice in the formulation of trade policies? To formulate, evaluate and reformulate good public policies, better data will have to be collected about the state of people's health, education, nourishment and political participation.

From a human development perspective, the major purpose of policy analysis is to bring policy change so that people's freedoms are expanded, and not reduced. A policy does not change because there is sufficient evidence to make the case for change but because there are powerful groups that have a special interest in not changing the policy. This is why advocacy is an important stage of policy analysis. Once the analysis is conducted, one needs to bring its major message into the public domain in order to mobilize public opinion and confront the special interests underpinning it. The use of 'killer statistics' – using statistics in a comparative mode to make people aware of a problem – can be particularly helpful. Here are some examples of 'killer facts' taken from the *Human Development Report* 2006: 'Most of the 1.1 billion people categorized as lacking access to clean water use about 5 litres a day one tenth of the average daily amount used in rich countries to flush toilets.' (p5); 'Some 1.8 million children die each year as a result of diarrhoea – 4900 deaths each day or an under-five population equivalent in size to that for London and New York combined.' (p6); 'The $10 billion price tag for the Millennium Development Goal seems a large sum – but it has to be put in context. It represents less than five days' worth of global military spending and less than half what rich countries spend each year on mineral water' (p8).

Box 12.5 Hunger amidst plenty

About half of all Indian children are estimated to be undernourished, and more than half of all adult women suffer from anaemia. Low birthweights (themselves reflecting the poor nutritional status of adult women) play a major role in the perpetuation of undernutrition and poor health.

There is some evidence of heightened nutritional deprivation during the (past) two or three years, a period of severe drought in large parts of the country. Over the same period, there has been an unprecedented accumulation of foodgrain stocks on the part of the central government – from about 18 million tonnes in early 1998 to well over 50 million tonnes as this book goes to press. To put these staggering numbers in perspective, it may help to think of the current stock as the equivalent of about one tonne of food for *each* household below the poverty line. If all the sacks of grain lying in state warehouses were lined up in a row, the line would stretch for one million kilometres or so – more than twice the distance from the earth to the moon.

While these massive food stocks are meant to contribute to the country's 'food security', that objective is clearly not well-served when the stocks are built by *depriving* hungry people of much-needed food during drought years. Further, the current stocks are more than three times as large as the official buffer stock norms. This huge surplus is, to a great extent, explained by the fact that the government is committed to unrealistically high 'minimum support prices' for foodgrains. This has boosted production, lowered consumer demands, and forced the government to buy the difference in order to sustain these artificially high prices.

The distributional effects of high support prices are not entirely clear. There is a widespread conviction that high food prices help the poor, because it is a form of subsidy to the agricultural sector, which is the main source of livelihood of a large number of poor households. But this reasoning is at best incomplete, since it is also the case that many more poor people in India buy their food on the market, and tend to be adversely affected when food prices go up. For casual labourers, migrant workers, slum dwellers, rickshaw pullers, rural artisans and many other deprived sections of the population, cheaper food would be a blessing.

As it happens, even poor *farmers* are unlikely to benefit much, if at all, from price-support operations. These farmers typically sell little grain, if any, on the market; instead, they tend to combine subsistence farming with labour migration and other income-earning activities.

The overall distributional effects of higher food prices can, thus, be quite adverse. A related issue is that it is not *possible* to sustain artificially high prices, short of destroying or exporting the surplus food. In fact, it aggravates the problem, by giving farmers mis-leading signals to the effect that they should continue growing more foodgrains instead of diversifying their crops. Sooner or later, this is bound to lead to a glut in the foodgrain market and a collapse of market prices, defeating the price-support policy, unless the intention is to accumulate large stocks indefinitely.

[O]pportunities exist today to make constructive use of the available food stocks. In particular, these resources could be used to implement social security programmes, such as employment schemes, school meals, in-kind transfers to the destitute, and an expansion of the public distribution system. These possibilities have received scant attention in recent policy debates, and there is little indication that the government has anything like a coherent plan for the constructive utilization of the country's food stocks. Instead, official policy seems to consist of postponing the problem of ballooning food stocks as long as possible.

This situation of 'hunger amidst plenty' is an extreme case of lopsided priorities, related in turn to sharp inequalities of political power. The government has been quite responsive to the demands of privileged farmers (the main beneficiaries of procurement operations), even boosting minimum support prices against expert recommendations. (In) contrast, the needs of the hungry millions have counted for very little in the formulation of recent food policies. The answer to this problem is not so much to undermine farmers' organizations, which have every reason to defend the interests of their members. The need, rather, is to build countervailing power through better political organization of underprivileged groups.

Extract from J. Drèze and A. K. Sen, *India: Development and Participation* (2002) Oxford University Press, Delhi, pp336–340.

Box 12.5 on food policy in India depicts a human development perspective on policy. First, Drèze and Sen describe the problem and assemble the evidence. They provide data about the rate of undernutrition, low birthweight and anaemia, and the existing foodgrain stocks. Note the persuasive use of facts in: 'it may help to think of the current stock as the equivalent of about one tonne of food for *each* household below the poverty line' or '(if all the sacks of grain lying in state warehouses were lined up in a row, the line would stretch for one million kilometres or so – more than twice the distance from the earth to the moon.' Second, they describe the policy content: the government support of a minimum price for food producers has meant that the government had to buy food surplus in order to maintain prices. Third, they evaluate the policy from the perspective of the freedoms of marginalized groups. While the policy has been beneficial for food producers who sell their products in markets, it has had detrimental effects on those who have to buy the food and who live on subsistence farming: they are unable to lead healthy lives and access other freedoms they might value. Fourth, they project the outcomes: if the policy of creating artificially high prices for grain continues, it becomes self-defeating. Fifth, they construct the policy alternatives: ceasing this support for a minimum foodgrain price would enable poor people to buy more food and be healthier. They propose to use the current available foodstock for implementing social security programmes. The criteria for assessing these alternatives are the well-being of the poor and whether they participate in the formulation of the policy that directly affects them. Will they be able to live healthier lives under alternative policies? Sixth, Drèze and Sen provide an analysis of power in the policy process. The main winners of the current food policy are the large-scale farmers because they have power over the subsistence farmers and rural labourers, and they dominate farmers' organizations. But any policy alternative to solve the hunger problem in India would need to count with the political empowerment of its most marginalized groups. Finally, the analysis of food policy has been conducted for the purposes of advocacy. It depicts an absurd (but powerful) narrative of 'hunger amidst plenty'.

Questions

12.1 Identify one policy in your country. Who is responsible for the policy decision? How would you describe the policy process?

12.2 In the country you know best, which areas of public policy would you say are best (and worst) managed? What are the primary private and public interests and institutions involved in each case? Can you think of ways of improving the worst ones?

12.3 Give examples of how Lukes' three dimensions of power are manifested in the policy processes in your country.

12.4 If you know about a sector in any country, such as agriculture, forestry, mining, ICT, health and education, describe how well you think it is functioning with respect to the expansion of human freedoms. Are there constraints that stem from poor or inadequate public policies? What policy-making institutions and stakeholder groups would or could be involved in improving sector policy and performance? What are the main obstacles, political or otherwise?

Notes

1   Initiatives such as IP Watch provide a wide coverage of issues and differing viewpoints (www.ip-watch.org).

2   This was one main point of agreement among economists and participants at the seminar 'How Are Globalisation and Poverty Interacting and What Can Governments Do about It?' OECD Development Centre, Paris, 9–10 December 2002.

3   One example of a growing set of human development policy analyses and methodologies is the *Human Development Impact Assessment Toolkit of Trade Policy* from the UNDP Asia-Pacific Trade and Investment Initiative (www.nsi-ins.ca/english/research/progress/05.asp). For an analysis of the growth and distributional impacts of trade, see the Alan Winters papers, Centre for Economic Policy Research (www.cepr.org/Pubs), particularly the paper on 'Trade, Trade Policy and Poverty: What Are The Links?'

4   A. Paterson, R. Adam and J. Mullin, 'The relevance of the national system of innovation approach to mainstreaming science and technology for development in NEPAD and the AU', draft working paper for the Preparatory meeting of the First NEPAD Conference of Ministers and Presidential Advisers responsible for Science and Technology, Nairobi, 13–15 October 2003.

5   For more information on ICT use in developing countries, see the LIRNEasia website at http://lirneasia.net/. Sister networks are linked to the Learning Initiatives on Reforms for Network Economies at http://lirne.net.

6   These have been reproduced in *Measuring Human Development: A Primer* (at http://hdr.undp.org).

Readings

Bardach, E. (2005) *A Practical Guide to Policy Analysis: The Eightfold Path to More Effective Problem Solving*, 2nd edn, CQ Press, Washington, DC

Drèze, J. and Sen, A. K. (2002) *India: Development and Participation*, Oxford University Press, Delhi

Ferguson, J. (1990) *The Anti-Politics Machine: Development, Depolitization and Democratic Power in Lesotho*, Cambridge University Press, Cambridge

Hill, M. (2005) *The Public Policy Process*, 4th edn, Pearson, Harlow

International Development Research Centre (2006) *Innovation, Technology and Science Programme Initiative Prospectus*, www.idrc.ca/uploads/user-S/11616331061ITS_Prospectus_English.pdf

Lukes, S. (2004) *Power: A Radical View*, Palgrave, Basingstoke

Sen, A. (1981) *Hunger and Public Action*, Oxford University Press, Oxford

UNDP (2006) *Human Development Report*, Palgrave, Basingstoke

Further Readings

Arrow, K. J. (1983) *Collected Papers of Kenneth J. Arrow, v. 1, Social Choice and Justice*, Harvard University Press, Cambridge, MA

Sen, A. K. (1979) *Collective Choice and Social Welfare*, North Holland, Amsterdam

Sen, A. K. (1982) *Choice, Welfare and Measurement*, Blackwell, Oxford

Sen, A. K. (1998) 'The possibility of social choice', in *Rationality and Freedom*, Harvard University Press, Cambridge, MA

The *Journal of Human Development* contains selected papers from annual HDCA conferences. Examples of policy analysis from the most recent issues include: water access and management, measuring gender equality, literacy, corporate social responsibility, income security systems and policies for reducing infant mortality.

The HDCA (Human Development and Capability Association) website (www.hdca.org) contains many policy analyses regarding such issues as health, HIV/AIDS, disability, mental health, girls and women's education, food security, higher education, child labour, rural poverty, ICTs, indigenous communities, decentralization and remittances. These can be accessed through the 'bibliography' or 'educational resources' sections and by entering relevant keywords. Thematic group activities (see website) include policy analysis in the areas of children, education, health and disability, indigenous people, religion and human rights.

Chapter 13
Policy Case Studies

Edited by Séverine Deneulin and Lila Shahani

Aims of the Chapter

- To identify policy problems.
- To understand the nature of development policy and the contexts in which it is made.
- To analyse development policy in its different aspects and to formulate policy recommendations from a human development perspective.
- To exercise one's creativity.

Key Points

When analysing a policy problem and seeking to address it from a human development perspective, some key questions have to be borne in mind:

- What is the problem that the policy seeks to address? What are the relevant data and information that need to be collected to highlight the problem?
- What is being done to address the problem?
- Does the existing policy respect the four human development principles of equity, empowerment, efficiency and sustainability?
- In what ways could the current policy be reformed so that it promotes valuable freedoms more effectively? In other words, how can policy respect key human development principles more fully?

The human development and capability approach is about social transformation: enabling people to become agents of their own lives and providing them with the opportunities to live lives they have reason to choose and value. But no social transformation is possible with ideas alone. It requires people to carry these ideas out, despite the infinite complexities – political, economic, social and cultural – of their lives. This chapter describes some 'real life' situations, where human development insights have been applied.

The case study method has been a widely used pedagogical method. It is, for example, used by management schools to form future managers, by challenging them with hypothetical business situations where management decisions need to be taken.[1] As Chapter 9 and the appendix on teaching human development have emphasized, the human development and capability approach does not lend itself to the 'banking approach' in education – to paraphrase Freire – where information is simply learned and recited. It requires instead a 'problem-solving' education, where students are invited to become active agents transforming the world in which they live, and building more just economic and social relations between people and societies. This is what this set of case studies hopes to achieve: to expose students to the complex realities of the world in which we live by creating hypothetical situations in which specific problems have to be resolved.

We begin with a fictive personal narrative of the life of a girl in Ghana, which powerfully depicts the type of harrowing reality many in the developing world struggle with everyday. We then set out to describe three different areas of policies (gender, taxation and security) in three different national contexts (Turkey, Syria and Haiti). We conclude by exploring the challenge of multi-sectoral policy in a post-conflict situation such as that currently facing Liberia.

A personal narrative of a woman's life in Ghana

Adib Nehmeh[2]

Ashanti's life begins in her family hut. But, as only 25 per cent of the Ghanaian population consults a doctor, her mother dies a few hours after delivery. The traditional midwife is not able to stop the haemorrhaging. Her mother joins the hundreds of women who die in childbirth every year – the maternal mortality rate in Ghana is 200 women per 100,000. Ashanti is underweight, born below 2kg. The under-five mortality rate is 111 per thousand live births.

The school is a big hut, with no equipment and running water. She is however lucky to go to school at all. In Ghana, 21 per cent of boys and 41 per cent of girls have never gone to school, and 38 per cent of men and 64 per cent of women are illiterate. Ashanti does not even finish her first year at school when she is subjected to a circumcision ceremony with other girls in the village: she is five years old. In the north of Ghana, 77 per cent of girls undergo female genital mutilation between the ages of 5 and 13.

Unfortunately, after three years of school, she is forced to leave in order to help her family. She begins to work with her family in the fields. In Ghana, 2.5 million children aged 5–17, or 40 per cent of children in that age group, work. The owner of one of the fields in which she works takes a liking to her. He is 50 years old. He tells Ashanti's father that he likes her and wants to marry her. The father agrees. In return, he can continue working in the field and receive a minor allowance.

When Ashanti reaches puberty, she cannot imagine herself to be the wife of the owner of the land, who is 38 years her senior. She decides to run away to the capital, Accra, where she will work as a 'porter' (*'Kayayee'*) in the market. She lives in the street, where she is subjected to all kinds of abuse. Of the children who work in the capital city, 23 per cent are attempting to escape poverty in the countryside. The majority of them are girls.

Ashanti's father calls her back, claiming that he is ill. When she returns, she finds out that, in reality, one of her brothers has stolen two cows from a family in another tribe. As a punishment, the family of the person who committed the theft has to send one of their daughters in servitude to the aggrieved tribe. To date, 4700 cases of tribal servitude for life ('Trokosi') have already been recorded in the country.

For 40 years, Ashanti lives in servitude to the other tribe, without any rights (or compensation) whatsoever. She gives birth to three children: two boys and a girl. Her life suddenly takes another turn when the son of the village chief dies from a fever. She is accused of witchcraft, and is sent, along with her daughter, to a witch camp: 3000 women and 500 girls are currently estimated to live in such camps.

Questions

13.1 Identify the areas of public policy which affect Ashanti's life.

13.2 If you were the members of a Ghanaian women's organization, which area would you prioritize? Why?

Gender policy in Turkey

Seyhan Aydinligil[3]

Turkey has been a constitutional republic since 1923; it became a multi-party political system in 1946. It is ruled by a parliamentary democracy, where the government is accountable to the parliament, which elects the president. Turkey is one of the world's 20 largest economies. Its GDP reached US$400 billion and GDP per capita US$5500 in 2006. Following a recovery from a serious economic crisis in 2001, Turkey has succeeded in reducing monetary poverty, from about 28 per cent of the population in 2003 to about 18 per cent in 2006. Less than 0.01 per cent of the population live on US$1/day. However, some social indicators continue to lag behind those of countries with similar incomes.

Turkey's five-year vision for development, as outlined in its Ninth Development Plan 2007–2013, is to become 'a country with an information society, growing in stability, sharing more equitably, globally competitive and fully (completing) her coherence with the European Union.' Equitable human and social development is a key government goal. But the development process does not always benefit men and women equally. A review of the situation of women in Turkey over the course of several decades reflects that, despite progress on many fronts, their status remains vulnerable.

Women received the legal rights to vote, to elect and become elected in the years immediately following the declaration of the republic in 1923. But other legal reforms aimed at greater gender equity in labour markets, and in the educational and health systems, were only implemented much later. In 1985, Turkey became a signatory to the Convention on the Elimination of all kinds of Discrimination against Women (CEDAW), eventually ratifying it. In line with the CEDAW recommendations, a General Directorate of Women's Status and Problems was established in 1990, under the auspices of the Ministry of Labour and Social Security. In 1991, the Directorate became administratively affiliated to the Prime Ministry, and the same year, the State Ministry responsible for Women's Affairs and Family was established. While these institutional and legal improvements have undoubtedly been important, particularly in terms of improving educational and labour participation, women in Turkey continue to experience significant setbacks. The evidence indicates that women's needs, and their concerns for equal participation with men, in the educational, health, economic and political domains have not yet been adequately addressed. Basic human development indicators for women are low compared to other middle-income countries and new EU member states, as Table 13.1 illustrates. There continue to be major challenges and structural barriers to attaining gender equity in all domains.

Table 13.1 *Gender equality-related statistics compared to other middle-income countries, 2005*

	Turkey	Argentina	Mexico	Bulgaria
Ratio of girls to boys in:				
Primary education	0.95	0.99	1.00	0.99
Secondary education	0.74	1.07	1.03	0.98
Tertiary education	0.73	1.51	0.98	1.16
Ratio of literate women to men	90.9	100.4	98.4	99.8
Share of female wage employment in non-agricultural labour force	19.9	45.5	37.4	53.0
Proportion of seats held by women in national parliament	9.1	36.5	25.0	22.1
Gender Empowerment Measure	0.289	0.697	0.597	0.595

Source: Millennium Development Goals Report, Turkey, 2005.

In the 2008/09 *Human Development Report*, the Gender-related Development Index (GDI), which is simply the HDI adjusted downward for gender inequality, is 0.780, compared to its HDI value of 0.798 (Table 13.2). Out of the 157 countries with both HDI and GDI values, Turkey comes in 126th position. A total of 125 countries have thus a better ratio than Turkey's. In terms of ranking, Turkey's HDI is 76th out of 179 countries with data.

Table 13.2 *The GDI compared to the HDI – with data for 2006*

GDI as % of HDI	Life expectancy at birth: female as % male	Adult literacy: female as % male	Combined primary, secondary and tertiary gross enrolment ratio: female as % male
1. Sweden (99.9%)	1. Russian Federation (123.1%)	1. Lesotho (122.5%)	1. United Arab Emirates (120.2%)
124. Singapore (97.9%)	64. Panama (107.1%)	92. Madagascar (85.3%)	128. Burundi (87.7%)
125. Burkina Faso (97.9%)	65. Rwanda (107.1%)	93. Syrian Arab Republic (84.7%)	129. Cambodia (87.7%)
126. Turkey (97.8%)	**66. Turkey (107.0%)**	**94. Turkey (83.7%)**	**130. Turkey (87.6%)**
127. Mali (97.8%)	67. Comoros (107.0%)	95. Rwanda (83.7%)	131. Morocco (86.1%)
128. Mozambique (97.8%)	68. United States (106.9%)	96. Tanzania (82.6%)	132. Korea (Republic of) (85.7%)
156. Occupied Palestinian Territories (92.8%)	157. Niger (96.9%)	135. Chad (31.3%)	157. Chad (60.4%)

Source: UNDP, Country Fact Sheet-Turkey 2008 (www.hdr.undp.org/en/statistics).

The Gender Empowerment Measure (GEM) reveals whether women take an active part in economic and political life. It tracks the share of seats in parliament held by women; of female legislators, senior officials and managers; and of female professional and technical workers; and the gender disparity in earned income, reflecting economic independence. GEM thus exposes inequality in opportunities in selected areas. In 2008 (with 2006 data), Turkey was ranked 101st out of 108 countries where GEMs were available, with a value of 0.371.

Legal reforms

Significant changes to the legal status of women have, however, been introduced in recent years. The Turkish civil and penal codes have been modified and revised to this end. A new clause on gender equality was introduced into Article 10 of the Constitution in May 2004. The close reads as follows, 'women and men have equal rights... The state is responsible for taking all necessary measures to realize equality between women and men'. This is a provision that paves the way for positive discrimination. Article 41 of the Constitution has been amended with a view to establishing and reiterating the principle of equality between spouses as a basis for the family. The 2001 Civil Code granted women equal rights as individuals and citizens, rather than recognizing these rights on the basis of membership to their families. The earlier Civil Code had recognized men as the sole family breadwinners and household heads. The new Civil Code also abolished the concept of the 'head of the family'.

The Penal Code, adopted in 2004, following extensive debates organized by civil society organizations and experts on selected articles of the draft, now recognizes crimes committed against women not 'as crimes perpetrated against the family or the social order' but as crimes and violations of individual human rights. In 2005, the Penal Code went through an additional paradigm shift, as it was further reviewed with respect to its full alignment with the universal principles of women's rights. References to customary concepts such as chastity, honour of the family, dishonour and shame have also been removed. The spokespersons for the Association for Women in Politics (KA-DER) confirm that these recent revisions in the legal codes are the outcome of the relentless and collective efforts of women's civil society organizations throughout Turkey. Over the years, actors in women's movements have worked together to amend many discriminatory clauses in the Civil Code, Penal Code and the Turkish Constitution itself. The amendments have now been incorporated into newly revised policies and regulations in the employment, education and health sectors. As such, these new legal revisions in the Civil and Penal Codes not only condemn and punish marital rape, and toughen the sentencing for honour killings, but also facilitate socio-cultural and political changes that provide greater social, cultural, political and sexual rights to Turkish women.

Despite these reforms, which have largely been adopted as responses to Turkey's EU accession process, the status of women throughout the country remains limited. According to data from official government reports and independent research findings, the number of women who are victims of honour crimes has not declined at the expected level. Data also indicate that domestic and sexual violence against women remains widespread. According to the World Watch Institute's 2002 'Women and Violence Report', Turkish women are subject to violence in about 34 per cent of the households surveyed. An earlier study, carried out by the Directorate of Women's Status and Problems in 1995, reported that, out of 1070 married women, 351 women experienced physical and verbal violence and/or intimidation of some sort. The national mechanisms to respond to and monitor these incidences on the other hand have not been fully developed or lacked effective implementation. In 2007, for example, there were only 38 shelter homes available to victims of domestic violence and sexually-abused women and girls in the entire country, with more than 25 concentrated in the cities of Istanbul, Izmir and Ankara. Further efforts are needed in Turkey towards gender equality in the judicial, institutional and administrative fields. There is also a need to further improve equal treatment between women and men in the labour market. Although equal opportunities and gender equality have yet to be fully achieved, the process of EU accession has generated and encouraged many important reforms, in law in general and in terms of gender equality in particular.

The educational participation of women and girls in secondary and higher education has also not reached desired levels over the past 25 years. Illiteracy among women is reported to be around 17 per cent. In an effort to monitor and reduce illiteracy among women and girls, compulsory education was raised to 8 years of schooling in 2000. The school dropout rate among girls in the 11–15 age group is also increasing, particularly outside large, metropolitan areas. This is a situation that is accompanied by an increase in the rate of early age marriages and maternal and infant death incidences. Turkey's National Human Development Report for 2007–2008 indicates that there is an 8 per cent school attendance gap between girls and boys at the primary school level.

Gender equality in employment and political participation are also among the problems that need to be recognized as priorities. According to the World Economic Forum's Global Gender Gap Index (GGGI), Turkey ranks at the low 105th place after such countries as Bahrain and Burkina Faso. In addition, Turkish women's participation in the labour force (currently at only 22 per cent) is one of the lowest in Europe. The salary gap between men and women for equal work is also estimated to be as high as 28 per cent.

Women's participation in decision-making

As an EU candidate country, Turkey has a much lower political representation of women at the national and local levels than the rest of the European community. The 2005 MDG report of the Turkish government acknowledges women's unequal access to political decision-making as a major democratic shortcoming. The report sets a target of 17 per cent women's representation in parliament by 2015. After the 2007 general election, the percentage of women in parliament increased two-fold to 50 women (out of 550 members), reaching 9.1 per cent of total seats in parliament. There are still many barriers that prevent women from taking up positions in political and legal spheres, however, and the figures above attest to this trend. Currently, there is one female cabinet minister in charge of gender and development affairs.

The proportion is also low at the local level, where only 0.6 per cent are mayors (18 out of 3234), 1.81 per cent are members of the provincial council (58 out of 3208) and 2.42 per cent are municipal council members (834 out of 34,477).

The Turkish government and a number of NGOs have implemented multiple projects with international development agencies over the past 25 years. One of them is the 'National Programme for the Integration of Women in Development,' which was implemented for the period 1993–2003, and partially financed by the UNDP. This programme led to the implementation of several studies aiming to analyse the situation of women in key development sectors. This programme led to the start of several women's study programmes at major universities, and initiated the first government and NGO dialogue series on selected gender equality issues. The National Human Development Reports, produced annually since 1995, made an annual attempt to include a detailed analysis of the situation of women in the country with new and disaggregated data, which was produced and analysed at provincial and regional levels. Other smaller-scale projects were jointly supported by the Turkish government, UN Agencies and NGOs during the period 1998–2008. One project, 'Women in Politics', implemented in 2006–2007, aimed to promote women's participation in politics, and train female candidates in electoral and political literacy issues while encouraging them to stand in the general elections. This and other programmes and projects involved training to empower women in the area of political literacy. A handbook, pamphlets and brochures were prepared and widely disseminated to prospective female candidates and to women as voters during municipal and general elections, providing information on political and candidature procedures, as well as information on political party visions relating to gender and development. Women in more than 24 selected provinces also went through training conducted by a consortium of experts and NGOs under the overall coordination of the Turkish NGO, KA-DER.

Economic empowerment

As the human development and capability approach indicates, economic empowerment is both a means and an end in itself. While improvement of income increases the quality of life of women and their households, the economic empowerment of women also strengthens their status as citizens, as individuals and in their role within their families and communities. Economic empowerment and improved social standing are therefore critical for achieving gender equality.

The 2004 National Human Development Report shows that most provinces in southeast Anatolia are ranked among the lowest 20 in terms of their human development performances. Similarly, the same report also states that the gender-based human development ranking of several of these provinces is even lower than their human development indicators. Women's participation in paid labour is 3.72 per cent, compared to the national average of 19.9 per cent, which is already very low when compared to the EU and other middle-income countries, such as Bulgaria, Slovenia, Argentina and Chile, where women participate in paid labour at not less than 30 per cent. In Denmark and Finland, time spent by women in market activities is at 58 per cent and 39 per cent respectively. In comparison, the unpaid family agricultural labour force in Turkey is predominantly female. These statistics further illustrate that the region presents many challenges that need to be overcome for improving the living conditions of women.

The South-Eastern Anatolia Regional Development Administration (with the help of UNDP in Turkey) has been supporting women's entrepreneurial activities since 1997, both at the grassroots and policy levels and in most of the provinces in the region. However, lessons from these programmes indicate that increasing women's entrepreneurship needs to be complemented by institutional reforms since both socio-economic and tradition-based barriers remain. Local ethnic and customary practices, lack of access to quality and specialized education, lack of business and entrepreneurial experience, and unequal access to credit, finance and other means of production continue to make women's employment difficult.

Policy options

The forces of customary laws, traditions, prevailing prejudices and religious pressures continue to undermine progress in human development and play a major role in relegating women into the private sphere, away from jobs, education and good healthcare, as well as public service opportunities. Women continue to belong to multiple layers of social realities that shape their lives. They often belong to collective identities – ethnic, religious, local, regional and international – in addition to being citizens of the nation state. In other words, women have a 'multi-layered citizenship'.[4] In Turkey, this fact is observable in several forms: in rural communities, women's lives are frequently influenced by local and ethnic traditions and by customary practices, which are often promoted by politically influential religious groups. Honour killings continue to be prevalent among ethnic communities, and many young women and girls are forced by their families to marry at early ages and to much older men in order to save their families from poverty and debt.

Like other Muslim societies, women's identity in Turkey often becomes the arena where power and politics converge. Women's bodies and the way they dress, cover and uncover their hair become the public issues over which political battles are often waged. This observation is therefore important for the identification of new policies that would bring about desired changes in women's lives. Some suggested areas for policy interventions that policy workers, government and civil society organizations could work on jointly in order to respond to the problem of women's marginalization in Turkey are as follows:

- *Human rights*: recognizing women's rights as human rights. This includes protecting and promoting the human rights of both women and men. It also means fighting violence against women, trafficking in women, forced prostitution and crimes of honour; promoting free choice in matters of reproduction and lifestyles; and granting migrant and minority women equal rights.
- *Representative democracy*: the persistently low representation and absence of women from decision-making at all levels of social, cultural and political life is a major policy challenge in which intensified efforts are needed.
- *Economic independence and education*: the position that men and women have in the economy is in many ways crucial to the balance of power between them. Fighting poverty and the feminization of poverty is significant in this regard. This is why gender equality should be specifically targeted in education. Education involves the ways in which societies transfer values, norms, knowledge and skills, as well as individual and social attitudes. It is crucial that education systems and the elements that constitute them – teachers, schools, textbooks, research institutes and education regimes – empower both girls and boys, taking care to counterbalance existing gender hierarchies. Media professionals can be a target group here, since they may have a very powerful position in the transfer and consolidation of norms and knowledge.
- *Gender-blind areas*: more attention should be paid to the so-called gender-blind areas, such as education and health, unpaid family labour, legal discrimination, low wages, violence, social security and women's rights. Gender has to be a central feature in all areas of social policy.
- *Citizen action*: giving voice to women's needs and concerns can force changes in public policy. The universal principles of equality and human rights and their far-reaching implications for the lives of women cannot be disregarded and must be buttressed by country-wide debates on social policy.

Question: Mock policy decision exercise

13.3 The UNDP has made €10 million available to launch a new programme aimed at tackling gender inequality in Turkey in the next five years. A committee of eight people have been invited to decide on the programme specification, budget allocation and timeline of the programme. The committee members are: representatives from the General Directorate of Women's Status and Problems; representatives from the women's NGOs; sociologists, economists, political scientists and lawyers specialized in constitutional, civil and criminal law and citizenship rights; the Turkish Minister of Education; the Turkish Ministry of Labour and Employment; the Minister of Health; the Minister of Justice and Security; the UN Resident Representative; the head of a women's shelter; and a female member of parliament or representative of the parliamentary commission on gender equality.

Students are invited to choose a role and draft a 5-page programme specification to address gender inequality in Turkey. Your programming document should also include a description of how you are going to use the €10 million budget in the five years and a justification of the budget allocation.

Fiscal policy in Syria

Rathin Roy and Khalid Abu-Ismail[5]

Macro-economic policies represent a key 'entry point' for activities fostering human development. Without revenues, the state cannot finance core human development activities such as paying teachers, nurses and doctors decent salaries. So far, Syria has had a healthy fiscal space, i.e. the amount of tax revenues it can draw from to finance direct or indirect human development expenditures. But the oil-dependence of its tax revenues has raised some concerns regarding the sustainability of this fiscal space.

The macro-fiscal picture

Table 13.3 presents a rudimentary summary of Syria's fiscal operations. While this data may somewhat underestimate total public spending, it does allow us to draw some preliminary conclusions. The first conclusion is that Syria has a fairly robust current surplus and is in fact able to finance all its development expenditures from total revenues, up to the year. In other words, Syria occasionally runs a small fiscal deficit and, at times, a fiscal surplus. Different data sources reveal no immediate fiscal crisis, in the medium-term, and hence there is room for focusing on the growth and distribution aspects of fiscal policy.

Table 13.3 *Syria's basic macro-fiscal picture, 1992–2002*

Percent of GDP	1994	1995	1996	1997	1998	1999	2000	2001	2002
(1) Total revenue	24.06	25.35	24.57	26.45	25.88	26.47	27.17	31.99	30.18
(2) Total expenditure	27.34	26.75	27.00	25.02	25.99	25.07	26.54	28.16	30.73
(3) Current expenditure	14.49	14.87	12.97	12.89	14.05	14.19	16.04	16.62	17.15
(4) Development expenditure	12.84	11.88	11.48	12.13	11.93	10.87	10.50	11.54	13.58

Source: Data provided by Ministry of Finance of Syria.

Discussions with authorities revealed that the likelihood of a fiscal deficit exceeding 3 percentage points of GDP was small, given high oil prices. Syria thus enjoys considerable fiscal space and is able to fund human development expenditures with little recourse to external or internal borrowing. The crucial question remains: is this fiscal space sustainable? Available Syrian budget data indicate that oil revenues and non-oil domestic revenues together contribute the bulk of revenue, accounting for 80 per cent of total revenue in the period 1992–2002.

Table 13.4 reveals some interesting trends in the mid 1990s, as Syria was able to meet its current revenue needs with non-oil revenues. In this sense, it might be argued that the fiscal position was stable and healthy since oil revenues were being used exclusively for investment purposes. The picture has worsened significantly since then and it is clear that oil revenues, increasingly, have to cover current expenditures, thereby leaving very limited room for the enhancement of fiscal space. In addition, it appears that oil revenues are increasingly being used for public consumption, implying a squeeze on resources available for public investment.

Table 13.4 *Non-oil surplus/deficit as a percentage of GDP, 1992–2002*

Year	Current expenditures/ GDP	Non-oil revenues/ GDP	Current non-oil surplus/deficit/GDP
1994	14.49	14.56	(–)0.07
1995	14.87	16.14	1.27
1996	12.97	13.95	0.98
1997	12.89	15.00	2.11
1998	14.10	15.12	1.02
1999	14.20	15.72	1.52
2000	16.00	14.84	(–)1.16
2001	16.60	13.47	(–)3.13
2002	17.20	16.11	(–)1.09
2003	18.60	15.00	(–)3.60

Source: Data supplied by Ministry of Finance of Syria.

It is clear from Table 13.4 that the current 'non-oil deficit' is not of an order of magnitude that would cause a fiscal crisis. The existing fiscal space is therefore sufficient to withstand fiscal shocks due to exogenous events including fluctuations in oil prices.

It is also clear that the macro-fiscal challenge that Syria faces is of a medium-term nature. Syria's ability to maintain a credible investment programme in human development sectors relies critically on it being able to deploy existing oil revenues entirely for productive public investment and to ensure that non-oil revenues fully finance current expenditure. In this sense, there exists considerable fiscal space for Syria to use its oil wealth to expand capital investments in activities promoting human development without recourse to the types of short-run stabilization policies the IMF employs. The next question to ask, therefore, is: what are the potential sources of non-oil revenue growth that would enable Syria to enhance public investment?

Sources of public revenue growth

Looking at the revenue structure (Table 13.5), what is immediately striking is the very low share of non-oil trade revenue, both in terms of GDP and in terms of total revenue. In the 1994–2002 period, these revenues accounted for 2–2.5 per cent of GDP and 7–9 per cent of total revenue. In comparative terms, across the region and in comparison with other middle-income countries, there appears to be considerable scope for enhancing revenue growth from this source, such as from import and export taxes.

Table 13.5 *Shares in total tax revenue of major types of taxes, 1994–2002*

Type of revenue	1994	1995	1996	1997	1998	1999	2000	2001	2002
1 Oil-related proceeds	0.390	0.360	0.430	0.420	0.420	0.410	0.450	0.580	0.466
2 Taxes on income and profits	0.130	0.180	0.120	0.160	0.160	0.190	0.180	0.110	0.140
3 Taxes on property and wealth	0.008	0.007	0.007	0.006	0.005	0.005	0.005	0.004	0.005
4 Excises	0.017	0.012	0.009	0.011	0.010	0.011	0.007	0.008	0.019
5 Taxes on international trade	0.100	0.100	0.090	0.080	0.090	0.080	0.060	0.070	0.080

Source: Calculated from data supplied by the Ministry of Finance of Syria.

Revenues from foreign trade can increase via two routes: (1) through an increase in non-oil foreign trade activity as a proportion of GDP, which increases the tax base and therefore tax revenues, and (2) through an increase in the incidence of taxation on foreign trade. The former provides a virtuous nexus in that there will be an automatic increase, ceteris paribus, in the contribution of trade taxes to total revenue. On the latter count, there is also evidence that there is scope to raise the relative incidence of foreign trade taxation relative to other countries in the southern Mediterranean Arab region. Although Syria has the highest trade restrictiveness rating in the sub-region, its effective import tariffs (i.e. customs duties on imports divided by value of imports) are very low (7.2 compared to 13.5 for Algeria, 21.4 for Lebanon or 15.1 for Egypt), and this is as much because of the low volume of non-oil trade as low customs duty collections.

Direct taxes

Discussions have revealed that there has been increased private sector economic activity in Syria over the past decade, particularly in the services sector and in construction. Even so, direct taxes constitute a very low proportion of total tax receipts in Syria. Direct taxes constituted 88 per cent of total tax revenues in 1955 but have witnessed a constant decline since then to less than 30 per cent in 2003.[6] Not more than half of the total direct tax collections are collected from the private sector, meaning that, in effect, direct taxes on private income currently contribute less than 10 per cent of total revenue. There are also a number of tax expenditures, which have no developmental impact but detract from fiscal revenue. These include: exemptions for the agricultural and tourism sectors; military salaries and wages; exemptions to the Syrian airlines, the Meridien and Sheraton Hotels; exemptions for private schools and religious orders; and exemptions for inheritance taxes for some bank deposits and properties. Reforming tax expenditures therefore appears to provide reasonable scope for enhancing direct tax revenues.

It might be believed that the withdrawal of the tax expenditures listed above would have significantly negative effects on economic activity in the sectors involved. However, there is no evidence to suggest that this would necessarily be the case, i.e. that a higher net tax burden would lead to lower levels of private activity in tourism, large-scale agriculture, aviation or private schooling. While precise empirical evidence on this would need to be gathered, the default assumption should be that a rise in the tax/GDP ratio as a consequence of withdrawal of tax expenditures would result in a net enhancement in revenue collection rather than the other way round.

Indirect taxes

The generic argument for reducing tax expenditures is as valid in the case of direct taxes as for indirect taxes. In addition, there is clearly a huge scope for increasing indirect tax collections. In terms of the tax burden, a snapshot analysis reveals that indirect taxes in Syria generate an extremely small proportion of GDP (Table 13.6) in absolute terms, as well as in comparison to other countries in the region and other middle-income countries. Data in Table 13.6 further indicate that there is ample scope for raising indirect tax collections in Syria by as much as 5–6 per cent of GDP. The combination of excise and sales tax/VAT (value-added tax) by which this can be done is an empirical issue and a full analysis needs to be carried out to determine the precise mix. Our purpose here is to establish that scope for such revenue-generation in fact exists at a macro-economic level. However, while the proposition that indirect taxes are always regressive when compared to direct taxes is no longer considered to be tenable, it is still not possible to design a generic progressive or distribution-neutral scheme of indirect taxes, unlike in the case of direct taxes.

Table 13.6 *Indirect taxes as a percentage of GDP in southern Mediterranean Arab countries and other middle-income countries, 1999–2000*

	Algeria	Morocco	Egypt	Jordan	Syria	Thailand	Chile
VAT	3.1	6.1	4.5	7.2	0.3	3.7	8.5
Excises	1.7	5.8	1.5	0.9	0.3	3.6	2.1

Source: Karim Nashashibi (2002) 'Fiscal revenues in southern Mediterranean Arab Countries: Vulnerabilities and growth potential', IMF Working Paper, 02/67, International Monetary Fund, Washington DC.

Another consideration is that revenue-neutral VAT is not always distribution-neutral. More conservative forms of taxation, such as excises and specific commodity sales taxes, are sometimes more desirable than VAT. Specifically, the existence of a large informal sector that escapes the VAT net has significant distributive and equity implications, which undermine its desirability. A VAT may create inter-sectoral and welfare-reducing distortions between formal and informal sectors.

Policy recommendations

Syria can significantly expand its fiscal space through three avenues:

1   considerably lowering tax expenditures to raise direct and indirect tax revenues;
2   raising taxes on international trade chiefly by enhancing the tax base and widening the coverage of import taxation;
3   exploring ways of expanding the indirect tax base, including (but not exclusively confined to) the introduction of VAT. Other ways of enhancing domestic indirect taxation could include: excises on luxury goods like cigarettes and tobacco, 'Tobin' taxes on foreign exchange-related transactions and a low-rated but broad-based taxation of key expenditures associated with increased private sector accumulation, such as private construction activities.

The most positive policy feature of the existing tax structure is that the tax base will grow automatically as Syria diversifies into non-oil based economic activities and accelerates its participation in non-oil international trade. This, combined with increased private sector activity, will automatically provide both an enhanced tax base and increased handles for the allocation of taxes on domestic production and consumption, and on international trade. A Tax Policy Master Plan should therefore detail proposed tax-enhancement measures with the envisaged changes in economic structure and should ensure that the incidence of taxation on poorer and vulnerable groups is minimized.

Question: Mock policy decision exercise

13.4 The Ministry of Finance has been asked to design a medium-term tax policy master plan over a ten-year period (2005–2015). The drafting committee is comprised of: the chief economist of the Syrian Central Bank; the Minister of Finance; the representative of the Syrian Association of Businesses; the representative of the oil industry; the representative of the national consumer organization; a World Bank economist; and the leaders of the main Syrian political parties (the Arab Socialist Ba'ath Party and the Arab Socialist Movement).

Students are invited to choose a role and draft a 5-page master tax plan. The plan should detail the target share of the components of Syria's tax revenues, as both a percentage of total revenues and a percentage of estimated GDP. The plan should pay special attention to the human development principles of equity and efficiency.

Security policy in Haiti

Carroll Faubert[7]

Since the departure of Jean-Claude Duvalier in February 1986, Haiti has been engaged in a seemingly endless political process punctuated by several military coups, outbursts of violence and foreign military interventions. The origins of the crisis go back to Haiti's the troubled past (Table 13.7)

Causes of the crisis

A culture of violence

The Duvaliers ruled Haiti for nearly 30 years, and their rule was marked by a widespread culture of violence. The infamous *Tontons Macoutes*, Duvalier's private militia, established a regime of terror beyond the imagination of most people: they had a free hand in arresting, detaining, torturing and killing whoever was considered to be an opponent of the regime, or whose wealth members of the ruling class coveted. Thousands were killed or had to flee the country. Violence became a means of achieving and preserving absolute political power.

Outbursts of violence and a round of bloody military coups followed the departure of Jean-Claude Duvalier in February 1986, lasting until the elections that brought Jean-Bertrand Aristide to power in December 1990. Aristide, a former priest, carried the hopes of the poor in Haiti. But, in less than a year, a military coup led by General Cedras forced Aristide into exile. The coup was one of the bloodiest in Haiti's troubled history: some 1500 people died, 40,000 fled the country and many more left the capital for the countryside.

The international community imposed an embargo as violent demonstrations rocked the country. International pressure and a US-led military intervention finally brought Aristide back to Haiti on 15 October 1994 to complete his term as president. Although not eligible for a second term in office because of the constitution, Aristide continued to pull many strings when he was replaced by René Préval, a close associate. In 2000, in a presidential election marked by massive fraud and the participation of only 10 per cent of registered voters, Aristide was declared winner, with 91.6 per cent of the votes.

Although the Duvaliers had long gone, 'Duvalierism' lived on during the Aristide years. Violence, human rights abuses and corruption continued unabated and remained the primary means of preserving power and amassing wealth. The *Tontons Macoutes* were replaced by other armed groups, some of whom continue to threaten security in Haiti to this day. Indeed, violence and impunity have become characteristic of the Haitian political scene in the past 50 years.

Table 13.7 *Haiti – chronology of key events*

1 January 1804	Haiti gains independence from France
1807–1820	Civil war between north and south Haiti
1821–1844	Haiti invades and occupies Santo Domingo (Dominican Republic since 1844)
1915–1934	The US invades and occupies Haiti
1957	Dr François 'Papa Doc' Duvalier is elected president through military-controlled elections
1959	Duvalier creates his private militia (*Tontons Macoutes*), following an attempted coup
1964	Duvalier proclaims himself President-for-Life
1971	Papa Doc Duvalier dies in office after naming his 19 year-old son Jean-Claude ('Baby Doc') as his successor
7 February 1986	Jean-Claude Duvalier leaves Haiti, following popular unrest and external pressure
1986–1990	A succession of military coups follows
16 December 1990	Father Jean-Bertrand Aristide is elected president with 67.5 per cent of the votes in Haiti's first-ever democratic election
30 September 1991	Military coup by General Raoul Cedras. Aristide goes into exile. An international embargo is imposed against Haiti in October 1991
19 September 1994	A US-led military intervention leads to the return of President Aristide in October
28 April 1995	Aristide abolishes the National Army
1996–2000	As Aristide is not eligible for a second consecutive term, René Préval, a close associate, is elected President
29 November 2000	Aristide is elected president in an election marked by fraud and extremely low participation. Economic sanctions are imposed on Haiti
29 February 2004	Aristide is forced to resign and to go into exile. The UN Security Council authorizes the deployment of a Multinational Interim Force to be followed by a UN Stabilisation Mission in Haiti (MINUSTAH)
17 March 2004	A government of transition is formed under Prime Minister Gerard Latortue
16 February 2006	René Préval is declared President-elect, following elections held on 7 February

The loss of moral and civic values

Under the Duvaliers, corruption and impunity became the rule for those in power. The three decades of dictatorship devastated the economy, destroyed tourism, drove out foreign investors and all but ruined rural production. Foreign aid agencies and religious and humanitarian organizations gave millions for development and relief, but the majority of the funds were appropriated by the ruling class. Regrettably, corruption, bad governance and impunity remained the foundation of politics during the Aristide years as well. This loss of moral and civic values continues to affect Haiti.

The criminalization of armed gangs

Fearing another military coup, President Aristide disbanded the National Army in 1995. As the army had been responsible for police activities and for the prisons, these services needed to be built up again. This left a weak police force to look after all aspects of state security and public order. Discontent among the former military and delays by the government in honouring its promises of financial compensation resulted in some members of the disbanded armed forces forming illegal armed groups or joining existing ones. Many of the armed groups operating today were created by President Aristide or his *Fanmi Lavallas* party as a substitute for an army they did not trust and that they had abolished. These armed groups became the unofficial armed wing of the regime and a means of intimidating opponents. In recent years, many of these armed groups have turned to purely criminal activities.

An erratic international response

Major national institutions have continued to function during years of political turmoil, in spite of their difficulties and weaknesses. This, coupled with the absence of geo-political interest in Haiti, partly explains the tendency of the international community to withdraw prematurely under the assumption that an election meant that the country could stand on its own. Between 1993 and 2001, no less than six different UN Missions were deployed to the country, each generally considered a failure. It was only from 2004 onwards that the international community acknowledged the need for a long-term commitment to secure Haiti's future through the creation of the UN Stabilisation Mission in Haiti (MINUSTAH).

Following the military coup of 1991 and the fraudulent elections of 2000, the international community reacted by imposing sanctions on Haiti. The intention was to disavow the violent coup and the democratic farce of the elections, but the effects were devastating, mainly for ordinary citizens. The 1991 embargo had particularly disastrous results: shortages of petrol, cuts in the supply of electricity, a sharp increase in consumer prices and the loss of at least 120,000 jobs. The political and military leaders whose actions justified the sanctions generally remained unscathed, while the poor were disproportionately harmed. The result was more poverty and the exacerbation of social tensions.

Consequences of the crisis

Physical security

The deployment of MINUSTAH led to the gradual improvement of security conditions. The larger towns outside Port-au-Prince and the rural areas are now relatively calm. Armed groups no longer operate in the open. Insecurity, however, has taken other forms and often concerns human rights abuses, the denial of justice or summary mob executions. In Port-au-Prince, the period leading to the 2006 elections saw a sharp increase in insecurity, mainly due to the activities of illegal armed groups operating from neighbourhoods where neither the national police nor the MINUSTAH forces dared to operate. These areas, known as '*zones de non-droit*', were the fiefdoms of gang leaders who exercised full control over the population. Cité Soleil, with its 300,000 people, is the most notorious of these enclaves. Today, violence and insecurity in Port-au-Prince are now characterized by:

- A shift from politically motivated violence to purely criminal activities, including kidnappings, drug trafficking,[8] rapes and murders. The criminal activities of illegal armed groups target all categories of citizens, irrespective of their social position or political persuasion.
- The development of linkages and collusion between illegal armed gangs, international drug smugglers, purely criminal groups or individuals, some members of the national police, and the political and business elite.
- The attempt by illegal armed gangs operating in Port-au-Prince to expand the territory under their control. For example, gangs operating out of Cité Soleil had reached areas just next to the international airport by the beginning of 2006.
- The acquisition of more sophisticated weaponry smuggled into the country and paid for by the proceeds of the illegal activities of armed gangs. At the same time, many in the middle- and upper-classes have acquired weapons as a means of self-protection, and the wealthier have often been members of quasi-militia protection groups.

The rule of law

Years of the abusive use of power by those in positions of authority – law enforcement agents, judiciary personnel and civil servants alike – have made it difficult for Haitians to trust the police, the judicial system and the state apparatus in general. After 10 years of international support, the national police force is still considered to be 'under construction' in 2006. The police force suffers from a negative stigma among the population in Port-au-Prince, and the Director General of the Haitian National Police himself is quoted as saying that some 25 per cent of his force is corrupt.

Deterioration of the environment

Over the past decade, Haiti has been hit by no less than 20 internationally-recognized natural disasters. In 2004, the southern part of the country was devastated by major floods, resulting in the death of more than 4000 people, while up to 330,000 had their homes totally or partially destroyed. Because of its geography, Haiti is prone to natural hazards, such as hurricanes, tropical storms, earthquakes, floods and landslides. The increased frequency and intensity of natural disasters is believed to be linked to severe environmental degradation. Chronic poverty, a high population density (nearly 300 inhabitants per square kilometre) and a weak institutional capacity to address long-term issues, such as the environment, have contributed to anarchic urbanization, deforestation and over-exploitation of agricultural land. The vulnerability of Haiti to natural disasters has been exacerbated by the recurring political, institutional and security crises that have weakened the capacity of the state to develop preventive measures and a national capacity to mitigate disasters.

Persistence of extreme poverty

According to the data contained in the Global Human Development Report 2007/2008, life expectancy in Haiti is 59.5 years; under-five mortality is at 120 per thousand live births; 46 per cent of the population is estimated to be undernourished, and 46 per cent does not have access to safe water. Among children aged five, 17 per cent are underweight for their age and the probability at birth of not reaching age 60 is 37.9 per cent. Only 30 per cent of the population has access to improved sanitation. While 53.9 per cent of the population has to live with less than US$1 a day, 78 per cent have less than US$2 a day; in all, 65 per cent of the population is estimated to live below the national monetary poverty line.

Exodus and brain drain

About one in five Haitians – a total of two million – is estimated to live outside the country, mainly in the US and the Dominican Republic. During the second half of 2005 and the whole period leading up to the February 2006 elections, when insecurity and kidnappings were at a height, many among the wealthier families of Port-au-Prince either left the country or sent their families away altogether. As in most similar situations, those who left were often the best educated, the entrepreneurs and those whose wealth or talents would have been needed by their country. It has been estimated, for example, that 80 per cent of college-educated Haitians now live outside the country.

However, this Haitian diaspora has had a significant economic impact on the country through remittances and tourism. It is estimated, for example, that remittances from the US alone amount to some 30 per cent of Haiti's GDP. Most of these remittances, however, are used for consumption needs and are not tapped for development or investment. Altogether, transfers from abroad directly to families amount to US$800 million, which is double the budget of the state.

Question: Mock policy-decision exercise

13.5 The Haitian government has been given a grant of €100 million by major international donors to improve its security situation. A committee, comprised of members of the Haitian Parliament and international donors, has been asked to draft a spending plan for the 2010–2015 period.

You are the members of that select committee. Draft a 5-page proposal for spending the €100 million in the five year period to address insecurity. Justify your priorities.

Technical assistance policy in Afghanistan

Mustafa Aria and Khwaga Kakar[9]

Background

Since 2001, Afghanistan has begun to rebuild its institutions, revive its economy, reform its administration, and extend control to the rest of the country beyond the capital city of Kabul. Despite more than six years of significant international aid,[10] the country continues to struggle with severe insecurity. Poverty remains a serious problem. According to a 2007 household survey, 42 per cent of the people live below the poverty line. Additionally, the country is faced with the challenge of a booming narcotics industry. Corruption is rampant, and many public services are not available to people unless they have personal networks or are willing to pay bribes. The government administration remains ineffective, and has difficulties in recruiting and retaining skilled professionals with management and administrative experience. Admittedly, it is currently making efforts to change this through administration reforms. However, the establishment of a true merit-based recruitment process, and the elimination of patronage and kinship from recruitment practices, still have a long way to go, thus hindering human development.

Technical assistance programme

The government's capacity has been damaged as a result of a long and devastating conflict, poor governance, and the exodus of qualified and experienced Afghans. To mobilize external resources, Afghanistan has relied on imported capacity, which, to a considerable extent, managed to jump-start crumbling government institutions, stabilize financial systems and initiate civil service reforms. However, what began as an emergency stabilization measure has now taken on a life of its own. That is because an absence of government leadership and a lack of coordination among those responsible for technical assistance, mean that efforts to train and empower Afghans remain insufficient.

This has also slowed down the transfer of technical and management functions to Afghans, and the progressive reduction of reliance on international advisors. In addition, a budgetary and regulatory constraint in recruiting qualified civil servants (while donors continue to pay foreign consultants high salaries) has undermined the government's capacity to build local expertise. In some cases, multiple advisors provided by multiple donors, mostly in the same department, are duplicating efforts due to a lack of coordination, making it difficult for the government to effectively manage them. At the same time, more needs to be done to encourage expatriate Afghans with skills to work in Afghanistan and sufficient incentives still need to be provided to encourage them.

Technical assistance, which is still largely supply driven, is dominated by expatriate companies and firms managing such contracts. The government and its development partners are aware that imported capacity is expensive and, if not coordinated and utilized effectively, can damage the building of sustainable local institutions. Furthermore, in the absence of progress towards building local capacity, Afghanistan is likely to remain substantially dependent on international advisors and resources for a long period. Both the government and donors realize that Afghanistan will not be able to afford imported capacity in the long-run, particularly when the flow of external assistance declines. It is therefore imperative that all technical assistance is efficiently utilized to build domestic capacity as soon as possible.

The uncertain security situation has further complicated the long-term retention of capacity in civil service and the military, that is, it has increased the government's dependency on external assistance – UN regional offices, international NGOs, Provincial Reconstruction Teams, and military and reconstruction experts. The Afghan government is thus less able to challenge donors in demanding or assuming greater leadership and responsibility for the delivery of services and the implementation of the rule of law.

Furthermore, weak project and programme appraisal mechanisms across the government line ministries have resulted in low quality projects, undermining the execution and implementation of its budget. In short, a lack of sufficient capacity has limited the government's ability to achieve its development goals in an efficient manner. In order to deal with capacity shortage, the donor community has hired international advisers to work in the civil service. Also, the donors have created 20 Project Implementation Units (PIU) within government institutions. PIUs have often been used to fill in the technical skills gap in the administration of donor-driven development assistance programmes.

National development frameworks

The government of Afghanistan, with support from the international community, has recently developed a fully fledged Poverty Reduction Strategy, called Afghanistan's National Development Strategy, and has agreed to implement the benchmarks for the Afghanistan Compact.[11] In 2008, the donor community pledged close to US$21 billion for the implementation of these two initiatives.

The government has also agreed to meet the principles of the Paris Declaration on Aid Effectiveness to improve the delivery and impact of external assistance. The major principles of the Paris Declaration include: (1) partner countries own and exercise leadership over their development policies; (2) donors align their overall support of partner countries' national development strategies; (3) donor actions are more harmonized, transparent and collectively effective; (4) resource management and decision-making are more results-oriented; and (5) donors and partners are accountable for development results.

Twelve indicators of aid effectiveness have been developed as a way of tracking and encouraging progress in respecting the principles outlined above. Targets for the year 2010 have been set for eleven of the indicators and are designed to encourage progress at the global level among the countries and organizations adhering to the Paris Declaration. Two indicators in particular deal with technical assistance and PIU. These are indicators 4 and 6.

Strengthen capacity by coordinated support (indicator 4)

Afghanistan received significant levels of technical assistance in excess of hundreds of millions of dollars. This reflects that capacity building is a key priority as a means of addressing the substantial drain in skills. Considerable progress has been made to increase coordination of technical assistance from 37 per cent in 2006 to 59 per cent in 2008. Afghanistan has exceeded the baseline ratio of 50 per cent, i.e. half of technical assistance should be coordinated, which the country was supposed to reach by 2010 (see Table 13.8). Much of this progress has been achieved through the expansion of the World Bank's Management Capacity Program, along with an increasingly collaborative approach to technical assistance.

Despite this progress, technical assistance has been largely a gap-filling exercise, which has failed to build self-reliance among government institutions. It has focused on fulfilling short-term outputs rather than providing training oriented towards the long-term. Generally, technical assistance in Afghanistan has not been integrated into institution-wide approaches based on comprehensive human resource assessments. In addition, there are no strong donor coordination mechanisms on technical assistance in specific sectors. Furthermore, technical assistance does not have the type of medium-term funding or pooled funding mechanisms they require.

Donors have cited that a key challenge is the contrast between the requested delivery of development results, on the one hand, and the very low capacities of the public and private sectors, on the other. Hence, development partners do not take, or do not have, the time to build up sustainable capacities, which create pressure for implementing parallel mechanisms. There is also a need for stronger counterparts on the government's side to take the lead on the use of technical assistance.

Table **13.8** *Coordination of technical assistance in Afghanistan*

	Coordinated technical cooperation[a] (USD m) (a)	Total technical cooperation (USD m) (b)	Baseline ratio (%) (a/b)
Asian Development Bank	11	11	100
Australia	2	2	100
Denmark	2	3	92
European Community	9	11	76
Finland	1	1	100
France	0	2	0
Germany	3	17	17
Japan	0	17	0
Korea	2	2	100
Netherlands	7	10	73
New Zealand	1	1	100
SIDA (Sweden)	1	1	100
UK	11	27	41
UN Agencies	14	62	23
USAID	69	164	42
World Bank	155	155	100
Total	**287**	**486**	**59**

Note: [a] Donor development support provided through coordinated programmes consistent with Afghanistan's national development strategies.
Source: Ministry of Finance of Afghanistan.

Parallel Project Implementation Units (indicator 6)

The Paris Declaration invites donors to 'avoid to the maximum extent creating dedicated structures for day-to-day management and implementation of aid-financed projects and programmes.' Donors have generally created parallel PIUs to ensure that projects have adequate capacity to be implemented, given that line ministries often lack skilled staff to perform accounting, financial management and reporting functions. The number of PIUs has decreased significantly from 28 in 2006 to 20 in 2008. This marks a reduction of about 32 per cent. It is expected that the target of achieving a two-third reduction by 2010 will be achieved.

Steps to reduce parallel PIUs include the World Bank approach, which encourages a programmatic approach where other donor-funded and government-funded programmes use the same implementation unit for their processing needs. In addition, the recently-approved Management Capacity

Program aims to attract skilled Afghans into government positions. Greater in-line Afghan capacity will serve to lower dependence on parallel systems.

Questions

13.6 Afghanistan is developing a nationwide capacity-building programme. You have been tasked with designing the programme:

(a) How will you involve donors in creating a nationwide capacity-building programme which ensures that technical assistance will be demand-driven and aimed at building government capacity?

(b) What specific policy recommendations would you propose to ensure that the delivery of assistance are effective and in line with government priorities?

(c) The government would like an exit strategy for foreign technical assistance. What policies should the government devise to reduce its reliance on this type of assistance?

(d) What should be done to encourage local ownership and avoid the involvement of international advisors in key decision-making processes?

Post-conflict policy in Liberia

Wilmot A. Reeves[12]

The first paragraph of Liberia's 2006 *National Human Development Report* (NHDR) opens as follows:

> The impact of the civil war and poor governance on Liberia's capacity for human development has been devastating. Loss of life through violent conflict or extreme deprivation, forced human displacement, the destruction of infrastructure and government capacity, and the collapse of livelihoods have left a perilous legacy of human insecurity. Even though the crisis of war has ended and the first steps towards reconstruction have been successfully made, the challenges are enormous. Indicators of human development in Liberia – covering employment, income, health, education, gender equality and child welfare – are among the lowest in the world ...[13]

Liberia has a history imbued with over a quarter century of political instability and economic mismanagement, resulting in 14 years of civil conflict (1989–2003). Its *NHDR* observes that the civil war had a devastating imprint on the country, affecting all indicators of human development. Presently, Liberia has a poverty rate of 63.8 per cent, unemployment rate is at 80 per cent in the formal sector, and the productive sector (agriculture, mining, forestry, fisheries, etc.) are almost completely paralysed.

Following years of civil conflict, the Accra Comprehensive Peace Agreement (CPA) was finally signed by all warring parties on 18 August 2003, including the government of Liberia, which was headed by President Charles Taylor,[14] the Liberians United for Reconciliation and Democracy (LURD), the Movement for Democracy in Liberia (MODEL),[15] and other political parties. After the signing of the CPA, President Charles Taylor was forced into exile in Nigeria, allowing his vice-president, Moses Zeh Blah, to preside over the country as president until the transitional government was inaugurated. In October 2003, the National Transitional Government of Liberia (NTGL) was inaugurated into office, eventually leading the country into democratic elections in October 2005.

Eighteen months after the signing of the CPA, Liberia continued to grapple with the daunting challenge of rebuilding the country. The CPA, brokered with the support of the international community, and guided by UN Security Council

Resolution 1509,[16] paved the way for one of the largest UN peacekeeping missions tasked with immediately restoring order and creating the political space to rebuild a viable state apparatus. The 2004 Liberia Reconstruction Conference (under the joint auspices of the Transitional Government of Liberia, the UN, the US and the World Bank, and strongly supported by the European Commission and other donors) led to a short-term stabilization plan, which served as the government-partner framework for dialogue and assistance. Because of its focus on verifiable results and inclusive institutional mechanisms, it elicited an unprecedented response from the donor community. Total pledges at the conference amounted to US$522 million, close to 80 per cent of the country's combined humanitarian and reconstruction needs.

In 2005, Liberia held general and presidential elections, which were free of violence and declared transparent by the international community. Mrs Ellen Johnson Sirleaf emerged as winner in these elections, setting the record for being Africa's first democratically elected female President, running on the ticket of the Unity Party (one of 21 political parties that had participated in the elections).

The years of conflict are behind the Liberian people, and relative peace now exists in the country, following disarmament (undertaken by a 15,000-strong UN Peacekeeping Force), demobilization, rehabilitation and the reintegration of over 100,000 ex-combatants. Support for this initiative was provided by the international community. However, there are still enormous development challenges because of high public expectations for the government to deliver on public services, including quality health and education services, jobs and the reconstruction and rehabilitation of roads and bridges. Given the severity of damage to the country's infrastructure, the restoration of basic services and the revival of the collapsed economy were the government's highest priorities.

The government set out to establish a concrete development framework, which was comprised of four pillars: enhancing national security, economic revitalization, governance and rule of law, and basic services and infrastructure. With the Liberia Reconstruction and Development Committee leading the development agenda, the government, with the assistance of international development partners, formulated its first 150 Days Action Plan. One of the deliverables in the Action Plan was the formulation of an interim Poverty Reduction Strategy (iPRS). This was followed by a Private Sector Day, which focused on investment opportunities in Liberia.

Using the experience and lessons learnt from the short-term stabilization plan, the 150 Days Action Plan, and the iPRS, Liberia now has a Poverty Reduction Strategy Paper (PRSP), which was formulated with the technical and financial assistance of its development partners. In June 2008, the PRSP was presented to partners in Germany, where a considerable amount of technical and financial support was also pledged. The PRSP is still built around the four pillars of the government's initial development framework, albeit with slight modifications: consolidating peace and security, revitalizing the economy, strengthening governance and rule of law, rehabilitating the infrastructure and delivering basic services.

Liberia is presently classified as a heavily indebted poor country (HIPC), with an external debt portfolio of more than US$4.5 billion (part of which has been waived by some donors, including the US and Germany) – a clear justification for preparing a PRSP. The PRSP serves as a framework for strong partnerships, donor assistance and debt relief. With this, Liberia is most likely to qualify for a complete debt waiver.

Liberia still faces huge development challenges in its traditional growth-driven sectors, including agriculture, forestry and mining. In addition, it is faced with the challenge of reforming a very underdeveloped financial sector, generating productive employment, and diversifying the economy. These challenges have the potential to undermine Liberia's progress on human development.

Questions

13.7 Assume you are ministers of the newly elected government of Liberia, faced with these demanding development challenges. What would be your immediate response? Briefly outline and discuss key poverty-alleviation measures that you would propose to the government to deal with some of the challenges described in the above discussion.

13.8 Assuming the development priorities listed below are just a few of the areas that need serious attention, which would you prioritize? Justify your selection from the perspective of the human development and capability approach (you can select more than one option):
   (a) revitalizing the economy through agricultural development, private sector development, and the mining and forestry sectors;
   (b) enhancing national security and consolidating the peace process;
   (c) creating jobs through labour-intensive projects;
   (d) creating jobs through capital-intensive projects;
   (e) rehabilitating the infrastructure (roads and bridges) and delivering basic services; or
   (f) all of the above.

Notes

1   The Harvard Business School case study method is probably the most well known. As its website puts it: 'There is only one way to learn the demanding art of leadership – and that's by leading ... By engaging students in business conflicts developed from real events, cases immerse students in the challenges they are expected to face. Challenges that require thoughtful analyses with only limited or even insufficient information. That requires effective responses within ambiguous circumstances or complex economic and political contexts.' See www.hbs.edu/learning/case.html.

2   Adib Nehmeh is Policy Advisor with UNDP in Lebanon. This fictional story, based on real data, is taken from a presentation made at the 2008 Human Development Oxford Training Course by Nuzhat Ahmed, Cesar Caballero,

David McLachlan-Karr, Rogel Nuguid, Rajasekharan Parameswaran, Nasser Shammout and Serge Yapo, with Adib Nehmeh as the lead author of the story. Data come from the National Human Development Report of Ghana, available at www.undp-gha.org. The presentation, entitled 'Ghana: An advocacy strategy to end violence against women, is available in PowerPoint® at: http://hdr.undp.org/en/nhdr/training/oxford/2008/presentations/.

3   Seyhan Aydinligil is Professor of Social Policy and Human Development, Middle Eastern Technical University, Ankara, Turkey. Data are mainly taken from 'Turkey: An Overview' at www.worldbank.org/tr, and the Turkish National Human Development Report.

4   Nuval-Davis, Nira (2007) 'Intersectionality, citizenship, and contemporary politics of belonging' in Jennifer Bennett (ed.) *Scratching the Surface: Democracy, Traditions and Gender*, HBF, Lahore, pp7–23.

5   This edited case study is drawn from chapter 3, 'Fiscal Space', in a UNDP report entitled *Macro-economic Policies for Poverty Reduction: the Case of Syria*, April 2005. It has been reproduced with the kind permission of Khalid Abu-Ismail/UNDP.

6   Nejmeh, Elias (2003) 'Economic reform, where to?' paper presented to the Syrian Scientific Economic Assembly, Damascus.

7   The case study draws mainly from a UNDP document entitled 'Evaluation of UNDP assistance to conflict-affected countries: Haiti' written by Carroll Faubert. It has been supplied by a group of participants at the 2008 Human Development Oxford Training Course (Olivier Adam, Judy Grayson, Patrick Kendall, Antonio Vigilante and Louisa Vitton). The presentation entitled 'Haiti: A New Beginning' can be accessed at http://hdr.undp.org/en/nhdr/training/oxford/2008/presentations/. For a glimpse of life in Haiti, see Sen's 'Foreword' to Paul Farmer (2005) *Pathologies of Power*, University of California Press, Berkeley, which has been reproduced in *Maitreyee*, the e-bulletin of the Human Development and Capability Association, October 2006, available at http://www.hd-ca.org.

8   It is estimated that between 18 and 20 per cent of illegal drugs entering the US transit through Haiti.

9   Centre for Policy and Human Development, Kabul University.

10   Since 2001, Afghanistan has received more than US$15 billion in Official Development Assistance (ODA), not including off-budget security spending, which is not formally reported. Current estimates for total assistance, ODA and security-related expenditures are US$40–50 billion.

11   The Afghanistan Compact establishes the framework for international cooperation with Afghanistan. The document is available at www.nato.int/isaf/docu/epub/pdf/afghanistan_compact.pdf.

12   National Economist, UNDP, Liberia.

13   A copy of the report, entitled 'Mobilising capacity for reconstruction and development', is available at www.lr.undp.org/NHDR'06_web.pdf.

14   President Charles Taylor is presently in the International Tribunal in The Hague, facing charges of war crimes, brought against him by the Special Court of Sierra Leone, for his alleged support of the civil war in that country in exchange for diamonds.

15   LURD and MODEL were the two rebel factions fighting to oust the government of President Charles Taylor. LURD was attacking the government forces from the northwestern region of Liberia, while MODEL attacked it from its southeastern and central regions.

16   UN Security Council Resolution 1509 was adopted at its 4830th meeting on 19
      September 2003 to support the end of the civil conflict in Liberia and to restore
      civil authority.

Appendix 1
Teaching the human development and capability approach: Some pedagogical implications

Melanie Walker[1]

Human development aims to expand people's capabilities to be and do what they value being and doing. Having knowledge and getting a critically-oriented education are crucial components in forming a good life plan with genuine choices. When we teach the human development and capability approach, we therefore need to keep in mind that our pedagogy ought to be consistent with the core principles of the approach itself. It ought to be both a critical and *humanizing* pedagogy. An education process that humiliates students or reduces their confidence as they learn about human development ideas would certainly not be appropriate for enabling transformation and the expansion of capabilities.

The crucial point is that we should not separate what we teach from the way we teach it. *Who* is teaching, who is *being taught*, and *how* they are being taught matter as much as *what* is being taught. If we value democracy and gender equality, we should foster them in the way we teach. We want our students to experience democracy and equality in their learning experience, not inequality or injustice.

The ideas of critical educators like Paulo Freire are particularly helpful. For Freire (1970, 1985), teaching and learning are both political and cultural processes. The political nature of education is evident in the values and perspectives teachers and students bring with them to a learning situation, in the way teaching and learning occur, in the forms of assessment and evaluation conducted, in the funding arrangements for education, in what appears or is left out of the curriculum, in the justifications provided for education, in the reading and writing completed or recommended, in the value placed on credentials and qualifications, in the language of instruction, and in government policies that frame the learning process as a whole. The cultural processes of education are meant to foster freedom. Thus, teaching and learning must always be situated within their respective political and cultural contexts. It also follows, therefore, that social and economic structures constrain what is possible and what is regarded as being legitimate and worthwhile in education.

Central to Freire's pedagogy is the idea of becoming more fully human. We are 'beings of praxis' and hence capable of transforming the world. This firmly links his pedagogical philosophy to that of human development. For Freire, we humanize ourselves when we engage in critical, dialogical praxis. We dehumanize ourselves and others when we actively prevent this. Knowledge and knowing is never complete, and both arise from dialogue and engagement with the messy realities of life.

Freire distinguished between what he called 'banking education' and 'problem-posing education' (see Box 9.8). The former is oppressive, involving the transmission or pouring of ideas into blank and docile containers, which then reproduce these ideas in an uncritical fashion. Criticism and questioning are suppressed and alternative ways of understanding the world actively discouraged. Learners are passive spectators rather than participants in their own learning process. In contrast, problem-posing education involves learners as agents with a dialogical and critical approach to education. A culture of silence thus excludes and oppresses, because speech/voice and freedom are intimately connected. Emancipation becomes the process of finding one's own voice and this can occur only in conditions of justice and equality (even if this justice and equality is only possible in the classroom). Freirean pedagogy builds on and from the experiences of learners (although not uncritically) and welcomes questions, debate and discussion. A critical mode of being is the key to pedagogical purpose and practice. Students learn to ask questions, not just to answer them. Education is something students do, rather than something that is done to them. This means that dialogue is central to learning.

Freire's work strongly underpins what is called 'critical pedagogy' (see Kincheloe 2004; Leistnya et al 1996). Critical pedagogy broadly draws on critical theory and a structural critique of formal education as a site where capitalism and its values and social relations are constantly being reproduced, but where proposals for resistance and change can also be compellingly made. Critical pedagogy argues that education is a site of symbolic control, where our understanding, our disposition to learn, and the formation of our identities are shaped and influenced by the culture of teaching and learning practices. The pedagogical is thus about the formation of learner identities and how we learn to see ourselves in relation to each other and to the rest of the world. We might learn to be ethical and compassionate or uncaring; we might learn to exercise knowledge to help others or to harm them; we might learn to respect diversity or fear those who are different from us. The key question is: what do I as a human being become as a consequence of what I experience in learning about human development? For teachers of human development, the essential question is therefore: what kinds of human beings do I hope my students might one day become?

Critical pedagogy pays careful attention to history, power and participation in educational settings. It is centred on critical thinking, which involves being able to interrogate the assumptions about life and power relations we routinely take for granted, to exert more conscious control over our lives, and to raise questions about the moral relevance of our actions. By challenging us to recognize and critique undemocratic social practices and the global relations that produce and sustain them, we are in position to engender transformation. For example, students and learners would have the knowledge to critique how race, gender and other forms of inequality and oppression are made to seem normal in the world.

Critical pedagogy is power-sensitive. It offers a framework to examine power and domination in education and uncover its selection and sorting functions. It critiques not just educational hurdles to educational success and agency, but also how these educational barriers are shaped by social, economic and political obstacles to social justice and democracy. It sees identity as fluid, contingent, dynamic and in-process, so that change is always possible and new identities might be produced when new opportunities (or freedoms) are opened. It is always evolving; it is not a pedagogy that we do or achieve but one that we continue struggling towards, always in committed dialogue with others.

A human development approach to pedagogy ought then to be a form of critical pedagogy, connecting education to the world beyond the classroom and the educational institution because conditions in society, such as forms of inequality, penetrate education. Our pedagogy should therefore foster reflection on freedom and inequalities, and pay attention to global processes that affect us all. We should *do* human development and social justice, and not simply learn about it. This entails that the classroom environment be one where students are able to influence activities. It also involves a high degree of self-regulation by students, and some degree of encouragement so they learn to take risks in their own learning experience.

For Freire, therefore, education ought to be 'the practice of freedom'. In that context, pedagogy has three key features: learners should be active participants and co-constructors of knowledge; learning should be meaningful to the learners; and learning should have a critical focus. Thus learners are engaged co-constructors of knowledge itself. This includes attention to history, participation and mutual engagement, connecting experiences to the learning encounter and a process of inquiry, critical dialogue and dissent. As Freire explains, through praxis, individuals realize their full humanity. Praxis is the reflexive relationship of theory and practice which involves acting with others to transform the world. It is the act of reflectively constructing and re-constructing the social (and educational) world. Knowledge (even knowledge about human development) therefore cannot simply be transmitted or written onto 'blank slates', but develops through the involvement of learners in invention and reinvention, and through curious, imaginative and hopeful inquiry.

Other pedagogical features might include the importance of hope and love in teaching and learning, so that students might aspire to decent futures for themselves and the rest of the world. Thus, Freire (1995, p3) wrote that teachers ought to 'unveil opportunities for hope, no matter what the obstacles might be', fostering our confidence to pursue our aspirations. Furthermore, in learning about human development in schools, colleges and universities, we acquire knowledge about human development not just for the sake of having knowledge, but to use this understanding in ways that might meaningfully improve the world in which we live.

In the human development approach to pedagogy, teachers become critical and reflective intellectuals. They have a questioning frame of mind, are open to learning from their students and other teachers, and are also active citizens. As critical intellectuals, teachers ought to be involved in social justice struggles to build a better world. Such struggles may be quiet, often unnoticed, forms of intellectual subversion, or they may be more public protests. By *doing* human development pedagogies in their classrooms – pedagogy *for* and pedagogy *as* human development – teachers enable students to experience democratic, critical and compassionate ways of thinking and being. In a human development classroom, diverse identities would have equal value: a student would not be undermined or overlooked simply because she was female, disabled, or old, or from a different cultural, national or racial group.

A human development approach to pedagogy should also pay attention to students having specific pedagogic rights (Bernstein, 2000). Without these, students may not develop the capabilities to participate equally and effectively in society and to function well in a democracy (Walker, 2006). These rights would further direct our attention to the normality of unjust hierarchies, where students might not be recognized as potential partners in the pedagogic process.

Bernstein therefore argues for three integrated pedagogic rights: the first is the right to 'enhancement,' which involves critical understanding and seeing new possibilities; this right is the key to the formation of confidence and agency. The second right is that of 'inclusion', which is the right to be included socially, intellectually, culturally and personally – which is fundamental to social exchange. The third is 'participation' in shaping and transforming political outcomes or, in other words, the right to 'civic practice'. These pedagogic rights allow each person to realize his full potential in acquiring knowledge. Like any other rights, pedagogic rights could be expanded through pedagogical and social arrangements which secure these rights.

A focus on rights directs us to the process aspects of freedom, which include the types of pedagogical processes we are specifically concerned with here. Sen (2004) is himself clear that, while capability is important for evaluating the opportunity aspect of freedom, it cannot deal adequately with its process aspect because capabilities point to individual advantage but do not necessarily tell us about the fairness of the (pedagogical) processes involved, or about the rights-based freedom of each learner to pedagogical processes that are equitable.

In summary, the fundamental elements of a human development pedagogy would be constituted by: theoretical ideas from Freire and critical pedagogy, a pedagogical practice focusing on the formation of each student's capabilities, and pedagogic rights.

Note

1   Melanie Walker is Professor of Higher Education at the University of Nottingham and Publications Editor of the Human Development and Capability Association.

Readings

Bernstein, B. (2000) *Pedagogy, Symbolic Control and Identity*, Routledge, London

Freire, P. (1970) *Pedagogy of the Oppressed*, Seabury Press, New York

Freire, P. (1985) *The Politics of Education: Culture, Power and Liberation*, Macmillan, London

Freire, P. (1995) *Pedagogy of Hope: Reliving Pedagogy of the Oppressed*, Continuum, New York

Kincheloe, J. L. (2004) *Critical Pedagogy*, Peter Lang, New York

Leistyna, P., Woodrum, A. and Sherblom, S. (eds) (1996) *Breaking Free. The Transformative Power of Critical Pedagogy*, Harvard Educational Review, Cambridge, MA

Sen, A. (2004) 'Elements of a theory of human rights', *Philosophy and Public Affairs*, vol 32, no 4, pp315–356

Walker, M. (2006) *Higher Education Pedagogies: A Capabilities Approach*, Open University Press, Maidenhead

Appendix 2
Didactic Pictures[1]

What is empowerment?

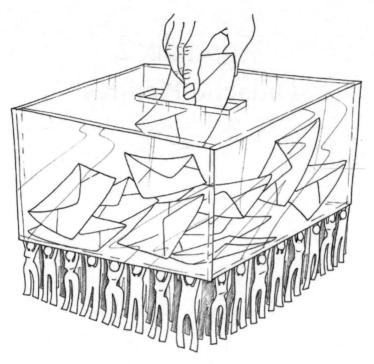

What is democracy?

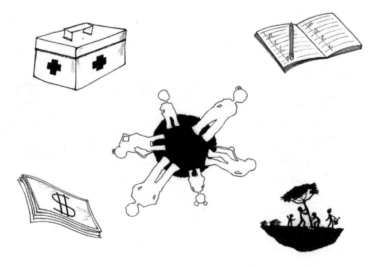

What is human development?

What is human freedom?

What is gender equality?

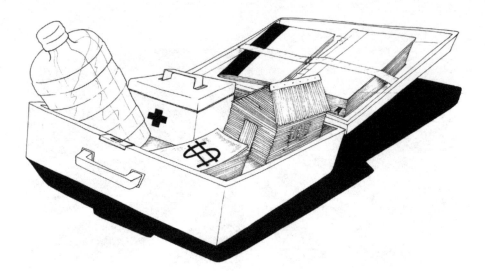

What are the basic valuable freedoms that the development process should promote?

What human development themes does this picture make you think of?

Note

1   The pictures are taken from 'Guías de aprendizaje sobre desarrollo humano: el país que somos, el país que podemos ser', published in 2006 by the Human Development Office of UNDP Dominican Republic. The didactic guide can be found at http://odh.pnud.org.do/publicaciones/. With kind permission of reproduction by the Human Development Office of UNDP Dominican Republic.

Index